Artificial Intelligence
and the
Future of Power

Rajiv Malhotra is an internationally acclaimed author and public intellectual. He combines his background in physics and computer science with his quarter century of path-breaking research on India's historical and future place in the world. As the founder of Princeton-based Infinity Foundation, he continues to change the global discourse with new and innovative paradigms. Rajiv Malhotra's work covers a broad spectrum including mind sciences, civilizations, geopolitics and the future of India.

Artificial Intelligence *and the* Future of Power

5 Battlegrounds

Rajiv Malhotra

RUPA

Published by
Rupa Publications India Pvt. Ltd 2021
7/16, Ansari Road, Daryaganj
New Delhi 110002

Sales centres:
Allahabad Bengaluru Chennai
Hyderabad Jaipur Kathmandu
Kolkata Mumbai

ISBN: 978-93-90547-03-6

First impression 2021

10 9 8 7 6 5 4 3 2 1

Printed at Parksons Graphics Pvt. Ltd, Mumbai

Dedicated to
the young scientists and technocrats

CONTENTS

Part Two: Battleground India

INTRODUCTION

It is extremely easy to find people who speak pleasantly. But it is rare to find people who speak and hear true words even when they are not pleasing to hear.

—*Ramayana*[1]

My love for both physics and philosophy, which started in childhood, went on to become a lifelong passion, a quest that continues to this day. As a college undergraduate, I immersed myself in the nascent field of consciousness studies and discovered that renowned theoretical physicists, such as Werner Heisenberg and Erwin Schrödinger, had been inspired by **Vedic** insights and used them as the philosophical lens for understanding quantum mechanics. This approach came to be accepted as one of the interpretations of quantum mechanics in the twentieth century and has, since then, influenced many scientists.

Later, while studying computer science in the US, I became interested in **algorithms**. An algorithm is a systematic, step-by-step process to achieve an outcome, like a recipe, whether for cooking, getting a driver's license, or managing payroll. Algorithms are typically used to describe streamlined, repetitive and predictable procedures.

The interplay between my spiritual quest and interest in computer science generated many questions that have intrigued me for the past several decades, such as:

- Physics can be viewed as the discovery of nature's algorithms. But is nature *only* algorithmic, or are there also natural processes that cannot be modeled as algorithms because they transcend all algorithms—such as exalted spiritual experiences?
- What are the limits of algorithms in modeling humans? In particular, is it possible to model human psychology, emotions, and intuitions as algorithms?
- If all processes could, in principle, be modeled as algorithms, what would be the implications for free will and the nature of consciousness?
- How is **rtam (rita)**, an important term used in the **Rig Veda** to refer to the patterns that comprise the fabric of all existence, related to algorithms? Is rtam related to algo-rithm?

In the early 1970s, a subject of intense discussion was the investigation of a category of algorithms under the umbrella term of Artificial Intelligence (AI). That is when I started out as a graduate student specializing in AI; the aim was simply to develop algorithms for activities like playing chess. At the time, the best computer program could only just beat an average human player. But that was then. It took a quarter of a century for the major milestone in 1997 when an IBM computer program named Deep Blue defeated Garry Kasparov, the reigning world chess champion. The rest, as they say, is history.

My lifelong quest has been to understand the nature of intelligence, both natural and artificial, and how it plays out at various levels. To pursue this quest, I set up Infinity Foundation in 1994, a nonprofit organization to promote dialogue between Eastern and Western schools of thought. Its first projects included investigations in consciousness studies.

DISRUPTIONS AND BATTLEGROUNDS

Fast forward a quarter century. I have recently reconnected with AI, a field of research that has been reborn as a new force. Artificial Intelligence is amplifying human ingenuity and is the engine driving the latest technological disruption silently shaking the foundations of society. My use of the term is not limited narrowly to what AI is specifically in the technical sense, but also includes the entire ecosystem of technologies that AI propels forward as their force multiplier. This cluster includes quantum computing, semiconductors, nanotechnology, medical technology, brain-machine interface, robotics, aerospace, 5G, and much more. I use AI as the umbrella term because it leverages their development and synergizes them.

On the one hand, AI is the holy grail of technology; the advancement that people hope will solve problems across virtually every domain of our lives. On the other, it is disrupting a number of delicate equilibriums and creating conflicts on a variety of fronts.

Given the vast canvas on which AI's impact is being felt, one needs a simple lens to discuss its complex ramifications in a meaningful and accessible way. After several rounds of restructuring the book, I zeroed in on using the following key battles of AI as the organizing principle. Artificial Intelligence plays a pivotal role in each of these disruptions, and each of these battlegrounds has multiple players with competing interests and high stakes:

1. Battle for economic development and jobs
2. Battle for power in the new world order
3. Battle for psychological control of desires and agency
4. Battle for the metaphysics of the self and its ethics
5. Battle for India's future

These battles already exist but AI is exacerbating them and changing the game. In each case, the prevailing equilibriums are disintegrating, and as a result, creating tensions among the parties held in balance. We are entering an epoch of disequilibrium in which a period of chaos is inevitable. Eventually, however, a new equilibrium will be established, and a new kind of world will emerge.

What follows is how AI is shaping these battles.

Battleground 1: Economic Development and Jobs

A recurrent debate surrounding AI concerns the extent of human work that could be replaced by machines over the next twenty years when compared to new jobs created by AI. Numerous reports have addressed this issue, reaching a wide range of conclusions. Experts consider it a reasonable consensus that eventually a significant portion of blue- and white-collar jobs in most industries will become obsolete, or at least transformed, to such an extent that workers will need re-education to remain viable. This percentage of vulnerable jobs will continue to increase over time. The obsolescence will be far worse in developing countries where the standard of education is lower. Forecasts, however, disagree on the precise timing of this disruption and on the types of human work that might remain safe from machines in the long run.

The routine assurance given to these reasonable concerns is that when AI eliminates certain jobs, those employees forced out will move up the value chain to higher-value tasks. This simplistic and misleading answer overlooks the fact that the training and education required to advance people is not happening nearly at the same feverish rate as the adoption of AI. Those that promise the solution of re-education have not thus far put their money where their mouth is. The gap of employee qualifications will inevitably widen.

Business owners and labor have always had certain competing interests, with the former looking to optimize profits and the latter concerned about wages and employment. Artificial Intelligence disrupts this precarious balance because it suddenly kills old jobs; it also creates new jobs, but the most lucrative new ones will be concentrated in communities with high levels of education and availability of capital. More broadly, AI will worsen the divide between the rich and poor, the haves and the have-nots. This will intensify the schism between the camps having divergent vested interests.

There is a real possibility that AI may trigger an unprecedented level of unemployment and precipitate social instability. Especially for countries like India, where a large percentage of the population lacks the education that is vital to survive a technological tsunami; the adverse effects could be shattering.

My approach to AI's social impact is neither haloed by utopian fantasy nor dipped in gloom. Chapter 2, *The Battle for Jobs*, discusses the potential for unemployment and economic upheaval from the widespread adoption of AI. It raises practical concerns: What will happen when AI makes large numbers of workers obsolete? Who will pay for the re-education of the literally millions of displaced workers? Will the new jobs be in places far removed from where the unemployment will hit hard? Will society's wealth become even more concentrated in the hands of a few than it already is because a minuscule percentage of humans will control the powerful AI technologies? How will the new haves and have-nots fight for resources, and how might such social disequilibrium ultimately play out?

This battleground is important for industrialists and labor activists, as well as for economists and policymakers. Civic leaders, politicians, public intellectuals and media cannot continue to ignore the evolution of AI. More voices must enter the debates to propose appropriate, coherent responses and policy changes.

Battleground 2: Global Power

China is using AI as its strategic weapon to leapfrog ahead of the United States and achieve global domination. Chapter 3, *The Battle for World Domination*, explains the battleground where the geopolitical competition between China and the US is playing out. Both these superpowers recognize AI as the most prized summit to conquer in their race for leadership in economic, political and military affairs.

While aerospace, semiconductors, biotech, and other technologies are also crucial in this race, AI is the force multiplier that brings them together and catapults them to new levels. Both these countries are heavily invested in AI, and between them they control the vast majority of AI-related intellectual property, investments, market share and key resources.

Besides competing directly against each other, the US and China will also compete for control over satellite nations and new colonies. This results from the fact that the disruptive technology will weaken many sovereign states and destabilize fragile political equilibriums. There is a realistic scenario for the re-colonization of the world differently, i.e. as digital colonies.

Furthermore, some private companies controlling this technology could become more powerful than many countries, just as the British East India Company—a private joint-stock company—became more powerful than any country of its time. This battleground is relevant to readers interested in geopolitics and the emerging world order.

Battleground 3: Psychological Control and Agency

A troubling trend is that as machines get smarter, a growing number of humans are becoming dumber. In a sense, the public has outsourced its critical thinking, memory and agency to increasingly sophisticated digital networks. As in any outsourcing arrangement, the provider of services becomes more knowledgeable about the client's internal affairs and the client becomes more dependent on the supplier. The quest for deep knowledge and critical thinking is becoming a thing of the past because it is easier for people to use internet searches whenever any information is needed. People are operating on autopilot rather than thinking and learning on their own.

Google is becoming the **devata**, or deity, that will instantly supply all knowledge. Mastering the rituals and tricks of interacting with this digital deity is considered a mark of achievement to be proudly flaunted among peers. Education is seen merely as a prerequisite for getting a job. **Deep learning** in machines is resulting in shallow knowledge in humans—an irony indeed. Cognitive skills like memory and attention span are atrophying, even as knowledge, authority and agency are being transferred from humans to machines. In effect, AI has managed to hack human psychology.

In an era of instant access, social media has confused people between knowledge, opinion and popularity; whatever is popular is assumed to be true. Individuals who lack followers, likes, shares and comments on social media often retreat into low self-esteem, depression, substance abuse, or even suicide.

Machines surreptitiously model individual psychological behavior by identifying the patterns of users' choices, and then use these models to manipulate and control their actions.

The paradox is that the manipulation is done under the guise of free services that are difficult to resist because they have now become an all-too normal part of our lives. Those who control the psychological models can use AI to influence human emotions and behavior. What concerns me is the psychological, emotional and mental hijacking in progress through these technologies.

Some readers will have a mental block that prevents them from accepting the viability of such psychological interventions. They need reminding that the Russians hacked the 2016 US presidential election with the use of Facebook and the British firm, Cambridge Analytica. Chapter 4, *The Battle for Agency*, explains how AI is taking advantage of emotional vulnerabilities and hijacking the agency of large numbers of people worldwide.

There is a vibrant branch of AI that continually refines the construction of individual psychological profiles. The technology has two parts: building individuals' emotional maps, and using those maps to intervene and produce targeted feelings and outcomes. Most people are uncomfortable accepting that machines can uncover their private selves to the extent of knowing them better than a spouse or close friend. The truth is, in some ways, machines know individuals even better than they know themselves, because people know only their conscious selves and cannot access their unconscious levels, and also because machines are capable of detailed and extremely long term memory that exceeds human capacity. Machines penetrate us far more deeply and analyze our personal behavior microscopically and intimately. They record how we unconsciously respond to online choices and use this to develop insights into aspects of ourselves that we might not want to publicly disclose or even privately come to terms with.

Machine learning is the field that trains computers through analysis of large quantities of data. This data can be acquired by seducing the public to part with it voluntarily; people are tantalized with online carrots and their responses are monitored, tracked and recorded. Using emotional hooks as a bribe, machines tease out users' motivations, both conscious and unconscious. An entire industry of AI-based artificial pleasures is emerging. Recently, litigation has started against the large digital platforms for surreptitiously gathering private data on citizens.[2]

The raw material required to develop machine understanding of human desires and the artificial manipulation of them is called **big data**. Most people happily and voluntarily give up this private data, often without realizing it.

Once the digital systems capture this data, they amass unprecedented power and wealth by analyzing and manipulating our subconscious thoughts. Shoshana Zuboff, a social psychologist, and author of *The Age of Surveillance Capitalism: The Fight for a Human Future at the New Frontier of Power,* characterizes the transfer of data from the public to the digital giants as an act of theft.

> During the last two decades, the leading surveillance capitalists—Google, later followed by Facebook, Amazon and Microsoft—helped to drive this societal transformation while simultaneously ensuring their ascendance to the pinnacle of the epistemic hierarchy. *They operated in the shadows to amass huge knowledge monopolies by taking without asking, a maneuver that every child recognizes as theft.* Surveillance capitalism begins by unilaterally staking a claim to private human experience as free raw material for translation into behavioral data. Our lives are rendered as data flows....[3] (Emphasis added)

People are being duped to part with their data in exchange for freebies and goodies that are disguised as services ranging from practical help for our physical health to emotional delights. The digital capitalists constantly reassure the public that data collection is for their own good using several pretexts. For instance, we are told that surveillance is a public safety service. The cameras capturing data everywhere are keeping us safe. Airlines claim that the use of facial recognition speeds up the boarding process and makes travel safer.[4] Medical information being captured helps develop custom diets and generates the appropriate grocery list for one's family. Cookies are installed on users' devices under the pretext that this provides more personalized experiences.

Many companies use AI to spy on us and collect our private information, justifying their behavior under the garb of serving the public. In a recent article, Zuboff exposes this hoax of free services in her powerful voice:

> We celebrated the new digital services as free, but now we see that the surveillance capitalists behind those services regard us as the free commodity. We thought that we search Google, but now we understand that Google searches us. We assumed that we use social media to connect, but we learned that connection is how social media uses us. ...We've begun to understand that "privacy" policies are actually surveillance policies....
>
> The *Financial Times* reported that a Microsoft facial recognition training database of 10 million images plucked from the internet without anyone's knowledge and supposedly limited to academic research was employed by companies like IBM and state agencies that included the United States and Chinese military....

> ....Privacy is not private, because the effectiveness of these and other private or public surveillance and control systems depends upon the pieces of ourselves that we give up—or that are secretly stolen from us.[5]

The private flow of data from consumer to machine also promotes the transfer of human agency from humans to machines. The data that surveillance companies capture is their source of power and is the fuel for the new economy of trillions of dollars. Zuboff has called this a "bloodless coup from above" and warns of a growing gap between "what we know and what is known about us".[6]

By figuring out the cognitive comfort zones for individuals, AI-driven systems can deliver emotional and psychological needs, thus gradually making people dependent on them. As machine intelligence increases people move toward living in a world of artificially induced emotions and gratification. Eventually this trend leads to a syndrome I call **moronization** of the masses. This mode of existence feeds into the business models of digital capitalism, as shown in Figure 1.

Those who know—or should know—about the wider consequences of this transfer of agency have been largely silent. There has been insufficient open debate in which the utopian view of AI could be counterbalanced by realistic concern. Though think tanks and industry consortia such as Open AI, Deep Mind Ethics and Society, and Partnership on AI do address concerns about AI, they tend to be founded or dominated by the big tech players and aligned with those companies' commercial interests. While I am enthusiastic about AI's potential, what gravely concerns me is the lack of open, thoughtful public debate on what an AI-dominated future could look like.

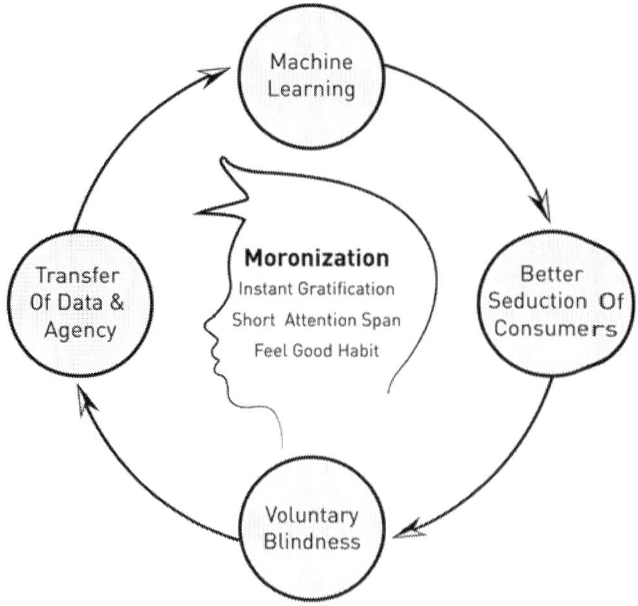

Figure 1: Moronization of the Masses

Artificial Intelligence technologies must be publicly debated as disruptors of the social structures that shape the world order—testing and redefining the limits of liberty, the future of democracy, and the meaning of social justice. Just like war is too important to be left only to the generals to discuss and resolve, AI is too important to be left to the tech giants.[7]

The asymmetric relationship between gigantic digital platform businesses—companies like Google, Facebook, Twitter, Amazon, to name a few—and their users, is of paramount importance. These companies deliver the most popular and widely used services in the world today, designed specifically to meet the demands of a public that is hungry for social media. However, beneath the surface the suppliers and consumers have opposing interests—in privacy, data rights, agency, intellectual property rights and free speech.

This battle is distinct from the other battles in one important respect, i.e., one player is largely ignorant that such a battle is under way. The suppliers of digital services understand the game and play it skillfully, while most consumers are not even aware that the interests of producers and consumers of digital media are at odds. In fact, when people are informed that they are voluntarily surrendering psychological control of their lives, they usually dismiss it as a conspiracy theory.

Fortunately, many consumer activists, social scientists and legal experts are already raising alarms about the conflict, and they will find this battle particularly significant. For instance, Pratyusha Kalluri, an AI researcher at Stanford, has written a short but powerful piece in *Nature*.

> It is not uncommon now for AI experts to ask whether an AI is 'fair' and 'for good'. ...The question to pose is a deeper one: how is AI shifting power?
>
> Law enforcement, marketers, hospitals and other bodies apply artificial intelligence to decide on matters such as who is profiled as a criminal, who is likely to buy what product at what price, who gets medical treatment and who gets hired. These entities increasingly monitor and predict our behavior, often motivated by power and profits.[8]

Chapter 4 explains the most difficult message of the book, because many people simply do not want to believe how remarkably successful AI has become at hacking our minds, psychology and emotions. This chapter is important for anyone who wishes to genuinely appreciate the emotional power of AI. Such persons include social psychologists, policymakers, consumer rights lawyers and activists, and most of all, the public whose agency is being hijacked.

Battleground 4: Metaphysics

The success of AI is based on training machines to achieve intelligent behavior. This has empowered a worldview according to which life, mind and consciousness are merely biological processes running on human beings as machines. In effect, AI has helped biological materialism sneak in through the back door while the leaders of the consciousness movement have been blissfully taken off guard.

I come from the diametrically opposite side in this battle: I have been deeply invested in philosophies based on the primacy of consciousness. And lately I have become concerned that this worldview is being undermined by the powerful trajectory of the AI revolution. Figure 2 illustrates my intellectual journey centered on physics and Vedanta as shown at the top, and my algorithm-based career shown at the bottom. The middle is where they intersect, or rather clash. My struggle to reconcile these conflicts is at the core of the creative churning and tension in this book.

What troubles me is that the digital industry empowering self-learning systems is proceeding in a direction opposite to that of consciousness movements. In fact, this is the real clash of civilizations under way: *the battle between algorithm and being*.

Chapter 5, *The Battle for Self*, explains how the technical and commercial success of AI is built on the assumption that biology and mind are algorithmic machines that can be modeled, mimicked and manipulated using artificial interventions. It describes the implications of the success of materialism that detaches us from our very sense of self and being. The digital dehumanization seems pleasant because the stimulation of pleasures and pains is being artificially managed to create a delusional life. This undermines the human concepts of free will, personal agency and the self in favor of artificially induced experiences. When the experiences become algorithmically controlled, what happens to the spiritual being that is the experiencer?

Readers with a background in philosophy, spirituality and ethics will be provoked by the battle between the metaphysics of consciousness and AI's reductionist challenge to spirituality.

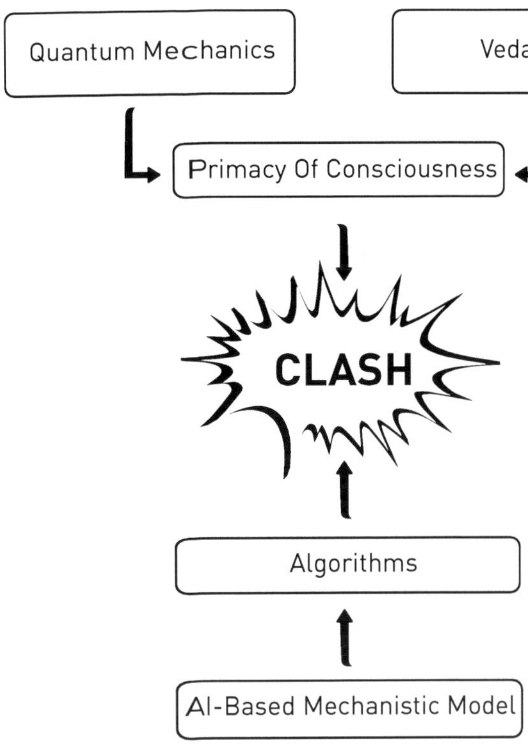

Figure 2: Consciousness of Mechanistic Models

Grid of Four Battlegrounds

As a way to position the four battlegrounds introduced above relative to each other, they can be arranged in the 2x2 table below.

	Physical/Sthula-Sharira	**Mental/Sukshma-Sharira**
External	Global/Geopolitical (Chapter 3)	Identity, Agency (Chapter 4)
Internal	Domestic Economics (Chapter 2)	Selfhood, Spirituality (Chapter 5)

In Indian metaphysics, the sthula-sharira refers to the physical body and the sukshma-sharira refers to the mental and psychological body. Though conventionally this framework is applied to individual persons, I am extending it and applying it to nations.

A nation's sthula/physical body consists of its geography, infrastructure, resources and other tangible assets. There is a further distinction between internal affairs dealing with the domestic economy and employment, and foreign affairs to safeguard its interests internationally. Both of them concern the physical wellbeing.

The sukshma/mental body of a nation is the state of its people's mind and psychology. It is publicly or externally expressed as their identity, confidence and pride. Internally, it is the people's experience of selfhood and spirituality.

Battleground 5: India's Future

India is an important case study on the impact of AI because that is where all the other four battles come together into one large and complex battleground.

As a preface to my discussion on India, I point out that Indian society has forsaken its metaphysical roots in **dharma** to chase the Americanization of **artha** (material pursuits) and **kama** (gratification of sensual desires). As a result, it is neither here nor there—having lost its traditional strengths both individual and collective, it is at best a poor imitation of the American dream.

Overpopulation, unemployment and poor education make India especially vulnerable. Many of its industries are technologically obsolete and dependent on imported technologies. India presently has a disappointing level of AI development and it needs to embark on a rapid program to catch up.

Meanwhile, the public as well as the leaders are mesmerized by the foreign social media, seeing it as the prestigious platform on which to prove oneself. I will explain that this is like welcoming back the East India Company with hugs and gratitude.

Indians love discussing India as a superpower—either already or soon to become one. Part Two: *Battleground India* offers a sobering picture of the country's prospects. It explains that not only is India lagging behind China in AI by at least a decade, it also routinely gives away its unique data assets to foreign countries because of the ignorance of its leaders. Part Two presents the thought experiment according to which, if the present trajectory continues, India could be heading toward re-colonization, this time as a digital colony under the domination of the US and/or China.

India is home to one of the largest talent pools of young brains, yet the shortsighted policies of its leaders continue to sell them out as cheap labor to make quick profits from wage arbitrage. In this way, India has squandered its software lead. This complex battleground is important to those for whom Indian issues and trends are of special interest.

Just as this manuscript was about to be sent for publishing, there was a positive development in India. I am glad to know that Kris Gopalakrishnan, a cofounder of Infosys and major venture capitalist in India, is leading the development of policies on data rights. India's approach to regulating non-personal data is commendable and a great beginning. Gopalakrishnan is one of the few brilliant thinkers on this issue in India, and his involvement makes this a credible initiative. It is too early to evaluate this development; hopefully, it will begin a new phase in India's relationship with AI.

THE PURPOSE OF THIS BOOK

My investigations into these disruptions have not been easy on a personal level in two ways. First, my **svadharma** (core purpose) since childhood has been based on the principle of the primacy of consciousness. This worldview is now being challenged by the opposite model of biological materialism, and AI is dramatically empowering this materialistic philosophy.

Second, as a patriotic Indian I have been doing **purva-paksha** (critical analysis) of forces that threaten its civilization. The stress test of India discussed in Chapter 6 suggests a diagnosis that many of my fellow Indians will object to. Some of the hard realities I unmask will shock readers and expose truths they would rather not hear. But as I have matured in my journey, it is time to reflect on my insights and crystallize some advice out of deep affection for the youth who will be custodians of the culture I was fortunate to be born in.

Supporters suggested that I should perhaps not write such a critical analysis. But facing a problem head-on is a crucial step toward resolving it. Determined to communicate this message in good faith and with the best of intentions, I have looked for role models in the Vedic tradition, exemplars who faced similar dilemmas and risked their popularity for the sake of presenting objective and logical arguments. I found Vidura in the *Mahabharata* a good role model in writing this book. He is considered a paragon of truth, integrity, and impartial and consistent judgment. People find in him the conscience of the *Mahabharata*; the principles he advocates have been compiled under the name *Vidura-niti*. His intellectual posture and tone have emboldened me in writing this book.[9] A sequel to this book which is underway will offer concrete solutions to the predicaments being exposed here.

We live in an epoch defined by major disruptions, both predictable and unpredictable, desirable and undesirable. Clearly, AI is a major disruptive influence, one that to date has not been properly understood, or even discussed, outside the circles of its experts. A great deal has been written on AI's gifts to the world, but not enough on its risks. My goals are to balance the discourse and empower the advocates that speak for the underdogs in these conflicts. The emphasis of this book is to examine society's vulnerabilities to the impending technological tsunami. I hope it will shake up the thought leaders that need to be better informed and more engaged.

Artificial Intelligence has spread throughout much of society, especially since the beginning of the twenty-first century—across health, military, entertainment, education, marketing, manufacturing, and just about every other sector. Even the least technologically savvy among us interacts with AI on a daily basis when we use social media via a smartphone or rely on a car's navigation device. Whether you are a social media fanatic and diehard AI aficionado, a paranoid skeptic that barely has a social media footprint, or something in between, it is impossible to escape the ubiquitous impact of AI technology.

But what if AI is like an iceberg with most of it hidden beneath the surface? And modern civilization, like the luxury passenger ship, Titanic, is on a collision course with it? Social and cultural thought leaders continue to embrace AI as a gateway to a technologically advanced utopia. They are equivalent to the band that continued playing on the deck of the ship even as it was sinking. This complicity must be challenged to give the general population a glimpse into AI as a potential threat to our society's rickety foundation.

Currently, people's reaction to AI is one of two extremes. Some optimistically imbue AI with an aura of seduction and magic. Others view it ominously, akin to the smarter-than-human robotic villains that take over the world in science fiction stories and films. Both these extremes overlook the practical realities of AI that we must confront.

We need institutions and regulations that guard against economic monopoly and environmental ruin; and conversation and debates are a critical first step in the process. The public must be made aware of—and help monitor—the unfair advantage companies have that can affect our liberties, our democratic processes, and our very concept of society.

Today, the charge into the future with AI technology is being led by American companies such as Google, Amazon, Microsoft, Apple, Facebook, Twitter and Netflix, as well as Chinese digital behemoths such as Alibaba, Tencent, Baidu and Huawei. To preempt public activism, technology leaders promote self-regulation, which unfortunately misses the point. Their seemingly benevolent stand furthers their own interests while creating a fog against public investigation. The problem is the lack of intellectual engagement from competent groups that do not have a vested interest in the digital industry.[10]

Policymakers and other leaders in industry and public life, however, need to stop reacting as followers and start to engage the industry more assertively and aggressively. The irony is that in most democratic countries, the public does not see itself as digitally colonized. The real challenge, therefore, is to convince people they are being lulled into complacency, and that they are explicitly giving up their agency because of the seductive power of social media.

This book aims to stimulate alternative thinking and dialogue that may avert the potentially harmful outcomes of AI. Just as a cardiac stress test is not intended to kill patients, but rather to reveal vulnerabilities and prevent future catastrophe, I want to stress test present society's ability to accommodate AI socially, economically and politically. India functions as an especially important case study on the likely disruptions of AI.

This book invites nonexperts into the conversation around AI. This is important because, unlike other technical fields such as nuclear energy and genetic engineering where the public actively debates the social implications, in the case of AI the public has not yet become energized.

Just as I had finished writing this book, the world was suddenly disrupted by Covid-19. The pandemic has created a cascading effect that is reverberating through every aspect of our lives. History books will define this hinge point as a discontinuity separating life before and after. This called for a re-examination of this book and I started asking myself: Does the pandemic effectively stop, or slow down, AI? If so, the book is already obsolete because the impact of AI would be overshadowed by the crisis. Or is it the other way around, namely, that its effect will solidify AI and accelerate its advancement?

I concluded it was the latter: The defeat of Covid-19 will be claimed as a victory for AI and the scientific materialism on which it is based, and this will produce a great leap forward in the march of AI. Though the Covid-19 pandemic has thrown economic forecasts into disarray, and many of the statistics cited in this book will need to be revised, the overall trend I explain is not likely to change. In fact, my prediction is that due to Covid-19, the effects of AI will accelerate even faster than before.

However, this crisis will also trigger greater ethical introspection. There will be a new level of concern for humankind's harmful exploitation of nature, including animals, by turning them into "property" like any other economic asset. The interconnectivity of all things, as captured in the Vedic principle of Indra's Net, deserves special attention. The pandemic is a reminder of materialism going too far and ending up disrupting its own equilibrium.

My goal is to educate and empower users and consumers of AI, as well as civic leaders, so they will be better equipped to engage the digital giants on a level playing field. We are not yet powerless in this battle but must play our cards strategically. I hope the information in these pages will inform, enlighten and provoke readers. As citizens we do have a say in how fast, and in what ways, we allow AI into our lives and becoming informed is the first step toward productive interventions.

PART ONE

ALGORITHM VS BEING

1

OVERVIEW OF AI TECHNOLOGIES

Artificial Intelligence is the future, not only for Russia, but for all humankind. It comes with colossal opportunities, but also threats that are difficult to predict. Whoever becomes the leader in this sphere will become the ruler of the world.

—Russian president, Vladimir Putin[11]

CHAPTER HIGHLIGHTS

- Two foundational concepts of AI described in this chapter are machine learning and big data. Machine learning is the use of diverse experiences to train the algorithms and build models that perform actions considered intelligent. Big data refers to the massive data sets—enormous collections of examples—that are used to train machines.
- Devices classified as smart homes, wearables and implants are fundamentally changing not only how humans interact with machines, but ultimately influence the way humans think, feel and behave. Virtual Reality (VR)- and Augmented Reality (AR)-based products are also among the latest expressions of AI.
- The limits of AI are the subject of much debate and controversy. Most people believe that jobs involving emotions are inherently beyond the purview of machines.

Confusion between consciousness and intelligence often clouds these discussions.

- As machine learning continues to advance and expand the boundaries of AI, its algorithms become better at emulating human emotions and intuition. Models are continuously learning and adapting, resulting in machines that eerily mimic human thought as well as creative and emotional responses. The gap between human and machine intelligence is shrinking and intelligent machines often exceed human characteristics—in speed, accuracy, durability, cost efficiency and endurance.
- Artificial Intelligence holds many promises for improving and enhancing human functioning in a wide range of applications such as medical diagnostics and treatment, agricultural science and production, education, transportation safety and efficiency, military weapons systems and strategy, financial investment and management, legal and judicial processes, and recreational and creative activities.
- Unemployment on an unprecedented scale is likely to result from the ever-increasing automation of more types of jobs. Over time, positions generally considered safe from AI will be impacted as algorithms become increasingly sophisticated.
- Current political systems are not prepared to deal with the radical changes that AI will engender. Social disenfranchisement, population changes, political upheaval, shifting perceptions of societal norms, and worsening class distinctions will create widespread unrest.
- As computers exert more control over individual lives, people give up their agency by allowing, encouraging and even preferring AI to make decisions for them.

- Of primary concern is the apathy of governments and intellectual elites to address, or even recognize, the potential severity of AI disruptions. Society is at a tipping point, and not enough people appear to be doing much about it.
- Big data creates an array of potential problems: security issues, privacy concerns and the transfer of usage rights.
- In the wake of the Covid-19 pandemic, both the development and the application of AI have accelerated. Artificial Intelligence-based systems play a useful role during the pandemic and simultaneously stretch the boundaries of personal invasion.

FUNDAMENTAL ADVANCEMENTS

Artificial Intelligence is rapidly becoming embedded in the world around us, often hidden yet ubiquitous. This is called ambient AI and it is becoming seamlessly integrated into the fabric of our lives. Our comfort level with machines in intimate settings is growing and people are increasingly speaking to their devices. According to researchers, the use of voice interface devices for online searches, shopping and other common tasks is on the rise. By 2022, over half of all US households will own a smart voice device and use it for shopping, with Amazon and Google being the dominant suppliers. Research has revealed that a majority of users keep smart voice devices in their living rooms because they feel comfortable with them, as if the device were an actual person and trusted friend.[12]

Even before AI's recent rise, computers had already taken over many repetitive tasks that can be described with algorithms. A new phase has begun wherein AI performs far more complex work based on machine learning, including tasks performed unconsciously by humans and not fully described by algorithms. Furthermore, some tasks require more data than the human mind can deal with and require faster speeds than any human could match. For example, automated recognition of speech, handwriting and facial recognition already surpasses human skill. Nor is AI limited to merely replicating what humans do. It exceeds human cognitive abilities in a growing number of applications. An important research frontier giving AI considerable power is the range of emotional, aesthetic and psychological applications discussed in Chapter 4.[13]

Machine Learning

Artificial Intelligence is an umbrella term encompassing a range of theories and technologies that have existed since the mid-twentieth century, undergoing numerous cycles of growth and decline. The emergence of the internet fueled the collection of large quantities of data and breathed new life into the field. The conditions for the maturation of AI technology became available at the dawn of the twenty-first century with the evolution of smaller, faster computer processors and a renewed interest in machine learning, a foundational concept central to modern AI.[14]

There are two aspects to the way we learn: the first being teacher-driven where a pedagogy or structure drives the process, and the second being student-driven where the receiver of knowledge draws from multiple sources. The former is typically bounded by the limitations of the teacher's own knowledge and methods. The latter allows the student to assimilate far more knowledge from diverse sources, both organized and unorganized, and develop original frameworks to become more knowledgeable than the teacher. Both these approaches, one supervised by a teacher or expert and the other unsupervised and self-directed, have their parallels in AI.

As an example of the second approach, when you teach children how to distinguish a dog from a cat, you do not provide a formal set of rules—an algorithm—to follow. Instead, you offer examples through which children can learn. You present an image of a cat next to that of a dog and point out the differences. The more examples you provide, the more accurately a child can differentiate. Similarly, children learn languages by exposure to examples of usage rather than being taught formal grammar. Children have a biological learning system that analyzes patterns based on experiences; this mechanism develops rules to interpret the experiences and these rules improve with each experience.

The idea behind machine learning is to train computers to perform intelligent functions through experience rather than relying on a formal set of instructions. This can lead to the discovery of new patterns and relationships. Unfortunately, the concept is often murky for those outside the field because many books and articles about it are jargon-heavy or conceptually dense, and some are works of fantasy about a futuristic world, utopian or dystopian.[15]

Machine learning does not rely on predefined rules but instead uses adaptive learning by trial and error. With each exposure to new data, the algorithm learns to recognize patterns better. As large quantities of examples are fed into the system, the machine learns to identify deeply buried patterns and correlations that it then codifies into rules.

Figure 3 shows one method of machine learning by trial and error, evaluating each outcome in a feedback loop. Positive feedback loops reinforce certain behaviors, while negative feedback loops teach avoidance of certain choices.

The more experiential data a system uses to learn from, the smarter it can become.

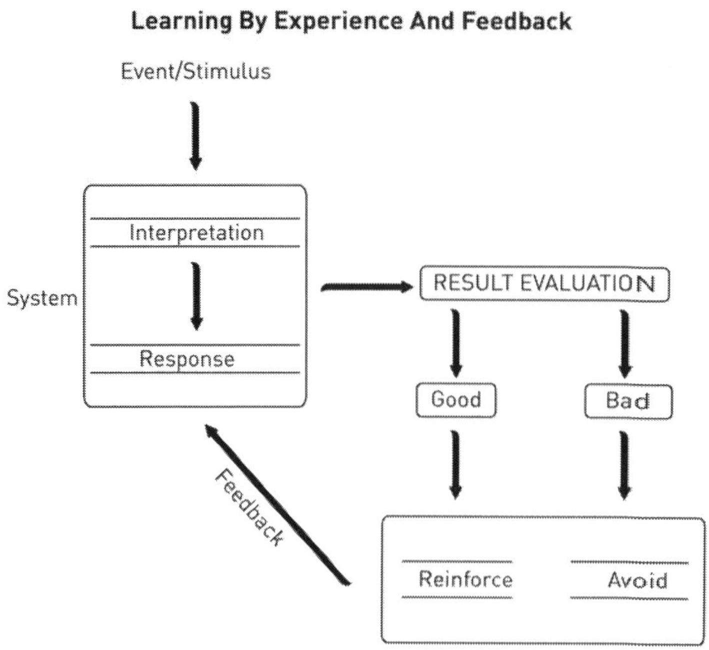

Figure 3: Simple Machine Learing

Data from past events is used to train algorithms and create models that are then used to predict the outcome of future events. The learning is iterative, and the system constantly becomes smarter with experience.[16]

Systems of Intelligence

Both natural systems and human-made systems have intelligence, but of different kinds. I use the term **natural causation** to refer to the rules by which natural systems function, and the natural sciences are the discipline by which we try to understand this causation. Scientists perform experiments and gather data to reveal behavioral patterns and create a model called a hypothesis—their best guess of how the system functions. Further testing either validates or negates the hypothesis, leading to revisions, retesting, and a stronger alternative. The process continues, and if no test negates the model, scientists might eventually reach a consensus that it can be considered a law. A law is merely a hypothesis explaining how something functions that scientists have not been able to disprove. In other words, science is our way of learning the cause–effect rules by which nature functions.

In the case of natural systems, there is no authority available to teach us the rules of causation. God does not provide a user manual or a customer support department.

The term **human causation** applies to processes that humans build. The creators of such a system can provide an instruction manual to explain how it works, so we can automate it using algorithms.

In the case of some human-made systems like ancient archeological sites or old scripts, the creators of those things are not available to explain their intentions. No design specification or training manual exists. Such human systems are like natural systems in that no authority is available to teach us the rules; we must independently investigate the system's behavior patterns to infer how it works. Without a teacher or defined rules, programmers cannot develop conventional software to instruct the computer. This is where machine learning can eliminate the need for an outside instructive authority because it figures things out by examining examples.

If a machine can learn on its own to use and imitate something made by humans, it should not be surprising that it can also learn to outsmart the human creators. The common statement that "Computers cannot perform better than their human creators" is *false*. Many AI systems beat human players in games even though the games were constructed by humans.

An interesting and important kind of intelligence is unconscious human intelligence, which is behavior that individuals cannot explain about themselves, commonly known as intuition. If someone doing a task is not conscious of *how* they do it, they cannot give us an algorithm to carry out the task. The question becomes whether the unconscious mind, though inaccessible to conscious thought, can be accessed externally by someone else. The practice of Western psychology is based on the premise that the answer is yes; through careful, targeted questioning, psychologists learn to delve into what lies hidden in a client's unconscious mind. A skilled questioner can extrapolate thoughts and feelings that people are unaware of.[17]

What is particularly significant about machine learning systems is that they can use numerous cause–effect examples to determine even unconscious patterns—effectively reverse engineering individuals' behavior, at times better than what the individuals themselves could explain. Because people are only partially self-aware, they cannot reveal what they do not consciously know. In contrast, machines can thoroughly observe and profile patterns of behavior that people exhibit unconsciously or unintentionally.

To summarize, there are three kinds of situations in which we cannot explicitly compile the rules for a system's behavior from an authoritative source.

1. *Natural* systems in the hard sciences such as physics, chemistry and biology;

2. *Human-made* systems created by individuals that are not available to explain or describe them, as in archeological sites and writings that have not been decoded; and
3. *Unconscious* behaviors, where people respond in particular ways but cannot explain how or why they do so.

Machine learning seeks to analyze and interpret these three kinds of systems by studying numerous examples of cause and effect to construct algorithms that replicate the system's behavior. The more examples a machine has of a given phenomenon, the better it can learn. Machine learning is inherently adaptive.

In some situations, a given individual may be conscious of how he or she does something but not know how others make decisions. For instance, a Covid-19 doctor might not know how thousands of other doctors worldwide are treating patients. Machine learning can also be used in these cases—for example, to model the collective experience of medical clinicians scattered around the globe generating millions of patient outcomes. The lessons learned from collective experience can be used to improve the diagnosis, management decisions, and therapies used.[18] The AI concept known as **swarm intelligence** refers to the collective behavior of decentralized, self-organized systems. This concept holds promise in studying cultures as collective systems and serves as a doorway for AI to enter into the humanities and social sciences.[19]

Humans and machines each have their own competitive advantages. Human intelligence spans multiple domains and contexts. If machines had this ability it would be called **artificial general intelligence**. However, machine learning as of now is highly context-specific because it uses examples from a specific environment. Consequently, AI systems tend to be applicable to only one kind of situation and have difficulty sharing what they have learned across multiple domains of knowledge.

Machines, on the other hand, are far superior in sharing with each other the models extracted from multiple machines in the same area of expertise. For instance, driverless cars share examples of their performance and each decision of a given car is stored for the collective learning of all cars. Human drivers cannot share each other's driving methods in a similar way; no single driver gets the benefit of every other driver's special experiences. Furthermore, when human drivers die, their knowledge is lost because the technology to transfer memory between humans does not exist. Knowledge accumulated by one generation passes to the next only to the extent that it has been recorded in books, manuals or transmitted personally and orally. In the case of machines, the demise of one does not lead to its memory loss. Even after a machine stops functioning, its data remains available for other machines.

Thus, machines are better at sharing across different members and across lifespans, whereas humans are superior at sharing across contextual domains.

Traditional machine learning can function with relatively small amounts of data, but the performance of the algorithms tends to plateau after a certain amount of data has been assimilated. The creation of **neural networks**—processes modeled after human brain activity—brought about a fundamental breakthrough in machine learning.[20] This enabled the approach called deep learning that involves training neural networks on vast amounts of data and building practical applications. Deep learning algorithms keep improving as more data is fed into the system (see Figure 4).

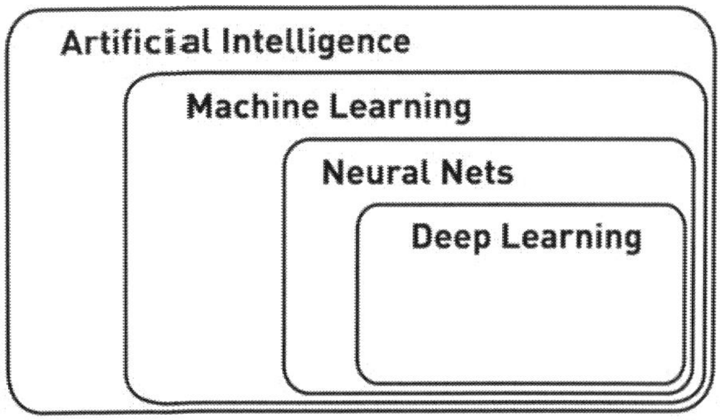

Figure 4: Relationship Among Computer Science Disciplines

Big Data

Billions of individuals are being minutely tracked from cradle to grave and their profiles are curated with private information. This includes information like voting histories, criminal histories, gun ownership, religious leanings, car and home ownership, divorces, litigations, health, credit history, interpersonal relations, and so forth. Massive amounts of such data—called big data—are the raw material required for machine learning to develop advanced intelligence. This raw material is vastly more valuable than any algorithm; better quality and a larger quantity of data help machines outperform any preconceived, fixed algorithm.

Big data may be characterized by the five Vs: variety, volume, velocity, veracity and value. These qualities exist in all types of data.[21]

- *Variety* represents the different types of data we collect and use. Data variety expands as it is gathered from increasingly diverse populations of humans, animals, plants and even the atmosphere. Data may be available in any number of different formats. In the past, almost all available data was structured (such as numbers in a spreadsheet), but today 80% of the data being added is unstructured and often informal, consisting of text, audio, images, video, or sensory information.

- The *volume* of data has been doubling every two years. Since 2005, there has been a 300-fold increase, and roughly 2.5 quintillion bytes of data are created daily. A major source is smart phones with their range of sensors.
- The *velocity* at which data is captured is accelerating because it is no longer constrained by the need for manual entry. The **Internet of Things** is a network of millions of devices that transfers data between them in real time.
- *Veracity* refers to the quality of data, a measure of the legitimacy and accuracy of this vast amount of data, in contrast to fake news, misinformation and viruses.
- *Value* refers to data as a form of capital—financial, social and political. As data is increasingly processed, it grows in value and becomes more monetized.

Leading digital companies have devised different ways to use practical applications for leveraging their big data.

- *Amazon* analyzes the purchase history of millions of customers, using machine learning to determine their purchase propensity and offering them targeted product recommendations. It pioneered the application of **recommendation systems**, which offer product suggestions to users based on their likelihood to purchase them.[22]
- *Facebook*'s popular Messenger and WhatsApp services are a goldmine of private information. They store every personal message that users generate, serving

as a laboratory for training its army of chatbots—programs that masquerade as humans by engaging in simple conversations—to become better at mimicking humans.

- *Twitter* analyzes each tweet in real time in correlation with the user's profile and preferences. Its machine learning system can rate each tweet using known policy offenders and inappropriate content to flag messages that violate the company's policies.
- *Pinterest*'s machine learning system is used to moderate spam, discover new content, and maximize revenue from advertising.
- *Yelp*'s large-scale machine learning system supports its human staff in compiling, categorizing and labeling images as well as understanding text-based reviews posted by members. It is highly effective at selling to consumers who have only a vague idea of what they want.
- *Salesforce* has a system called Einstein that helps digital marketers score each sales lead and develop targeted marketing campaigns.
- *Baidu* is a Chinese company with a research lab known as Deep Voice that is considered a technology leader in mimicking the voice of any person. By becoming trained in the unique subtleties in pitch, cadence, pronunciation and accent, Deep Voice can create a synthetic voice for a specific person that is difficult to distinguish from the person's real voice. Many other start-ups are beginning to offer similar products that mimic human speech. Some organizations are now producing video-based **deepfakes**, where machine learning systems pose as realistic human personalities, both visually and aurally.

To illustrate how big data is used to train a machine, consider driverless cars. To teach a driverless car, engineers do not program the car's computer merely with a set of driving rules. Instead, the driverless cars *teach themselves* how to drive just as humans do: through experience and practice. With dozens of onboard cameras and sensors feeding data into the system in real time, the cars learn to recognize traffic patterns and adjust their responses accordingly.

Each car's AI system can recognize shapes and differentiate between pedestrians, bicyclists, cars, trucks and tractor-trailers. It builds a real-time detailed map of its immediate physical environment, identifying each object nearby. By applying what it has previously learned, it can predict not only the speed of each type of object but also how it might suddenly change direction. Equipped with this predictive model of everything in its vicinity, the system can compute every possible scenario for the next second, the next two seconds, the next three seconds, and so on. Hence, it can choose options to minimize the chances of a collision.

Further, the collective practice of all driverless cars, as an example, is far more extensive than the total lifetime experience of even the most sophisticated individual human driver. The reason is that the skill of human drivers remains in their isolated memories, encoded as individual reflexes and habits, and passes on with the drivers. But the proficiency of each driverless car is systematically analyzed and shared with other cars. Eventually, as driverless vehicles are interconnected via 5G, they will directly communicate with each other, allowing vehicles to collectively negotiate decisions to optimize the flow of traffic.

Once machines are trained to perform tasks, they are often able to do them better than humans. Even AI's most critical detractors cannot deny this simple truth: AI-powered applications do, indeed, have certain advantages over those operated solely with human intelligence. Machines are not restricted by the limitations of human memory or lifespan. Their clock speed and memory can be continually increased. Their behavior is more consistent and predictable than that of humans. They possess more stamina and can operate under conditions that are unsafe or unsustainable for humans.

The potential of machines to improve does not mean they are progressing toward some perfect outcome. Computers are still susceptible to subtle influences and omissions. Ideological biases do sneak into machine learning applications, whether consciously or unconsciously. One example of bias was exposed by a report in the journal *Science* about an algorithm used by US insurance companies and hospitals to identify patients requiring high-risk care. The algorithm contained an unconscious bias against Blacks because it used historical healthcare spending patterns—which varies between Blacks and Whites—to determine patients' current needs. The US Senate demanded a review of this practice, temporarily undermining the public's trust in AI.[23]

The use of AI to screen job applicants has also been called into question. If machines' training is based on data that is not balanced, bias may occur at various points in the process and routinely eliminate qualified applicants that do not fit precisely into the categories developed by the machine learning system. At Amazon, a machine learning model demonstrated a gender bias against the resumes of female candidates based on the historical preponderance of male candidates.[24]

Bias also crept into Microsoft's attempt to build a bot that could interact on Twitter. TayTweets was inadvertently trained on a vast amount of mostly biased tweets in a twenty-four-hour period, and as a result when TayTweets interacted on Twitter, its responses were downright racist! Microsoft had to backtrack and quickly took down its bot.[25]

Evolution of AI Devices[26]

In the decade spanning 2005 through 2015, the growth of smartphones positioned them for large-scale data collection. These devices, equipped with ever more advanced sensors, wireless networking, imaging, and voice capabilities, have been capturing much larger quantities of data than desktop or laptop counterparts. Social media companies grabbed this opportunity and became dominant platforms supplying a variety of services. Many mobile-friendly technologies and applications emerged in this decade and continue to be important sources of big data.

Then the wearables space took off in a big way with the pioneering Fitbit and Pebble smartwatch. Several fitness-tracking watches quickly emerged, with their functions eventually absorbed into smartwatches such as the Apple Watch. The development of these devices established a new kind of data to mine at scale: personal health and fitness. In the medical industry, such data often captures the most intimate details of a person's physical performance and is considered extremely confidential. Through the social gamification of fitness and health, as well as other subterfuges, technology companies have acquired medical datasets that may well rival that of some large healthcare organizations. However, because they are classified as nonmedical companies, it is unclear whether they will be held to the same standards of data protection as the medical industry.[27]

With smartphones and wearables proving the value of mining private data, the next step pushed the boundaries even further by positioning data gathering under the guise of safety and convenience. In 2014, Amazon's Alexa successfully overcame the first barrier to household penetration of smart home technologies, putting its always-on ambient conversational AI at users' beck and call to perform simple tasks around the house. Amazon, Google and Apple have made huge investments in home automation technologies and partnerships with appliance manufacturers to capture a plethora of data from households, including voice, video, temperature, soil humidity, air purity, Wi-Fi strength, how often someone opens the refrigerator, eating habits, and every other imaginable parameter measurable by a gadget that's connected to the AI hub at home.

These voice interfaces will soon be embedded into ambient surfaces like ceilings and walls and furniture instead of being standalone devices. Amazon has tied up with a prefab construction company to pursue this.[28] Users will not even have to think about whether they are in the same room as a smart device—the interface will be omnipresent.

Smart home products with voice-activated assistants, light bulbs, appliances, entertainment systems, and security systems are now powered by AI. Video face recognition, speech recognition, and **Natural Language Processing (NLP)** for understanding personal conversations is taking the surveillance monitoring of private lives deeper than ever before.

Data privacy issues have not been adequately addressed vis-à-vis transparency on where and how all this data is stored and handled, who has access to it, and the relationship between the manufacturer and local law enforcement to govern its usage.

From wearables, the industry is progressing to implants that physically fuse technology into our bodies and tinker with the creation of a new kind of augmented human being. These technologies may monitor our physiology and emotional responses in new ways and do so very accurately because of their proximity to the source of emotional responses in our bodies. They would serve as a token of our physical identity and encode crucial information about us. It is also plausible that implantation of technologies may become the norm for applications like communication, health monitoring and physical identification. The data harvested from such devices would model personal consumer behavior and be extraordinarily invasive and intrusive in terms of privacy.

Each of the modalities mentioned above has broken new ground in creating a new kind of data about individuals that was hitherto unavailable or difficult to obtain—*variety*, one of the 5 *V*s. The more kinds of data that corporations can mine, the more complete the psychological and behavioral profiles of individuals that can be built; hence, the more sophisticated the ability of corporations to manipulate individuals and entire societies, by providing subtle nudges and cues through their every interaction with technology.

While each modality enables a greater variety of data to be collected, the veracity of the data also benefits. Rather than depending on humans to voluntarily provide information, the devices are an always-on ambient surveillance mechanism continuously gathering data. Along with variety, the volume and velocity of data collections are catalysts to the big data value chain.

The following table shows the evolution of devices working from outside the human body to ones with increasing proximity to internal processes, and finally to ones implanted within the body.

	Web Browsers (Laptop/ Desktop) →	Smartphones →	Smart Homes →	Wearables →	Implants
Data captured	Online activity	Online activity; location, motion, and audio; biometrics	Indoor location and activities; appliance usage; video and audio; environmental data	Location; sleep, ECG, pulse oximetry, motion, body temperature, other vital signs, and biometrics	Biological-mental; multiple vital signs, medical and mental data; physical identity
Modality	Conventional	Mobile	Ambient	Personal	Intimate
Level of privacy control by individual	Controllable: can be restricted, turned off, or left behind	Limited: harder to restrict, can be turned off or left behind	Low: usually always on and hard to bypass	Low: typically turned on to provide value; may be left behind	None: always on and impossible to bypass
Marketing focus	Internet access and entertainment	Ubiquitous connection with the world	Convenience, security and peace of mind	Fashion, functionality, personal connectivity and fitness	Health, identity, personal safety and medical management

The AI-based products that are expected to shape the next decade will initially include non-invasive gear people wear on their bodies, and eventually, devices that will be internally implanted. These devices will deliver a wide range of user experiences—from completely synthetic/virtual activities to various hybrids that enhance the real world with virtual experiences.

A totally virtual experience is one in which nothing perceived is real. Virtual Reality goggles create a three-dimensional experience in some distant, or even fictional, location, and special clothing can simulate the experience of an imagined climate. A major trend, however, is to mix and match physical surroundings with virtual objects beyond the user's own senses. While VR systems substitute a synthetic environment for the real one, AR enriches the actual physical environment with superimposed virtual objects. Users remain immersed in real space as AR seamlessly integrates visual information such as virtual objects or tools to help users perform actual tasks.[29]

Augmented Reality technology will usher in a whole new generation of AI-based technologies, with applications ranging from medicine, manufacturing, warehousing, retail sales, real estate, tourism, the military and education all the way to consumer entertainment.

Physical environments are being enhanced with AR to enrich the information available, especially visually, in the performance of a variety of tasks. For example, in conventional surgery, surgeons can see either the patient's physical body or images of the surgery site, but not both simultaneously. Augmented Reality allows surgeons to superimpose details from various scans directly over their patients' body. Human vision and machine vision get merged into one.

People may enjoy a real, physical dinner at a fancy restaurant in the AR company of a distant person who appears to be sitting next to them and sharing conversation. The experience will feel like an intimate two-person dinner when, in fact, each is eating alone and far away. Sports fans wearing glasses, gloves and other wearables will experience the thrill of making the game-winning play, while thousands of spectators cheer from the stands. By wearing a **haptic** suit along with goggles, even people who are not physically fit would be able to experience the thrill of mountaineering, going down Niagara Falls, or skydiving.

Apple and its competitors are racing to deliver a completely new generation of products based on AI technology. In recent years, a large number of patents have been filed in this field, countless start-ups have been acquired by the digital giants, and several groundbreaking trials are under way in specific applications. Just as apps were the big trend in the previous decade, AR will be a game changer in the present decade.

We are on the verge of the next revolution in electronics; this time fueled by AI systems. This change also represents a fundamental break from existing media, as significant as the shift from radio to television was two generations ago.

INTELLIGENCE VERSUS CONSCIOUSNESS

Science fiction that depicts AI in the form of conscious beings has fueled popular misconceptions of AI and done a disservice by trivializing the imminent AI revolution. Fantastic narratives have generated lively speculation and debate regarding the consciousness of machines.

People often confuse intelligence and consciousness. Intelligence exists in many forms and can be conscious or unconscious. Human intelligence is only one kind of intelligence.

Artificial *Intelligence* and Artificial *Consciousness* (AC) are vastly different. Machine intelligence simply refers to machines' ability to function in practical ways *equivalent* to humans. Consciousness is neither necessary nor sufficient for a system to be intelligent. An intelligent system could be unconscious. Conversely, a conscious system could be unintelligent.

When a truck driver loses work to a driverless vehicle, it does not matter whether the vehicle is conscious or not. What matters is that machines can replace human workers by doing the same job and performing it better and/or at a lower cost. We recognize that horses are conscious while automobiles are not, but this distinction did not prevent automobiles from performing the work previously done by horses. In the same way, the advent of driverless cars and trucks will eventually make today's automobile industry obsolete.

Similarly, when computers analyze X-rays and other medical diagnostics more efficiently and accurately than human experts, the implications for the healthcare field have nothing to do with whether the machines are conscious.

To differentiate between Artificial Intelligence and Artificial Consciousness, the linguistic framework of classifying statements as first, second and third person is useful.

- In first-person statements, I discuss something about myself, such as my feelings or something going on inside me. The first-person voice expresses the speaker's selfhood, or the "I". "I am happy" and "I am at home" are examples of first-person statements. This ability to experience oneself is known as sentience.
- Second-person statements are those made *to* another person or persons, for instance, "You are early".

Second-person speech is interpersonal and tends to be direct with one or more persons that are present.
- Third-person statements are used to refer to an object or entity: he, she, it, or they. The entity referenced may be another person, an inanimate object, or an abstract idea, such as "It is hot today". Speech *about* something or someone is a third-person statement.

Humans possess all three qualities: the first-person is our selfhood; the second-person consists of our interpersonal relations; and the third-person is the realm of mental objects such as cognition and concepts.

The term philosophical zombie (or p-zombie) has been used to refer to an entity that exhibits second- and third-person capabilities but lacks first-person awareness. As individuals we know that we are not a p-zombie but have no way of ascertaining whether someone else is a p-zombie or not. Humans have no window to see another person's inner being. We cannot determine whether another person is self-aware or merely a robot pretending to be human.

No matter how much someone externally appears to have an inner sense of self, no test exists that can definitively rule out the possibility that they are a machine simply pretending to have a self. P-zombies are indistinguishable from any normal human being. If a p-zombie were poked with a sharp object it would not experience any pain, yet outwardly it would behave exactly as if it had. From a purely practical perspective, an entity's ability—or lack of ability—to function from the first-person perspective is irrelevant to others.

Human intelligence is partly conscious and partly unconscious. For instance, I am not conscious of several biological mechanisms within my own body, such as my cardiac functions and my digestion, which are functioning all the time. While these functions are extraordinarily complex and intelligent, we are not conscious of them, and more importantly these processes are not themselves self-conscious. Similarly, we are also unconscious of large portions of our mind, where intelligent processes go on all the time without self-awareness.[30]

Our body grows, adapts, heals itself, and deals with unexpected threats and attacks from external forces through unconscious intelligence, i.e., by learning from experience and feedback the same way machine learning does.

Clearly, intelligent learning does not require consciousness—neither in the case of our body nor of a machine.

Artificial Intelligence's third-person capability allows it to run complex algorithms *about* all sorts of entities, and to become better at solving problems defined in terms of objects and ideas. Machines' second-person capability gives them the uncanny ability to interact *with* humans just as other humans would. However, an AI system does not need to experience first-person self-awareness to do its job.

The question of a machine's selfhood is inconsequential to the practical benefits and challenges that AI presents. Considerations of selfhood belong, instead, to the field of Artificial Consciousness. Many thinkers that fail to comprehend the multilayered and practical impacts of AI are focused on tangential philosophical questions more appropriate to Artificial Consciousness. They present arguments about machines lacking sentience, but such arguments are irrelevant to the impact of AI.

Experts on the nature of intelligence like to debate between the top-down and bottom-up models of the emergence of natural intelligence. According to the top-down model, God or some creative force makes intelligent beings. The initial approach used in AI followed the top-down model: Human programmers wrote the algorithms for machines to perform specific functions and tasks, analogous to God creating the universe and its systematic rules.

The bottom-up model is based on Charles Darwin's theory of evolution (1859), according to which intelligence emerged by unconscious natural selection. Darwin postulated a trial-and-error system intrinsic to nature, with no grand design, purpose, or plan determining the outcomes. Nature's intelligence develops through the feedback of results produced.

The latest AI revolution is based on bottom-up neural networks that rely on many examples and feedback from the outcomes. Machines learn how to perform tasks by developing their own rules from the bottom up.

Figure 5 shows the top-down and bottom-up approaches. Artificial Intelligence is a bottom-up approach in opposition to the primacy of consciousness, which is top-down. It is not fundamentally interested in understanding human intelligence from a philosophical perspective, but in finding pragmatic approaches that work best for a particular activity.

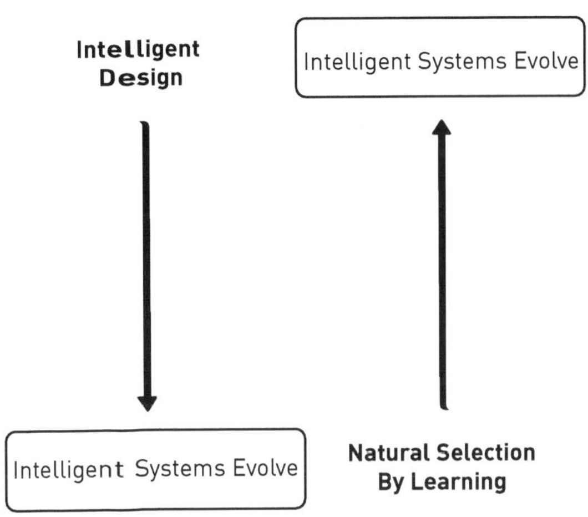

Figure 5: Models of Evolution

APPLICATIONS

To understand how AI is permanently transforming the social, economic and geopolitical landscape, it is important to take note of the broad range of applications of AI in all dimensions of society. The following pages give a brief survey to illustrate sone of the applications.

Healthcare

Healthcare is one of the most important domains in which AI technology is bringing positive effects. This is not surprising since medical practice is based on protocols and a protocol is basically an algorithm. Algorithms help medical doctors diagnose conditions efficiently and effectively; experts who compare the quality of human versus machine diagnoses find machines to be gaining an advantage in many specialized areas.

In times of crisis like the Covid-19 pandemic, when medical emergencies overwhelm the capacities of even the best of public health systems, AI is used for rapid diagnosis with less reliance on human involvement than ever before and with superior diagnostic accuracy. For instance, in San Diego, health radiologists and other physicians are using AI to analyze lung imaging to rapidly detect Covid-19.[31]

The outcomes of every diagnosis and patient consultation at major institutions are being channeled into a central diagnostic database for machine learning. As a result, machines are accumulating more medical knowledge and clinical experience than human doctors ever could, and AI will gradually replace, or at minimum supplement, doctors in making diagnoses, except for highly specialized situations.[32]

Machine learning techniques are already being used in studying the effects of different medical interventions such as lockdowns.[33] Technology helps monitor disease progression, track and control logistics and supply chains in real time, monitor public health to pinpoint infection hotspots, identify and classify infected individuals to help optimize public health systems, and coordinate responses.

The pandemic has forced physicians and their patients to use telemedicine, and the response has been universally favorable. Machine learning is augmenting doctors and at the same time telemedicine can capture new kinds of patient data such as facial expressions, emotional states, etc. The pandemic is also accelerating the commercial availability of health and fitness wearables to facilitate doctor-supervised health monitoring, remote diagnostics, and even certain treatments. With new kinds of devices there will be new kinds of data captured as well.

The field of AI in epidemiology specializes in building models to predict how diseases spread. In cases where the data set is far larger than usual, AI epidemiological models are better than conventional models for tracking and predicting the spread of diseases. For instance, a start-up in Malaysia developed an AI model to predict which neighborhoods are likely to have a dengue fever outbreak.[34] The Canadian company BlueDot developed an AI system to accurately predict when Covid-19 would migrate from Wuhan to Bangkok, Seoul, Taipei and Tokyo, based on analysis of airline ticket data and the locations of travelers' mobile phones.[35] Artificial Intelligence is now harnessing medical big data on individuals in order to model the spread of the pandemic and to manage real-time public health policies. Public health systems around the world are analyzing big data on human responses to the virus and to government policies, as well the effectiveness of different kinds of treatments.

Artificial Intelligence, in combination with mobile robots, will provide a much-needed support ecosystem for the care of the elderly. As the aging population increases worldwide, their care will have to be entrusted to robotic nurses, doctors and other helpers because the cost of human caregivers will become prohibitive.

Another area witnessing huge breakthroughs is research on the human genome. The study of how genes behave and influence physiological functioning is an exciting new frontier. Human DNA contains more than 20,000 individual genes. Because of its inherent complexity, gene analysis requires the help of AI. The benefits of this research range from improving understanding of diseases and developing more effective treatments to furthering doctors' ability to predict patients' future health. However, a downside is that the same AI technology developed for cures can also be applied to create intelligent germ warfare.[36]

Another pioneering example is the Fortune 500 American multinational, and one of the world's leading healthcare companies, Johnson & Johnson's project known as *Mellody*, which stands for "Machine Learning Ledger Orchestration for Drug Discovery", whose purpose is to leverage "the world's largest collection of small molecules with known biochemical or cellular activity to enable more accurate predictive models and increase efficiencies in drug discovery".[37]

Neural networks can be trained to model and replicate the behavior of pathogens and biological systems that constantly learn. Once Covid-19 is modeled as an algorithm (regardless of how complex it is), treatments can be developed as counter-algorithms that neutralize the mechanisms of the disease. Such advancements can then be applied to fight many other diseases.

In a different kind of application of AI, the Pentagon,

the headquarters of the US' Department of Defense, has developed a system that uses infrared lasers to identify individuals by reading their heartbeat from as far as two hundred yards away. The lasers can detect a cardiac signature that is unique to everyone.[38] The initial goal will be to identify combatants on a battleground, but such technology will quickly extend far beyond this application. While most current commercial technologies of this kind require users to wear a physical device, remote sensing technologies of the future will be able to read detailed personal data without the awareness or permission of individuals.

Biotechnology and information technology are already combining to create a new era of body and mind management. Applications such as medical implants that can intervene in mental functions will increasingly manage (and perhaps manipulate) human emotions and psychology. Once these applications are installed, the floodgates could open for implants that offer all kinds of virtual and augmented lifestyle enhancements.

Breakthroughs in neuroscience will eventually lead to products that enable the manipulation and management of human behavior. For instance, the US government has granted a permit to a treatment for Attention Deficit Disorder (ADD) using a digital game.[39] Some of the laudable goals of such technology would be to prevent or treat serious mental health problems and even avert criminal behavior.

In the long run there will be technologically enhanced humans that will exhibit all sorts of novel qualities, both physical and mental. Parents will have the option to choose the physical and mental genetic characteristics they want for their children. The concept of creating designer babies is no longer science fiction; it is an achievable reality currently blocked by legal and ethical concerns.

Transportation

One of the highest profiles and most impactful AI applications already in play is the driverless car. Much of the pioneering work in this field was stimulated in the US by the Defense Advanced Research Projects Agency (DARPA), the same agency that also developed what later became known as the internet. To help build driverless vehicles for the US military, DARPA organized a competition with a million-dollar prize for building a self-driving car that would drive the fastest through the Mojave Desert, a distance of 142 miles. In the first challenge in 2004, every car crashed, failed, or caught fire in the early phase of the race. But the event galvanized the imagination of young technocrats, and a research ecosystem emerged with the commitment to build practical driverless cars. In the 2005 race, there were five finishers, and this took the AI and robotics world by storm. Many of the contenders in DARPA races went on to play leading roles in what is now the driverless vehicles industry.[40]

Advances in this field will virtually eliminate the need for human drivers, just as a century ago automobiles eliminated the need for horses. At that time, critics of cars argued vociferously in favor of the horse-drawn carriage. Some even argued that important characteristics of the horse—such as its instincts, feelings and sensibilities—could not be replaced by an unfeeling machine.

Similar arguments against driverless cars are rampant today. Despite a lack of emotions and so-called common sense in cars, the pragmatic reality is that mainstream adoption of driverless vehicles will result in millions of drivers worldwide—long-haul truckers, delivery drivers, taxi and personal drivers—losing their ability to earn a living. Uber recognizes the business challenges inherent to maintaining a fleet of human drivers[41] and is investing heavily in self-driving taxi fleets.[42] Disruptions in the industry are inevitable when AI effectively turns taxis into the latest high-tech appliance.

Agriculture

Much of the technology developed for driverless cars has been deployed on farm equipment as well. The American corporation John Deere, already has autonomous tractors that can operate long days, under adverse conditions, and even in coordination with other unmanned and manned equipment on farms. Caterpillar is another heavy-equipment manufacturer that has integrated AI-based autonomy into its fleet.

Artificial Intelligence will also bring about smart agriculture that enables plants to survive climate change: for instance, dramatically reducing the amount of water required to grow certain crops. Mass population migrations from arid regions in search of water and the ability to grow food would be eliminated.

Artificial Intelligence can be effective in conjunction with what is called a **digital twin**, which is a virtual replica of a complete physical environment such as a farm that is recreated using data collected from a variety of sensors. In effect, the twin is the video-game equivalent of a real-world farm. Farmers can simulate conditions in the virtual landscape just like someone playing a video game—changing environmental conditions, choice of seeds, pests encountered, and other factors. By modeling how the digital environment responds, farmers can generate better results on their real farm. Artificial Intelligence can effectively eliminate the decision-making and practical role of human farmers to improve agricultural production.

The US agriculture administration has been developing robotic solutions that utilize,

> AI technologies to assist in pollination, weeding, pesticide applications, and fruit harvesting; AI algorithms that assist in identifying plant, animal and tree species that contribute to pest control and ecosystem management; and adaptive groundwater and watershed models to maintain resilience of agricultural systems. [...] monitoring livestock, using robots to sort harvests, analyzing irrigation systems, and utilizing UAV technology to analyze crop health and efficiently apply pesticides. [...] aerial monitoring of fungi levels on corn and other crops using computer vision and deep learning.[43]

Already, machines equipped with cameras and tactile sensors can identify crops that are ready to harvest. Elimination of the labor-intensive monitoring and harvesting will be another devastating blow to farm workers.

Military

The US military has one of the most advanced drone-based weapons systems in the world. It combines drone technology with satellite imaging and AI-based vision. Drones equipped with facial recognition can be programmed to attack a specific individual or individuals. While such precision minimizes collateral damage, in the wrong hands the technology has the danger of becoming the future of organized crime gangs or even rogue governments that could assassinate targets merely by supplying AI devices with facial images and other biometrics.

The Central Intelligence Agency (CIA) and the Chinese military are among those developing AI systems that multiply a single fighter plane into a squadron or mini air force of drones at the push of a button. Pilots will be able to launch drones and control their navigation remotely, forcing the enemy to deal with a multitude of aircraft instead of just one.

Similarly, artificial foot soldiers will be adept at negotiating potholes, rocks, landmines, shrubs—any natural or artificial land features that create significant obstacles for the average soldier. Robotic warriors will perform more efficiently and effectively than human soldiers in any terrain and climatic condition. In addition to having superior strength and endurance, they will withstand adverse conditions and hostile environments. Moreover, the military will benefit from robots' enhanced performance without having to manage supply lines with the food, medicine, or waste removal systems required for a human army.

Futuristic warfare systems are being funded in a big way.[44] In the fiscal year 2020 budget, the US Pentagon asked for a nearly tenfold increase in the Navy's spending on large AI-empowered unmanned surface, underwater and aerial vehicles, including four unmanned submarines. The US Navy deploys the Phalanx Close-in Weapons System (Phalanx CIWS) and is building the next-generation Boeing MQ-25 Stingray, a drone aircraft intended for aircraft carriers. The US Air Force is testing the concept of an armed Unmanned Aerial Vehicle (UAV), the Kratos XQ-58A Valkyrie drone, which will accompany fighter aircraft to attack enemy air defenses and shield the piloted aircraft. The US Army is likewise boosting its robotics R&D.

Both China and the US are upgrading their weapons systems to fight wars with smart autonomous weapons, and the strategic and tactical decision-making will be supported by AI-based systems capable of analyzing complex situations and taking independent actions.

Several other countries are following suit. For example, Israel has deployed the Iron Dome missile defense system. The United Kingdom's Brimstone missile system and Israel's Harpy Air Defense Suppression System are almost autonomous. South Korea deploys a sentry robot with an automatic mode called SGR-A1 on the North Korean front. Norway is likely to deploy the Joint Strike Missile, which can recognize an enemy ship or land-based weapon without human intervention.

Boston Dynamics, a company once funded by Google, has developed many biped, quadruped, and insect-like robots that can perform a variety of manual tasks such as opening doors, lifting heavy objects, and even doing backflips.[45] While their cognitive skills are currently comparable to humans in specific domains, their physical prowess already far exceeds the organic beings they are modeled after. It is plausible that this technology will improve weaponry to such heights that a military without comparable sophistication will effectively be using bows and arrows to fight tanks. Clearly, the disparity raises the stakes for survival in an increasingly dangerous world.

On the other hand, the capability of mutual destruction might instead inspire the achievement of peace through deterrence.

Financial Services

The US financial services sector is increasingly adopting AI to increase operational efficiency across several functions. Banks are making large investments in AI for compliance, risk management, fraud detection systems and credit decision making. JPMorgan Chase has developed an AI system that automatically analyzes and summarizes complex legal documents in seconds, which would otherwise have taken over 300,000 manual hours. BNY Mellon's robotic process automation program aims to automate repetitive manual tasks and has resulted in 88% improvement in processing time, and a 1,000 to 10,000 times decrease in failed trade reconciliation times.[46]

The insurance industry in the US is investing heavily in machine learning technologies to improve business effectiveness. Insurance claims and underwriting are the specific areas where insurers are seeing the biggest opportunities for AI. Popular AI applications among insurers include driver performance monitoring and insurance market analytics. For example, Progressive Insurance has collected fourteen billion miles of driving data from client drivers and used it for machine learning-based predictive analytics. Liberty Mutual is experimenting with an app to perform real-time assessment of vehicular damage during crashes and provide customized repair cost estimates based on an AI model trained with a dataset of large number of car crash images. However, there is also increasing concern from insurance companies that lower accidents on account of AI will reduce the need for auto insurance.[47] There is also the looming question of how to determine liability in driverless auto accidents.

In the stock exchanges, tens of thousands of traditional traders worldwide have already lost their jobs to algorithms. Artificial Intelligence is also replacing economists who build price models and evaluate investment portfolios and risk.

Artificial Intelligence helped to make market abusers and manipulators more sophisticated and difficult to trace than in previous eras. In response, regulators are deploying their own AI systems to look for abusive behavior.[48]

In a significant development, a Hong Kong venture capital firm has appointed an algorithm to its board of directors, a position that includes responsibility for making investment decisions.[49]

Education

E-learning is already capturing a significant market share from brick-and-mortar universities every year, and the trend is expected to accelerate as distance-learning technology becomes smarter and more accessible. Only disciplines in which a laboratory or other physical facility is necessary are temporarily secure from this digital revolution. E-learning levels the playing field by making high-quality education equally available to every person in every corner of the world, and on an unprecedented scale.

China has introduced the use of AI in schools from kindergarten to universities to accelerate learning and intensify competitiveness even further. Many classrooms are equipped with facial-recognition cameras and brainwave trackers that students wear on their foreheads using a headband. Parents and teachers see these as tools to improve grades. The AI system interacts with children by giving hints and, at the same time, gives the teacher real-time tracking of students' attentiveness and overall cognitive functioning. Robots take attendance, serve as teaching assistants, and help evaluate students. Besides boosting grades as well as safety, China's educators say the system makes education more personalized by understanding the learning habits of individual students and analyzing their physical and mental health. The AI system claims to make more scientifically based decisions about education policies, and China expects to lead the world in the next-generation technology of smart education.

> This increasingly aggressive and sometimes intrusive use of high-end technology in education is pivotal to Beijing's goal to make the AI industry a fresh driver of economic expansion. Virtually unobstructed access to a potential sample pool of around 200 million students

> allows Chinese scientists and researchers to amass an unrivaled database, which is indispensable to develop advanced algorithms. That provides a key advantage for China in an ongoing race with the U.S. for global dominance in the field.[50]

One US company that has already supplied 20,000 headbands to China now plans to introduce this system of education in US schools as well.

Social Sciences

The academic discipline of anthropology involves gathering field data, and sociologists then plug this into their models. The rough analogy is that anthropology generates what we know as big data, while sociology uses this data to train its models that explain some social process. Social scientists ideally should start with a clean slate and let the data drive their discovery of social models, rather than making the data fit into pre-existing models. In practice, however, social scientists' internal biases, derived from their own background brimming with preconceived ideas, serve as a lens that filters the data to build social models. The discipline still uses many colonial assumptions that were developed to study and interpret ostensibly primitive societies.

The AI-based approaches of knowledge discovery and knowledge mining could revolutionize the social sciences. The term **unsupervised learning** refers to machine learning in which the system is turned loose to explore and discover structures on its own. It can be effective in building entirely new models of society. The quality and quantity of big data being generated by the digital platforms in a single day far exceeds all the data gathered by social scientists over the past two hundred years. However, the mere fact that the machine learning is unsupervised does not mean it is free from biases.

The fact is that any AI-based discovery of social structures would depend on the goals and values of the developers. These values serve as the guiding principles to implement the deep mining of knowledge about society and discover its structures. Such principles are bound to be conditioned by the developers' worldview.

For instance, each time Facebook flags a post for "violating social norms", its algorithm is premised on a subjective principle of what these social norms ought to be. Imagine the algorithms making such decisions were based on the ethical principle that animals are spiritual beings like humans and deserve respect. Such an algorithm would reject many posts that promote animal products, animal laboratory testing, and so forth. Or, if the criteria were controlled by a radical Islamic republic that considers women exposing their faces a criminal act. Contrast that with a principle that considers the burqa a violation of human rights. The list of such subjective social norms is endless.

Even in the same country values change drastically over time. Had there been AI-based algorithms enforcing **community standards** in the US a century ago, Presidents Teddy Roosevelt and Woodrow Wilson would have been heroes and posts praising them given high rankings. But today the Black Lives Matter (BLM) movement in the US is fighting against what it considers white supremacy and has disgraced these iconic presidents; praising them can violate present-day community standards. Likewise, Christopher Columbus, for whom there is a US federal holiday, is now branded racist and many organizations boycott his birthday. Bias also creeps into AI models by the pre-selection of the data used for training the model as well as from the choice of model to be used. There is no universal or consistent set of principles that Facebook, Twitter, Google, and others could claim to be implementing in their algorithms to prioritize the social merit or demerit of content.

The risk for a society like India is that Indians have not pioneered research in this field and are importing foreign biases through the AI models of companies like Facebook, Google and Amazon. Data-driven social sciences have been in use for decades, and Indians in particular, are importing biases in the form of the model and data being used.

Figure 6 compares the old social science approach to new AI-based methods.

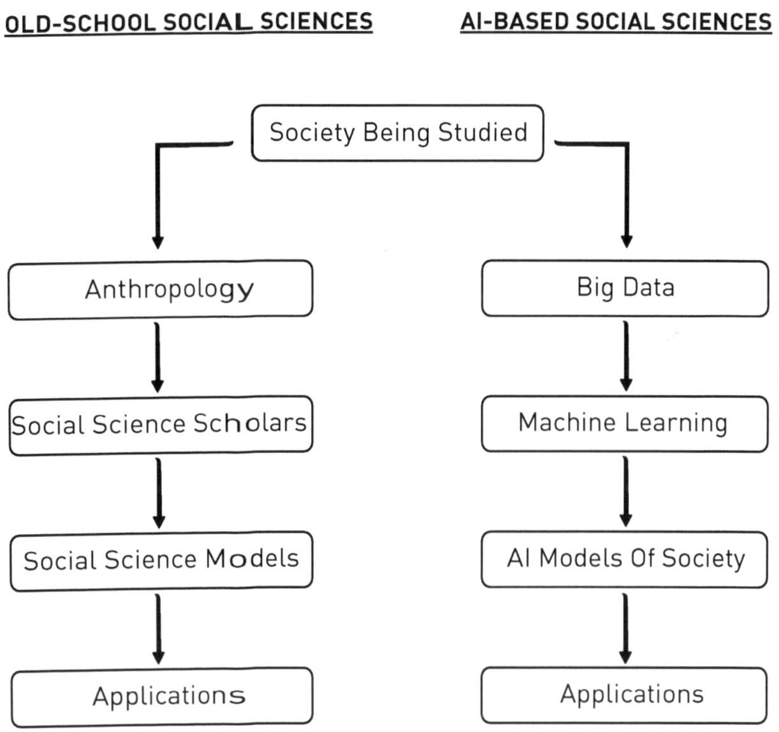

Figure 6: Models of Social Sciences

Gamification and Social Engineering

The term gamification refers to a formal set of techniques that were experimentally developed in the video and computer games industry to entice users into desired behaviors by encouraging them toward victory. The intention is to make entertaining computerized games where players can compete against themselves, or the machine, or each other. This is done by taking advantage of their psychological predispositions. The cognitive science and neuroscience of human motivation and response to pleasure/pain has been used by game developers over the past few decades to perfect their ability to maximize players' engagement.

In parallel, a field emerged that adds game mechanisms and psychology of competitiveness into nongame environments such as consumer marketing. By tracking each individual consumer's interactions using a scorecard, the marketers stimulate the consumer's behavior to reinforce positive responses and increase participation. Typically, the marketer starts a gamification project by defining its objectives in measurable terms, and the target audience's motivations are researched.[51] In principle, one can gamify any set of rules, principles, or values as the criteria that define victory and defeat.

For this book, I am adapting the concept of gamification beyond its normal usage and applying it to describe *interventions in politics and social engineering*. Such applications already exist even though the term gamification might not be in formal use to describe them. I find it a useful framework to understand the application of AI to manipulate social behavior.[52] Once these cultural and social activities are looked through the lens of gamification, many more ideas emerge—such as the possibility of gamifying the grand narrative of a nation or civilization.

The principle of gamification to reward good habits could be applied to optimize good dharmic behavior (i.e. karma gamification), good environmental behavior, good behavior in advocating and practicing human diversity, and so forth. The list is as long as the list of social causes.

Figure 7 shows how one could start with a social theory, use it as the foundation to build policies and principles for social, economic and political systems, and then develop concrete rules for measuring behavior, and finally gamifying it to modify social behavior. One can gamify any grand narrative and expand it in powerful ways without necessarily using hard power over the citizens. This AI-driven gamification amplifies whatever values and goals are built into it, and there is no such thing as an absolute, universal or neutral worldview. This is the future of social sciences and politics.

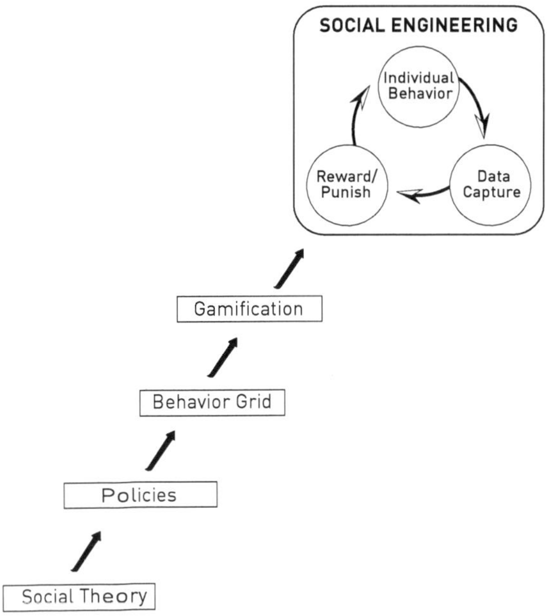

Figure 7: Gamification and Social Engineering

Shoshana Zuboff, a harsh critic of gamifying society, writes:

> The power of games to change behavior is shamelessly instrumentalized as gamification spreads to thousands of situations in which a company merely wants to tune, herd, and condition the behavior of its customers or employees toward its own objectives.[53]

She has been one of the foremost critics of the digital industry's agenda to program humans as though they are machines:

> Automated machine processes not only *know* our behavior but also *shape* our behavior at scale. With this reorientation from knowledge to power, it is no longer enough to automate information flows *about* us; the goal is to *automate us*.[54]

Zuboff has popularized the term "Instrumentarian society" to describe the emerging society in which individuals are herded as machines operating collectively under the control of algorithms:

> Just as industrial society was imagined as a well-functioning machine, Instrumentarian society is imagined as a human simulation of machine learning systems: a confluent hive mind in which each element learns and operates in concert with every other element. In the model of machine confluence, the "freedom" of each individual machine is subordinated to the knowledge of the system as a whole. Instrumentarian power is to organize, herd, and tune society to achieve a similar social confluence, in which group pressure and computational certainty replace politics and democracy.[55]

Google's Eric Schmidt is one of the tech leaders with a long track record of promoting that instead of the typical focus emphasizing machines to become more like humans, it is necessary for people to become more machine-like.[56] This view is shared by many other leaders of the digital revolution including Microsoft CEO, Satya Nadella.[57]

There can be as many ideological applications of gamification of society as there are social-political theories. A civilization's grand narrative can be used explicitly or implicitly to define the goals and objectives of an AI system. Such a system can be used to facilitate social engineering according to the contours of a given value system. China has been doing this very openly for several years, initially in its Muslim regions and subsequently across the country. All top-down rule-based societies have a similar social engineering impact on their populations.

- China's AI-based social engineering system of reward and punishment is based on its strict ideas of governance, society, ideals and values resulting from a combination of Confucianism, Taoism, communism, modernity and postmodernity unique to defining the Chinese civilizational identity.
- The US's value system is based on the capitalist principle of maximizing financial success and the value of human rights that spring from a fragile deal between liberalism and Judeo-Christian values. The war over Facebook's censorship of hate speech or lack thereof illustrates the power of algorithms to modulate the discourse even while claiming to champion free speech.
- An Islamic country that wants to develop AI-based social engineering will naturally formulate goals and objectives using Islamic criteria.

A system trained with big data based on Biblical premises would gamify to nudge the players in that direction just as one could gamify social systems to encourage Islamic, Vedic, or any other ideological beliefs. Recently, Christian theologians have started discussing the notion of baptizing robots to make sure they evangelize properly.[58] The future of evangelism, missionary work, and NGOs transforming society will use this technology and this will shape the ideological winners and losers of tomorrow.

Given the immense leverage of gamifying AI-based systems for social engineering, it is inevitable that this amazing power will fall into the hands of totalitarian regimes. Or, perhaps even more dangerous would be to have such power in the control of those who appear benign and even philanthropic in their motives. Zuboff describes them as follows: "They [are] dressed in the fashions of advocacy and emancipation, appealing to and exploiting contemporary anxieties, while the real action is hidden".[59] She is referring to the billionaires who own and manage organizations like Google, Facebook, Twitter, Microsoft and Amazon. While the publicly declared autocrats are well identified and people are wary, these billionaire string-pullers are the hidden puppet-masters seen as giving away free services; what is hidden are the gamification mechanisms that manage social behavior on an unprecedented scale.

The Chinese Communist Party has developed a sophisticated Social Credit System to standardize the assessment of citizens' and business organizations' economic and social conduct, and each entity is constantly tracked by an elaborate system of what is called "social credit". There are multiple, different forms of social credit systems being experimented with and advanced. Every individual and collective entity is tracked and evaluated for trustworthiness and good citizenship. China uses its mass surveillance systems and big data from conventional sources for this purpose.

Examples of bad behavior that have a negative impact on one's score include dishonest and fraudulent financial behavior, playing loud music or eating in rapid transit systems, violating traffic rules such as jaywalking and red-light violations, making reservations at restaurants or hotels but not showing up, failing to correctly sort personal waste, fraudulently using other people's public transportation ID cards, and so forth. Examples of behavior officially listed as positive factors for credit ratings include donating blood, donating to charity, volunteering for community services, paying taxes and bills on time, promoting traditional Chinese morals values, and so on.

High-speed rail tickets have been denied to people who were deemed untrustworthy (i.e. blacklisted, and once on such a blacklist it can take two to five years to be removed from it, but this can be accelerated by performing certain prescribed remedies. Public shaming is also a part of the system to expose and embarrass the worst violators. Such shaming information is displayed online as well as at movie theaters, buses, and other public places. Some local municipalities have also banned children of "untrustworthy" residents from attending certain schools and colleges.

China has been openly using these methods to socially engineer its Uighur Muslim population in the Jinjiang region.

Those with high credit ratings receive rewards like priority at hospitals and government services, discounts at hotels, better employment opportunities, etc.

The US has a plethora of credit systems that have not been unified under one comprehensive system as in China and gamified as such. But there are many such isolated systems, such as financial credit, points assigned for traffic violations that insurance companies use for rating risk, legal history records, and so forth. All these are easily available, and many specialized entities compile them for clients seeking to investigate someone. Social media has taken this to a new level: In the guise of helping their specific ideas of human rights, social justice and community norms, Facebook, Google and Twitter decide which posts get boosted and which ones get banned or shadow banned, warned and even publicly shamed as a branded "violator". Interestingly, US visa applications have started requiring declaration of social media accounts.

India, too, has its complex maze of privileges doled out by the government based on status determined by birth rather than by conduct and merit. One could debate whether behavior-based social credit would be better than birth-caste-based politics.

What might be an equivalent approach to install Vedic principles in society? First, the goals and objectives would have to be defined using Vedic social theory. This would establish the non-negotiable principles that must serve as the foundation for such a society. Hypothetically, there could be a social gamification system based on the principles of dharma with the goal to maximize good karmas.[60] Before the advent of AI, Brahmins filled the role of defining the social narrative and embedding it in the application of dharma in society. Implementation was the role of the **Kshatriya** (ruler). One could implement the social narrative within the machine learning system and penetrate the functioning of all civic organs. This AI-based digital-kshatriya system would control, measure, modulate and shape the civilizational ethos in society. It would optimize the outcomes in accordance with the prescribed values.

Any long-term gamified social engineering might result in changes in the biological algorithms through **epigenetics** from one generation to the next. The epigenetics system is also like a machine learning mechanism similar to the neurology of the brain.

Games

The abilities of machine learning systems are illustrated by the success of AI systems in learning the board game Go, which is far more complex than chess in terms of the number of possible moves available at each step. After the first two moves in chess, the next move has around 400 possible options; in Go, the number of possibilities is 30 times higher, making it impractical to hard code the complete set of options. Yet Google's AlphaGo learned to play the game without being programmed with rules, merely by playing and observing hundreds of different players. The system can even play against itself and improve while doing so! AlphaGo ultimately defeated the reigning human champion without a human coach teaching it any strategy. Similarly, Google's DeepMind program has demonstrated the amazing feat of becoming an expert in forty-nine different classic Atari games by analyzing numerous examples of each game.[61]

While such research may seem trivial, AI for gaming is not merely an entertainment product. Its deeper function is to develop methodological breakthroughs in AI that can be implemented in other applications.

Tourism

The Covid-19 pandemic's shock to tourism has given a boost to haptic interfaces like full-body suits that provide tactile sensations of VR or AR. Such technology was already on the rise as a new form of entertainment and is now advancing even faster. For the price of a physical trip to a destination, many young consumers will invest in devices that enable them to enjoy a variety of VR and AR vacations. These virtual journeys will be more varied and exciting than their physical equivalents.

For instance, users will be able to experience climbing Mount Everest, which most people could never physically do. Vacationers may be able to journey into deep oceans, venture inside the mouth of a large whale, and even become a tiny creature swimming inside the bloodstream. Many such practical and affordable apps and innovative services will be popular in the next decade, just as the previous decade was defined by novel apps based on conventional smartphones.

Art

Imagine a famous painting like the Mona Lisa coming to life as an animation—speaking and smiling from within her frame. Researchers recently accomplished exactly that effect with AI.[62] With the advent of such videos, called deepfakes, distinguishing between the real world and AI-enhanced imitations is becoming almost impossible.

Could another Wolfgang Amadeus Mozart be in our near future? Perhaps not a human one. Artificial Intelligence-based composition of music, however, has achieved a significant milestone: Machines are now able to generate original compositions so realistically that music critics are unable to distinguish between human-composed and machine-composed pieces. Interestingly, experts have praised computer-generated music for its "soulfulness" and "emotional resonance", characteristics that until now were a result of human creativity. Machine learning has also enabled programs to respond to audience feedback and mood in real time and adapt the music being played accordingly.

Another interesting creative use of AI is in selecting specific music for each individual listener. Pandora has developed a technology known as the Music Genome Project, which captures the mathematical essence of music as parameters analogous to the human genome. Machine learning is used to personalize recommendations to users.

The creation of such products and applications will accelerate with the imminent arrival of AR devices. Facebook founder Mark Zuckerberg's vision for the decade starting 2020 is that AR glasses will be the next ubiquitous platform, taking over from today's phones, because they will be "delivering a sense of presence—the feeling that you're right there with another person or in another place". In an ironic twist, a group of developers created a deepfake of Zuckerberg that quite literally put fake words in his mouth![63]

DEBATES AND CONTROVERSIES

This book contests many widely held, popular beliefs about the nature of AI and its impact, such as the following:

1. Machines are objective and trustworthy because they follow rules without prejudice.
2. Data rights are being protected or at least a framework has been widely established in which to protect them.
3. Because machines lack human emotions, activities that are emotional or involve **aesthetics** and creativity are permanently beyond the reach of automation.
4. Unemployment caused by AI will self-correct because market forces will demand retraining programs and create new, better jobs.
5. Advancements in AI cannot disrupt or threaten human agency and free will.
6. As new technology continues to affect our way of life, existing social and political systems will be adequate

to manage the disruptions; such systems are robust and will not be undermined.

7. The leaders of the tech industry have the public's best interests at heart. Economists, political thinkers, media and public intellectuals are well informed and have adequately protected the interests of ordinary citizens.

I submit that all these assumptions are false, as summarized in the following pages. It is important to note that the arguments on different issues are independent in the sense that a reader may disagree with my logic in some instances while agreeing on other issues. My goal is to equip concerned citizens who want to participate in these debates with fact-based information and insights. Chapters 2 through 4 provide more details on each topic.

Biases in Machine Learning

Artificial Intelligence models and algorithms are touted as being objective and neutral, which is far from the truth. Biases of the people that control the AI systems enter in at least two ways. Figure 8 illustrates that in addition to the data sets, a precise definition of goals and objectives is required for training machines. As explained earlier in the section on gamification and social engineering, this definition is selected at the discretion of the AI developers. Consequently, the final model is vulnerable to both intentional and unintentional biases.

Item A in Figure 8 depicts the purpose, objective, or goal of the AI system to be built. The developers must clearly establish what they expect the system to do. This is determined by the client, whether an individual, a government, a private company, or NGO.

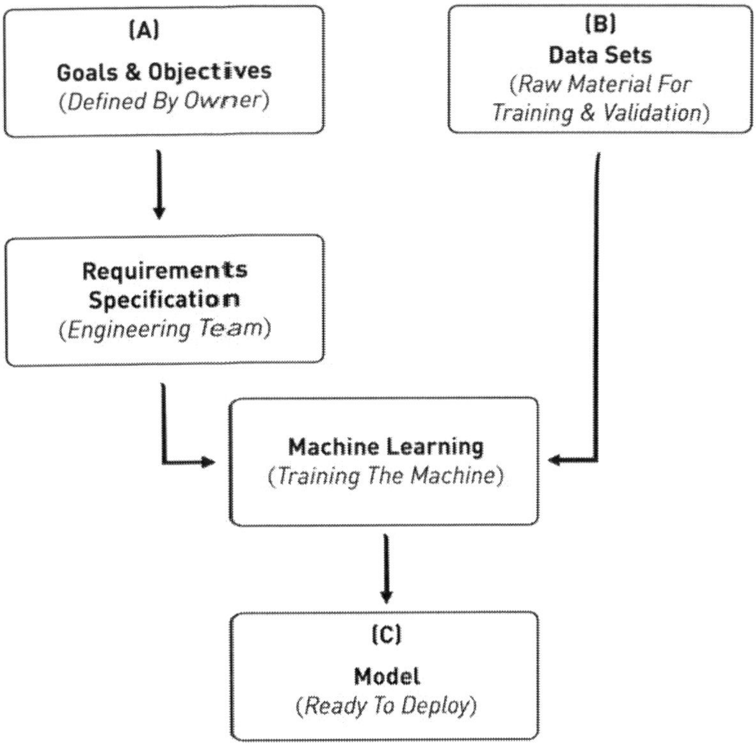

Figure 8: Potential Sources of Bias

From this definition of the end goals, the engineering team formulates its own specifications. The goal does not have to be fixed; it can evolve as the system progresses depending on user needs and market/environmental conditions. The requirements are often expressed in terms of a specific measure of performance, and the criteria for optimization may bc based on a combination of factors.

Item B depicts the big data sets that are used as raw material for training. Some data may be used for the actual training while other parts may validate or test the system's performance. The big data used could also contain biases and tilt the training.

The box in the center is the machine learning process itself. Many approaches and technologies are available within the machine learning field, which keep evolving. Specific methodologies are selected as appropriate for a given project.

The outcome shown as C represents the model ready for deployment in the AI system. The machine has been trained according to the original goals and objectives.

Clearly, the choices of A and B are arbitrarily made by human beings who control the machine learning process. Biases can easily creep in.

Data Rights

An important issue concerns the use of raw data to derive models: Who owns the models of personal behavior developed by such data? Do individuals have the right to demand a full disclosure of all models that use their data in any manner, and the right to challenge the biases in these models? Should data owners have a share in the intellectual property rights of the AI models created with their data?

I can list at least four separate and distinct, though interrelated, issues that should frame the discussions on this matter. Only the first is being adequately appreciated by the public.

1. *Privacy*: Keeping someone's personal data protected from unauthorized disclosure.
2. *Neutrality*: Providing a level playing field without bias from the digital platform.
3. *Data Usage*: Getting consent prior to using someone's personal data to engage with them in any way.

4. *Intellectual property rights of data*: Giving an ownership stake in the models developed to those whose data is used in the development.[64]

Neutrality

There is a folk theory of democracy and freedom of press that claims media represents the wishes and desires of the people. But genuine free speech requires a level playing field for deliberation, argumentation and debate, and this is far from the actual situation. In fact, the history of systemic propaganda and misinformation is incredibly old, for which the term "manufacturing consent" has been used. This has been described as the use of "effective and powerful ideological institutions that carry out a system-supportive propaganda function, by reliance on market forces, internalized assumptions and self-censorship, and without overt coercion".[65]

Some examples follow:

- In the medieval era, the Church had a powerful office of propaganda.[66]
- In the 1890s, the famous American media tycoons Joseph Pulitzer and William Randolph Hearst created what became known as "yellow journalism" that competed for inciting public opinion with sensational and fake news. It led to the justification of US invasions abroad.
- The twentieth-century sophisticated propaganda machine of the Nazis is infamous.
- More recently, Julian Assange of Wikileaks and former US intelligence official Edward Snowden incurred the wrath of the US government for exposing secret surveillance and propaganda machines.
- In India, during the government under the control of Sonia Gandhi of the Congress party, it was an

unwritten rule that the media should never name her explicitly in criticism. More recently, Narendra Modi (currently the prime minister) is also protected in certain circles.
- Donald Trump and his opponents each accuse the other camp of planting fake news.

Today's clickbait journalism and marketing is the most advanced version of this kind of system that has ever been developed, and every sophisticated marketing or political organization uses it for persuasion. Grabbing eyeballs is more important than accuracy or truth.

Data from social media trains the algorithms, which, in turn, feed the user what is likely to produce the desired effect. This echo chamber perpetuates itself. Google's search engine has tilted the field by using algorithms that are inevitably trained by some subjective criteria. Facebook has become powerful through its "Like" *economy*. Its WhatsApp is among the biggest propagators of misinformation.

The fact is that Facebook, Google, Twitter, and other social media platforms use their proprietary AI algorithms to screen content being posted, and these algorithms are trained to flag violations of the company's policies on appropriate behavior. The algorithms embed the companies' official censorship ideologies to decide which posts will be given priority for promotion, which will be ignored or even shadow banned, in what instances will users be warned about their posts or asked to delete certain content, and on what basis will users be blocked.

Machine learning models routinely make arbitrary decisions that the companies rationalize as an enforcement of community standards and community guidelines. But what are these standards and guidelines, who defines them, and how are they interpreted for enforcement? Social media companies have publicly established generic criteria like authenticity, misrepresentation, false information, respect for intellectual property, insensitivity to the dignity of others, hate speech, and so forth. These lofty principles are too broad and give the algorithms too much discretion. Though commendable at face value, in practice the implementation is inconsistent, biased, and in many cases, outright unfair. Worst of all, their algorithms lack transparency because the models that drive them are closely guarded secrets. Many posts have been rejected on spurious grounds that expose the digital platform's cultural, racial, or ideological prejudice.[67]

In the face of numerous complaints, Facebook recently established an independent board to adjudicate challenges against the company's treatment of content.[68] The move is intended to preempt litigation against the firm in public courts. Interestingly, the authority of the oversight board does not include review of, and modifications to, Facebook's secret algorithms and models. Further, the choice of the board members is itself arbitrary; inclusion of individuals with good credentials from diverse backgrounds does not necessarily mean freedom from bias. Reasonable cynicism suggests that this board is a decoy to deflect attention away from the heart of the problem by offering a partial solution that does not address the root of the problem.[69]

True protection against bias would require the full disclosure of the model and all the algorithms, as well as *the optimization targets and data sets used for training*. Only then would it be possible to audit its neutrality. Alternatively, the digital platforms would have to stop all censoring done in the name of public good because public good is subjective.[70]

At the heart of the matter is the ambiguity enjoyed by the digital platforms as to whether they are governed by telecom or media norms. Telecom firms cannot show prejudice against a subscriber based on the type of person. Nor can the carrier listen to calls and block them based on content. In other words, the carrier cannot censor. By the same token, the carrier is not held accountable if its network is used for anti-social activities.[71] Media companies, on the other hand, have the right to decide the content and from whom they will carry, and correspondingly, they also have the liability if the content violates the regulations.

Digital platforms enjoy the best of both worlds. They exercise their prerogative to decide the merits of content—that too very arbitrarily—and yet claim immunity from prosecution if the content violates individuals or society.

The table below summarizes the rights and responsibilities of telecom, media and digital platform companies regarding content.

	Telecom	Media	Digital Platform
Right to censor content	No	Yes	Yes
Liability for content violations	No	Yes	No

Use of data without breach of privacy

The demands being made for data protection focus mainly on privacy, but these debates are missing the main point. Privacy merely requires that the data on given individuals will not be disclosed to others. The behavior profile based on users' buying habits, analysis of personal messages, financial transactions, travel history and other metrics is used to develop models, typically with names and identities of the individuals kept secret from third parties a restriction that seems to have satisfied naïve regulators and public activists. The real issue isn't that Amazon, for example, will reveal someone's personal data to others. Rather, my concern here is that having the individual's profile gives the company an unfair advantage in dealing with users. Once a good model has been developed, the data has served its purpose. At that point, the model becomes the prized asset of the company, and the raw data could even be deleted.

The point being made is that some companies owning big data make it anonymous by replacing personal identities with numbers that are not linked to individuals, thereby satisfying the superficial privacy requirements. However, the data is still used to build behavioral models for groups and communities, if not individuals. Simply dissociating customer data from actual identities gives insufficient protection and merely provides better optics in the eyes of regulators who do not know better.

Using private data to make personalized shopping offers seems benign. However, the same advantage is afforded to a political group that seeks to influence votes, garner support for a cause, mobilize a revolt, or predict an individual's behavior in a given negotiation or dispute. Such profiling of individuals is being used to develop psychological and emotional models that exploit weaknesses and vulnerabilities, pinpoint the inducements most likely to succeed, identify what threats and fears make the most effective deterrent, and enable other manipulative opportunities. Keeping personal information secret from third parties does not imply that the AI company is not using it for its own benefit. Even when data is kept private, the strategies built on the data can be deployed to deal with users.

For instance, imagine if a marketing company, political group, religious group, terrorist group, or foreign government wants to infiltrate the lives of a community with the help of AI-based psychological behavior models. The target community could be defined on criteria like its location, religion, political leanings, ethnicity, age, or other variables. The effectiveness of such a model-driven manipulation does not require knowing the identities of individuals whose private data was used to train the model. *Anonymization is an exercise in futility.*

The only way to solve this problem would be to *declare individuals' data to be their intellectual property,* such that any use of it must require their specific permission for every instance. Users, as the owner of their own data, should be able to control its use under a license arrangement. In particular, a model derived by training a machine learning system should be considered intellectual property. Doing so would redefine the debate on Facebook's entry into India through its investment in the telecom company Jio—discussed in Chapter 6. Rather than offering mere assurances that Facebook will protect individuals' privacy, the company would have to take a stand on who owns the models that its machine learning system develops using the personal data of Indians.

These issues remain even after personal raw data has been deleted from a database. The distinction between the rights to the raw data and the rights to the finished model or an algorithm has not been addressed properly. The *disclosure* of someone's private data and the *use* of that data to build intellectual property assets represent two different kinds of advantages. The public needs protection against the use of private data to train models that are deployed to negotiate, entice, trap, deceive and even blackmail users.

Current discussions on data protection are incomplete and misleading. The irony is that well-intended but ill-informed lawmakers tend to give technology-savvy companies significant latitude in interpreting what data is considered *essential* to their services. For example, websites often allow access only after users give full consent to all levels of cookies even though such cookies are nonessential to the company's services. This practice employs convoluted language to nudge users toward a choice that serves the company's vested interest. Ironically, the very companies that pride themselves on being user-friendly in their apps deliberately adopt interfaces that obscure how a user's data will be used. The option that is in users' best interest often lies buried several clicks deep, shrouded in lengthy legal text. Tech companies typically deploy strategies that make users increasingly frustrated and fatigued with the dizzying number of privacy-related choices they must make. The companies want users to give up messing with privacy settings after finding them too complex and to simply accept the default settings.

Amidst all the confusion and anxiety surrounding Covid-19, people have dropped their guard on privacy concerns and accepted the fact that giving up personal data is beneficial for their own survival. People are willing to forego privacy to have their geolocation monitored so they can stay away from those infected, and hence there are increasing threats from surveillance by both government and the commercial sector. The power balance has dramatically shifted in favor of the digital platforms. According to a marketing industry report, "...nearly 90% of consumers have changed their behavior because of Covid-19".[72]

More data than ever before is flowing into the leading digital media companies about our health concerns, families, financial status, the kinds of products we purchase and other aspects of our lives. The big digital companies are touting that the real-time geo-surveillance continuously monitored from their mobile devices, wearables and apps is helping health experts keep the public safe. The altruistic talk of serving the national interest is a form of immunization from attacks against their monopolistic and surveillance behaviors.[73]

Zoom conferences have replaced business and personal gatherings; people are spending considerably more time online for everything from education, work and healthcare, to interpersonal relationships and social roles. All this virtual activity generates big data that feeds the insatiable appetites of the digital platforms. The pandemic gives those platforms more power than ever before.

The case study of India is the subject of Chapter 6. It explains in detail how India's present approach to data protection from foreign companies is muddled and dysfunctional. With its focus limited to making sure users' private data is not leaked, India's laws do not appreciate all the subtle issues mentioned above. Legal restrictions demand the data to be physically located in servers based in India. But *physical location has little relevance in the digital world.* Foreign entities can still mirror the data outside India. Also, Indian authorities would have no way to make sense of the data without knowing the models and algorithms that use it—and those remain secret in the custody of the AI companies.

A good analog for demanding fair data rights would be the UN's Convention on Biological Diversity, whose goals include the fair and equitable sharing of benefits arising from genetic resources. The treaty establishes conditions for access to genetic resources and ensures sharing fairly and equitably the results of research and development, and the benefits that arise from commercial and other utilization of genetic resources. The spirit of the treaty is based on the concept that developing countries providing genetic resources should receive a transfer of the technology that uses those resources. It stipulates that special attention be given to the development of national capabilities to reduce the vulnerability of developing nations.[74] The AI field needs to deliberate along similar lines as an international treaty on data rights.

Cognitive Limits of AI

Many experts in the field believe that there are "uniquely human characteristics such as empathy, creativity, judgment, or critical thinking" that will never be within the scope of AI.[75] Machines, after all, are unconscious and hence inherently incapable of understanding or replicating human emotions. The problem with this perspective is that it assumes that intelligent behavior requires consciousness. However, as noted earlier, whether a machine has any inner experience or sense of self is irrelevant to its pragmatic performance.

A machine does not need to *be* emotional for it to *act* emotionally with others or be able to obstruct or modify the emotions of others. The purpose of AI is served if machines can mimic humans' external behavior *as though* they had the same inner experience. What matters is whether a machine can model how emotions shape human behavior. This emotional mimicry is akin to actors performing a role; if they can replicate the emotional experience of a character, they have no need to internally experience the emotions. As a matter of fact, emotional mimicry is becoming a key factor in the adoption of AI as an effective replacement for human healthcare workers. Artificial Intelligence applications have a strong future in caregiving, given the increasing number of the elderly in developed countries and the shortage of healthcare workers.

Another popular notion is that because machines lack common sense, they cannot compete with humans in using ad hoc techniques and improvisation to solve problems. However, Autodesk, an American software developer, used AI to develop an autonomous drone simply by specifying the parameters of the design and letting the program create the actual design. The result was a drone that looks remarkably like the pelvis of a flying fox! When it is professionally trained, AI can incorporate common sense features, illustrating how neural networks can match humans even in areas involving the use of improvisation.[76]

Even more daunting is the way AI's collaboration with neuroscience is revealing neurological patterns that correspond to specific perceptions, emotions and actions. Artificial Intelligence and neuroscience are being combined to send signals to the brain that create artificial sensory experiences and emotions. This process amounts to an intervention in the neurological system, hijacking signals going to the brain by inserting artificial signals and thereby creating an experience in the brain that did not really happen and is entirely made up.

In other words, research is disputing the cherished belief that emotions cannot be reduced to algorithms. While it is true that not all emotions have been or will ever be successfully modeled as algorithms, machines have had considerable success replicating some human behaviors said to require judgment, gut feelings, creativity, and so forth. The scholar, Daniel Susskind writes:

> The temptation is to say that because machines cannot reason like us, they will never exercise judgment; because they cannot think like us, they will never exercise creativity; because they cannot feel like us, they will never be empathic. And all that may be right.

> But it fails to recognize that machines might still be able to carry out tasks that require empathy, judgment, or creativity when done by human beings – by doing them in some entirely different way.[77]

Susskind's point is that just because humans use a specific faculty and method to produce a given outcome does not make that the only approach for achieving the outcome. Driverless cars do not need to follow practices followed by human beings; they learn how to navigate by using sensor data from large numbers of real and simulated test drives. Susskind takes the view that machines could surpass human capabilities because the human approach is only one of many potential approaches.

> If machines do not need to replicate human intelligence to be highly capable, there is no reason to think that what human beings are currently able to do represents a limit on what future machines might accomplish.[78]

Economists tend to classify jobs using categories such as manual, cognitive and interpersonal, and then evaluate to what extent each of these techniques can be automated. However, even this type of classification is applicable only to the way humans work, and machines need not be limited to doing work in the same manner. Machines could discover their own original approaches to achieving desired outcomes.

Unemployment and Inequality

It is troubling that although most reports from the past fifteen years on the economic impact of AI do recognize the likely job displacements, most industry reports tend to dispel the alarm bells. They claim that the unemployment problem will self-correct based on the assumption that losses will be offset by the new jobs created in AI. However, their assumptions are overly optimistic. Such reports, written by economists and think tanks, fail to explain how the new jobs will be created. Additionally, the new jobs created will likely not be in the same geographical areas as the old labor-intensive jobs. New jobs in Silicon Valley, for instance, will not do much good to the millions of workers displaced in poor countries. Chapter 2 explores in greater detail the devastation AI will potentially cause through massive unemployment.

Nor is the argument that the unemployed workforce will be re-trained for new kinds of job, a convincing one. For one, many displaced workers might be past the age where they could learn new technologies or simply, lack the necessary education or intellectual background to acquire these skills. The cost of such re-training would be enormous, and it is at best naïve to assume that corporate employers that are eliminating old jobs to boost profits will generously re-train displaced workers. Especially vulnerable are workers that perform ultra-specialized repetitive tasks and become unemployed when they are no longer young enough to easily get re-trained.

Another issue is that AI will further promote the concentration of wealth. We seem headed toward a society of oligarchs that use AI-based systems to control the masses, thereby leading to a new type of serfdom.

Transfer of Agency and Power

The overarching power of the digital network derives from its use of data to exert psychological influence and its ability to hijack emotions. The more successful these new technologies are in providing what may be called artificial pleasures and gratifications, the more humans are subject to manipulation. The surrender of personal agency amounts to a loss of selfhood.

Research suggests that millennials and Generation Z youth do not mind giving up their privacy and autonomy in exchange for the delights offered by new technology. In many cases, it is claimed: "If the AI-based system is better at making my decisions than I am, better at delivering my sensory pleasures, and I can go through life on autopilot, what could be wrong with it?" Chapter 4 addresses the loss of free will and human agency on the part of the public.

Of special concern is the stealth mode for collecting private data and using it to manipulate emotions without the full knowledge of the users. The author and speaker Yu-kai Chou calls this the Trojan Horse without Greek soldiers, meaning that sneaky methods are like Trojan Horses but instead of soldiers with hard power, the psychological conquest is carried out by gamification.[79]

Social and Political Disequilibrium

The problems of unemployment and increased inequalities will only worsen with the rising population, especially in poor countries. Forecasts from the past twenty years have been predicting a leveling off of the world's population. Though birth rates have declined significantly, the drop has been largely balanced by a decline in death rates due to medical advances. Lifespans have extended and that trend is expected to continue. A realistic view of the future should not assume the total population will level off before the end of the twenty-first century.

Economists, public officials and members of the new tech elites need to come to terms with the fact that concerns about the social disruptions of AI are realistic. Once past this mental hurdle, leaders must address the social and political turmoil likely to result from the large-scale combination of problems: overpopulation, mass unemployment and concentration of wealth in the hands of a few. It is not enough to say that similar situations have been resolved before. They have not. The scale of the population today is by itself enough to make the dangers unprecedented.

On the other side of this crisis are the elite digital oligarchs that wield unprecedented power. Artificial Intelligence, with its associated technologies of robotics and artificial behavior management, could augment or replace traditional governing bodies and armies of bureaucrats. This is made worse by the fact that the masses are vulnerable to the lure of exotic mental and emotional escapes available through AR systems. Chapters 4 and 5 explain the use of artificial emotional management and artificial aesthetics as an opium of the masses to keep the public sedated and under control.

The powerful impacts will pose serious challenges to social and political systems. But for now, AI is being hailed as a platform for utopia. The views of many futurists assume that society will proceed directly from the present social order to a superior one in the future. However, I foresee a prolonged period of disequilibrium in between, starting in the next decade and lasting till the end of this century.

The youth of today will feel the brunt of this transition. By the time those born in 2020 are in their teens, the crisis of the present equilibrium will become obvious. And except for the lucky, sheltered elites that enjoy positions of power, most people will face uncertainty and turmoil.

Eventually, society will sort itself out and we will arrive at a new equilibrium. This new society might have a much smaller population that enjoys many of the utopian AI benefits, as speculated in Chapter 5. But in the interim, humanity has a long and dangerous road to travel.

Complicity of Public Intellectuals

Far too many public intellectuals that function as authors, media personalities, public officials, academics and various kinds of activists seem hopelessly uninformed. When the topic is raised, they tend to either escape into science fiction or dismiss concerns about AI as a conspiracy theory.

Among those who have written about the impact of AI on society, few appreciate these concerns enough to face the dilemmas. The majority is in denial and prefers to ignore a crisis that does not have easy solutions and that cannot be wished away.

2

THE BATTLE FOR JOBS

CHAPTER HIGHLIGHTS

- Big data will have a major economic impact as a new kind of capital asset, a phenomenon we could think of as **data capitalism.**
- The large digital platforms are the key engines today that mine the data and curate, analyze and apply it. Social media brings together disparate parties to interact and captures their data in the process.
- The business model of digital platforms is inherently monopolistic. A virtuous cycle of success generating ever greater success keeps new competitive entrants at a disadvantage that is tough to overcome.
- Influential organizations have produced reports in recent years that forecast AI's impact on jobs. An exhaustive review of their predictions reveals a wide range of opinions divided between those that fear a job crisis and others that think the economy will self-correct by creating new jobs in the AI-based economy.
- Artificial Intelligence is already beginning to make inroads into more creative and intuitive white-collar work. But certain tasks are more difficult to enhance or replace and some AI applications are not yet economically viable.

- Artificial Intelligence will be a force multiplier that makes the strong even stronger and the weak weaker. New haves and have-nots will be created, especially hurting the elderly, women and people of color that are already most vulnerable.
- A recurring optimism is that philanthropy from the elite AI companies and the superrich will fill in the gap in employment—creating jobs that are not economically necessary but artificially created to help the unemployed. However, this wishful thinking is unsubstantiated, and it distracts from the root of the problem.
- Eventually, the loss of jobs will lead to a decline in the consumer economy as the buying power of people decreases. The decline in consumption will in the very long-term lead to a decline in production and an overall downward deflationary spiral.
- The economic meltdown precipitated by AI's impact on jobs could lead to social unrest with potentially catastrophic results.

DATA CAPITALISM

There is a tectonic shift under way wherein the new means of production are AI-based machines trained with big data. Data has been called the new oil because it fuels the digital economy. Google, Facebook, Amazon and Microsoft, among others, create trillions of dollars in value largely from data and distribute it to every sector of the economy.

A fundamental aspect of data capitalism is the concept of a **platform**—a company with a collection of mechanisms bringing together a set of parties to interact with each other. A platform has been defined as "a business based on enabling value by creating interactions between external producers and consumers. The platform provides an open, participative infrastructure for these interactions and sets governance conditions for them".[80] A platform can be any avenue that facilitates decentralized interaction. Examples include:

- Facebook connects a community that could comprise friends, members belonging to a common interest group, or buyers and sellers. It provides a range of services that make interactions among the parties more efficient than if the parties were to engage with each other on their own sans the platform.
- Uber connects riders and drivers and manages their transactions with one another.
- Google's search engine brings together consumers of information with millions of websites that supply information.
- LinkedIn connects hundreds of millions of professionals with each other, at the same time giving them control over who they will interact with and on what basis.
- eBay brings together a wide range of buyers and sellers.
- Kickstarter provides a forum for entrepreneurs to connect with potential investors in the online phenomenon known as crowdfunding.
- Robinhood is a popular trading platform that has demystified and democratized stock market investments for millennials.

Many platforms also serve as the infrastructure on which participants can build something unique. Users develop personalized profile pages on Facebook; software developers build apps for Apple's App Store. Companies can use platforms for their internal needs as well as to sell products and services to customers, leveraging the R&D investments of the platform.

Platform companies are growing far faster than any other sector of the world economy. In just a few years, they acquired trillions of dollars of market capital, mostly concentrated in the US and China. The United Nations Conference on Trade and Development report on the digital economy describes the powerful position platforms hold in the economy.

> Both their high market valuations and the speed at which global digital companies have attained high capitalizations attest to the new value associated with being able to transform digital data into digital intelligence. Investors are betting on the disruption and reorganization of whole economic sectors, such as retail, transport and accommodation, or health, education and agriculture, by investing in long-term, digital-intelligence-based control of those sectors, which, they believe, will enable the generation of high profits in the future. Such disruption may involve sweeping away traditional players as well as preempting the emergence of new digital competitors. By introducing new products, services and business models, global digital companies become factors of disruption in sectors as varied as transport, accommodation, banking, education, and the media.[81]

The vast quantity of user data the platform companies gobble up every second is the chief source of these companies' power and wealth. Individuals and organizations voluntarily (or involuntarily when they are ignorant) hand over massive amounts of data to them. The platforms systematically record all the data that passes through them. Cloud companies are also becoming huge data collection enterprises, and their large investment in infrastructure makes them difficult to compete against. All this data is machine-readable and can be mined, curated, organized and monetized.

Digital capital consists of the mechanisms that capture and monetize the data, and this is the very heart of the new digital economy as shown in Figure 9.

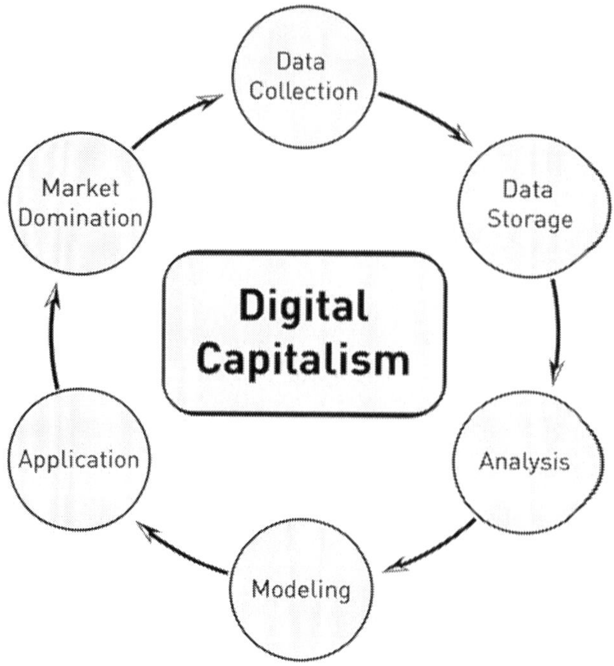

Figure 9: The Cycle of Digital Capitalism

This intelligence is vital to every marketing organization that wants to reach consumers efficiently and quickly to sell something, be it products, services, information, or ideologies. The digital platform is able to deliver advertisers' message in a targeted manner because it exploits private user data and leverages its AI algorithms to produce good response rates (called click-through rates or conversion rates), and the marketers pay the platform handsomely for such targeted and intimate access to consumers.

A platform's business model is to offer a variety of services free of charge to billions of users in exchange for taking control of the data that travels on the platform. The value chain for data resembles the manufacturing value chain and includes capturing raw data, organizing and processing it, building application models, and using these models for decision-making. The data's value increases with each stage.

Isolated data is seldom valuable. Only when data from millions of users is aggregated, processed, stored, analyzed and exploited in various applications does it become valuable. This is the reason individuals do not feel they are giving away anything of significant value.

The value of data is not uniform like that of a commodity, such as gold or oil, but depends on specific kinds of data and what the companies do with it. Different platforms aggregate it in different ways for different ends. The table below gives some prominent examples.

Platform	Type of Big Data
Google Search, YouTube	General interests & information
Facebook	Personal relationships
Apple iTunes & App Store, Google Play	Emotional & recreational interests
Apple Siri, Amazon Alexa, Google Assistant	Conversations & requests
Amazon, Walmart, Reliance Jio	Shopping habits
Microsoft AI	Office work habits, corporate client metadata

Given the wealth and power enjoyed by the leading platform companies, the question arises as to how they have managed to secure their position so firmly. Why can't new competitors enter the market more easily and challenge these companies' dominant share?

The answer is that the resources required for success in an AI-driven revolution are data, software, hardware, trained models, applications, customer relationships, brands and financial capital—and these resources tend to become concentrated in a few hands. Deep learning produces a virtuous cycle of success leading to more success. More data leads to superior products, which brings more users, who produce even more data, which increases profits, which further expands the business model and allows companies to collect and exploit even more data. The gap between winners and losers widens and becomes almost impossible to close. A few well-known examples will illustrate this.

- Google is hard to beat in search engines. Microsoft tried competing by investing heavily in Bing but has failed.[82]
- Facebook has cornered the market on social relationships and interpersonal interactions. No competitor has come close to overtaking it.
- Amazon dominates e-commerce. Even companies with huge financial backing have failed to supplant it.

A more comprehensive list of factors protecting the monopolies of platforms is given below.

1. *Ability to extract data and turn it into proprietary applications*. Dominant platforms like Google, Facebook, and Twitter are those providing the public free online access as a way to acquire huge amounts of data. The big established players have the economy

of scale to offer marketing solutions to corporate clients, something a new player cannot match. Success perpetuates and leads to greater future success.

2. *Networking effects.* A platform with a critical mass of users naturally attracts many more new users. This trend is partly the bandwagon effect of a popular brand, but pragmatic reasons also play a part. The large number of consumers on a given platform makes it more attractive to advertisers; more advertising results in a greater number of users, which ultimately leads to higher revenue, which allows the platform to offer better services. The greater the number of people that use Uber, the more it makes sense for new drivers to work for Uber, and the more drivers that work for it, the better the service becomes for users. The greater the number of women that sign up for a dating service, the more men want to sign up, and vice versa. The platform's success on one side of the market increases its attractiveness for other groups—the virtuous cycle. The business of being a platform intermediary can become monopolistic and winner take all. Each new user benefits from the existence of many existing users. New platforms do not have enough resources or stamina to scale such a high barrier.
3. *User investment in the platform.* Once users are invested in a platform, they do not want to walk away. The public has spent a lot of time building personal pages on Facebook, accumulating friends and participating in lively discussions. All this time, energy, and sometimes money invested, would go to waste if they migrated to a different platform. Entire business models and communities have been

built, and users are reluctant to abandon them. Many video producers have tailored their videos' content, length, frequency, targeting and other parameters to fit Facebook's or YouTube's algorithms; they would have to start from scratch if they moved.[83]

4. *Deep pockets.* Given their first-mover advantage and huge vaults of cash, the big platforms can afford to sacrifice short-term profits for aggressive long-term growth. Emphasis on long-term strategies enables them to strengthen their market position and further extend their lead.
5. *Acquisitions.* Leading platform companies have accumulated so much wealth that when their monopoly is threatened, they can simply buy out smaller companies, as illustrated by Facebook's acquisition of WhatsApp and Instagram. In fact, a common exit plan among start-up entrepreneurs is to build up a business to the point that a leading platform will want to acquire it. If a start-up refuses to get acquired, the platform company may incorporate similar features, being careful to not violate copyright or patent laws.[84]
6. *Vertical integration.* Large platform companies expand into new business areas made possible by the amount of data accumulated. For example, Amazon sees the sales details of independent companies that sell merchandise through its platform and uses this data to decide when and in what ways to compete with its own clients. Amazon is now producing movies, directly competing with the leading streaming service, Netflix. It also bypassed FedEx and other delivery services by using its own delivery trucks and is planning to further expand its local delivery service

with drones and robots.[85] Facebook now produces its own TV shows and is entering the field of VR through acquisitions such as Oculus. This kind of expansion is tough for new entrants to replicate because they lack the large platforms' activities across many industries.

7. *Artificial Intelligence as a strategic weapon.* Given the research lead in AI enjoyed by the dominant platforms, they constantly look for new industries where their strengths can be leveraged to siphon off market share from conventional players. We should not be surprised to see them getting involved in the defense industry and even leveraging their political influence. Once VR and AR products are perfected, platforms could acquire entertainment giants like Disney or compete directly against them. Newcomers simply do not have that kind of leverage.
8. *Privileged insights into the market players.* With all the market data from their advertisers, producers and users, digital platforms often know more about a company's customers than the company itself does. The platforms use this data as an invisible hand to influence interactions and outcomes between producers and consumers. Much of this influence is not apparent because it is carried out through the platform's algorithms. For example, platforms can boost any political ideology and gray-list or outright ban any public figures. Blatant bias is enforced through ad hoc filtering and censoring criteria called community standards that offer no transparency.
9. *Lobbying and policymaking.* The large platforms are global players. Their lobbying budgets have increased considerably in several countries.

The global consulting firm PricewaterhouseCoopers summarizes the power of the AI giants:

> AI front-runners will have the advantage of superior customer insight. The immediate competitive benefits include an improved ability to tap into consumer preferences, tailor their output to match these individual demands and, in doing so, capture an ever-bigger slice of the market. And the front-runners' ability to shape product developments around this rich supply of customer data will make it harder and harder for slower moving competitors to keep pace and could eventually make their advantage unassailable. We can already see this data-driven innovation and differentiation in the way books, music, video and entertainment are produced, distributed and consumed, resulting in new business models, new market leaders and the elimination of traditional players that fail to adapt quickly enough.[86]

UNEMPLOYMENT

Many reports on AI's economic impact categorize human labor in a grid that separates routine from nonroutine work, and manual from cognitive work. Researchers assume that routine work is more vulnerable to AI replacement than nonroutine work, and that manual work is more easily automated than cognitive work.[87] Historically, the most difficult tasks to automate have been those that do not follow a structured, predefined flow: jobs that require creativity, intuition, emotion, complex coordination, mechanical dexterity and complex spatial reasoning.

However, this view is outdated and whether a task is routine is unimportant; what matters is whether the rules for performing it are well-defined. Any set of explicit rules can be turned into a computer program. Furthermore, as discussed in Chapter 1, even when the work involves ad hoc judgment, and even if the rules are not explicitly known, neural networks can be used to develop AI algorithms. The advances in unsupervised learning allow machines to explore and create novel approaches in an unstructured setting. The fact is that AI is a moving target with major breakthroughs that cannot be fully anticipated. Increasingly, it enhances the productivity of well-paid white-collar workers in developed countries and is beginning to augment or replace them. Each year, advancements enable systems to perform at higher cognitive levels.[88]

Expert forecasts of AI's impact on work vary a great deal, with a variety of factors to consider, such as the following:

- In many cases, a job involves performing a collection of tasks. Only some of them can be automated, and the job survives because the multifaceted worker is still necessary for other tasks.
- Economic forecasts have not caught up with major breakthroughs in AI and the job-eating technologies have not been fully taken into consideration. For instance, until a few years back, machines could not reliably recognize different kinds of images. But by 2017, deep learning had taken machines' cognitive capabilities to new heights. Now machines surpass human cognition in accuracy and speed in several applications. Once AI can effectively execute a cognitive task, it can be implemented quickly. In contrast, replacing manual workers with robots takes longer because the process involves investment in hardware and complex installation. Consequently, white-collar

workers will, in many instances, be impacted far more dramatically than production-line jobs.

- Some industries are being reinvented so dramatically that their entire way of performing tasks are discarded and replaced by something entirely new. For instance, human telemarketing operators are being phased out as the public becomes more comfortable purchasing online directly. There is an intergenerational aspect to this shift: Millennials prefer going online, while their parents' generation, the baby boomers, typically prefer to talk to a human on the phone. Likewise, iTunes did not merely replicate the old functions of music publishing and distribution; it effectively destroyed the old music industry and invented an entirely new one. As a result, many of the old industry players went out of business, and start-ups emerged in a completely new ecosystem.
- Regulatory restrictions and the momentum of doing things the old way will slow down job losses in many situations.

One trend is the adoption of devices called **cobots** (collaborative robots), which are robots that do not work independently of humans. Cobots work *alongside* humans and amplify their productivity, which means that automation is introduced gradually. Once in the door, however, the cobot's dexterity increases, and over time it can assume more tasks. This means there will be both human-centric and robot-centric advancements—the former leading to machine-augmented humans and the latter leading to human-augmented robots.

The result of all these trends is a general increase in productivity which implies that fewer human workers will be required. Businesses will benefit, but wages will remain low as more workers chase fewer jobs.

Some economists and industry leaders assure us that the elimination of old jobs will be compensated by the birth of new kinds of jobs. The **Luddite Fallacy** states that rather than eliminating jobs, new technology simply changes the nature of jobs. When the British textile industry was mechanizing during the nineteenth-century Industrial Revolution, skilled handloom weavers rose in protest and destroyed the new power looms. They became known as Luddites, after their leader Ned Ludd.[89] However, their fears were unrealized; productivity gains from industrialization resulted in greater wealth that was reinvested into society and created new jobs. Though the Luddites were right in the short term, they were wrong about the long-term impact of the new technology.[90]

The pattern has repeated itself in economic history over the past two centuries. Agricultural automation in the West induced farmers to migrate to cities for factory jobs. And subsequent industrial automation led workers to move into the service sector. In each of these instances, the automation revolution went through three stages:

1. It reduced the number of old style of workers in a given sector.
2. Surplus workers migrated to other sectors and boosted production in new jobs.
3. The cost of goods dropped which raised overall standards of living.

The Luddites did see an immediate loss of jobs and suffering from wage reduction, but their future generations were better off. The question now being debated is this: Will the pattern repeat itself with AI-driven automation? If so, the latest AI threat to jobs will merely be a short-term disruption eventually offset by long-term economic gains. Or will the paradigm be different this time?

My position on this is that *AI is different compared to prior technological disruptions for several reasons.* For one thing, the disruption is occurring faster and more dramatically than during prior waves of automation. Because the pace of automation was slow in previous revolutions, displaced workers had the opportunity for re-training, and the education system had time to adjust and provide workers with the latest skills. Farming automation was a slow process; it took multiple generations, allowing society to adapt to the economic shift. Middle-aged farm workers could continue in their jobs, while their children went on to get factory work. In other words, it was an intergenerational shift and did not necessarily affect the workers mid-career.

A report by Bain & Company titled *Labor 2030: The Collision of Demographics, Automation and Inequality* predicts abrupt changes in the next decade compared to the slow transitions of the past.[91] *Worker displacement will occur two to three times faster than during the prior shifts from agriculture (early 1900s) and from manufacturing (late 1900s).* This is because the adoption rates for new technologies have been accelerating. When the telephone was invented, it took seventy-five years to reach fifty million users; the mobile phone only took twelve years after invention to reach that level. The adoption of smartphones took only four years to double from one billion to two billion.[92] Artificial Intelligence adoption is thus likely to achieve dramatic penetration because of its exponential adoption rates across different applications.

Many workers will be caught mid-career when they expect, and need, to work for many more years. They will be too young to retire but too old to retrain easily.

Previous revolutions had other redeeming factors as well. The limits on the availability of capital hindered companies' ability to scale up new technology rapidly, and implementation also depended on slow product R&D. But today's high-tech society has an abundance of well-organized venture funding and a frenzy of R&D for lightning-fast introduction of new products. China is a major catalyst in this revolution, making the global economic change more rapid than ever before, and hence far more disruptive.

Another difference is that in the past disruptions, machines could not replace the well-identified and economically valuable faculties of human intelligence which served as a haven not vulnerable to automation. But as machine learning advances, will any human skills remain beyond the reach of AI? Will humans have anything left to offer employers once smart machines take over their essential tasks? In other words, are the Luddites finally being proven right?[93]

Finally, the current population levels are far larger than in earlier times, so the scale of the unemployment problem will be worse. The Bain & Company report argues that comparisons with past revolutions should not make us complacent.

> Contrary to popular notion, the absolute number of workers in agriculture actually changed very little during that period of automation. Rather, change happened slowly enough that younger entrants to the workforce were steered into new jobs—the children of farmers moved to cities to work in urban factories. In effect, employment in agriculture was frozen in place for a generation while the rest of the economy rapidly grew around it. Despite this fairly optimal scenario—one that mitigated the full disruptive force of

> agricultural automation—the historical record indicates that this period was tumultuous for those working the agricultural industry and other fields experiencing large-scale displacement. The automation of manufacturing in the 1970s concentrated on a narrower subset of industries, and the equivalent rate of jobs lost now plus those not created in the future would have been about 800,000 workers a year scaled to current population and labor force. Even today, the negative economic effects of this transition linger in the Rust Belt region of the US and areas of Western Europe.[94]
>
> Historical comparisons suggest tackling massive job loss from automation—including the eradication of entire job functions that are not replaced in the future—will be a serious macroeconomic and social challenge for most advanced economies. The common thread will be that disruption will have highly uneven impacts.[95]

With so many moving parts in this complex problem, it is difficult to make specific forecasts on unemployment. Many prestigious and influential organizations have published detailed studies predicting the level of unemployment likely to result from AI and related automation. Appendix A summarizes these forecasts. Though these forecasts were made before the Covid-19 pandemic and will have to be revised, the pandemic will not change the long-term trends and will probably accelerate and exacerbate the impact of AI.

The hard reality is that human labor is becoming costlier while the cost of machine substitutes declines. Although humans are still able to outperform machines in several ways, it will become increasingly challenging to find jobs in which humans will continue to have an inherent advantage. The incentives to find such work will diminish over time as mobs of job seekers fight over the diminishing number of openings suitable for humans. Political projects to create employment just to provide jobs are not indefinitely sustainable. No degree of re-training will solve this problem either. And no number of new positions created by the AI-based economy will compensate for the loss of work.

Economists, social scientists and political thinkers are not trained to address the issue that robots do not pay taxes or buy houses and consumer goods to support the economy. Entirely new laws and public policies will be necessary, but as of now world leaders are in denial.

INEQUALITIES AND SOCIAL DISRUPTION

Automation will create a dichotomy between new haves and have-nots. Massive unemployment will occur simultaneously with shortages of professionals in the latest technologies. Those who are technically qualified, possess the latest knowledge, and can work competitively in the new economy will be rewarded with high-paying jobs. These will be the new elites. Unfortunately, most workers will be left behind to face unemployment or eke out a meager living.

In the imminent future, society will have to acknowledge the existence of what I call the unemployable class. Additionally, the greater longevity that results from medical advances will further increase costs for the nonproductive elderly. Income disparity will become glaringly large and foment increased stratification between social classes. The middle class might virtually disappear, leaving a small upper class of elites and an exceptionally large lower class. Labor shortages will exist at the upper end, with a surplus of obsolete workers at the lower end.

The new haves will be privileged to enjoy all the benefits that new technologies afford them, while those that are not among the high-value producers will lack the income to afford such indulgences. Society will effectively establish a new kind of caste system. Intellectual property developers and their investors will occupy the top position, followed by the technology workers, and finally the masses at the bottom.

Bain & Company is concerned that advanced technologies are worsening the gap between the haves and have-nots across the world.[96] Those that are involved in the new AI-based economy will thrive at the expense of many who will be left behind.

> As competition grows for scarce talent, leading companies will invest more to attract, grow and retain scarcer high-end talent and ensure that their workforce is as productive as possible. To increase their allure, employers may enhance existing incentives with monetary benefits, culture and flexible work arrangements.[97]
>
> Yet, the growing gap between the majority of workers who suffer automation's negative impact and the highly skilled few who benefit from it is likely to increase income inequality dramatically.[98]
>
> We expect the 2020s to be a period of greater macro turbulence and volatility than seen in decades. It is also likely to be a period in which extremes become more extreme. Technological innovations will give rise to new corporate powerhouses, but at the same time, pervasive insecurity may haunt ordinary families and global enterprises alike.[99]

Artificial Intelligence will exacerbate economic divisions by worsening the disparity that already exists. In the *Global*

Wealth Report 2019, Credit Suisse Wealth Institute indicates that the top 1% of the world's richest people own 45% of the world's wealth; it provides the breakdown for major countries.[100] According to one report the world's 2,000 billionaires have more wealth than the bottom 4.6 billion people combined, and the richest 1% have more than the combined wealth of 6.9 billion people.[101]

The top 1% in the US doubled its share of national income between 1980 and 2016. By 2017, the top 1% of Americans had almost twice as much wealth as the bottom 90%.[102] India, too, is one of the top five countries in the world in terms of the most wealth concentration. The World Bank estimates that almost 50% of the world's population lives on less than $5.50 a day.[103] The impact of AI threatens to worsen these inequalities suddenly and dramatically.

The economic boom of recent years did not reach the lowest strata of society. From 2011 to 2017, average wages in G7 (Group of Seven: Canada, France, Germany, Italy, Japan, United Kingdom and United States) countries increased by only 3%, while dividends to wealthy shareholders increased by 31% in the same time period.[104] Bain & Company also concludes that the owners of tech giants will further consolidate the world's wealth.

> In addition to job loss and wage suppression, automation may also increase income inequality by increasing the share of income going to profits vs. wages. The share of income produced by labor already is declining, and with automation, it likely will fall further.... Under those conditions, increased profitability would largely flow to owners of capital and further reduce the share of national income allocated to labor. Capital ownership is already highly concentrated.... Because capital

> ownership is tilted toward those already in higher-income brackets and also much more narrowly concentrated than income, this shift toward capital income is likely to contribute to rising income inequality.[105]

Jamie Susskind, author of *Future Politics: Living Together in a World Transformed by Tech*, reaches a similar conclusion.

> Over time, more wealth flows to capital-owners, and less to workers. Using productive technologies, capital-owners control an increasing amount of economic activity while employing a shrinking number of workers. Capital comes to be concentrated in the hands of a small number of firms, themselves controlled by a small number of people. Relying on the network effect, these firms accrue huge cash reserves that enable them to acquire more capital and expand into new markets. With the data they gather, they develop AI systems of astonishing capacity and range. Large swathes of the population – former workers, failed capitalists – find themselves with no capital and no way to earn a living. Those with a stake in the successful firms enjoy a growing slice of an expanding economic pie. The wealth gap between the tiny elite of owners and the rest expands radically.[106]

Inequities are also facilitated by laws that exempt huge amounts of inheritance tax. Contrary to popular claim that wealth creation is mostly the product of hard work and merit, the fact is that a significant portion of the wealth of the ultra-rich comes from their inheritance.[107]

Most economists like to pacify the public with the claim that new jobs created by AI will compensate for the loss of old jobs, but this assertion does not address the problem for several reasons. As stated earlier, AI's new jobs will not be located where old jobs are eliminated, but wherever the AI industry's innovations and implementations are located. The Oxford Economics report indicates that job losses and gains will be unevenly distributed between countries, between regions of the same country, and even between different communities in the same region. The consumers who benefit from cheaper goods due to automation will be scattered around the world, whereas the communities that lose manufacturing jobs will be locally concentrated. In fact, Oxford Economics states: "increased industrial automation will tend to *exacerbate the regional inequalities* that already exist within advanced economies".[108]

The World Economic Forum's (WEF) 2020 report on global risks notes:

> Within countries, wealth gaps could also increase: automation is forecasted to hit low-skilled workers and women the hardest. Societal divides could also widen between rural and urban areas in developing economies, and between smart and non-smart cities in developed countries.[109]

The report further highlights the irony that this trend is a form of exploitation, because the data collected from the masses will be used against those very people:

> Data are increasingly being collected on citizens by government and business alike, and these data are then monetized and used to refine the development and deployment of new technologies back towards these citizens, as consumers. Amassing of data by a handful of small entities leads to a further entrenchment of gaps between advanced and emerging economies.[110]

A United Nations report adds yet another dimension: The low-wage advantage of workers in some areas is currently being eroded because digital platforms reduce workers' bargaining power.[111]

There is a lot of wishful thinking about the inequality problem, but precious little action. A recent report calls out the hypocrisy:

> Over the past decade leading academics, and even mainstream economic institutions such as the IMF, have produced robust evidence of the corrosive effects of inequality. Affected communities, activists, women's rights organizations and faith leaders have spoken out and have campaigned for change around the world. Recent protests, for example against inequality and climate chaos, from Chile to Germany, are huge. Mainstream economic meetings, such as those of the IMF and the World Economic Forum, have placed economic inequality on their agendas time and again. However, the inequality crisis remains fundamentally unaddressed.... Despite much handwringing about the divide between rich and poor, and the evidence of its corrosive effects, most world leaders are still pursuing policy agendas that drive a greater gap between the haves and the have-nots.[112]

In my youth, the divide between haves and have-nots was not at the same scale as it is now. Millionaires were a rarity in India, as in most countries. I remember reading about how business magnate John D. Rockefeller was a *billionaire*, which was a big deal. Several decades later, I learned of some individuals surpassing ten billion dollars in wealth. Today, several individuals possess personal wealth in the *tens of billions* of dollars. And recently, at least three individuals crossed the one hundred-billion-dollar threshold. I predict that in the next twenty-five years, the world will have at least a few *trillionaires.*

Simultaneously, at the other end of the spectrum, the poor are now poorer than ever before. The unprecedented concentration of wealth contrasts with unparalleled misery on a large scale in many parts of the world. Furthermore, inequality has a particularly disturbing gender component. The combined wealth of the world's richest twenty-two men is more than the total wealth of all the women in Africa. In terms of worldwide political power, only 18% of government ministers and 24% of members of parliament are women.[113]

The coronavirus pandemic will make the unemployment situation even worse for the most vulnerable people, exacerbating the problems caused by AI. One estimate is that this latest crisis could plunge another half a billion people into poverty and will adversely impact women more than men.[114] The well-recognized gender pay gap even in developed countries like the US is likely to worsen due to the pandemic.

> Part of the reason for the uncontrolled gender pay gap is that women are more represented in lower-paying jobs compared to men, who comprise a higher percentage of the professional sector. Women are also more represented in occupations with a social or service component. ... The coronavirus has hit service workers particularly hard, but the vast majority of the occupations dominated by women are at risk, as most depend on social interaction. With businesses and schools closing to enforce social distancing, women are more likely to face unemployment.[115]

Ultimately, the disruption will also impact the capitalists because only well-paid workers make good consumers. They are the same people who buy the products and services that fuel the economy. But when workers become unemployed, they lack purchasing power. In other words, while automation will enhance the capacity to produce sophisticated products, the lack of sufficient consumers that can afford to buy those products will lead to an underutilization of production capacity. Extreme economic disparity eventually causes a downward spiral in demand and could precipitate a deflationary economy that contracts.

In the long run, such a downward spiral can start with unemployment, followed by a reduction in consumption and eventually a decline in revenue and profit. Each stage leads to the next in a ripple effect. As profits decline, companies further reduce their workforces, leading to even greater unemployment—the spiral accelerates, and the economy shrinks.

Bain & Company supports this point, arguing that inequality will ultimately lead to a decline in the demand for economic goods that shrinks the economy.

> The primary macroeconomic consequence of higher inequality is to constrain growth by limiting the growth of effective demand vs. the growth in supply. Despite many technological innovations that will increase the capacity for goods and services, the inability of effective demand to keep pace may ultimately reduce growth. Effective demand is consumption supported by income. Supply growth may be temporarily sustained by other forms of demand, such as that generated by capital investments or consumption supported by borrowing. But when the investment or credit cycle ends, demand can drop precipitously.[116]

In other words, while automation will increase the capacity for production, it will diminish demand by compressing income at the bottom.[117] The initially booming AI-based economy will end badly. According to Bain & Company, the growth in capital investments for automation is likely to end around 2030 and usher in a new phase of low demand.

> As the investment surge comes to an end (likely around the end of the next decade), a newly automated economy will likely slip back into demand-constrained conditions. Many of the companies that invested heavily in automation may be saddled with assets that are out of step with the level of demand needed to utilize them fully. At the same time, millions of consumers who have lost their jobs to automation are likely to curb their spending.[118]

Such a profound disruption in the labor market will trigger social unrest. Sir Angus Deaton, a Nobel Laureate economist at Princeton University, has analyzed how the white American middle class has been suffering from an epidemic of suicide, drug addiction and alcoholism in recent decades, set off by the economic disruption caused by the Reagan Revolution of the 1980s. President Ronald Reagan broke the traditional labor unions that represented a safety net for the white middle class and its American Dream. The American Dream was the promise of lifetime employment that afforded workers good medical benefits, a real chance to own a home, and the ability to educate their children in college. Then globalization opened the floodgates to foreign competition from countries with cheap labor. Multinational corporations became more powerful and created a whole new class of wealthy individuals.

Unfortunately, society failed to adequately address how this affected blue-collar workers and disenfranchised the American middle class. Gone in a flash was the American Dream: For the first time in three generations, the next generation was less upwardly mobile than their parents and grandparents. Much of the white American working class, especially those without a college education, has been riddled with broken families. As life became harder, society saw an associated rise in what has been called *deaths of despair*.

This economic disruption triggered the current social crisis that brought Donald Trump to power in 2016; the white American middle class wanted to "take America back" in a desperate attempt to mitigate its plight. The implicit assumption is xenophobic: that some intruders have "taken away" America, and now the real owners want to take it back. The phenomenon recalls the rise of Hitler in Germany, also fueled by a major economic crisis. Germans were desperate to forge a new narrative that would restore their entitlement to prosperity. Nazism was, in a sense, a movement to "take Germany back" from groups accused of taking it away from its real owners.

My argument is not that all stressed countries run the risk of a Nazi-like outcome, but rather, an economic meltdown anywhere that leads to high unemployment could precipitate social calamities on a large scale. Though strong Gross Domestic Power (GDP) growth is one measure of success, the *quality and equity* of GDP growth is also a salient point. If the megatrends discussed in this book trigger mass unemployment, social unrest would inevitably follow. Economic divisions will tear at the social fabric and undermine human dignity. Widespread unemployment, combined with increasing inequality, will lead to social disorder, political unrest, and even threats to the sovereignty of many nations.

The Bain & Company report vindicates my thesis that AI-driven inequalities will lead to social disruptions that the business and political worlds need to come to terms with.

> Populations suffering severe economic dislocation could view jarring levels of income and wealth inequality as a form of social failure—a failure to provide the vast majority of the population with the chance to earn a decent living despite the nation's technological and economic wherewithal. Today's level of inequality already has prompted growing public concern and debate. It seems reasonable to expect that at significantly higher levels, popular criticism would intensify and increase pressure for social policies to address it.[119]

The impact on the aging world population will be uneven as well. The American management consulting firm McKinsey & Company states that AI will actually help *developed* countries' aging populations, because it would "give a needed boost to economic growth and prosperity and help offset the impact of a declining share of the working-age population in many countries".[120] However, the WEF report reveals the other side of the story. The data highlights the large deficit in retirement funds, a time bomb that threatens aged people in those countries. In India, the retirement savings gap was $3 trillion in 2015, and is forecast to grow at 10% annually to a staggering $85 trillion by 2050.[121] In the US, the gap will worsen at 5% annually and become $137 trillion by 2050. Further, retirees will be forced to compete with the working-age population for both resources and social services.

All these disruptions are magnified by the fact that the world population is forecast to increase to 9.7 billion in 2050 and to 11.2 billion by 2100.[122]

Despite these trends, a sizeable segment of millennials, especially those employed in the tech industry, subscribe to the optimistic view that AI will usher in an age of abundance and freedom for all. This attitude is an oversimplification resulting from a collective unwillingness to acknowledge reality and inability to reason with sophistication when confronted with uncomfortable truths.

CHALLENGING THE OPTIMISTS

To solidify my arguments, it is worth summarizing my response to the optimists. Their common counterargument to the potential devastation of AI is that the current wave of automation differs little from previous occurrences. During previous waves, machines were not replacing judgment, intuition and creativity. Artificial Intelligence is, however, encroaching even the highest levels of human cognition and intellect in fields like medicine, transportation, sports, media and the arts. Of course, some residual human jobs will remain, but these will be fewer and fewer. The open question is this: Is there a level of human function *higher than what AI can replace*? If so, what is it? The answers are speculative at best.

Contrary to popular reassurances by many economists, there is no guarantee that market forces will create enough new jobs to replace the old ones. Lawrence Summers, former Harvard president, chief economist at World Bank, and treasury secretary under former US president, Bill Clinton, told *New York Times* that we cannot stop technological change, nor can we "just suppose that everything's going to be O.K. because the magic of the market will assure that's true".[123]

Reports that do admit to the seriousness of the problem often pass the responsibility for solutions over to some unnamed billionaires. They assume large-scale altruism and philanthropy on the part of the top 1% to help the unemployed. Yet the idea of redistributing wealth from the rich to the poor through taxation is, at best, idealistic. Most proclamations on the importance of doing good fail to propose how to transform the human ego dramatically enough to make such altruistic visions real. How can we shift the rich and successful away from the intoxication of materialism and personal grandeur? The problem of limitless greed is old, and not easily solved.

Most of the ultra-wealthy prefer to remain silent on this uncomfortable challenge. They may even fear becoming targets of mob violence. Publicly they support that somehow the masses will be taken care of, but do not attempt to answer the questions of how and by whom. Daniel Susskind, author of *A World Without Work: Technology, Automation and How We Should Respond*, explains the hypocrisy of the superrich.

> At the 2019 World Economic Forum in Davos, the *New York Times* reports, business leaders talked a good game in public about how to contain "the negative consequences that artificial intelligence and automation could have for workers," but in private these executives had "a different story: they are racing to automate their own work forces to stay ahead of the competition".[124]

Another idea being floated is to reduce the hours and days of work—but that solution would also reduce take-home pay. Some people propose the expansion of emotion-based and care-based professions that nurture the spirit, such as yoga teachers, entertainers and life-coaches rather than production jobs. But the numbers do not add up because such jobs will be far fewer than the jobs lost.

Economists, politicians and commentators keep reassuring us that education and retraining can solve the problem. But the roles that will be in demand cannot be predicted. Daniel Susskind explains:

> It is hard to escape the conclusion that we are headed toward a world with less work for people to do. The threat of technological unemployment is real. More troubling still, the traditional response of "more education" is likely to be less and less effective as time rolls on.[125]

Even if labor markets do rebalance in the long run, until then billions of lives will be ruined. Many past inequities that became unsustainable were resolved only through apocalyptic events—such as the Black Death in the fourteenth century and the two World Wars of the twentieth century.

The leaders we put our faith in are merely kicking the can down the road. It is time that industrialists introduce these issues into the ethics of their business management. McKinsey states:

> For business, the performance benefits of automation are relatively clear, but the issues are more complicated for policy makers. They should embrace the opportunity for their economies to benefit from the productivity growth potential and put in place policies to encourage investment and market incentives to encourage continued progress and innovation. At the same time, they must evolve and innovate policies that help workers and institutions adapt to the impact on employment. This will likely include rethinking education and training,

> income support and safety nets, as well as transition support for those dislocated. Individuals in the workplace will need to engage more comprehensively with machines as part of their everyday activities and acquire new skills that will be in demand in the new automation age. [126]

The Bank of England's chief economist sets a good example by urging governments to increase worker retraining and prepare itself for a welfare state to cushion automation's blow.[127] Both businesses and governments should be directly involved in worker retraining. It is inevitable that governments will intervene with higher taxes and regulations to control the social and economic disruptions.

PANDEMIC AS ACCELERATOR OF TRENDS

The Covid-19 pandemic will likely worsen the economic crisis and hasten AI's pervasive influence. The adoption of robots has accelerated to keep factories running and maintain supply chains in the absence of human workers.

Companies that supply AI-based commercial products are enjoying unprecedented financial rewards as a result of their rapid response to the pandemic. Systems for remote work, online commerce, drone technology, medical systems that are less dependent on physical human contact, military systems that are not vulnerable to human illness, driverless trucks that support supply lines with less vulnerability to illness—have received a sudden boost. Our dependence on digital systems including social media and cloud services has never been so high. Cloud-based digital systems are providing a variety of pragmatically useful and psychologically enriching services. The digital czars' unquenchable thirst for more of our data has empowered an Orwellian surveillance culture. A noteworthy byproduct is that neural network systems are gobbling up big data from the public on an unprecedented scale and level of detail.

The prolonged devastation of the economy, the workforce, government programs and budgets, and public concerns about security are definitely triggering serious reflection on the fundamental premises of modern life. Modern civilization will hopefully survive and become stronger, but it will certainly become radically transformed in the process.

3

THE BATTLE FOR WORLD DOMINATION

The kings have become like dogs
that snatch meat from one another.

—*Mahabharata*[128]

CHAPTER HIGHLIGHTS

- China's rise to power in this century must be compared with Britain's emergence as the world power in the 1700s. Britain achieved dominance through the Industrial Revolution, and China aspires to achieve it through the AI revolution.
- The US and China have become a duopoly that owns most of the AI-based economy at the expense of much of the developing world, a trend I call **digital colonization.** China has successfully catapulted itself from a poor country to an imperial power, asserting its influence over Africa, Latin America and parts of Asia.
- A key contributor to the consolidation of AI-based global power is the harvesting of big data from poor countries. Raw data is being mined from populations in remote places where it is easy to take advantage of ignorant and corrupt leaders.

- Multinational digital platforms are rapidly consolidating immense power the same way three centuries ago the East India Company became the world's most powerful empire in history—as a private firm.
- China has been preparing for digital dominance for two generations by developing its human capital since the days of Chairman Mao (1893-1976) and his successor Deng Xiaoping (1904-97). It used its educated population to position itself initially as a labor-intensive manufacturing base for various countries, mainly the US. Then it climbed the ladder of value-added manufacturing by educating its youth at higher levels of competitiveness than its rivals like India. In the past decade, it has set its sights on becoming the world's dominant supplier and user of AI.
- China's Communist Party worked with private entrepreneurs to nurture a culture of gladiator-like intense competition for domestic development and use of advanced technology. Chinese firms were encouraged to beg, borrow, or steal whatever technology they could, in the belief that the end justified the means. China's high technology rat race has become a brutally competitive culture. Artificial Intelligence conferences around the world are dominated by speakers from China presenting serious research that is on par with, or even ahead, of the US in many areas.
- China has gambled its entire nation-building strategy and global ambitions on a digital vision of the future. It is taking huge risks and making bold long-term investments. No other country has bet so much of its future on AI.
- Given its form of government, China can gather data about its population better than other countries. In fact, its citizens are accustomed to the loss of privacy and have

become convinced of the benefits to the collective good. There is no serious resistance to surveillance in China.

- China is projecting its technology and financial capital to colonize other countries, most notably Pakistan and developing countries in Africa. Colonization secures the strategic trade routes, the sources of raw materials, and the captive markets for its industrial goods. In some places China has already started using AI facial recognition to monitor populations on behalf of totalitarian regimes. Such applications are a new kind of colonization facilitated by AI.
- Just as Rome used roads as a major instrument for expanding and controlling its far-flung empire, so also China is using the infrastructure of roads, railways and seaports in addition to digital highways to build its empire.

DISRUPTING THE WORLD ORDER

Comparing Britain's and China's Industrial Revolutions

Prior to the mid-1700s, Britain was merely a regional European player. Extreme poverty at home and constant warring with neighbors had stifled British growth and development. According to European writings, India's textile and metallurgy workers were more prosperous than their European counterparts in the 1600s. But within a century of the East India Company's arrival, most Indians had become impoverished while the working class in Britain got jobs in their country's new factories. Over more than two centuries, a massive transfer of jobs and wealth from India to England ensued.

Britain's encounter with India catapulted the previously isolated nation into a position of global dominance. Three main factors transformed Britain from a small, poor island into the world's mightiest empire:

- *India's trade and technology*: The East India Company accumulated massive amounts of wealth through its lucrative trade with India. The innovative corporation gradually started co-opting India's traditional manufacturing capabilities, especially in the areas of textiles and steel production. At first, it established its own manufacturing plants in India to reverse engineer the knowledge, but eventually transferred the expertise—and the factories—to Britain. This influx of knowledge and technology was an important factor in facilitating Britain's Industrial Revolution.
- *Colonization of India*: The colonization of India provided Britain access to huge amounts of capital. Besides profiting from trade, Britain became the tax collector in large regions of India where it imposed high levels of taxation. It also secured India as a captive market for selling its finished goods.
- *Britain's technology*: Britain developed mass production using the technologies of the water wheel and steam engine, paving the way for the first Industrial Revolution between 1760 and 1830. From 1870 to 1914, the second Industrial Revolution was brought about by the electrification and mechanization of factories.

The Industrial Revolution enabled Britain to surpass its European rivals and become the world's largest empire, a position it held for almost two centuries.

There are some parallels between Britain's rise to world domination and China's ambitions to achieve the same.

Artificial Intelligence is to China's twenty-first-century rise to power what the Industrial Revolution was to Britain's ascendance in the late 1700s.

However, unlike Britain, China's recent rise to power is not its first experience of historical greatness. China has a long history as a preeminent nation with an advanced, regionally dominant civilization. Through ancient and medieval times, China enjoyed a high culture that produced technological innovations such as paper, movable-type printing, gunpowder, the compass, the mechanical clock, silk, acupuncture and porcelain. Few inventions are developed entirely in isolation; for millennia China enjoyed bidirectional intellectual trade with other countries that further enhanced some of its technologies.

Later on, China declined and became impoverished over several centuries. At the end of the Second World War, China's people had been entrenched in poverty for several generations. *China's recent rise is a redevelopment*—that is, China is a redeveloping, not a developing, nation. The ancient roots of its earlier prominence play an increasingly important role in defining its future identity on the world stage.

What is an entirely new kind of experience for China—in which it has a long learning curve ahead—is to build an empire that is global and not just in its geographical neighborhood. In this respect, its projection of hard power into far-flung places like Africa and Latin America are bold experiments.

DIGITAL COLONIZATION

The industrial revolutions of prior eras produced different effects in different countries and in different communities within countries. This is also likely to be the case with the disruptions of AI. The initial disruptions will primarily be in developed countries where automation is strongest, but the reverberations will gradually be felt in every corner of the world.

The new AI-based power centers are located firmly in the US and China. A new era of colonization—namely, digital colonization—is already underway. The associated economic, social and political effects will devastate other countries, which will be relegated to the status of colonies or satellites. And China's grip on its colonies will strengthen—including large parts of Africa and Latin America as well as Asian countries like Pakistan.

To understand the huge disparities between this duopoly of AI leaders and other countries, we must look at where the new AI investments are being made. The AI investments in recent years, as well as forecasts for the future, have resulted in a heavy concentration of intellectual property, industrial assets and wealth generation in the US and China. PricewaterhouseCoopers has forecasted that the total world GDP will increase by up to 14% by the year 2030 as a result of AI, suggesting that almost sixteen trillion dollars of *additional* economic activity will be added to the world economy during this decade alone.

The table below offers a breakdown of AI's boost to the world's GDP by region. China is at the top, even ahead of the US. Despite having the world's second-largest population, India is at the bottom, subsumed into the "rest of the world" category.[129]

Increase in GDP by 2030 resulting from AI	
Region	**GDP increase by 2030**
China	$7.0 trillion
North America	$3.7 trillion
Northern Europe	$1.8 trillion
Southern Europe	$0.7 trillion
Developed Asia (Japan, South Korea, Taiwan)	$0.9 trillion
Latin America	$0.5 trillion
Rest of the world (Africa, South Asia, Oceania)	$1.2 trillion

Source: PricewaterhouseCoopers, Sizing the Prize, 2017[130]

A United Nations 2019 report also offers an interesting perspective on technological dominance.

> China, the United States and Japan together account for 78 per cent of all AI patent filings in the world. USA and China account for 75 per cent of all patents related to blockchain technologies, 50 per cent of global spending on internet-of-things, at least 75 per cent of the cloud computing market, and 90 per cent of the market capitalization value of the world's 70 largest digital platform companies.[131]

An important new technology related to AI is the Internet of Things, in which all sorts of physical devices are digitally connected with the internet, the same way computers and digital phones are. These interconnections include ubiquitous home appliances like lighting fixtures, refrigerators, and cars and office buildings as well as commercial devices including entire factories. The US and China account for half the world's spending on the Internet of Things. Figure 10 makes this trend clear.[132]

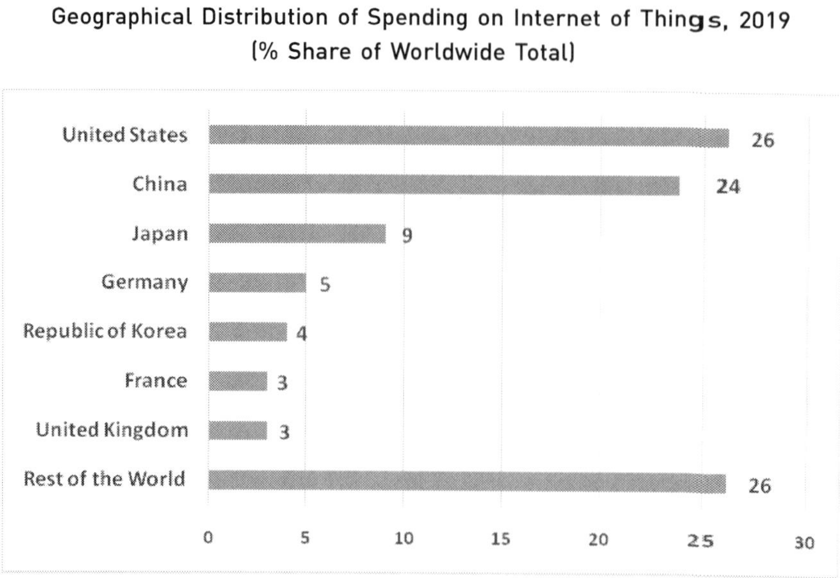

Source: UNCTAD, *Digital Economy Report 2019, 7*

Figure 10: Country breakdown of spending on Internet of Things

China and the US have surpassed all other countries in spending with their vibrant AI developers, venture funding, and huge databases already in place. Their resources create an insurmountable barrier to competition for all other countries at this stage.

Bain & Company analyzes a different aspect of the disparities between rich and poor countries that AI will exacerbate. It warns that poor countries will no longer be able to use their low wages to climb the development ladder. Another report exposing the deepening divide between developed and developing countries states:

> The winners of the digital revolution are, on the other hand, likely to be the highly developed Asian countries with good education systems, such as Singapore, Hong Kong, Taiwan and South Korea. These countries—together with the Scandinavian countries—have been undertaking research and working to find digital solutions for complex issues for a long time. The digital interconnection of people in these countries is also very far advanced.[133]

Unfortunately, the newly emerging markets that have been hoping to copy the export-led growth model of Japan, the Asian Tigers (South Korea, Taiwan, Singapore and Hong Kong), and China are likely to face shrinking global demand. As automation spreads, large pools of unskilled labor will become less valuable as labor becomes a smaller proportion of overall costs. At the same time, new technologies are poised to make smaller-scale manufacturing more cost efficient, allowing advanced economies to rely more on domestic production.[134]

In fact, the next generation of robots will become cost competitive against workers in developing countries. This trend will adversely impact poor countries, especially those burdened with large populations, as smart computers take over more and more jobs.[135]

A report from Oxford Economics also warns that

> the effects of these job losses will vary greatly across countries and regions, with a disproportionate toll on lower-skilled workers and on poorer local economies. In many places, the impact will aggravate social and economic stresses from unemployment and income inequality in times when increasing political polarization is already a worrying trend.[136]

It goes on to state that automation is likely to hit the poorest people hardest.

> On average, a new robot displaces nearly twice as many jobs in lower-income regions compared with higher-income regions of the same country. At a time of worldwide concern about growing levels of economic inequality and political polarisation, this finding has important social and political implications.[137]

The WEF report agrees that the digital divide between rich and poor countries creates a vicious cycle from which the poor cannot escape.

> A widening digital divide between countries risks a vicious cycle, as increasing wealth gaps and a brain drain make it harder for those left behind to catch up.... Hence, countries could lose out on the compounding effect of investments and subsequently lack the R&D capabilities needed to thrive, contributing to yet further brain drain.[138]

In summary, AI-driven disruptions will precipitate the dawn of the age of digital colonialism. Because economies of scale figure significantly in the development and management of AI technology, the haves and have-nots in AI will be a decisive factor in determining the fate of nations. Some will win big, and others will be forced out of the race. The countries with the biggest databases, the largest budgets, and the most experience with deployment will eclipse others in AI. Digital domination will translate into profits and, consequently, increased investment capacity over those that fall behind. The gap between leaders and laggards will be practically impossible to close; in fact, due to the exponential growth of technology, the gap is likely to widen. The low-wage comparative advantage of developing countries is rapidly fading away because AI-based automation will eliminate most low-level factory jobs.

Those countries left behind are destined for digital colonization in the same way the Industrial Revolutions enslaved many parts of the world. Countries starting late in the AI race will eventually give up, forced to accept their fate as a second-tier player and becoming, in effect, a dependent nation or even a virtual colony.

Data Exploitation

When European colonizers were plundering the natural resources and wealth of their colonies, they did not always keep detailed records that would expose them to accountability for the carnage they wreaked. Similarly, there is no accountability today for moving data across borders. Even though all countries systematically track the movement of physical goods through their ports via customs and the movement of human labor via immigration, they simply ignore tracking the movement of data. The logic of movement across borders applies selectively when it suits those that dominate the global system.

Poor countries lack the sophistication and clarity to negotiate, and therefore their valuable data is pilfered by foreign parties over whom they have no control. In most cases, these countries do not even know who has taken what data or how it is being used. Consequently, they are unable to assert sovereignty claims over their own native data. *Rich countries, led by the US, aggressively complain about stolen intellectual property, but they have conveniently avoided classifying data as intellectual property.*

Perhaps the most egregious form of economic exploitation today is the export of free raw data and the import of value-added information products that use this data. In some cases, biased agreements spell out how developing countries receive modest amounts of technology and network connectivity in exchange for giving up vast amounts of data. Zimbabwe, for example, has signed such a deal with the Chinese company CloudWalk. The Zimbabwean government receives surveillance technology, and in return CloudWalk receives facial recognition data on Zimbabwe citizens. The Chinese will effectively own and control private data on Zimbabwe's citizens, a potentially powerful political weapon in the future.[139]

The Chinese are also gathering vast amounts of surveillance data in Pakistan as part of their transfer of surveillance technology to the Pakistani government. The Pakistanis see the technology as a gift, but personal data about Pakistan's citizens, including political leaders, could be used to blackmail future Pakistani governments. Imagine the Chinese knowing more about the whereabouts and activities of persons of interest in Pakistan than Pakistan's own intelligence services. And imagine the leverage such knowledge gives the Chinese authorities.[140]

India has already given away a mountain of precious data on the Kumbh Mela (a pilgrimage and festival celebrated once every twelve years attended by millions of people; the last one attracted nearly one hundred million) to foreign researchers from Harvard. The study compiled sociodemographic, DNA, and psychological data on tens of millions of people from every corner of India. Additionally, precious genetic data from India's immense biodiversity has been collected as part of medical collaborations with foreign organizations. Part Two discusses in detail how the appropriation of its citizens' data is sabotaging India's future.

Western agriculture companies are gathering data from farmers in remote developing countries. These nations provide a unique ecosystem of diverse climates, soil and water conditions, seed varieties, and other parameters that agricultural scientists want to study. Conditions on each farm are distinct, because farms in poor countries are not large-scale, mechanized, or standardized the way they are in developed countries. Such varied data is invaluable in training machines to optimize the algorithms. The AI-enabled companies build models of the farmers' choices and variables like climate, soil, fertilizer, etc. Often the monitoring technology is classified as foreign aid or implemented as part of a trade deal. In return, some labor-intensive data services are outsourced to the poor countries, creating more wealth for a few rich middlemen in that country but doing nothing for the millions whose data has been siphoned off.

In another example, a subsidiary of UK-based Babylon has partnered with Rwanda's Ministry of Health to provide technology for free online healthcare consultations and appointments—in exchange for the patients' medical data that can be used for research.[141]

Developing countries face a dilemma: Connecting to global networks is critical to their development, yet those networks are controlled by the West or China. Consequently, poor nations must compromise their data assets, and potentially their sovereignty, just to get connected. In contrast, rich countries acquire huge amounts of valuable data, usually without paying for it.

A UN report describes this exploitation:

> Users of Facebook are suppliers of raw data; Facebook as a company produces the value-added data products, which are then given back to the users for free (social

> interaction) and sold to companies seeking marketing opportunities (targeted advertising space). From a geographical perspective, this emerging global "data value chain" sees the positioning of most countries as data suppliers while only a handful of platforms and countries that receive most of the data can turn them into value-added data products, which, in turn, can be monetized.[142]

Google's high-altitude balloons and Facebook's drones are projects that those companies claim will benefit millions in Africa by connecting them onto the global knowledge highways. But such deception merely panders to the feel-good headspace of ignorant politicians of poor countries that happily give up their data sovereignty.

We know about the horrible debt traps that have yoked many developing countries to creditors in rich countries. The UN warns that in the future, "Developing countries may risk ending up in a 'data trap,' at the lower levels of the data value chains and become dependent on global digital platforms".[143]

Return of the East India Company

Throughout history, the dynamics of power has shifted from era to era. A new epoch is dawning, where power will be concentrated in the hands of those that control AI-based algorithms that drive the digital platforms.

The AI-based concentration of power has taken on a terrifying new aspect. When we think of global power, countries like the US, China, and Russia readily come to mind. But today, *private* companies are accumulating immense power based on their ability to leverage AI and big data as tools to influence, manipulate and even control the minds of people.

Some of these private companies may soon become more powerful than many nation-states, but the shift will not be obvious. They will not fly a flag or manage a currency (although some are attempting to launch their own cryptocurrency), and they will not wield military power, at least not directly. However, their unprecedented knowledge of people and things around the world, coupled with their ability to disrupt and alter the physical world and manipulate people's choices, will lead to a new nexus of power. Such companies will decide who will, and who will not, be given access to this new form of power, and on what terms.

Amy Webb's (author, futurist and CEO of Future Today Institute) book *The Big Nine: How the Tech Titans and Their Thinking Machines Could Warp Humanity* discusses nine companies—six American and three Chinese—that own and control most AI and big data intellectual property. They achieved control through intermediary structures, venture capital funds and complex networks of interrelationships.

Not one Indian company is a player in this league. Most unfortunate is that a large number of talented Indians work for American and Chinese companies in an *individual* capacity, including in top executive positions, but not as owners. Indians who do own companies tend to sell their stake when the right offer comes along. Whenever innovative entrepreneurs anywhere in the world develop a promising breakthrough, digital giants or venture firms that serve as their proxies are waiting to buy them out. As a result, hundreds of instant millionaires are being created at the individual level, including many living in India.

I view this trend as the return of Britain's East India Company, which started out in 1600 as a modest private company for the purpose of making profit from lucrative trade with India. Over its 250-year history, the East India Company became the world's largest private business, amassing more wealth, income and military power than even its own British government. Despite being a private company, it became a colonial power—collecting taxes, operating courts, and running the military and other functions of state across many kingdoms within India. At the time, the East India Company had more ships, soldiers, money and territory under its control than any European government, though now it is remembered as a rogue machine. Since then, the lines between government and private companies have often blurred.

The People's Liberation Army, the communist party machine that controls China's government, directly or indirectly owns and controls many of China's capitalist enterprises. The government uses technology from these companies for its AI-based surveillance and control of citizens. Similarly, private companies supplying mercenaries are hired by the US military and the CIA in various parts of the world. There are many ways private companies work in alliance with, or as proxies, for certain governments.

Sometimes the digital giants outweigh the governments they claim to support. For instance, in one year, Google received more than 10,000 requests from the US government to turn over private user information, and it decided to comply 93 times.[144] The question becomes: Do private companies decide who to compromise by turning over their private data to a government?

The power of businesses differs from that of nation-states in certain ways. Democratic governments can be held accountable, at least in theory, because they claim to exist for the public good and must get votes to stay in power. Private firms, on the other hand, exist solely to benefit the interests of their owners and do not have the same level of accountability to society.

India seems to have forgotten its experience with the East India Company. The government has failed to halt the continuous outflow of private data to foreign firms. If data represents national wealth, India is for sale. The threat to its national security and sovereignty needs to be called out.

CHINA'S AMBITIOUS PLAN

Long-Term, Systematic, and Disciplined

China's recent rise as a global superpower can be traced to several factors. Chairman Mao's tumultuous Cultural Revolution, lasting between 1966–76, provided the initial impetus. The Cultural Revolution was a controversial grassroots movement that used draconian methods to achieve economic and social transformation. The sacrifice of basic human rights empowered the government to pull China out of abject poverty through rapid modernization. Any aspect of traditional Chinese culture that interfered with the modernization agenda was brushed aside. For instance, religious places were closed but not destroyed, the vision being to reopen them after the economic and social transformation had been accomplished. Mao did not want to destroy ancient culture; rather, he put it in mothballs for revival by a later generation.

Mao believed that the foremost priority was to build a solid foundation for China's prosperity and international power; only once that goal was accomplished could the population return to appreciate its old civilizational assets.

One of the most impressive characteristics of the contemporary Chinese population is how educated the people tend to be—a trait that is the direct result of the aggressive agenda of Deng (Mao's successor) to educate all citizens, both men and women. As a result of this educational policy, today's Chinese youth for the most part belong to families that have been educated for multiple consecutive generations.

Thus, prior to this latest spurt in economic, political and intellectual growth, the Maoist revolution and the follow-on foundation established by Deng had already laid the groundwork for the country's societal goals. Of course, the price society paid in terms of human rights abuses was unprecedented in scale and intensity. China, however, has consistently defied Western attempts to demonize its government as an abusive, totalitarian state. China controls its own narrative. Its citizens' education has been built on the foundation of the grand narrative of past greatness and its future as the world's foremost superpower. It is clear among Chinese people today that the long-term destiny of their country's greatness has been drilled into them as non-negotiable. This collective self-confidence is a remarkable asset. This is the reason the sale of cheap labor to the West was strategic, and not a sellout of its national interests.

Based on the principles for which two generations of Chinese people made extreme sacrifices, China began its love affair with American globalization. The US multinationals' drive to expand required cheap labor, and China boldly configured itself in the global value chain as the prime supplier of low-cost manufacturing. It offered the most favorable terms, on a large scale, and supplied labor characterized by efficiency and discipline, along with managers that made it easy to do business.

But the results were not visible for a long time. In 1975, when Bill Gates founded Microsoft, China was still bogged down by the Cultural Revolution. Almost a quarter century later, when Google was founded in 1998, only 0.2% of China's population had internet connection, compared to 30% in the US.[145] Persistence eventually paid off. By 2017, less than twenty years later, nearly half of all AI venture funding worldwide was coming from China's investors.

For instance, China's information technology company iFlyTek has demonstrated that it is on par with, or ahead of, Google, Facebook and IBM in NLP systems, specifically in the ability to grasp overall meaning rather than merely individual words, and is becoming the world's most valuable AI speech company. China is already the world's top market for robots, nearly as large as Europe and the US combined.[146]

These gigantic leaps are not only in information technology. In 2007, China had no high-speed rail lines, yet by 2019 it had more miles of high-speed rail lines than the rest of the world combined.[147] The country has also made substantial advancements in its domestic aerospace industry. It has successfully launched its own space station, the Tiangong-1, has put astronauts into space, and is building regional and medium-range airliners to compete with the Boeing-Airbus duopoly. In the past twenty years China has vaulted to the forefront of development in one industry after another.

A prominent reason is that the Chinese government made huge bets on high-risk initiatives that led to game-changing transformations. Democratic governments are less willing to take such extreme risks because failure can lead to political ruin. The Chinese political system also does not require the time-consuming consensus for high-tech development that is needed in democracies at each stage and for each decision. Nor are Chinese leaders preoccupied with domestic fragmentation as a serious diversion. Despite numerous internal rebellions, none have threatened the equilibrium of either China's sovereignty or government stability in any practical sense.

Furthermore, multinational corporations operating in China have no need to contend with messy domestic politics. While American human rights activists have constantly accused China of labor abuses, and the US government regularly issues official protests, US manufacturing giants nonetheless have become increasingly addicted to the profits made possible by maintaining manufacturing bases in China. Against all odds, China became the factory of the world at a dramatic pace.

China started out with a long-term strategy for climbing the ladder of higher value-added manufacturing. Its strategic planners identified futuristic industries to target and with remarkable precision, determined which technologies would become critical to the future AI revolution. Today's game-changing technologies were anticipated by China ahead of most countries and the country positioned itself based on that vision.

The Chinese realized they faced a serious talent shortage in critical domains of competence. To fill these gaps in skilled labor for advanced technologies, it adopted a multipronged approach that included a menu of human resource development programs:

- Raising educational standards for schools and universities to achieve the world's best practices.
- Sending its high potential students abroad in the nineteen eighties and nineties, mostly to American universities, to learn and bring back vital knowledge required to advance their technology. These students were not chasing individual opportunities disconnected from the national plan. Most were part of comprehensive government designs to identify critical domains and acquire the levels of knowledge

for China's overall economic development strategy. Most of them returned to China to work.

- Recruiting the world's best brains to come and work in China by luring them with attractive compensation packages.

Each of these programs was well planned and integrated across various governmental ministries and civic institutions. China's rise to technological superiority has not been an ad hoc development out of chaos. Rather, it has been a meticulously organized strategy.

India has tried similar tactics, but the efforts were not as strategically planned or comprehensively implemented as China's. Young Indians pursued their studies and careers solely as personal opportunities, and not as part of an overall societal goal directed by a centralized, coordinated plan. An example of China's distinct approach is that not many Chinese students study sociology or human rights with a career goal of bringing down China's social organization. In contrast, India's youth have been lured into various kinds of "breaking India" career paths.[148] China wisely chose to import Western science and technology while deliberately resisting the integration of Western social theories into the management of China's domestic matters.

China's vision statements are not just talking points meant to impress audiences and make the public feel good. These strategies are implemented at the deepest levels of society and its institutions. China has stronger government–industry alliances than any other major country, its R&D investments are paying off, its standard of public-school education has been rising at a rate typical of world leaders, it has harnessed more data into its AI systems than any other country, and its population is sold on the idea that surveillance using big data is in the long-term national interest.

China innovates in several cutting-edge technologies. At the center of the advanced technology being developed and produced in China is AI, and the technology permeates each industry to its core. In fact, China is currently producing more patents in certain advanced technologies than any other country, *including* the US.

The export surplus from manufacturing has stocked China's treasury with cash to finance an impressive war chest. In fact, China is currently a major lender to the US government and utilizes this economic clout to successfully negotiate with US authorities, both governmental and corporate.

Gladiator Culture

A few decades ago, China made a commitment to develop sports as a nation-building project and set the target to be among the top medal winners at the Olympics. A nationwide infrastructure initiative helped the country achieve this goal, and the Chinese consider this one of their assets in social cohesion. China's rise in international sports laid the foundation for a strategic plan to not only build physical health but also enhance psychological qualities such as strong character, team spirit and pragmatism. This path to emotional robustness serves as a useful foundation to the society.

Kai-Fu Lee is a leading venture capitalist developing China's next generation high-tech companies, and a former president of Google China as well as executive at other US tech giants. He has explained the secret behind China's sudden rise in AI technologies. He compares China's internet entrepreneurs to the gladiators who fought to their deaths in ancient Rome's Coliseum.[149] Such a mentality came naturally to the Chinese people; the past few generations had been raised on the scarcity of everything, which made them good at hustling. The entrepreneurial coliseum was a natural arena for applying this experience.

Today's life-or-death technology battles recognize no ethics or scruples—they are a winner-take-all game, a cutthroat competition in which success is obsessively pursued at any cost. To survive, players cannot be complacent for even one moment because new competitors are always at the gate. Constant innovation and ruthless self-preservation are the only rules. Chinese companies assume that their best ideas are being plagiarized and their employees being poached.

The way neural networks use feedback from massive amounts of data is a good analog to understand how the gladiator battleground works. China's gladiator entrepreneurs incorporate data from other gladiators' experiences to improve their own performance. In a sense, all competitive free markets work this way; China's happens to be more intense and operates on a scale larger than others.

Understanding how this market approach has evolved deserves a quick recap at the various stages of industrialization in China over recent decades.

1. As noted earlier, China began the process by selling cheap labor to American companies.
2. Chinese companies quietly and humbly learned from their American clients, then reverse engineered and imitated US business models and products.
3. Inspired by US entrepreneurs, several thousand Chinese start-ups rapidly emerged, adapting American models for Chinese market conditions.
4. The surge in technological competition turned China's start-up business ecosystem into a coliseum in which thousands of companies fought for market supremacy. Just like in ancient Rome, the ethos was either kill or be killed. What mattered was rapid deployment,

the ruthlessness to survive and thrive amid chaos and bloodshed. Using cleverness, tricks and subterfuge, entrepreneurs blatantly copied ideas and techniques from wherever they could to get ahead.

5. The scale and intensity of mimicry forces Chinese companies to innovate incrementally. They constantly refine their products, cut costs, implement new ideas, and hustle to raise money. Companies unable to sustain constant innovation are frozen in copycat products and will not survive.
6. The result is that China has a formidable, and unparalleled supply-chain ecosystem. In contrast, most other countries' supply chains lack any central operating plan and tend to function as fragmented silos.

This model of entrepreneurship is how China so rapidly climbed to the top of the AI ladder. The most valuable asset resulting from their process was not a product, but the culture of the coliseum encouraged by the government. Because the Chinese people traditionally show deference toward authority figures and are raised to conform to established norms, the government's support for fierce entrepreneurship in the domestic internet market, especially since 2014, boosted this new culture.

In contrast, such practices are not easily accepted in Silicon Valley, at least not so openly and blatantly. Many Silicon Valley entrepreneurs belonged to elitist families like well-educated computer scientists and other technocrats. According to the moral code of Silicon Valley's gentry, the jungle-warfare tactics of China are less than respectable, even crude. China's coliseum, where devious tactics are commonplace, is more fiercely competitive, nimbler and shrewder than Silicon Valley.

Neither has India's traditional **jugaad** culture (putting ad hoc pieces together to improvise) developed an ecosystem like China's to drive collective competition in a positive direction. In the Indian jugaad culture, **jatis** (communities) do not compete directly against each other. Experience gained is kept private within a family or close community and not shared, used instead for personal micro-optimization that is nowadays rife with corruption. China's coliseum has no such rules according to Kai-Fu Lee's thesis, and even if there were, no one would follow them.

In summary, China learnt the innovation engine model that the Silicon Valley had pioneered; but today its economy is five times that of India and is competing with that of the US in purchasing power parity. China is ahead of the US in publishing AI research papers, filing AI patents and in the number of leading AI companies created. It has created a large capital pool for taking risky bets with potential game-changing outcomes.[150]

Betting the Future on AI

The Chinese government made a bold bet by placing AI at the center of its strategic vision to leapfrog ahead of the US in every major field by 2050. Its ambitious plan established milestones and measurable benchmarks to assess progress along the way. They have achieved their benchmarks thus far. China is committed to becoming the worldwide center of AI innovation by the year 2030, including not only AI itself but also the wide array of breakthrough technologies enabled by, and associated with it, such as quantum computing and microchip design.[151]

These comprehensive plans address educating the Chinese people in the latest technologies as well as deploying these technologies in every aspect of their public and private lives. To this end, Chinese venture capital investing in AI constituted a massive 48% of global venture funding in 2017, surpassing the US for the first time.

The Chinese Communist Party has declared its intent to pursue a "first-mover advantage" in order to establish itself as "the world's primary AI innovation center".[152] Its 2017 strategic plan for AI made strong statements of vision and commitment.

> AI has become a new focus of international competition. AI is a strategic technology that will lead in the future; the world's major developed countries are taking the development of AI as a major strategy to enhance national competitiveness and protect national security.[153]

In 2017, at the 19th National Party Congress, President Xi Jinping issued a bold statement that China would become the world leader in technology. The pronouncement galvanized the nation the same way President John F. Kennedy's 1961 speech calling for the US to land a man on the moon by the end of the decade had roused Americans.

China's ambition is based on forecasts that predict AI technologies will engender a productivity leap on a scale comparable to that of the eighteenth-century Industrial Revolution. It is estimated that AI-related products and services will cause a sixteen trillion-dollar increase in global GDP by 2030. The Chinese intend to capture almost half of this total increase, approximately $7 trillion, while North America's share is estimated to be lower at $3.7 trillion.

China's universities and tech companies are at the forefront of the country's ambitions. Its AI experts have become the world's most prominent contributors in the field, surpassing Americans in many specialties. Tsinghua University in Beijing has surpassed Stanford University in the number of times its research papers are cited in the top 100 AI institutions.[154] One of China's top technology entrepreneurs summarizes this trajectory.

> Artificial intelligence will be the first general-purpose technology of the modern era in which China stands shoulder to shoulder with the West in both advancing and applying the technology. ... China's progress allows for the research talent and creative capacity of nearly one-fifth of humanity to contribute to the task of distributing and utilizing artificial intelligence. Combine this with the country's gladiator entrepreneurs, unique internet ecosystem, and proactive government push...[155]

Tsinghua University is heavily invested in advancing China's military–industrial complex. It houses the High-End Military Intelligence Laboratory, with the support of the Central Military Commission. The technology company, Baidu, and the China Electronics Technology Group Corporation collaborate on the development of the Joint Laboratory for Intelligent Command and Control Technologies for the benefit of the Chinese military.

China has additionally founded two major research organizations completely focused on the development of AI-based unmanned systems. The exact level of its funding remains a military secret, but it is estimated to be in the billions of dollars. Western scholars have conceded that China, not the US, leads the world in the military application of drone technology. A few hundred development and manufacturing companies of Unmanned Aerial Vehicles (UAVs), as well as many private entrepreneurs, are funded and directed by the Chinese military.

China's drone-powered air force includes supersonic drones, unveiled at the 2019 National Day parade. According to the *South China Morning Post*: "This suggests the PLA (People's Liberation Army) is prioritizing the development of the most cutting-edge technologies that will change the game of war".[156] The PLA has also developed autonomous killer robots, cloud-based drone squadrons, and autonomous landing vehicles. All these systems use machine learning to make independent decisions, such as plotting routes and avoiding obstacles.

Artificial Intelligence is being used to upgrade simulations and improve training and combat readiness. The PLA has implemented what is called the algorithm game, which predicts events in the battleground to give soldiers a cognitive advantage. US intelligence suspects that China has also developed malicious code to invade enemies' network in order to steal secrets.

China is strategically investing its large capital reserves well beyond its borders. As with everything else, this capital diversification is being implemented in a centrally planned and targeted approach. Among the bigger initiatives being undertaken are:

- Building an AI-based economy that achieves global supremacy within the next twenty-five years.
- Building a military force on par with the US in most respects using the latest technological innovations, and especially prominent in the neighborhood of the Indo-Pacific region.
- Building and controlling major trade routes worldwide. All roads led to Rome in ancient times, but all roads will lead to China by the middle of the twenty-first century according to their ambition. Such a broad logistics network will give China access to precious raw materials in places ranging from Africa to South America. It will also enable China to gain end-to-

end control over supply chains, enabling the efficient transport of Chinese finished goods to every corner of the world. For instance, by 2040, Africa will have two billion people, 40% of the world's renewable energy, and the world's fastest-growing economy. China has already captured the strategic high ground in Africa by buying long-term positions in natural resources, logistics and government relations.

CORE ASPECTS OF CHINA'S AI

Big Data

China has surpassed the US in the quantity of data being automatically entered into its AI systems daily. Its internet companies developed products and services based on their own unique perspective and social systems. Therefore, it is a mistake to characterize any Chinese company as the Facebook of China, Twitter of China, or Amazon of China. The Chinese have created an alternate digital universe with no clear mapping drawn from the US digital ecosystem. For example, WeChat, owned by the Chinese giant Tencent, enables users to perform any number of activities and daily tasks—send text and voice messages, pay bills, make appointments, file taxes, buy tickets, engage in group activities—without ever leaving the platform. In the US digital ecosystem, the vast spectrum of applications that WeChat encompasses are dispersed among many different apps. Consequently, the data collected by the US apps is scattered, not centralized.

The alternate Chinese digital universe started in 2013 when it went beyond merely copying Americans and started innovating in a major way. In part, this innovation was required because of China's different starting point. Before the advent of the new digital giants in the US, American society already had a high penetration of credit cards and a network for charging payments, a system that was in place before the internet became ubiquitous. China, on the other hand, lacked significant credit card penetration, and therefore it developed new systems in which cheap smartphones serve as credit card devices.

In the US, data from credit card payments is not controlled by the same companies that supply other internet services. But in China, internet companies that supply an abundance of services also collect massive amounts of data from routine payments. The same database includes users' physical financial transactions as well as soft data from their personal messages, emotional propensities and social interactions. China not only has a higher quantity of data than the US, but the quality of the data is superior in certain ways.

According to Kai-Fu Lee, China is the Saudi Arabia of data.

> If artificial intelligence is the new electricity, big data is the oil that powers the generators. And as China's vibrant and unique internet ecosystem took off after 2012, it turned into the world's top producer of this petroleum for the age of artificial intelligence.[157]

This appetite for big data has triggered alarm bells in Washington. For instance, the US government has flagged the ownership of Grindr as a national security risk and ordered the Chinese owner to divest a majority stake by 2020.[158] Grindr, a hook-up app for the LGBTQ community, is an example of how the US fears data can be misused. Grindr was acquired in 2016 by Chinese gaming company, Kunlun. During the Cold War, homosexual blackmail was used by Stasi, the former state security service of German Democratic Republic, and the KGB, the former secret police force of the Soviet Union, to target vulnerable officials in the West. It is feared among some US policymakers that the Chinese might be fishing for private data they could use for blackmail.

President Donald Trump also ordered a Chinese company to sell its ownership of a hotel property management software that poses a potential national security risk. The software manages over 90,000 rooms worldwide and collects vast amounts of personal data on hotel guests. In 2017, another Chinese entity unsuccessfully tried to invest in a US company that streams movies to airline and cruise passengers by satellite. Federal laws were then passed to regulate foreign acquisitions of any US business that has access to data on more than one million people, including certain genetic and biometric data, financial data and health data.[159]

Another example is the US' decision to ban the popular Chinese commercial product TikTok internally for its employees, claiming that China can use the technology to collect data on users.[160] Almost two months after the US Transportation Security Agency invoked the ban, India banned it more broadly, but this was in retaliation to a border security incident.

Surveillance

China is the acknowledged world leader in the use of AI for the surveillance of large populations. It is already leveraging AI technology to manage portions of its own population, having deployed a large AI system to control the Xinjiang province's Uighur Muslim population. China is considered a testing ground for perfecting this technology, which might be exported to other governments.

Artificial Intelligence-enabled technology can track and monitor an entire society using a variety of pervasive automated surveillance techniques. Individuals under surveillance know only a portion of the tracking to which they are subjected. The system tracks movements, activities, communications and behavioral patterns and continually scores each individual in a complex matrix to profile who is, and who is not, a loyal citizen, according to criteria established by Chinese authorities. The system also dispenses rewards and punishments based on its determination of individuals' loyalty. Some rewards and punishments are explicit, while many are surreptitiously delivered to brainwash citizens on a subtle, unconscious level.[161]

Chinese citizens are being trained in large military-style camps designed to transform them into obedient workers. The official directive states that the goal is to "turn around their ingrained lazy, lax, slow, sloppy, freewheeling, individualistic ways so they obey company rules".[162] There are also reports that China is planning to edit the Quran and the Bible to force its citizens into widespread compliance with the national ideology.[163]

Such surveillance and control systems might one day be used more widely. Once China perfects its AI-based control of society, the system could be expanded to impose control on its satellite countries. China is rumored to be providing such systems to the ruling elite in places like Pakistan (already a virtual colony of China) to help keep the Pakistani population in check. The Pakistani government is in effect turning into a mere puppet in the hands of its true Chinese masters. China would be able to disrupt the existing regime and install their own proxies—a high-tech version of the way the British Empire ruled India via the local rajas.

China is the world leader in facial recognition technology. The AI companies SenseTime, Megvii, and Yitu are the recognized front runners in this field. Chinese law enforcement leverages this technology for the large-scale tracking of individuals of interest. Also, Chinese-designed 5G networks are acquiring a large market share worldwide, and this will enable real-time acquisition of data from around the globe that could potentially be sent back to the Chinese government. The US has banned these companies, asserting that their technology is used to violate human rights. However, many observers suggest that America's real motive is to set back China's lead in AI-related technological development.

China has utilized the big data from the Covid-19 catastrophe to further train its AI machines. The post-pandemic world will be one with even more powerful AI systems deployed in society. Ironically, the pandemic will give a boost to technologies like AI, robotics, and both virtual- and augmented-reality systems.

Genetics

China has a centrally planned, joint military–civilian national strategy with exploration and innovation in biological research as a priority.[164] For over a decade, academic and military researchers have been developing their ability to exploit AI in order to weaponize biotechnology. China's military–industrial complex has formally identified areas such as brain-control weapons and specific ethnic genetic attacks as promising areas for future innovation and development.

The PLA, controlled by China's Communist Party, is actively involved in military research using AI combined with neuroscience. According to US reports monitoring China, the PLA is pursuing technologies to boost the performance of troops in combat. The US fears that China is currently developing genetic weapons for the purpose of winning a bloodless victory. The way is to manipulate the psychological behavior of a population or spread specially manufactured microbes to defeat an enemy without the need to wage conventional war.

China also leads the world in the number of human gene-editing trials, some of which have caused worldwide controversy. The PLA's medical institutions have become major centers of research on the military applications of AI-based medicine and biotechnology. Artificial Intelligence is a key tool in the advancement of gene editing technology, especially for a genome as large as humanity.

The city of Shenzhen is home to China National Genebank, a massive collection of genetic data slated for application in AI-based research. Its stated aim is to "develop and utilize China's valuable genetic resources, safeguard national security in bioinformatics, and enhance China's capability to seize the strategic commanding heights".[165]

BGI Genomics is China's national leader in this technology project, with massive amounts of diverse genetic data at its disposal collected from a variety of sources over decades, including its surveillance in the Jinjiang region of China. Though based in China, the company has a global reach, boasting laboratories in California and Brisbane (Queensland) and a series of collaborative research agreements with academic and medical organizations around the US. American policymakers worry that BGI has too much access to US citizens' private genetic information, claiming that the company is studying military applications, including human gene editing.

Such applications are just the tip of the AI iceberg. For China, AI is clearly inseparable from their nation-building agenda. If AI were to founder for some reason, China would suffer a definitive setback to its ambitions. The country has literally bet its entire future on AI.

CHINA'S QUEST FOR DOMINATION

China has formulated a strategic roadmap for becoming a world leader in every respect, effectively replacing the US as the foremost global superpower (see Figure 11). Its use of AI is deeply embedded in its ambitions.

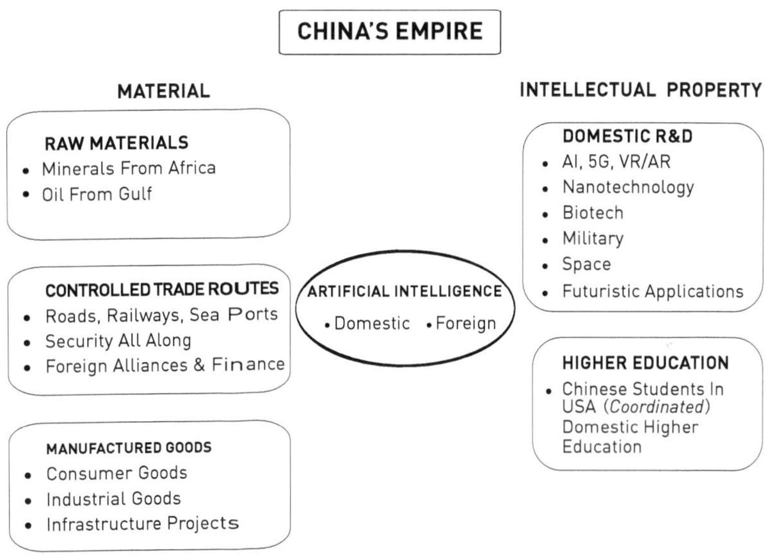

Figure 11: China's Roadmap to Power

Knowing quite well that data leads to power, China has replaced the leading US digital giants—Google, Facebook and Amazon—with Baidu, Alibaba and Tencent in its home market. China's massive companies are now successfully taking on US corporate giants in many parts of the world.

As explained in Chapter 7, Indian tech giants like TCS, Infosys, Wipro and HCL enjoyed an early lead in the export of software and services. At one time India had a legitimate claim to world-leader status in this arena but then squandered its advantage due to myopic thinking. As a result, China catapulted ahead of India in seminal technologies like AI. Part Two will delve into the details on how India lost its competitive lead.

The US–China rivalry centers on competition to lead the world in AI as the engine that will shape the new world order. The US recently announced a ban on American tech companies exporting AI software to China.[166] China, from its side, banned the use of all foreign technology in its government offices.[167]

Based on its sociopolitical priorities, China has successfully pursued a stunning path to bring economic prosperity to its massive population on a scale and at a speed unprecedented in world history. According to a recent report by Credit Suisse Research Institute, it has replaced Europe as the world's principal source of global wealth. In addition, it has surpassed the US as the country with the largest percentage of its population in the top 10% of global wealth. The report further indicates that China's wealth per adult is five times that of India's, and the gap with Western countries is steadily closing. And in terms of human rights criticisms, an interesting observation is that China's wealth is far better distributed throughout its population than is India's or US's.

Figure 12 illustrates how China's hard power nourishes, and is nourished, by a variety of strategic initiatives. The breadth of these supporting initiatives requires coordinated planning, and other aspiring countries will have difficulty catching up with such a large-scale enterprise that has been implemented over several decades.

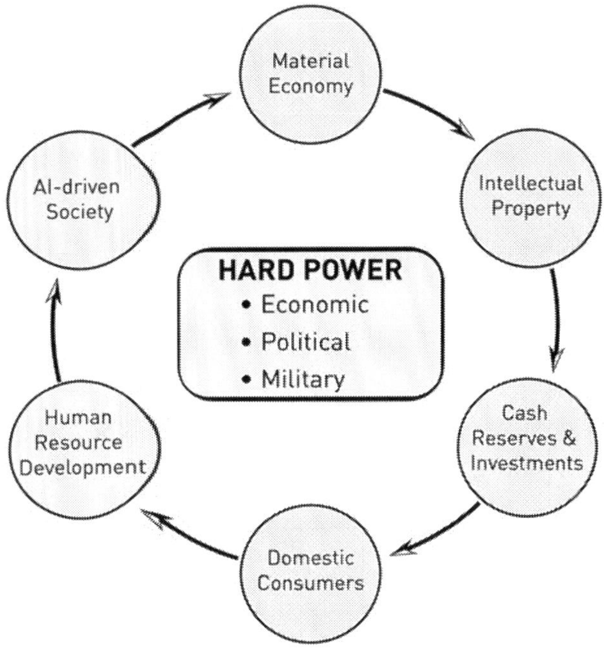

Figure 12: China's Strategy for Domination

Ambition to Become the New Rome

I have explained the parallels between Britain and China in historic terms. Ancient Rome's history also provides some interesting parallels with China. The Roman Empire was built on hard power. Its unparalleled network of roads provided a strategic advantage that enabled its economy to flourish. A dominant military and strong economic might enabled Rome to quickly conquer and assimilate many other nations and smaller empires.

China is likewise building an ambitious network called the Belt and Road Initiative, which includes infrastructure investments in seventy countries across Asia, Africa and Europe. The project uses cutting-edge technology to develop, operate and maintain end-to-end control over roads, railways and sea routes. Many strategically located seaports around the world will also be under China's control and operation. Besides physical transportation, the initiative includes an electric grid and a communications network—the largest and most sophisticated global logistics network ever undertaken by any country in history. China has been accused of neo-colonialism because of the debt incurred by the host countries and terms of operation being imposed on them. These agreements give China disproportionate ownership, whether direct or indirect, of the new infrastructure. China claims it is creating employment in the short term as well as helping these countries' long-term economies by providing sophisticated infrastructures; critics respond that China is creating persistent dependency.

The second parallel with Rome is in its use of hard power to defeat and assimilate the soft power giant of its time, Greece. The Mediterranean region had been divided conceptually into two main civilizations. The term *Occident* referred to Rome and the territories to its west, while *Orient* referred to Greece and the lands to its immediate east. Rome's strengths were its military prowess, centralized administration and proficiency in engineering. Greece was strong in philosophy, art and culture. In modern parlance, the Romans wielded hard power while the Greeks possessed soft power. The encounter between them, beginning in the eighth century BCE and lasting nearly one thousand years, resulted in what is now known as Greco-Roman civilization.

Over several generations, Rome waged a series of wars to ultimately conquer Greece's loose confederation of city-states. Romans were fascinated with the ancient classics of

Greece, its philosophy, and the work of major figures such as Plato and Aristotle. At the same time, they had no qualms about colonizing Greece, and eventually almost destroyed the roots of the culture they so admired.

Once the Romans had scored a decisive hard power victory over Greece, they appropriated what they considered the best of Greek knowledge, art and spirituality. They adapted the original form and expression of Greek culture (such as architecture) through the process of cultural digestion, and finally incorporated it into their own framework and Latin language.

The history of the clash between Rome and Greece can provide insight into the present dynamic between China and India. China enjoys a clear hard power edge over India, an advantage that is likely to grow in the next several years in the absence of India's acceleration. India, on the other hand, prides itself on its soft power. It is the world's largest democracy; its civilization is founded on a vast spiritual heritage including yoga, meditation, plant-based medicine, mathematics and other significant contributions to world culture. When the subject of China's power comes up, Indians commonly bring up their country's soft power as a counterbalance.

But the example of Rome versus Greece illustrates that *soft power cannot be supported or maintained without adequate hard power*. Victors in war are not determined by cultural sophistication. The big question to consider would be the role of Chinese technological advance in any military encounter it has with India, including through Pakistan. In evaluating such a scenario, one cannot assume that soft power will protect against a hard power attack. India's own texts like the *Mahabharata* demonstrate that soft power by itself is not enough to counter an enemy's hard power advantage. India would be foolish to ignore the gigantic ambitions and appetite of China as the world's latest, and likely fiercest, colonial hard power.

Pandemic and the Pushback

Recently, many countries feel a sense of betrayal by China. Supply chains are trending toward deglobalization as manufacturing companies return to onshore production. This shift will have a major impact on the shape of the world economy and geopolitics. Local and nationalistic ideologies are strengthening, populism is surging with blame leveled against multilateral institutions such as the World Health Organization (WHO), the G7, the G20, the UN, and other mechanisms of global governance.

Human rights studies are one of the US's primary weapons against China. When the US government publishes its annual report on human rights violations in different countries (a report that, incidentally, excludes the US itself from any evaluation of such violations), Chinese authorities quickly respond with their own report on US violations. Beneath this annual face-off is China's philosophical position that it determines its own criteria for what constitutes human rights, or any abuses thereof. It sees economic prosperity as the foundation on which a sustainable quality of life can be built, including human rights. This approach differs drastically from the Western criteria, for which individual freedom (but not economic freedom) is the top priority.

Amidst all this, the Covid-19 pandemic will only worsen the existing fault lines between different countries and different religions. The West and many other countries are likely to re-evaluate their dependence on China. The US trade war with China might worsen in this environment, potentially leading to a meltdown of global systems of cooperation. The big question will likely be: Will China be ostracized by the global community?

The pandemic appears to have given a boost to the China-like command societies and economies in times of disaster when the pragmatics of rapid decision-making and implementation take priority over aesthetic values like individualism and freedom. Ironically, the US government's economic bailout can be seen as socialism overriding capitalism in the world's largest free-market society.

In times of prosperity, an open society has the competitive edge of making creative breakthroughs, but debate will rage over whether a different approach is better for catastrophic times. Some issues that will be debated include:

- Should faith in capitalism and globalization be questioned because of the sudden nationalization of economies like the US?
- Should democracy's superiority be questioned because of how China managed its crisis and the way the major democracies were forced to use heavy-handed government dictates after voluntary, freedom-based efforts to contain the virus failed?

US GOVERNMENT RESPONSES

Though China was quite open about its global ambitions during the past two decades, the US did not consider it a serious threat until recently. The US had bought into China's public posture that both would be friendly superpowers and the rise of China would expand the global economy for the benefit of all. Also, the US felt that converting China into free market capitalism would be a moral and ideological victory.

However, China's recent behavior and the economic and geopolitical price the US is paying has triggered the alarm bells. The most shocking impact on US thinking toward China has been the US military's assessment that China is rapidly catching up in weapons technology, and that this has been based on the theft of intellectual property.

What has been presented to the public as a trade war with China is a much deeper US concern: that China's advancements in the cluster of technologies I have classified under the AI umbrella directly threaten the US military-industrial complex's world domination. Even the allegations against Huawei, TikTok and others for surveillance of US data is only the tip of the iceberg of this concern. The Pentagon and CIA have always been suspicious of China in this regard but now for the first time, the White House has accepted China as the new cold war enemy.

Unlike in China, in the US, the government and private industry largely pursue their own separate initiatives, although there is overlap when the government funds an industry program. Companies such as Google, Microsoft, Apple, IBM and a whole range of aerospace and defense contractors have led the US side in this tech battleground. The government has had its own internal projects as well, but much of the fundamental research is left to independent contractors. Recently, the government has dramatically expanded its direct involvement in AI in addition to the work being done in private industry. The US government is directly a stakeholder in guiding the cutting-edge developments and has made significant commitments to these initiatives.

President Trump's head of technology policy, Michael Kratsios, wants the "collective power" of the government and private sector in the US to keep the country ahead of China. The National Security Commission on Artificial

Intelligence (NSCAI), a government commissioned panel led by Google's former CEO Eric Schmidt, is supporting this unified government-industry complex to counter China. In November 2019, the NSCAI report urged the US government to increase investment in AI by showing that China is investing more and progressing rapidly in several areas.[168] The US government is now also concerned that China has used the Covid-19 pandemic to give a boost to its technology and get ahead of the US.[169]

President Trump issued an executive order to focus on AI with the statement:

> Continued American leadership in Artificial Intelligence is of paramount importance to maintaining the economic and national security of the United States.[170]

The White House AI Report elaborates on this commitment:

> The age of artificial intelligence (AI) has arrived and is transforming everything from healthcare to transportation to manufacturing. America has long been the global leader in this new era of AI and is poised to maintain this leadership going forward because of our strong innovation ecosystem. Realizing the full potential of AI for the Nation requires the combined efforts of industry, academia, and government. The Administration has been active in developing policies and implementing strategies that accelerate AI innovation in the U.S. for the benefit of the American people.[171]

The White House Office of Science and Technology has recently issued a plan to fund long-term investments in AI technologies, human capital development, big data, evaluation and testing of AI, and public–private partnerships to accelerate AI advances. It notes: "...our country's AI R&D

will benefit from the largest integrated health care system in the country and the largest genomic knowledge base in the world linked to health care information".[172]

The US government is now actively throwing its weight to counteract China's AI initiatives that pose a national security threat. For instance, *the hardware technology for AI has been declared a national security asset by the US and bans have been imposed to prevent this technology from getting into Chinese hands.*[173]

The trade war with China is only the tip of the iceberg of a much broader program to re-establish US's lead in technology, especially AI. For instance, in 2019, President Trump signed an executive order, *The American AI Initiative: The United States' National Strategy on Artificial Intelligence.* The strategic intent is to advance and protect AI technology and innovation as a national asset. The initiative channels funding for AI in a variety of concrete ways and includes wide-ranging collaborations with both the private sector and academic research. It identifies fundamental research and applications in science, medicine, communication, manufacturing, transportation, agriculture and security. The goal is to build a unique and vibrant American R&D ecosystem to accelerate AI discoveries.

The US Defense establishment has historically been at the forefront of developing numerous game-changing technologies for military use, and some of the most crucial technologies in public domain today, like the internet and the Global Positioning System (GPS), have their origins in such military projects.[174] Similarly in the area of AI, the Department of Defense has large ambitious projects in the pipeline and has established the Joint Artificial Intelligence Center (JAIC) to "harness the game-changing power of AI".[175] The goal is to use AI to address large-scale problems in domains as varied as cybersecurity, military healthcare, warfare decision-making, humanitarian assistance and disaster relief.[176]

The US Navy is increasingly leveraging AI-based technologies to increase its lethality, which is considered a giant military leap that easily surpasses previous advances like radar, nuclear power, and space travel. Artificial Intelligence is envisioned not merely as a tool for faster decision-making and reduced operational costs, but also as a major component of real-time feedback mechanisms for different platforms and systems. The Navy is implementing machine learning solutions to anticipate and restock supply bins, update command training devices on system change, predict dangers and provide potential solutions.[177]

Plans are also under way for futuristic machines like Unmanned Undersea Vehicles (UUVs) with highly accurate and lethal advanced autonomous features without the drawbacks of traditional submarines and sea mines. Similar to the strategic role of drones in the Air Force, the intent is to develop UUVs and allied systems and "integrate them into broader undersea warfare operating concepts as a whole".[178]

> Our opportunity today at this information inflection point is to see things differently, as a complete culture, as a team—to see data and advanced analytics in the proper sense: as warfare enablers that pulse through every ship, aircraft, submarine, sensor, weapon, and perhaps sooner than later, every sailor. [179]

The Air Force is using predictive AI models for aircraft maintenance. For example, the F-35's Autonomic Logistics Information System uses real-time data from the aircraft's engine and other onboard systems to predict the next maintenance date and the issues that need to be addressed.

This system has helped streamline the earlier processes, where maintenance was done either according to a standardized schedule or when actually required for repairs.[180] Another development is the Multi-Domain Command and Control system, which will use AI to consolidate data from air-, space-, cyberspace-, sea-, and land-based operations. The system provides a unified, seamless platform to visualize friendly and enemy forces and increase the lethality of the Air Force.[181]

Military defense contractors including Lockheed Martin, Boeing, General Dynamics, Northrop Grumman, and Raytheon are working on cutting-edge AI technologies like machine vision and NLP. Huge sums are being invested in research and development on autonomous drones and crafts for sea, space and air; semi-autonomous military vehicles; enemy detection systems; and robotics. In conjunction with quantum computing and encryption, such projects will define the future direction of military research.[182]

In 2019 the US Director of National Intelligence started *The AIM Initiative: A Strategy for Augmenting Intelligence Using Machines* to augment the reasoning capabilities of intelligence analysts by combining commercial AI and proprietary algorithms. The program aims to counter the threat of Russia and China's massive AI initiatives to transform their militaries and intelligence operations and to blindside the American intelligence community. This program includes partnerships with industry, academia and the Department of Defense to create new policy frameworks and invest in significant research. It includes work on fake image or audio detection, human language technology, identity intelligence, automated planning, and several other areas.[183]

DARPA's Media Forensics (MediFor) program is another major defense program that uses AI to tackle the issue of image and video manipulation and deepfakes. The program attempts

> to level the digital imagery playing field, which currently favors the manipulator, by developing technologies for the automated assessment of the integrity of an image or video and integrating these in an end-to-end media forensics platform. If successful, the MediFor platform will automatically detect manipulations, provide detailed information about how these manipulations were performed, and reason about the overall integrity of visual media to facilitate decisions regarding the use of any questionable image or video.[184]

Artificial Intelligence is increasingly being used in surveillance, reconnaissance, logistics, command and control, and in developing lethal autonomous weapons. The CIA has around 140 AI-related projects in image recognition and predictive analytics. Computer vision and machine learning algorithms are being used to analyze video footage and identify hostile targets. Advances will augment the efforts of numerous analysts who painstakingly comb through videos to extract actionable intelligence. In fact, AI has already been used in military operations in Iraq and Syria. The intelligence community has been working on numerous cutting-edge and potentially game-changing AI initiatives for some time.[185]

> Some examples include developing algorithms for multilingual speech recognition and translation in noisy environments, geo-locating images without the associated metadata, fusing 2-D images to create 3-D models, and building tools to infer a building's function based on pattern-of-life analysis.[186]

In 2019, the US Department of Energy announced plans to build "the Frontier supercomputer, which is expected to debut in 2021 as the world's most powerful computer to maintain US leadership in high-performance computing and AI".[187] It will be up to fifty times faster than currently available supercomputers and will leverage second-generation AI systems with advanced capabilities in deep learning and data analytics to "deliver breakthroughs in scientific discovery, energy assurance, economic competitiveness, and national security".[188]

In January 2020, the Department of Transportation released a report on developing advanced driverless vehicles, *Ensuring American Leadership in Automated Vehicle Technologies: Automated Vehicles 4.0*. The goals include US government standardization of the industry to ensure US dominance. Over 90% of automobile crashes are attributed to human error; automated vehicle technologies could significantly address these failings.[189]

Newer modes of automated transportation could potentially solve the connectivity needs of demographic groups like the elderly and challenged people to provide greater independence and dignity. The Accessible Transportation Technologies Research Initiative (ATTRI) program aims to help everyone travel independently and conveniently, regardless of their individual abilities, and also to address the crucial problem of first-/last-mile mobility by connecting all travelers to existing public transport infrastructure.

> ATTRI applications in development include wayfinding and navigation, pre-trip concierge and virtualization, safe intersection crossing, and robotics and automation. Automated vehicles and robotics are expected to improve mobility for those unable or unwilling to

> drive and enhance independent and spontaneous travel capabilities for travelers with disabilities. ... In addition, machine vision, artificial intelligence (AI), assistive robots, and facial recognition software solving a variety of travel related issues for persons with disabilities in vehicles, devices, and terminals, are also included to create virtual caregivers/concierge services and other such applications to guide travelers and assist in decision making.[190]

The Federal Highway Administration is working on projects to enable cooperative automation of vehicles, thereby allowing vehicles to communicate with each other as well as with various vehicular infrastructure systems to improve safety and reduce travel bottlenecks.[191] The Maritime Administration and Federal Motor Carrier Safety Administration are working on a joint project to automate trucks in order to improve operations at ports. This project has the potential to transform the freight transportation system by enabling seamless transfer of goods, reducing wait time for commercial drivers, and streamlining truck access and parking at busy ports. Such improvements will in turn lead to increased productivity and have a multiplier effect on the economy, given that every sector of the economy depends on the freight transportation system.[192]

These aggressive AI initiatives demonstrate the seriousness with which China's AI is being taken. In some respects, it is at least on par with the US and in other areas it is rapidly catching up and hopes to surpass the US. The threats are across the entire spectrum of American and Western civilization's domination in recent centuries: technology, economics, military, geopolitics, prestige, culture, and even moral authority. This is something the US simply cannot afford to accept. Nor are the Chinese likely to pull back from their march ahead. Therefore, we have entered a new period of cold war between these two superpowers. The importance being given to AI is such that Eric Schmidt, presently chair of the US Department of Defense's Defense Innovation Advisory Board, has announced ambitious plans to create a US government-funded AI university.[193]

Unlike the cold war with the Soviet Union, in this instance the US faces a more serious opponent. China is a much larger country than the Soviet Union in population and economy. It has adopted the competitiveness of Western capitalism to spur its original research and development, whereas the Soviets were bogged down with dysfunctional bureaucracies. The Soviet military machine was powerful as well, but it was based on a weak economic foundation and eventually it had to collapse under its own weight. China's military might is being funded by its own powerful economic engine and hence it has a superior staying power over the long haul. The Chinese have literally infiltrated the US economy as the factory supplying US consumer and industrial goods of every kind imaginable. In other words, China has hacked into the American success factors, imitated them, and is in the process of surpassing them.

What this means to the book's thesis is that all other countries, especially India, will feel the impact of the US vs China cold war. India will face increasing challenges in its attempt to become a totally independent and neutral country with superpower status. At the same time, India is far too large and complex to become a satellite of either the US or China.

The impact on other countries will be severe as well. There is a real danger of the world slipping into a phase of recolonization in which the US and China compete for territories and imperialistic influences just as the European powers—Britain, France, Holland, Portugal and Spain—did in the sixteenth to nineteenth centuries. The strategic weapons that were the game changers were devices like navigation and canons. Now there are the new technologies we have been discussing—with AI as the umbrella bringing them together and serving as the force multiplier.

4

THE BATTLE FOR AGENCY

CHAPTER HIGHLIGHTS

- Corporations like Google, YouTube, Facebook, Amazon and Twitter surreptitiously use machine learning techniques known as emotional analysis to profile users' behavior patterns and use these models to influence their choices. The goal is to identify the conscious and unconscious patterns that drive human actions and use this knowledge to build predictive models of both individual and group behavior. Machine learning can psychologically model individuals to such an extent that AI systems are at times better at understanding a person's behavior than even family and friends.
- Advances in emotional and intuitive machine learning are at the cutting edge of AI research. Artificial Intelligence algorithms learn through sophisticated analysis and scoring of users' online comments and engagements. The development of detailed profiles for not only individuals but also communities, identity types, nationalities and other categorizations takes digital surveillance to new levels. Deep learning gives machines astonishing insights into people's logical and emotional lives.

- The age of artificial pleasure and artificial addictions is upon us. The AI industry promises to deliver designer-customized experiences, and these services are orchestrated to continue the cycle of dependence. Digital systems are fulfilling desires to such an extent that users become emotionally and psychologically dependent on them, and even addicted to the gratification they supply.
- People feel relieved that many tedious parts of their lives are on autopilot. However, it results in AI's encroachment on agency and free will. This surrender of individualism can become a form of digital slavery.
- Machine learning models have embedded biases of their developers and pass these in search results, promotion or suppression of posts, and evaluation of content in general. Customized content subtly directs users toward specific responses and inculcates greater trust and reliance on machines. This has a powerful influence on the public discourse.
- The aestheticization of politics and power is a Marxist theory explaining how the ruling elites can advance their goals under the cover of feel-good aesthetics. In the context of AI influencing human psychology, we must differentiate between an aesthetic posture and a pragmatic posture. Pragmatics refers to empirical effects in the external world, whereas aesthetics refers to emotional effects.
- Most people readily accept that AI can deliver pragmatic services of various kinds, such as self-driving cars, personalized automated grocery delivery, and robotic labor in factories. But they have difficulty accepting that aesthetic functions are also being successfully performed by AI.

▸ Sneaky deployment of AI can camouflage a pragmatic agenda behind an aesthetic mask. Free services like email, search results and customized experiences are used to win over users while collecting their personal information. Through the targeted use of AI, big digital corporations are applying aesthetic interests to achieve pragmatic ends.

ARTIFICIAL EMOTIONAL INTELLIGENCE

Computer science originated in mathematics and electrical engineering departments. Hence, it is a *hard* science, and the hard sciences demand precision and predictability. Early AI efforts inherited the requirement of being logical and provable, which excludes the possibility of concepts like paradox and intuition that cannot be precisely described. To remedy this limitation, the field of AI has changed dramatically. Machine learning has successfully entered the realm of satisfying the aesthetic and emotional needs, and this enables technology to penetrate ever deeper into our lives.

Emotions, as distinguished from reasoning or knowledge, are feelings typically involving pleasure or displeasure, and often intertwined with mood, temperament, personality, disposition, creativity and motivation.[194] Without a doubt, machines do not *have* emotions. Based on this fact, it is often incorrectly concluded that emotions are entirely beyond the purview of machine intelligence, that humans have some ephemeral quality machines can never penetrate. Writers frequently claim that human emotional and aesthetic sensibilities make us unique, and therefore a non-human entity could never successfully replace humans in emotional contexts or successfully manipulate someone's emotions.

Nevertheless, even though machines are unemotional and lack consciousness, the issue is whether they can outwardly *perform* certain emotional functions in a purely practical sense. In Chapter 1, I used the analogy of an actor who performs as a character in a movie or play. The acting job is successful if the audience feels that the character is realistic. It is irrelevant how the actor feels internally as that is invisible to the audience; all that counts is how authentically the actor can project externally. Likewise, a machine is successful in its emotional role if it *acts* appropriately according to people's expectations. Whether the machine *feels* any actual emotion is simply irrelevant.

The key point is the difference between *being* emotional (an internal response) and *behaving* emotionally (an external response). Machine learning in the realm of emotions and intuition is at the cutting edge of AI development.

In 1950, the computer pioneer Alan Turing introduced what became known as the **Turing Test**, a way to measure how closely a machine's response resembles a human one. It is a game of imitation in which the machine mimics human behavior as closely as it can. Both machine and human responses are presented to judges, who must decide which response is from the human and which is from the machine. The more often the machine can fool the judges, the higher its score. Such a test can be designed for any topic of conversation. The longer the test continues, the greater the challenge for the machine, because it is easier for machines to deceive the judges with a relatively brief conversation than a more complicated one.

Artificial Intelligence has already passed the Turing Test.[195] Contrary to popular belief that computers are inherently incapable of acquiring emotional and social skills, considerable progress is being made to develop machines' ability to sense and reason, and to mimic human emotional states and social situations. These capabilities are already being used for human–machine interactions, including situations that involve emotional caring, negotiation and persuasion.

The term artificial emotional intelligence refers to the following kinds of abilities:

- *Predicting* individual behavior by modeling emotional patterns. Artificial Intelligence can develop emotional profiles of individuals that enable a machine to evaluate someone's psychological state.
- *Substituting* for human contact by providing emotional interaction. Artificial Intelligence is becoming adept at reading and responding to emotions like a human.
- *Influencing* moods and shifting people's choices toward a product or idea with emotional value. With the ability to masquerade as human, AI can make people feel good about themselves, boost their self-esteem, and reinforce specific ideas. It can make them feel happy or sad or convince them to choose a certain movie, buy a specific product, fall in love with someone, start hating someone or something, and so forth.

In performing emotional functions, the machine is not expected to achieve perfection—but neither can human beings perfectly perform such tasks. If the machine's emotional performance is sufficiently on par with that of humans, it will replace humans at some point or at least augment the emotional work of humans.

Intuition can be viewed as a hypothesis that helps humans make decisions when the purely rational mind cannot make sense of a situation—amid confusion, changing conditions, paradoxes, ambiguity and fake news. It is not the logical approach of linear, discursive analysis. Rather, it makes choices based on feelings, hunches and random factors. Although it is not illogical, intuition operates at a lower level of certainty than logic. Like any hypothesis, intuition is fallible. Intuition is heuristic and improves with practice. It gets reinforced or diminished in a given situation based on its success in predicting outcomes. In contrast, logical computation produces the same output regardless of practice.

The branches of AI dealing with artificial emotional intelligence are galloping ahead because machines are no longer limited to well-structured tasks and can now deal with ambiguous situations. Ad hoc tasks involving instincts, intuition and creativity are also subject to automation. While the extent to which AI will be able to perform such tasks is uncertain, some cognitive functions are already becoming automated.

Natural Language Processing (NLP) is the branch of computer science that analyzes human languages to make sense of speech and written works. It is vast and sophisticated and brings lexical, grammatical, semantic, psychological and pragmatic knowledge into computer science. As machines learn to mechanically generate meaningful natural language statements, they will have the ability to hold conversations with people with increasing sophistication, nuance and complexity. The goal of NLP is to replace or augment normal human conversation among people.[196]

One of its subfields is **sentiment analysis**, which strives to understand attitudes, opinions and emotions being expressed either consciously or unconsciously. It is a powerful tool for monitoring public opinion on a given topic at any time and place.[197] An even more sophisticated level is **emotional analysis**, which looks at the levels of intensity associated with emotions. It analyzes emotions from texts, audio and video as well as facial expressions, body movements, gestures and speech. **Emotive internet** is a research field that analyzes emotional content, develops **internet memes** and spreads them to influence public emotions.

Artificial emotional intelligence, also called **affective computing** or **emotion AI**, integrates computer science and cognitive science.[198] The goal is to develop systems that recognize, interpret, process and simulate human agency in various ways. It emulates human empathy by giving appropriate emotional responses, thereby enriching human–machine interactions. Affective computing systems can look at a face and determine the person's mood—happy, sad, delighted, angry, etc. They can listen to a conversation between two people and successfully guess whether the people are related or not. Affective computing capabilities are being added to AI-generated movies with multiple plots and endings that dynamically change depending on the measured emotional state of the viewer.

An interesting example of an emotional machine is a Japanese robot available on the market to provide companionship to lonely men. The female-styled robot goes to work with them, listening to and learning the clients' behavioral patterns, and offering them customized advice and comfort. Continuing feedback from the clients' responses improves the robot's effectiveness. The goal of these robotic companions is to serve as therapist, counselor, or friend and act as the first line of defense and protection in the event clients consider actions that might be a danger to themselves or others.[199]

The broad goal of all these fields and subfields is to understand human cognition, replace or augment humans with machines, and influence people's choices. These functions are already being widely used for clinical medicine, political analysis, customer service, market research, and business strategy. Considerable research, however, is still needed before models can understand and replicate human common sense, which is implicit knowledge and often unconsciously ingrained in human interactions.

EMOTIONAL HIJACKING

Dumbing Down the Masses

Figure 13 shows how digital technology is also dumbing down the masses. People's memories are atrophying because they constantly depend on online searches and intelligent devices for information. As memory atrophies, attention span shortens, leading to a decline in study habits. At the same time, digital users artificially inflate their egos through social media platforms like Facebook and Twitter, with instant popularity measured by the number of likes or followers, sometimes running into millions. While these activities enhance social status—indeed, some social media stars consider themselves a new class of celebrities and intellectuals—they also contribute to a greater dependency on, and addiction to, social media. Ultimately, such users become dependent on social media for their self-esteem and psychological well-being. This cognitive reengineering is not a passing fad but the likely future being driven by the latest AI technology. I use the term 'moronization' to refer to this dumbing down of large portions of humanity.

This is unlikely to reverse because, contrary to popular belief that human cognition is somehow sacrosanct, algorithmic modeling of emotions, psychological characteristics and mental faculties is already delivering practical applications. Such applications, of course, render humans highly susceptible to emotional seduction by digital systems.

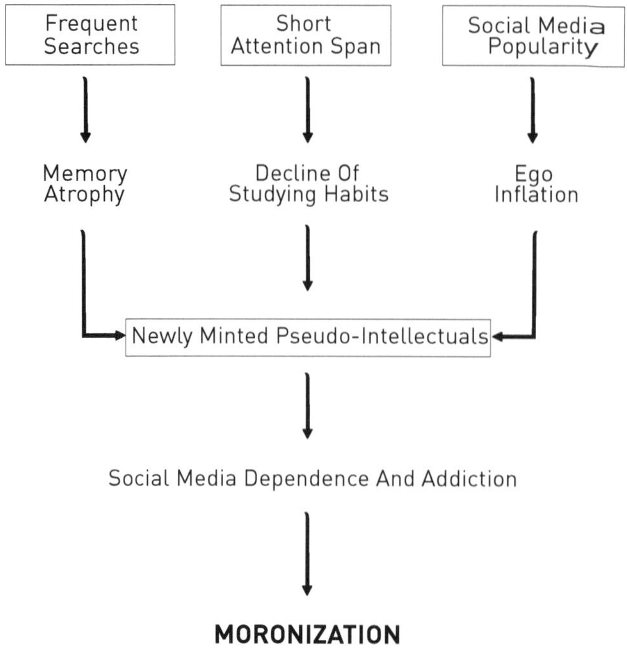

Figure 13: Moronization of the Masses

A machine's emotional engagement with people advances through a few definable stages:

1. Learning about users' emotions to build a psychological model or map of likely responses.
2. Establishing an emotional relationship that users learn to trust.
3. Offering personal, intimate advice, starting with gentle, harmless suggestions.

4. Substituting a mechanized form of companionship that seems human.
5. Manipulating human psychology by influencing users to behave according to mandates determined by the machine's developers.

Cognitive scientists and machine learning experts claim that no aspect of human functionality is ultimately beyond the scope of AI-based emotional analysis and manipulation.

There are many supporters for the idea of machines managing humans. Yuval Noah Harari, the international bestselling author and public intellectual, supports the cognitive takeover by machines, hailing it as a public service and a worthy addition to people's lives. Harari explicitly advocates that everyone would be better off if they surrendered their decision-making power to companies like Google. Giving Google unfettered access to our private data would enable the company to become "a system that monitors your bank account and your heartbeat, your sugar levels and your sexual escapades. It will definitely know you much better than you know yourself".[200]

Harari says that humans are prone to "self-deceptions and self-delusions that trap people in bad relationships, wrong careers and harmful habits".[201] In contrast, Google is a more reliable decision-maker precisely because it cannot be hoodwinked by emotional delusions. He goes much further and says,

> Many of us would be happy to transfer much of our decision-making processes into the hands of such a system, or at least consult with it whenever we face important choices. Google will advise us which movie to see, where to go on holiday, what to study in college, which job to accept, and even whom to date and marry.[202]

In fact, he shows sympathy for the voluntary surrender of our individuality.

> In exchange for such devoted counseling services, we will just have to give up the idea that humans are individuals, and that each human has a free will determining what's good, what's beautiful and what is the meaning of life. Humans will no longer be autonomous entities directed by the stories their narrating self invents. Instead, they will be integral parts of a global network.[203]

Indeed, Harari's notion is that all people should relinquish their humanity to Google. The ubiquitous and all-powerful global digital network is poised to digest our selfhood. The network should, and will, define our meaning in life.

It is worth noting that Harari's books are endorsed by many technology luminaries such as Microsoft founder, Bill Gates. In fact, in 2013 Microsoft filed for a patent that it updated in 2016, for making devices that monitor users' behavior. Its purpose was to preemptively detect "any deviation from normal or acceptable behavior that is likely to affect the user's mental state". Such surveillance functions could be embedded in operating systems, browsers, phones, or wearable devices and monitor a person's behavior while interacting with other people or with online systems. The system was designed to detect "when the user engages in excessive shouting by examining the user's phone calls...." A baseline of "normal" behavior would be developed and constantly updated, and this baseline would be used to detect any deviations from this so-called normal behavior. The device would be capable of alerting "trusted individuals" like doctors, caregivers, insurance companies and even law enforcement. In effect, this would be a system of surveillance of any kind of behavior it is trained to detect. The big question is: Who decides what is normal behavior and what should be done with people who deviate from it?[204]

Artificial Pleasures and Emotions

By manipulating hormones, neurotransmitters, neural networks, and eventually artificial memories, machines are rigging our human physiology to produce pleasure and avoid pain. Certain kinds of private experiences are already being technologically engineered to alter individuals' emotional states.

One active area of research is the modeling of human weakness and vulnerability. Machine learning systems score the likelihood of users being diverted from reading something on their screen. When a pop-up appears on the screen, the machine learning system tracks the messages that are most successful in grabbing a given user's attention. Various kinds of cognitive stimuli are devised and tested, and the responses are recorded and stored in a database that can be accessed by AI systems and used to construct a detailed map of an individual's psychology.

This map provides insights into psychological behavior patterns. How likely are users to be diverted by, for example, an ad for a product for which they recently searched? Or perhaps by pornography? Or by a specific political conspiracy theory or the news of an impending alarming event? Models identify how specific individuals are fickle or susceptible to flattery, to techniques that feed their hunger for attention, and to the types of entertaining diversions that make their humdrum lives more exciting.

The cognitive mapping of hundreds of millions of people's emotions, likes, dislikes, preferences and vulnerabilities is taking place in a very scientific manner. Their activities are recorded in a variety of formats including voice, text, images, handwriting, biometrics, buying habits, interpersonal communications, travel options and entertainment preferences. Machines have become extremely clever at not only capturing private information but also understanding the meaning and purpose of human activities.

Besides these predictive models for individuals, AI researchers also model communities, cultures and subcultures. This data helps develop psychological profiles that anticipate reactions and can be used to manipulate or influence groups that have their own distinctive habits or tendencies.[205] Such systems can detect patterns and understand how, for example, a Uighur Chinese is emotionally different from other Chinese. Artificial Intelligence can determine distinct psychological and emotional templates for hundreds of groups, whether African Americans, white Americans from the US red states, Punjabis living in the US, students at Jamia Milia University in Delhi, potential leftist troublemakers in West Bengal, or whatever grouping of humanity one can imagine.

Marketing firms and political groups are buying access to services that model the consumers' psychology and thereby improve their ability to engage the subcultures in their target group, taking marketing propaganda to a new level of sophistication. We are witnessing the commodification of emotions.

Once built, these psychological profiles weaponize the social media platform into a means for manipulating any individual's private psychology. And for what purpose? For the benefit of whomever, or whatever, is in control of the machine. The beneficiary could be the digital platform itself, such as Facebook or Google, or their commercial clients—advertisers, political candidates, or anyone else willing to pay to influence a target audience. Such models of personal psychology are always learning from the feedback and getting smarter. The more a model is used, the better it gets, just like human psychologists get better at understanding clients the longer they interact with them.

Breakthroughs in hardware devices are a part of this AI-based emotional management industry. As noted in Chapter 1, several types of artificial reality systems are currently being developed: VR, which places users in a virtual surrounding; and AR, which leaves them in their physical surroundings but augments the environment to make it more interesting or useful. Their goal is to personalize the experience by catering to individual needs that have already been meticulously mapped. Initially this technology will customize experiences through wearable devices, such as glasses, watches and gloves; eventually, implants in the human body will replace wearables.

Researchers are experimenting with physical implants that will take VR and AR systems to new heights for the gratification of sensory delights. Just as talkies replaced silent movies, a new generation of movies in which feelings are transmitted directly to viewers through implants is predicted to be available in the future. Virtual Reality can be used, for example, to provide the sense of walking around the neighborhood, even if one is physically confined at home.

This field has attracted a frenzy of collaborative research programs with biologists, neuroscientists, computer scientists, psychologists, artists, and a host of other disciplines. Such technologies for managing the human mind are expected to expand exponentially. The instant gratification of whimsical desires has led to the widespread availability of on-demand entertainment and the commodification of luxury tourism. Self-indulgence has taken moral decadence to new levels.

At the outset of the Covid-19 pandemic, people's psychological vulnerability increased because uncertainty and insecurity disrupted their sense of security and their comfort zone. In such times, people tend to respond with panic and fear and grasp at straws to preserve whatever normalcy they can. When individuals are more prone to follow the herd, the agencies controlling social trendiness become even more empowered. The temporary emotional shifts engendered by the pandemic will eventually become normalized as the new psychological equilibrium. As online gatherings increase, so does the amount of data collected, and this normalization further advances people's use and acceptance of digital influence in their lives.

Addictive Behavior Programming

Numerous books and consultants specialize in teaching AI companies how to capture users through their emotions. *Hooked: How to Build Habit-Forming Products* by Nir Eyal examines human desires and weaknesses to make what are called *sticky* apps.[206] The intent is to map out users' emotional characteristics, especially their vulnerabilities, and then tap into that map to create a customized AI intervention that manipulates a specific desire. Sticky apps provide outlets for suppressed desires, such as the urge to watch pornography, go on an exotic journey, or indulge the fantasy of being a popular public figure. Once someone's hidden desires are identified, the content is selected to satisfy them. Those who long to travel can do so via AR goggles that will transport them to the place of their dreams. Designers of online hooks exploit people's tendency to seek relief from stress. Based on the idea that people prefer excitement to boredom and contentment to anxiety, digital marketing companies substitute artificial gratification to intervene and manipulate users' emotions.

Some manipulative systems contrive scarcity as a gimmick to enhance the perceived value; online retailers often state "only three items left" to create a sense of urgency and play on the user's fear of missing out. Other systems encourage users to invest in experiences which deepen their dependence on the system. For example, the exciting conversations held on a social media platform could become a precious part of one's social relations, making it difficult to abandon them and start all over again on a new platform.

Another hook is progression toward defined, achievable goals. Encouraging progress toward specific outcomes motivates users to continue investing if the goal seems close. This psychological principle is called **gamification**, and it is a cornerstone of designing addictive games and platforms. Computer game designers and social media companies are leading this type of psychological research and product development, hiring experts to build addictive products that effectively re-engineer users' cognitive systems.

A great example of gamification is the GPS navigation app Waze (acquired by Google), which gamified driving by rewarding drivers that reported potholes, traffic jams, and even police radars. The more one plays and sends such data to the system, the better one's score in the game, while Google merrily collects a ton of traffic data on a real-time basis. In effect, Waze uses the psychology of gamification to achieve free crowdsourcing of data that gets fed into Google's analytics.

The point of gamification is the free harvesting of enormous amounts of data from human players that can be used to train machines.

The process of psychological manipulation is designed to change behavior. The initial hook offers users a perceived benefit that the target group cannot resist; the system then makes it progressively harder for them to disengage. The resulting transfer of power is both gradual and unconscious.

Facebook, YouTube and Twitter freely deliver a wide range of user experiences that consumers find difficult to resist. Artificial Intelligence systems have figured out the most powerful, irresistible desires for all kinds of individuals, and fulfills them. An entire field of research specializes in designing systems of instant gratification and addiction.

Facebook's strategy is to make people excited about their number of followers and engagement. It reinforces their emotional cravings and distracts them from realizing that they are enthusiastically giving away intimate knowledge, and hence transferring power to the digital platform. Most users do not realize or understand this and would rather not know the long-term implications of gratifying their social needs online. The path seems to be paved with gold and is hard to resist.

Frequent engagement with a particular kind of stimulus increases the probability that the behavior will become a habit. Artificial Intelligence algorithms track how successful a given stimulus has been in triggering a craving. And constant gratification of the desire generates emotional dependency, which eventually leads to addiction. The figure below depicts the cause-effect chain leading to addiction.

Initial Hook ➔ Repetition ➔ Craving ➔ Gratification ➔ Loyalty ➔ Habit ➔ Addiction

The chain of causation starts with an *external* trigger, or hook. Users gradually develop an affinity for certain triggers over others. Successful hooks are repeatedly fed to specific users, eventually causing more robust and predictable behavior.

Neuroscientists believe that these triggers and responses are stored in a part of the brain associated with involuntary actions. In effect, the cycle of gratifications gradually programs the brain to produce an automatic response at the slightest external stimulus or indirect suggestion. It is well known that, once addicted, chain smokers no longer need to see a cigarette advertisement to reach for a cigarette. The triggers have become internalized, transformed into biological algorithms. All humans possess certain pre-existing biological desires that have evolved over thousands of years—sex, food, safety, shared bonds and love, self-esteem, and so on. Each of these urges can be used as a foundation on which to hook new habits programmed by the digital systems after hacking into our cognitive behavior maps.

The ultimate goal is to instill an increased reliance on the system to make default choices for users. For instance, typing systems are programmed to predict the next phrase or even sentences users are likely to type. Each time users accept what the predictive typing proposes, two things happen. First, the user becomes unconsciously more trusting of the system's choices. Second, the system learns which choices a given user is likely to accept or reject and refines its algorithm. Both sides are learning: the user to trust the machine, and the machine how to win more trust. The long-term effect is a loss of users' agency and this eventually leads them toward autopilot mode.

This type of predictive functionality can be expanded gradually to select which products users will buy, the books they will read, the movies they will watch, and so on. A victory for the system is its ability to make users subconsciously anticipate some reward, whether tangible or imaginary, because reward anticipation increases the brain's production of dopamine, a chemical associated with feelings of pleasure.

Self-esteem and reputation are a significant type of stored value critical to human existence. Human biological algorithms have evolved to incline us toward acceptance, recognition and inclusion by our peers. It is natural to seek social approval and avoid feeling rejected. The number of likes, followers, or subscribers on social media is a primary measure of self-esteem in today's digital world.

The drive for acceptance is why people are addicted to social media—continually checking for messages, notifications and emails, and anxious about whether their posts are liked and reposted or tweets re-tweeted. All this activity, mediated by the AI system, gratifies their biological desire for social validation.

Social media does give us the power to articulate and assert ourselves, but this sense of empowerment is at the discretion of the platform. Ultimately, the more dependent we become on the provisional liberty granted us, the more the platform controls us. One way it controls us is through exploitation of our deepest desire to be treated with dignity and respect.

Algorithms assign our social rankings. They identify us, sort us to fit into different templates, and then evaluate, compare, judge and categorize us. We are ranked according to the criteria used to train the machine learning system. These rankings are used to decide who is to be given more visibility, which videos go viral, and which messages and messengers go into obscurity.

At the same time, commercial reputation systems that use AI can be hired to perform the role of publicity agents; services such as ReputationDefender try to hack into the algorithms of the digital ranking systems. As a commodity that can be bought and sold, social ranking influences each individual's chance of success in various facets of life.

Digital giants can slant their algorithms to support content that aligns with their ideology. They filter what news is selected to be reported, the level of detail given to each item, and the nuance with which it is to be treated. They can also popularize specific fashions, trends, beliefs, interests and fads.

These biases are often buried implicitly in the training of their neural networks. Naturally, the rich and powerful have a greater say in the values and interests that are targeted for optimization. Much of this power is arbitrary: For instance, there is no regulation on where to draw the line on freedom of speech, to determine when extreme speech is too extreme. Who should decide when to block a post because it is disgusting, scary, offensive, or vulgar? The right to adjudicate others' speech is a powerful one. The consequences of noncompliance can bring shame, ridicule and feelings of rejection—all powerful ways to damage the modern ego.

This power over our egos has granted Facebook what we can think of as *bullying rights*. It routinely attempts to bully people into compliance with its rules on the boundaries of free speech, using tactics such as arbitrarily blocking users or reducing the visibility level of particular posts and videos. Facebook has developed algorithms—incorporating its own highly subjective and debatable values and premises—to adjudicate and reinforce its idea of social justice. How popular various users are among their peers is influenced by how much they obey, or resist, Facebook's ideological norms.

Facebook routinely sends warnings and even blocks posts for what it claims is a "violation of community standards". Those accused are given no opportunity to discuss with a real human being exactly what such standards imply and in what way someone might have violated them. The best response users get is that "the algorithms made this determination".

The hard reality is that the more you interact with Facebook, the more control it will assert over you. The company's tactic is to encourage people to comply by intimidating them enough to internalize Facebook's way of thinking. Users are reluctant to walk away from the platform because they have invested time and energy in it and are unwilling to abandon their relationships.

Social media has emotionally empowered scores of mediocre individuals. Those who quickly rise in popularity rankings mistakenly believe themselves to be thought leaders. The number of followers and retweets is the new yardstick by which the ego measures success. Unfortunately, because social media is a system rigged to emotionally manipulate people on a large scale, it attracts and rewards mediocrity. Those who invest excessive time on various social media platforms are conforming, and even catering, to the demands of mediocrity. Popularity among one's peers is hardly an objective measure of merit. In fact, social media is counterproductive in the long run because it misleads individuals and even communities by providing an artificial barometer of success.

Platforms like Facebook are successful because they have made a science out of fulfilling human desires for social engagement, and because they help people form habits to fill the vacuum of boredom and loneliness. The platform's value grows in proportion to the amount of personal psychological data users surrender to it. This data allows it to provide better and better targeted, personalized gratification, which in turn encourages us to keep returning for even more reinforcement. Dependence on social media for emotional wellness can, and is having, serious consequences: Research on the rise in suicide rates among American youth has identified social media as a factor.[207] Despite the ethical consequences, control over emotions and minds is the holy grail being sought aggressively by big firms.

The market for feeding pleasure and satisfying humanity's cravings, animal instincts and aspirations is exploding, encompassing fantasy travel, virtual sports experiences, games, pornography, and whatever else people can imagine and desire. This trend is the direct result of how successfully AI and neural networks have decoded human desires and developed solutions that cater to these desires. Such industries are generating massive fortunes as well as accumulating unprecedented power over our freedom.

Figure 14 depicts the typical psychological process by which users become addicted to social media and eventually conform to the systemic bias buried within the algorithms. By promoting posts and giving users greater exposure with peers, the system reinforces acceptable behavior; negative reinforcement techniques include shadow banning, blocking and eventually deactivating users' accounts.

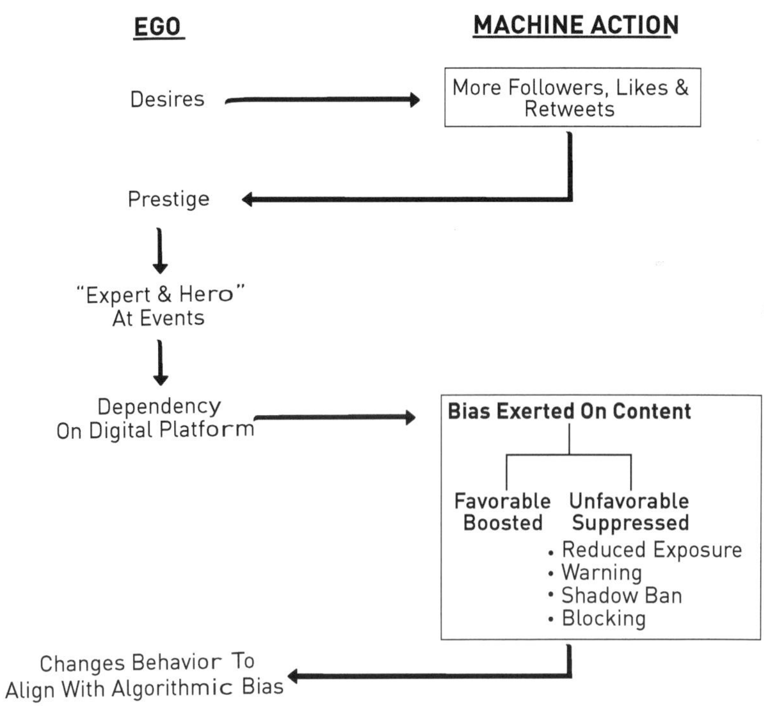

Figure 14: Reinforcing the Bias

Users assume that going along with the flow is in their best interest, especially since everyone else seems to be doing this. Jamie Susskind explains:

> Filtering is an incredibly powerful means of perception-control. If you control the flow of information in society, you can influence its shared sense of right and wrong, fair and unfair, clean and unclean, seemly and unseemly, real and fake, true and false, known and unknown. You can tell people what's out there, what matters, and what they should think and feel about it. You can signal how they ought to judge the conduct of others. You can arouse enthusiasm and fear, depression and despair. You can shape the norms and customs that define what is permitted and what is forbidden, which manners are acceptable, what behavior is considered proper or improper, and how shared social rituals like greeting, courtship, ceremonies, discourse, and protest ought to be performed; what may be said and what ought to be considered unspeakable; and the accepted boundaries of political and social conduct.[208]

Essentially, consumers are negotiating a trade: receiving benefits in exchange for modulating their behavior and surrendering their data (and hence power) to an inanimate stranger. The digital network has fooled us by styling itself as an innocent device that facilitates a variety of useful benefits. But such systems have outsmarted us to give away our personal and most confidential information to institutions owned by a concentration of elites with no accountability.

The playbook of the AI giants is eventually to have the maximum number of humans go through life on autopilot. People find comfort in automatic behavior that demands little or no conscious thought. Delegating one's agency to a machine is like trusting a friend. This frees up the conscious mind to pay attention to more important activities. One day, consumers—and voters—will make very few free choices and will be rewarded for living mostly in autopilot mode.

Yet few people ever consider the ramifications of this transfer of power because they are blinded by the fulfillment of their desires. Most people are not balancing—nor even conscious of—the trade-off between the gain in gratification and efficiency and their loss of free will.

Digital Slavery

A common technique for training AI systems is to throw a variety of stimuli at people simply for the purpose of measuring their emotional response. By tracking and analyzing responses, machines develop ever more sophisticated psychological maps of people, and in the process become emotionally savvy.

Figure 15 illustrates two distinct processes. On the left is the machine learning process by which users' personal psychology is determined. The system monitors users and creates a personalized predictive model, or map, of their private psychology. The right illustrates how digital platforms use these personalized predictive models to create what I call **happy morons.** Exploiting their predictive models, machines offer inducements (or threats) to drive behavior and addict users to the platform and its alleged benefits.

At first glance, Amazon's Kindle e-reader appears to be a benign, passive system. Unbeknownst to users, however, it monitors which parts of a book you spent more time reading, on which page you took a break, what definitions you looked up, what you highlighted, and other silent metrics.[209]

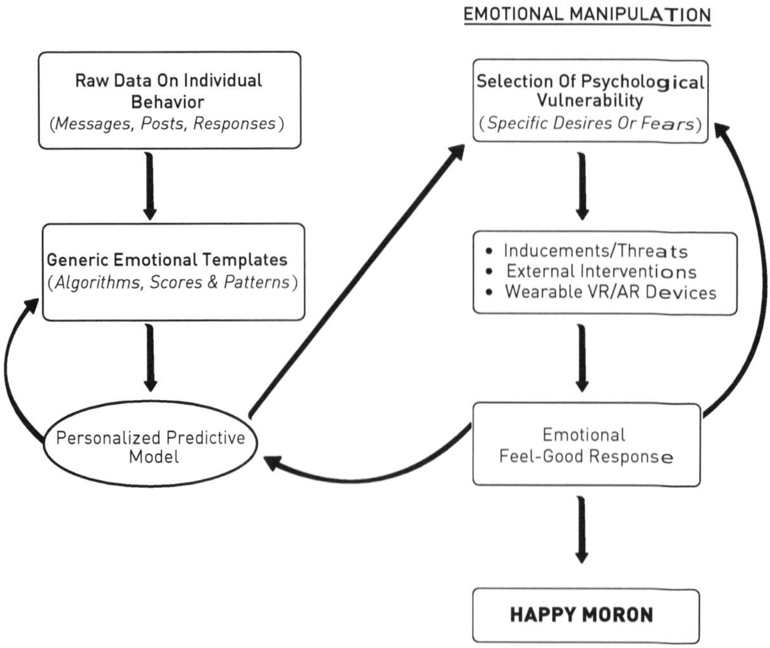

Figure 15: Machine Learning of Individual Psychology

In the future, with upgraded facial recognition and biometric monitoring, Kindle will be able to record what makes you happy, sad, or angry while you are reading. With that information it will be able to select books for you to read and might even customize a book that would be appropriate in each set of circumstances.

Likewise, Netflix has developed the ability to choose movies for individual members with incredible success. Individuals' response profile and what gratifies their inclinations are classified by types of desire, ranging from prestige to lust. It has recently launched the "choose your own story" interactive show where users make decisions on what happens to the characters. Tracking these choices enables Netflix to profile the psychology of its viewers as it can predict what users might do when presented with situations similar to what is in their shows. Netflix brags about its growing success in predictively modeling user behavior.

Facebook uses tens of thousands of factors such as clicks, likes, shares, comments and personal interests to determine users' news feed. Its marketing material solicits advertisers by bragging how well it can influence the emotions of users by such manipulations. Depending on what is in the best commercial interests of Facebook, its algorithms decide how to filter the information presented to each individual user. It is important to note that there is no such thing as an objective choice of content being made on our behalf. Susskind summarizes this phenomenon aptly.

> News and search services, communication channels, affective computing, and AR platforms—will determine what we know, what we feel, what we want, and what we do. In turn, those who own and operate these systems will have the power to shape our political preferences. ...Our very perceptions are susceptible to control, sometimes by the very institutions we would seek to hold to account. It's hard to contribute rationally when your political thoughts and feelings are structured and shaped for you by someone else.[210]

The more this type of customization succeeds, the more it will empower machine algorithms and strip humans of their autonomy. In *Homo Deus: A Brief History of Tomorrow*, Noah Harari explicitly recommends that you should surrender your feelings and let the algorithms run your life:

> The Google and Facebook algorithms not only know exactly how you feel, they also know myriad other

> things about you that you hardly suspect. Consequently, you should stop listening to your feelings and start listening to these external algorithms instead.[211]

The credibility of such systems is based on their success in many worthwhile applications that provide undeniable benefits. For example, IBM's Watson computer recognizes facial expressions for a variety of emotions, tones of voice, personality types, and numerous other signals combined with physical biometrics.[212] This ability is being used in leading hospitals to help doctors and caregivers understand patients and provide enhanced treatment. Empirical evidence collected in hospitals debunks the popular myth that physical human touch and personal engagement are critical to healing: Medical outcomes managed by machines are frequently found to be on par with, or even superior to, human management of patient psychology. In the current pandemic situation, robots have become preferable over humans to perform routine logistical and healthcare duties.[213]

All of these trends result in machines that can anticipate behavioral responses and manage people's feelings. The figure below illustrates how such innovations move into widespread use.

Experimental ➔ Early Adopters ➔ Legitimization ➔ Mainstream Acceptance

Social media has become the newest opium of the masses. Digital platforms distract and control the masses with addictive content to keep them mesmerized. Users' reactions are then analyzed, and the responses incorporated into the system in a never-ending cycle that makes algorithms ever more effective at manipulating behavior. In effect, people surrender their agency and willingly enter a system of digital slavery.

Alexis de Tocqueville, the political scientist and historian wrote in his description of life in America (1835):

> Every individual lets them put the collar on, for he sees that it is not a person, or a class of persons, but society itself which holds the end of his chain.[214]

This is a profound insight. Though people abhor the idea of being slave to another human, they are willing to become slaves of an impersonal entity like society. Tocqueville's collar today is the invisible hold that AI technology has on those that have become digital slaves. People are intoxicated with belonging—in particular, craving to belong to the internet community and then to steadily advance in that community, eventually becoming a virtual slave to it. The collar they wear gives them new forms of freedom, new tools of expression, and new opportunities of all sorts. But in return, they must accept the rules of the game they have chosen to play.

Artificial Democracy

Noah Harari has questioned the future of democratic elections in an age where AI-engineered elections could predict outcomes:

> What's the point of having democratic elections when the algorithms know not only how each person is going to vote, but also the underlying reasons why one person votes Democrat while another votes Republican.[215]

Furthermore, beyond merely predicting the outcomes, digital systems can also influence, and perhaps even manufacture, the outcomes of elections. The success of conventional politicians has depended on how well they understand and communicate with their constituents. To win elections, politicians are required to relate to their constituents on a personal and emotional level, and to relate better than their opponent does. However, spending personal time with voters, getting to know them on a personal level, is the old-school way to get elected. The new method is digital. Digital giants have invested heavily in deep learning to offer such digital interpersonal capabilities to the market. In their mapping of groups and sub-groups, neighborhoods are segmented into even smaller groups, each with its own psychological profile and signature qualities.

The approach of letting machines learn the psychology of individuals and then apply this knowledge for specific purposes has already had success in politics. Former US president, Barack Obama's 2012 presidential campaign was the first time that machine learning was used in a major democratic election. Using AI software, his campaign team compiled a database of voter information using social media and other sources. Machine learning algorithms then used this data to build individual voter profiles and predict responses to various kinds of canvassing. Each night, his team ran 66,000 simulations of the election, and the system determined where to assign resources—whom to call, whom to visit, what to say, etc. His victory was a watershed event in the use of AI for political campaigns.

Four years later, Donald Trump's son-in-law, Jared Kushner, led Trump's presidential campaign using AI on an even larger scale. Their database of 220 million citizens covered nearly every US voter. The machine learning system used 5,000 separate data points to build each individual's psychological profile, enabling the campaign to accurately pinpoint where and how to advertise and what message to send to each individual voter. The amazing success of this method was a shock to everyone in politics. Only much later did people discover how the shift in public opinion had been successfully maneuvered on such a massive scale. Susskind calls this process the "engineering of consent" and the "weaponization of AI".[216]

The Power of Surveillance

Artificial Intelligence is far more ubiquitously present in a person's life than any human companion is—watching and collecting more data daily than is humanly possible, observing and recording unconscious patterns. Interestingly, individuals are less self-conscious and more trusting of machines than they are of other humans because they do not suspect technology of invading their privacy. People let their guard down to machines more easily than while being under the gaze of other people. They fool themselves into believing that the AI system is harmless because it is inanimate, thus giving them a false sense of security. This tendency is evident in the way people say things in their internet chatter that they would never say in face-to-face discussions. Exposing oneself to a machine feels less intimate and psychologically threatening than exposing oneself to a human.

Often invisibly and anonymously, systems are capturing intimate details about the work we do, what we earn, the things we own, who we associate with and in what ways, what we like, dislike and find important, and who our family is. Actions, utterances, emotions, transactions, relationships, plans, ambitions, and even our exact location at any moment, are all fair game for the ubiquitous surveillance mechanisms. Systems can use this knowledge to determine the carrots that will work as the best inducements, and what threats or punishments will make effective deterrents.

This scrutiny is becoming more intimate than ever, monitoring spaces previously considered private. The French philosopher and social theorist, Michel Foucault explains that merely being conscious of the fact that we are being observed can be enough to discipline us.

> There is no need for arms, physical violence, material constraints. Just a gaze. An inspecting gaze, a gaze which each individual under its weight will end by interiorizing to the point that he is his own overseer, each individual thus exercising this surveillance over, and against himself.[217]

An invisible, subtle influence is being exerted over us by the mere fact that we are self-conscious of being watched and evaluated.

> Power does not need to be violent or threatening. It can be gentle, even tender. Some power is so subtle that it's almost invisible. Often the weak are not even aware that they are being dominated by the strong. Sometimes they do know they are being dominated, but they welcome it. The most skillful leaders know that to force someone is to gain power over their body; while to influence or manipulate them is to gain power over their mind. This can be the deepest and richest form of power of all.[218]

The public is being duped by a false sense of openness and transparency. Big companies have the power to create scandals and fake news, and then manipulate people's emotions to garner more social media hits—all with the goal of inciting large numbers of infuriated citizens to action or lulling them into complacency.

Even the common perception that Wikipedia provides a level playing field on which humanity can freely share all its knowledge is a pretense. The reality is that while all such digital structures behave like free and unrestricted systems, they are in fact controlled by gamification algorithms at the hands of those who own and operate them. Very few people grasp the profound deception of the system.

A subtle result of the Covid-19 pandemic is that several European leaders have explicitly stated that privacy rights must be overshadowed by the rights of establishments to know the health status of individuals entering their space.

THE BATTLE FOR AESTHETICS

Aesthetics as the Opium of the Masses

When Karl Marx (1818–83) called religion the opium of the people, he was not referring to a top-down imposition of power by the church. His point was that people *wanted* religion because it gave meaning to their lives. The same principle applies to digital media today. Nobody is forcing it on the public; people seek the external stimulation and gratifications of social media to fill a void. Like religion, AI uses cognitive and emotional manipulation to further the process of appropriating our agency and power: dumbing down the masses, feeding them customized feel-good gratifications, and winning over their hearts while influencing their minds.

The Marxist theory of the **aestheticization of politics** is a useful framework for explaining how digital platforms use emotions to manipulate the public. In the early twentieth century, Marxist scholars contemplated a puzzling question: When Germany was plunged into economic depression, it did not turn to a communist revolution as predicted by Marxist thought. Instead, Germany turned to Nazism. Why?

To understand this anomaly, Marxists theorized that Germany's depression did not trigger a proletariat revolution (as it previously had in Russia) because the ruling elite had created *an emotional narrative about Germany's past glory.* The fabricated theory of Aryans of German origin as the ancient supermen gave suffering people pride in their ancient roots. This false historical narrative was presented to the masses with aesthetics using poetry, dance, theater and fiery speeches.

By producing an explosion of aesthetically oriented art and literature about German patriotism and greatness, the Nazis convinced the German people that reinstating this imagined golden era of their past glory would solve all their practical problems. In essence, the economic catastrophe was a *pragmatic* concern, and the substitution of ancient glory an *aesthetic* solution.

Until the medieval era (fifth-fifteenth century) in Europe, religion functioned as the opium of the masses, administered by the church. Marxism objected to religion on the grounds that the church was an aesthetic instrument that kept people placid and happy to prevent them from rebelling. But in Nazi-era Germany, religion was not widespread enough to avert a popular revolution. The Germans were, in fact, a well-educated and highly scientific people when Nazism emerged.

Marxism seized on the idea that the aestheticization of politics could serve as a new kind of opium for the masses, and the elites could use aesthetics to emotionally manipulate the public. For the principle to work, the elites need to understand the aesthetic architecture of the masses. They must exploit the psychological hot buttons that trigger happiness and pleasure to brighten the dreary, depressed daily lives of common people.

The Sanskrit scholar Sheldon Pollock also uses this Marxist principle to explain events in India several millennia ago. He broadened this theory by referring to it as the aestheticization of *power*, because politics is only one type of power among many, such as cultural, religious, or economic power.[219] He theorizes that the *Ramayana* was enthusiastically adopted by the rulers across Southeast Asia as an aesthetic tool to glorify the populace's heritage. People did not feel a need to revolt against autocratic rulers because the aesthetics of performing *Ramayana* in public dance and theater, and chanting Sanskrit mantras in royal ceremonies, mesmerized them into complacency. In essence, Pollock claims that the *Ramayana* became successful as the opium of the masses. My book, *The Battle for Sanskrit*, offers a rebuttal to this thesis.

I feel that a better application of the theory to India is to explain that the British colonizers used aestheticization to appease Indian society and seduce it into becoming loyal to foreign rule. They put rajas on elephants, gave them twenty-one-gun salutes, and invited them to play polo. They distributed charity at Hindu festivals, allocated funds for temple building, and in general conferred a sense of importance on the rajas. These token benefits convinced people to believe that their raja was well and happy, that the attention indicated respect for the local culture, and that the British were good people who were looking after India. As a result, the larger questions of whether Indians were being ruled fairly or whether the raja was merely a figurehead were obscured. Many people in India did not see British rule as a problem they needed to solve, much less revolt against. In fact, Gandhi and Sri Aurobindo mentioned that one of the greatest challenges during India's struggle for independence was to rouse the Indian public into realizing that they were being oppressed under British rule.

In 1837, long before the Marxist formulation of this theory, Alexis de Tocqueville described aestheticization as special kind of political power:

> It does not break men's will, but softens, bends and guides it; it seldom enjoins, but often inhibits, action... it is not at all tyrannical, but it hinders, restrains, enervates, stifles, and stultifies so much that in the end *each nation is no more than a flock of timid and hardworking animals with the government as its shepherd.*[220] (Emphasis added)

The strategy of aestheticized power is a brilliant method to deceive people and give them a false sense of pride. It pushes emotional buttons that influence people's psychology and override their pragmatic interests.

The latest aestheticization of power is now being implemented by the digital platforms—the delivery of customized user experiences that machine learning has identified as those to which given individuals are most susceptible. Dumbing down users and addicting them to sensual gratification and intense emotions makes them more prone to aestheticization as a method of exploitation.

The use of aesthetics can be an effective means to capture power in a pragmatic sense. A crude example would be winning over someone's heart and using the emotional attachment to siphon off their money. A more sophisticated example is the diplomatic offer of military support to another country to achieve the pragmatic goal of getting troops into that country. We are also familiar with the way missionaries win over poor people by giving them gifts at a time of vulnerability, only to convert them and turn them into a political vote bank. The sequence of events is depicted in the figure.

Aesthetically attractive offers ➔ Trigger pragmatic actions ➔ Achieve hard power outcomes

In the same way, Harvard University's project "Mapping the Kumbh Mela" was sold to the Indian government and public. University researchers have been visiting India over the past decade to collect vast amounts of biometric, socioeconomic and demographic data from pilgrims and visitors to Kumbh Mela, which has the distinction of being the world's largest gathering. The Harvard team comprises scholars in religious studies, caste studies, anthropology, minority studies, gender studies and a multitude of scientific disciplines. The project is linked, conceptually and otherwise, with other large-scale data-gathering projects such as the Christian evangelist-led Joshua Project, which compiles ethnologic data to support Christian missions. The pragmatic significance of so much data is camouflaged behind the veil of clever aesthetics.

The rationale offered for this project was that it would help the Indian people by analyzing their data to improve public health, the physical and social environment, and the overall management of the event. Harvard used powerful aesthetics to conceal the pragmatic goals of its data-gathering plan. Aside from its impressive public relations campaign, the university brought Indian politicians and bureaucrats to their American campus to honor them publicly. Selfies on social media and private meetings with prestigious Americans were among the enticements for Indian leaders to sell out their country's pragmatic interests.

Similarly, when the CIA tracked down Osama bin Laden in Pakistan, it used a Pakistani doctor to collect DNA samples from local populations. Because the doctor needed an excuse to approach the villagers, the CIA established a fake vaccination program as cover. The aesthetics of a supposedly altruistic program was used to camouflage the CIA's pragmatic agenda. Sadly, one lingering effect has been that many people in Pakistan no longer trust medical workers who offer to vaccinate them.

The militant group ISIS brainwashes Muslims and converts them into suicide bombers by convincing them that the good life awaits them in jannat (paradise). This aesthetic manipulation commonly targets disenfranchised young men with emotional vulnerability. Such Islamist projects have evolved out of psychological experiments with thousands of men over centuries. Because some personality types are more easily turned into suicide bombers than others, ISIS classifies the psychological profiles of young Muslim men during the selection process.

With its recent rise to power in the last half of the twentieth century, China used the diplomacy of aesthetics to manipulate several US administrations and the high-tech industry. The US failed to understand the Chinese mind and underestimated its commitment to become the most powerful nation in the world. By selling the US on the idea of cheap labor, China negotiated a massive transfer of intellectual property, manufacturing capacity, jobs and overall power from the US. The Chinese executed their plan so brilliantly that the Americans never even suspected that China would be able to overtake them.

Aesthetic cover can also be applied in positive ways, such as concealing the messy side of a system. Disney World in Orlando employs several thousand people that keep the park functioning without being seen because much of their work is literally underground. The park is built on top of an underground city that houses the unsightly infrastructure, machinery behind the props, maintenance equipment, computers and staff. An underground railroad efficiently and invisibly transports employees around the park. Part of the magic of the Magic Kingdom is its aesthetic sophistication in concealing this gigantic machinery.

The converse can also be true: Power can define what is considered good aesthetics. The notion of the beauty of the human body is a good example. The history of white people's power over others led to fair skin being considered more beautiful than dark skin. Before the arrival of fair-skinned foreign invaders, positions of authority and reverence in many societies typically featured dark-skinned people. Paintings in India's Ajanta Caves from the second-century BCE depict fair-skinned maids serving dark-skinned women. Most of the ancient Hindu deities are dark-skinned as well: Kali, Durga, Krishna, Shiva and Hanuman to name a few. But today, fair skin is given a premium because of millennia of foreign rule by lighter-skinned people.

In early Christian art, Jesus was shown as a dark-skinned man with Middle Eastern features. But during the Italian renaissance (fourteenth-seventeenth century), it became fashionable for artists to paint Jesus with European features, because European elites of the era had developed a self-image of superiority over dark-skinned people. Historical records make clear that white skin was not always considered superior; it is plausible—even likely—that the prevailing aesthetic norms have been and still are shaped by those in power.

AESTHETIC-PRAGMATIC FRAMEWORK

Two Cognitive Postures

Pragmatics and **aesthetics** are the two cognitive postures that define a framework of power and manipulation. It is important to understand how AI invades our lives both pragmatically and aesthetically.

The intent of a pragmatic outlook is to drive an empirical outcome or specific goal. Pragmatics is goal-oriented and concerned with practical actions geared toward accomplishing a defined objective. Problem-solving is pragmatic, and hence algorithms are pragmatic. For instance, the criteria for choosing a surgeon are likely based on the doctor's success rate and ability to perform surgery, not the aesthetics of personality or appearance. Only the results matter.

In contrast, aesthetics involves beauty, artistic impact, feelings, and emotions. Artists and musicians would no doubt find it bizarre to be asked, "What is your algorithm for creating this piece?" or "How do you measure your efficiency?" or "What is your success rate?" Aesthetic worthiness is independent of its practical utility. Its value is in the emotional realm, so it is inappropriate to judge aesthetics in practical terms. This fact in no way devalues the importance of aesthetic productions such as art, music, poetry, and theater.

Most people accept that machine intelligence is useful for pragmatic applications that replace repetitive human labor, like driving, performing medical procedures and shopping. But the public is less inclined to believe that machines can also mimic human-like aesthetic effects. They doubt AI's potential in aesthetic areas because they consider aesthetics, emotions and other subjective functions to be beyond the ability of machines. The previous pages have argued against this assumption.

Pragmatics corresponds to left-brain functions (paying bills, repairing a machine, studying, analyzing data), whereas aesthetics relates to right-brain functions (music, pleasure, emotions). Aesthetics and pragmatics are not mutually exclusive and are often combined. For instance, while using aesthetic faculties to produce art, artists can also consider the pragmatic aspects of being on time for an art showing and managing their budget. In the entertainment industry, the products are aesthetic—music, movies, theater, sports, and so on—but companies set pragmatic goals such as maximizing profits and market share. Even when combined, however, aesthetics and pragmatics are distinct functions.

A crucial tenet of this book is that machine learning's neural networks can successfully construct a detailed map of both these modes of cognition. Although many people insist that AI cannot possibly replicate creativity, machines are already developing the ability to simulate and even intervene in the aesthetic side of our brains. Artificial Intelligence-generated writings have been accepted mistakenly by leading conferences, AI-generated music is climbing higher on popularity ratings, and AI-generated art has already made its way into museums.

Pragmatic responses are measurable and can be tracked, assessed and judged objectively. In contrast, aesthetics is subjective and much more culture-specific, and the impact differs from one individual to the next. Aesthetically inclined individuals are vulnerable to manipulation because they can become addicted to the feel-good factor or praise. They may miss the pragmatic implications of an event, enjoying it purely as a **tamasha** (grand public spectacle); the emotional experience serves as the end purpose. Pragmatic people would consider aesthetically manipulated people to be deluded escapists, lost in a feel-good comfort zone and diverted from serious, practical work. Pragmatists feel that those that are too artistic, emotional, or abstract at a time when empirical decisions are needed are counterproductive, because their words and actions have no practical consequences.

This framework of pragmatics and aesthetics is related to AI in important ways. As noted earlier, machine learning systems are capable of deciphering and modeling aesthetic, as well as pragmatic, responses from people. Using these insights into their psychology, AI systems can exploit human desires as gateways to their innermost thoughts, and eventually hijack their mind. Aware of these potentials, machine learning developers are pouring massive amounts of money into the field. They are opening the floodgates of our minds.

Pragmatists make good AI developers. After filtering out inconsequential information, they prioritize the available options. Feedback loops continually update their algorithms and recalculate the best path forward. Global Positioning System navigation works on this process; the system constantly monitors all variables that contribute to calculating the best route—traffic patterns, road work, accidents—and continuously recomputes the best choice in real time. To build a pragmatic model of a system, developers must know how different causes produce corresponding effects. Every effect is produced by a set of causes, and nothing happens without a cause.

Aesthetics and pragmatics frequently work in tandem. Systems designed to capture users' private data must accomplish their task in an aesthetic manner, so that users enjoy the experience and do not suspect an invasion of privacy. Suggestions for designing systems that induce the voluntary surrender of personal data include ideas like feeding young men with pornography, with the expectation that they will dish out all their data just for that experience.

An important insight is that AI often achieves its pragmatic goals under the cover of aesthetics. Clever AI systems achieve their pragmatic goals by using aesthetics as the doorway to users' minds and gain their trust.

Even in real life, the aesthetic and pragmatic dimensions often complement one another, with aesthetics serving as a means to pragmatic results. Professionals who engage with clients must have both capabilities, producing pragmatic results while maintaining a pleasant posture with clients. Likewise, the pragmatic goals of government can be greatly assisted by the adroit use of aesthetics. People working in politics, public relations, diplomacy, and other public fields need to achieve pragmatic goals by exhibiting political correctness and concern for their constituents.

Traditional kshatriyas (political leaders, warriors, or those with power) are required to govern and control the public. Their job is primarily a pragmatic one: formulating good policies and ensuring the safety of the people. Others in their kingdom might be preoccupied with singing, dancing, and pop culture, but while kshatriyas also patronize such aesthetic pursuits, they must understand that popular culture should not either hinder or obstruct the pragmatic outcomes.

The Covid-19 pandemic has created a shift in social priorities from aesthetic concerns to pragmatic issues like delivering necessary supplies and saving lives. An enhanced sense of pragmatics is replacing aesthetic norms. Being humane, being politically correct, and following social protocols and etiquette are sometimes being overridden and replaced by new attitudes aligned with the pragmatic reality of dealing with the deadly coronavirus. Online dinners, virtual political rallies, and even virtual weddings are pragmatic solutions to the crisis and have become acceptable aesthetically and even part of the *new cool.*

The use of the aesthetic–pragmatic framework is illustrated with two analytical applications. The first examines the type of work that is most vulnerable to automation as well as the kind that is relatively secure. The second application of the framework examines the dynamics between digital platforms as suppliers of services and their consumers, and this analysis provides insight into the nature of transactions between both players.

Vulnerability to Automation

Artificial Intelligence is becoming increasingly successful at understanding and replicating human psychology. Machines can mimic human emotional responses and even tailor their aesthetic interface for individuals. However, aesthetic tasks are relatively more difficult to automate than pragmatic ones because aesthetics is subjective.

Another factor in the difficulty of automation is whether the task entails interpersonal communication among people. The larger the group interaction, the more complex the task and the harder it becomes to train machines to fill the role. In Figure 16, *I-tasks* (shown at the bottom) refer to tasks that require one individual, and machines can be easily trained to perform them. *We-tasks*, in the top half, involve interactions among multiple persons. These tasks are more difficult for a machine to learn because they involve many variables. Machine learning will take longer to master and efficiently perform tasks of this type.

The two axes in the diagram create a four-quadrant grid. The nature of work in these quadrants is not mutually exclusive, and many jobs involve a combination.

A. Quadrant A indicates work that involves pragmatic we-tasks requiring social interaction, such as the work of medical internists and sports coaches. Even though there is social interaction, the outcome expected is of a pragmatic kind.
B. Quadrant B entails aesthetic we-tasks performed by professionals such as social workers, psychologists, public relations agents and salespeople, who must

be skilled at emotional management. Compared to Quadrant A, such tasks involve more subjectivity and personalization.

C. Quadrant C refers to workers that perform I-tasks to produce aesthetic works, for example, artists.

D. Quadrant D encompasses pragmatic I-tasks, such as the work done by tax preparers, bookkeepers, and computer programmers that can work without much social interaction. These tasks are the easiest to automate.

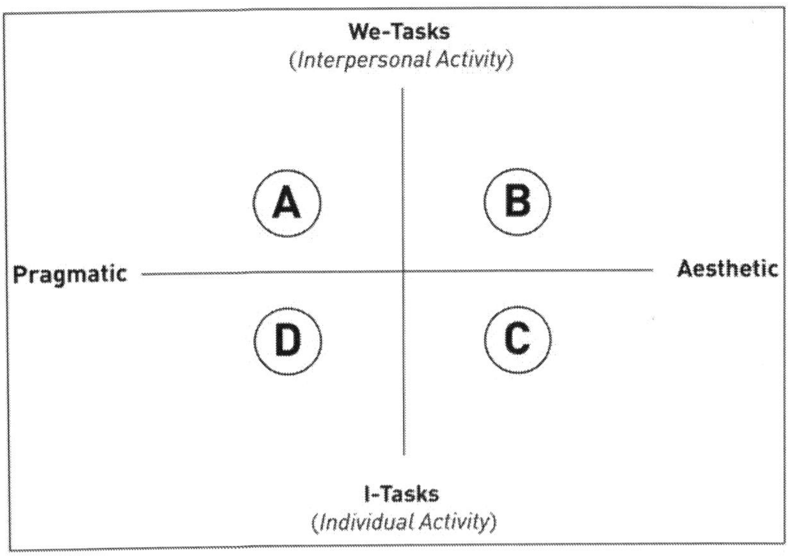

Figure 16: Four-Quadrant Grid of Vulnerability to Automation

In performing we-tasks, workers must have strong interpersonal and social skills, while for I-tasks, workers produce output in isolation. Therefore, we-tasks are more difficult to automate than I-tasks. The grid only serves to discuss the *relative* difficulty of using AI and should not be taken quite literally.

Quadrant B tasks are the most difficult to automate because they combine the collective dimension with aesthetic skills. Some experts cite such professions as the protected domain where human labor will be safe from automation. They may be relatively safe compared to the other segments, but the nature of work in B will change dramatically as machine learning evolves and augments the human workers.

The Gameboard

A similar four-quadrant grid is useful as a gameboard to simulate how digital platforms and the public interact. Understanding the respective goals of both players—the digital platform and the public—is crucial in such interactions.

Artificial Intelligence systems are designed to advance toward two goals: (1) *pragmatically* to increase wealth and political power for the likes of Facebook, Google, Twitter, and their affiliates; and (2) *aesthetically* to keep the masses feeling good while people voluntarily surrender their private data, agency and power.

The relationship between the major digital platforms and the public may be modeled as a gameboard, with the digital platforms indicated as players at the top half and the public as players at the bottom half (see Figure 17). Each side has both pragmatic and aesthetic interests in the transactions. This model demonstrates how the digital platform offers something to users and in return, receives something that the public willingly gives.

A. Digital platforms want private data from their users in order to test and perfect algorithms that pertain to their behavior. The data is also a commodity for sale to marketers to generate billions of dollars from targeted advertising.

B. Digital platforms also seek to build their credibility as a trusted entity by gifting free services to the public. They want to be considered champions of human rights and contemporary liberal values. They brand themselves as social-justice warriors that give the social underdogs a voice in global forums and help to build local and global communities.

C. Users want to increase their status and be perceived as leaders. They want to feel good about themselves by articulating their opinions and having others "Like" and "Follow" their posts.

D. Users also crave tangible and pragmatic benefits such as jobs, easier shopping experiences, and opportunities to increase personal income.

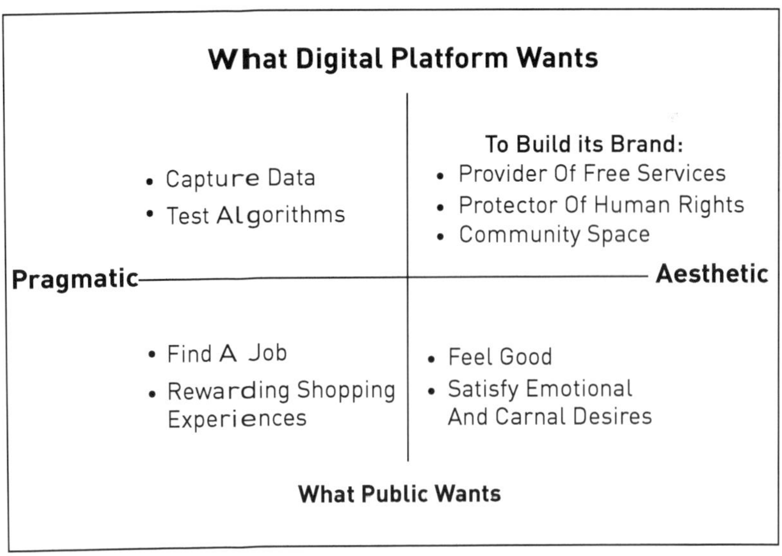

Figure 17: The Gameboard

For meaningful transactions to occur among these competing interests, both sides must be satisfied. Transactions commonly occur in various combinations and the following are illustrative examples:

- *A & D*: This is a purely pragmatic transaction for both sides. Consumer shops or looks for a job online and the platform gets the person's data.
- *B & C*: This is purely aesthetic for both sides. Consumers post their jokes, video clips, personal stories, and the platform uses this content to spread its aesthetic appeal to many more people. If the platform also gets useful data in the process, it becomes an *A, B, & C* type mentioned below.
- *A, B, & C*: In these transactions, users feel aesthetically rewarded by enjoying a wide range of free services while digital platforms obtain their private data. Users and their peers become subconsciously addicted to the platform and increasingly trust it to satisfy desires, which in turn boosts the platforms' presence and clout in the public. Increased visibility and influence help platforms increase their advertising revenue.
- *A, B, & D*: In these transactions, users derive practical benefits—whether buying or selling goods and services, landing jobs, or finding a spouse. Platforms acquire precious user data and further build their brand.

The institutions that control AI-based technologies employ them as instruments for achieving their own pragmatic outcomes. The CIA, the Chinese government, and American digital media giants all apply AI technology toward various pragmatic ends in which emotional and moral considerations are secondary and merely a means to an end. The digital giants use this technology to manipulate and manage users' feel-good psychological needs. They want to help emotional people daydream. The strategy will ultimately produce a false sense of agency in which the dumbed-down masses exist happily, never realizing that they have surrendered their power to the machines.

5

THE BATTLE FOR SELF

CHAPTER HIGHLIGHTS

- The two most foundational theories of consciousness are spiritual and materialistic, and they explain consciousness in entirely different, opposing ways. I have invested deeply in the spiritual approach to consciousness, and one of the primary reasons for writing this book is to expose how AI's influence is empowering the opposite camp of materialism.
- Artificial Intelligence and the life sciences are being combined to develop collaborations between computer algorithms and biological processes. New technologies combine computer science with medicine, biotechnology, nanotechnology, cognitive psychology, and several other fields to enhance the human mind–body complex. This intelligence will migrate from external wearable devices and the cloud to human implants. Artificial Intelligence-based systems will supply stimuli, narratives, fantasies, and other forms of cognitive and emotional manipulation. A range of intelligent medical, entertainment, and other applications will emerge over time. This will be entirely market driven, and not guided or limited by any moral, ethical, or ideological considerations.

- The notion of self will erode as a result of greater external dependency on algorithms that disrupt the natural sense of human individuality and free will. Humans will move away from the direction espoused by Vedanta and other spiritual traditions, taking materialism to new levels.
- Humankind's earliest narratives for giving meaning to the world offered transcendental accounts centered on a supernatural force or deity. Over the past few centuries, the success of science superseded the supernatural and spiritual. The new metaphysics in the West became humanism, a worldview in which there is no transcendental intelligence and humans are considered the center of existence and meaning. Humanism gave rise to liberalism, the basic tenets of which are individualism and free will. Liberalism is now at a new threshold of self-defeat: The outsourcing of gratifications to external technological agencies undermines the notions of self, individualism and free will. The current AI revolution threatens the metaphysics of its own origin.
- Postmodernism has created disrespect and cynicism toward all grand narratives. Social media has furthered this trend by relativizing knowledge, and facts have become nothing more than popular opinions. Objective truth is being replaced by whatever is most popular.
- Meanwhile, AI has succeeded in developing huge databases and models of psychology, social behavior and political patterns. These new data analytics are in the process of replacing traditional social science methodologies. Beyond introducing new methods of collecting and analyzing social data, the effect of AI will be to shift us away from the foundations of humanism, liberalism, individualism

and free will. A new AI-based mythology is being invented that undermines human agency.

- We are at the dawn of the age of endowing individuals with artificially enhanced bodies and minds with extended lifespans. Some futurists predict that technological breakthroughs will result in an entirely new type of human as different from us as we are now from animals. Authors like Yuval Noah Harari refer to these enhanced people as superhumans.[221]
- Very few elites will be able to afford the augmentations required to become superhuman. Technological advances at this level will not be available to most of the billions populating the planet today.
- The advent of superhumans will lead to what I call the *crash of civilization,* characterized by unprecedented social disruption that supersedes the metaphysics of humanism and its notions of free will, individualism and human rights.
- Humans craving carnal pleasures, fantasies, and other aesthetic stimulation will devolve into happy morons managed by digital intelligence trained in psychology. Although they will numerically be the majority, they will lack agency in any realistic, pragmatic sense.
- At some point, the elites will argue their case for depopulating the earth. The AI technologies of emotional manipulation and gratification will be used by the elites to seduce the masses to acquiesce and voluntarily surrender their agency to AI-based digital systems.
- A new mythology will arise in which digital intelligence will be akin to the all-powerful ancient gods of Greece.
- Depopulation will eventually lead to a new equilibrium and an entirely different world. But in the interim, there will be a few decades of dystopia in the world system.

MATERIALISM VERSUS THE SELF

Algorithmic Biology

Modern Western medical science is now discovering what the ancient philosophical system of Vedanta has always espoused, namely, that there is no hard boundary between mind and body, and that one influences the other. However, contrary to Vedanta's worldview, there is the opposite approach today in which the mind and physical body are being modeled as biological mechanisms using the scientific method known as reductionism. This method assumes the human to be a purely material system built of parts just like a machine. New reductionist approaches to medical treatment are emerging, which model the entire mind–body complex as a collection of discrete parts. Except for the fact that its algorithms operate on hardware made of organic material instead of silicon, biology is being understood to function just like a computer.

Such a reduction of the human being into biological algorithms is a modern breakthrough that makes it possible to go the next step: transferring these human algorithms from natural biological hardware to run on silicon or some other man-made hardware. This is where AI is headed.

The success of reductionism is simply a pragmatic issue validated by empirical evidence. In the world of commercial success, metaphysical debates between spirituality and science are becoming irrelevant. Few persons refuse treatment for an ailment just because it is based on a metaphysical model they disagree with. Suppose a computer chip implant can intervene in the biological algorithms of the body to solve a problem such as epilepsy or a mental health disorder. Its commercial success is not likely to be hampered by the ideological consideration that it boosts a purely materialistic model of human beings. Consumers will make a strictly pragmatic choice to take advantage of such solutions.

The commercial success of such mind–body technologies is not limited to medical applications. In the foreseeable future, an explosion of AI products will provide people with emotional, aesthetic and psychological enhancements. Whether these enhancements cater to genuine needs or trivial indulgences will be a subject of debate, but that will not slow down the adoption of technology. Initial public acceptance will come when hard medical science legitimizes the use of such technological infiltrations into our lives. The floodgates will then open for broader adoption in other industries such as entertainment.

As explained in earlier chapters, machine learning is seeing immense success modeling human psychology as a collection of algorithms programmed into biology. Once a person's psychological states are modeled as algorithms with known inputs and outputs, the machine can be trained to reverse engineer the person's psychology and artificially stimulate a desired experience. This rapidly expanding field enables machines to intervene in our cognitive systems and override our natural mind–body complex. It hijacks our natural human experience and replaces it with just another designable—and marketable—experiential product.

Furthermore, these experiential products will be independent of one another just like many different apps of a mobile device or lifestyle products on the market. The amazing success of purely materialistic instant gratification suggests that the emotional mind share of people is shifting away from higher pursuits in life to a portfolio of disconnected pursuits, each of which can be optimized in isolation through technology. Like the app stores of today, a marketplace may emerge where people can download moods and emotions on demand, and send them as gifts to others.

The power and influence of this AI breakthrough is worth restating. The underlying premise of the marriage of biology and computer science, continually reinforced by fresh discoveries and applications, is that all living beings—from the simplest single-cell organisms all the way to humans—are merely collections of algorithms. Researchers in neuroscience and other branches of medicine are studying the biological algorithms that the body has evolved over eons, and reverse engineering living systems to figure out behavioral models with increasing levels of sophistication.

The physical hardware that these human algorithms run on happens to be an organic machine, but this hardware can be switched. Once the model for any organ or mind–body function is sufficiently established, it can be ported to run on a different hardware platform, which may happen to be nonorganic, such as silicon. The future will see a rise in hybrid organic/nonorganic computing.

An important point about the new bio-AI technology is that, as argued in Chapter 1, intelligence is separable and independent from consciousness. An unconscious system can outwardly perform many of the same intelligent functions as a conscious being. The question of consciousness—what it is, what it does, and why it is important—is completely irrelevant to the recent rise of AI in a pragmatic sense.

Many technologists and futurists view living organisms as mere algorithms in which concepts like free will are meaningless. They model a human as a bag of meat driven solely by biochemical and electronic processes that we recognize as sensations, emotions, thoughts and even selfhood. Artificial Intelligence and neuroscience collaborate to produce interventions at various levels of our cognitive apparatus (see Figure 18); in effect, creating the means to hijack all the natural mechanisms that produce our emotions and thus drive our behavior.

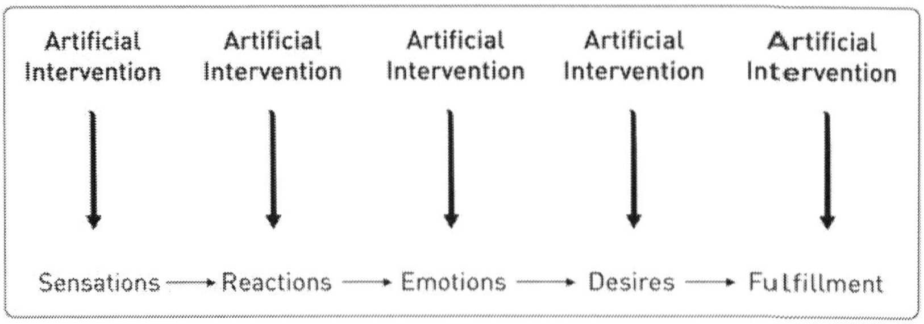

Figure 18: Artificial Behavior Modification

The world's largest wealth creation in recent times is emerging from the digital economy driven by computer algorithms that model human behavior at the deepest levels. This economy is going to get even bigger. The corporate giants of the future will deconstruct people into separately manageable biological processes and then use neural networks to monitor, understand and manipulate them. The self is being broken down into a definable series of sensations, emotions and thoughts. Each component of the self lends itself to external engagement by AI machines.

In these reductionist models, the self is nothing more than a pragmatic construct that serves as the nexus of individual desires and actions. The computerization of physiology and the use of AI to exploit biology and neuroscience will revolutionize commerce and industry, including shopping, entertainment, tourism, sex, games and sports, socializing and politics. Hardly any field will remain untouched.

Once the algorithms are figured out, intelligent systems can be installed both inside and outside the human body to provide enhanced functionality. As technology invades our bodies to deliver various applications, the human body gets reduced to a complex system of biological parts, with each organ as an autonomous module connected to other modules through inputs and outputs.

In this scenario, the paradigm of a human operating a machine may well be reversed—the machine could be driving the human. According to Noah Harari, humans will

> "become accustomed to seeing themselves as a collection of biochemical mechanisms that is constantly monitored and guided by a network of electronic algorithms".[222]

Hacking Nature's Learning Systems

The marriage between the life sciences and AI will disrupt existing societal norms. A new paradigm—considering the physical body as an organic computer—is emerging. In this paradigm, organic computers carry out biological processes the same way that silicon-based computers perform algorithms. Human physical and mental functions can be modeled as a set of algorithms running on the organic hardware that we know as our physical body.

Life scientists also claim to be able to use non-living mechanical systems to replicate the behavior of living systems. In effect, although they will not say so explicitly, this development is tantamount to creating what may be called artificial life. It is worth reiterating that such systems are *not* conscious, and further, that intelligence can be independent of consciousness. If our concern is with *functionality* in the world and not with the metaphysics of what we call life, it does seem reasonable to consider that such systems in fact behave *like* artificial life. This is to say, these are non-living systems that mimic the outward behavior of living systems.

Figure 19 shows the ways life sciences and computer sciences are already collaborating.

Once a living system's behavior has been replicated on computers, the technology will progress through the following stages of implementation.

1. Initially, the AI system will be in an external device operated on the cloud and/or a smart handheld device, or as a wearable item. Interactions with the user serve some specific purpose, often medical or entertainment, or whatever the application is designed to achieve.[223]
2. Research is under way to implant devices into the body to perform certain functions and even complex algorithms. These implants would then collaborate with the body's own biology in addition to interfacing with computers outside the body. Such developments are currently an active area of research and are considered very promising.
3. At some point in the more remote future, the body's own biology could be re-programmed to replace or augment implants. In other words, we as a society are headed for a synthesis of biotechnology, nanotechnology and information technology. Artificial Intelligence is the engine running all this.

The direction of modeling can also be reversed to decode nature as a learning system. *We can think of nature as a learning system in which each entity uses its environment to get trained.* Figure 20 shows a natural learning system—whether a cell, species, pathogen, or even a human community—interacting with its environment and training itself to perform better, learning to mutate and evolve by using the big data of its environmental experience.

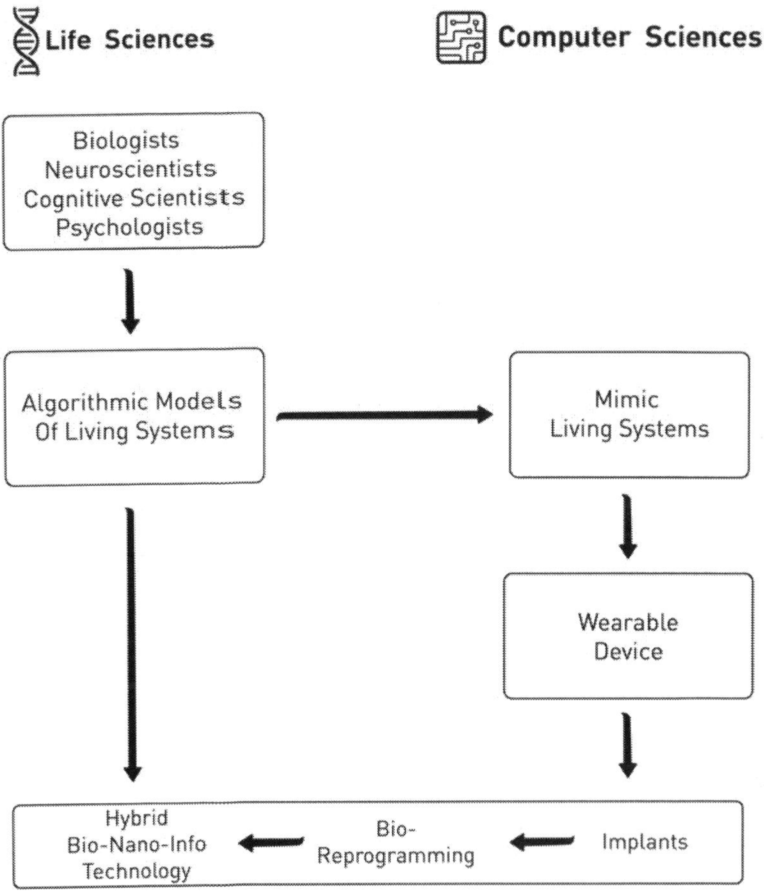

Figure 19: Collaboration Between Life Sciences and Computer Sciences

My point is incredibly significant in the philosophy of sciencc: machine learning and biological learning seem to share conceptual similarities in the way they learn from experience. This is shown in Figure 20.

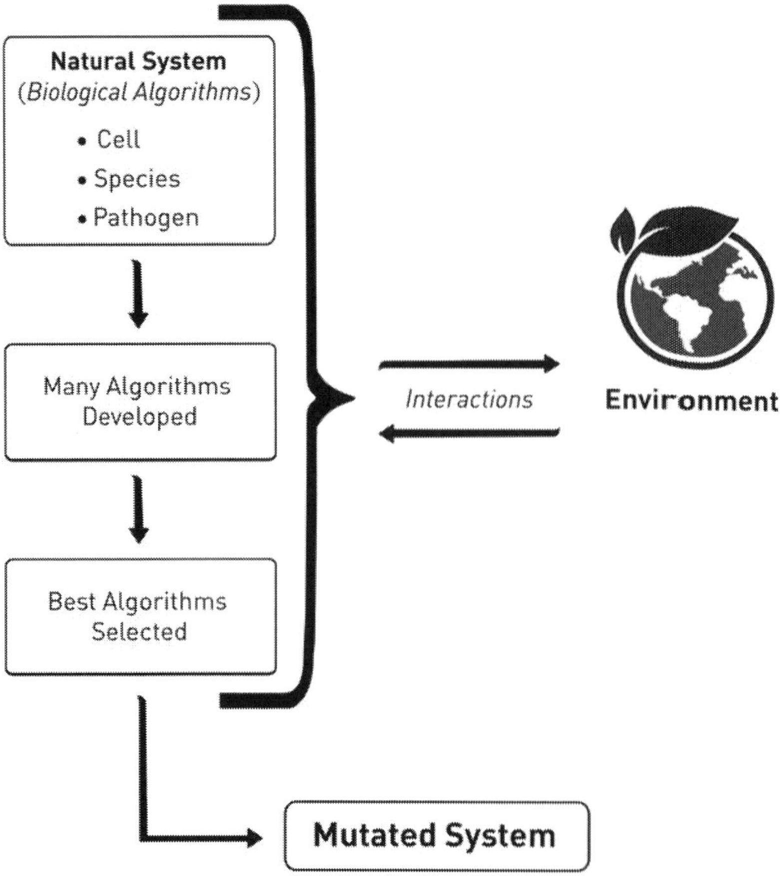

Figure 20: Machine Learning of Individual Psychology

For instance, the epigenetic system in biological cells is a mechanism analogous to a learning machine; it uses interactions with the environment and the responses it gets to learn about the environment and improve its own performance. The experiences of a cell are stored in the epigenetic material surrounding the DNA in the cell.

The epigenetic mechanism learns and generates multiple genetic algorithms; these are tested and the algorithms that perform well in a given environment (as measured by some criteria such as the rate of survival) carry more weight than the ones that do not perform as well. Over time, the successful algorithms become the new normal mechanism for a given type of cells.

The same theory can be applied to an entire species: a learning system that interacts with its environment. Natural evolution is essentially a trial-and-error learning system, with the responses from environmental encounters being equivalent to big data.

While the body's cells are evolving through training in the environment, so also the pathogens are learning and mutating. Pathogens are also biological mechanisms that learn by attempting to outsmart the body of a host and overcome the antibiotics and other medicines meant to kill them. Like any other learning system, pathogens can be modeled as algorithms whose parameters adapt to optimize survival in a given environment. Because a virus or bacteria functions like an algorithm, scientists can develop designer viruses and bacteria for purposes both good and bad.

Genetic mapping research is rapidly advancing to help customize treatments in specific populations. Machine learning could be useful to model a patient's biological system and develop a customized response. The successful conjunction of biologists, neuroscientists, psychologists and computer scientists that has delivered such practical benefits has commercially strengthened the reductionist perspective.

ALGORITHM VERSUS BEING

The Assault on Spiritualism

Reductionism is an analytical method that breaks down a system for deeper examination. These constituent parts are themselves composites of smaller parts, or subsystems. The reductionist process of dividing systems into ever smaller parts is carried out at as many levels as one can. As the reductionistic models move further from the holistic sense of a unified selfhood, systems are, simply speaking, considered nothing more than the sum of their parts.

Basically, algorithms can be broken down into smaller algorithms, which consist of even smaller algorithms. But in the end, *an algorithm has no self*. The notion of an algorithm having a self is meaningless in the reductionist approach.

A similar process takes place in the practice of Vedanta, where the self (often referred to as the ego) is deconstructed as a false sense of unity. In the perspective of ultimate existence, no ego actually exists. However, Vedanta and scientific reductionism differ in one critical aspect: The deconstruction of parts leads in opposite directions.

In the case of Vedanta, the deconstruction of the objects of inquiry—physical, mental, and emotional objects that occupy our cognition—is only one step. The subject of inquiry—the *who am I* question—is what leads to the final outcome. The process of deconstruction is carried out through various prescribed means. One method is **jnana** or knowledge; another is through **dhyana** or deep meditation; yet another is through **karma** at the level where action occurs spontaneously without any sense of being the agent of action; and finally, **bhakti** or complete surrender of the algorithmic self (i.e. ego) to the divine. Upon the cognitive dissolution of the ego, all experience is recognized as springing from a deeper level of being and a sense of more profound Absolute Self—with a capital *S*—known as the **Atman.**

Although the conventionally experienced self is discovered to be false in Vedanta, it is replaced by the permanent, and far more profound, Atman.

In the case of biological materialism discussed in the preceding pages, only a collection of physical parts exists with nothing beyond the physical.

Figure 21 compares the two systems of deconstructing or dissolving the ego.

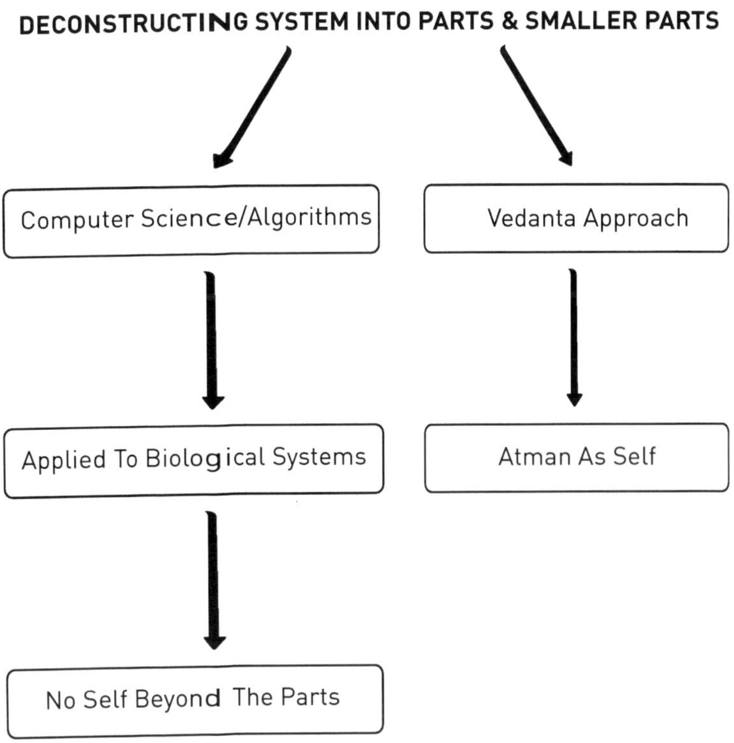

Figure 21: Two Systems of Deconstruction

Both these systems conclude that the self is illusory, but they differ in their final outcome. In Vedanta, the unified Self is the non-physical foundation, the ground on which all the parts and the ego holding them together exist. When the ego and its parts dissolve, the Self alone remains. In computer science, the reductionist process has no means of accommodating a unified sense of self as an ultimate reality.

A computer algorithm is fully capable of modeling any physical process because a process is merely a mechanism consisting of parts that comprise subparts ad infinitum. A system is fully characterized by the algorithms that describe its functionality. Consequently, there is no such thing as the indivisible self of a computer system. Computer systems have no need for a self, and in fact, it is impossible for a computer to accommodate the notion of the self as an autonomous being. The question, "who performs the algorithm?" is meaningless and irrelevant to the computer scientist. There is no "who-ness" in a material process.

What applies to computers also applies to the materialistic models of biology. When constructing scientific models of life forms, biologists have difficulty including the notion of selfhood as a fundamental entity with an autonomous existence. Whether the system is built of biological material or of silicon is inconsequential in this discussion.

At the pragmatic level, the reductionist model prevails over the model of a unified ultimate Self. The attention, funding and empowerment accorded to the products and services of the reductionist model are dominating today. Replicating human functions and responses into products that augment or replace the corresponding human components has a huge market, and in serving the market, AI will make a lot of money. At least thus far, reductionism is enjoying greater success, although the victory is not due to its metaphysical superiority. The market reality is that algorithmic models of human behavior are proving to be especially useful—and thus profitable—in many applications both pragmatic and aesthetic.

The ability of machines to mimic human emotions and psychology has been advancing based on the conceptual model that sensations and emotions are nothing more than algorithms that have evolved over thousands of years to help humans survive. Of particular importance is the fact that the technology of these reductionist models has been immensely successful in providing gratification to distinct components of individual psychology. We saw in Chapter 4 that the new systems can successfully entice humans, seizing on specific carnal desires, fantasies, hopes and aspirations. They offer instant gratification and turn this into habits, and eventually into digital addictions.

This mechanization of desire management hacking humans' innermost life in shown in the figure below.

Machine Learning ➔ Behavioral Algorithms ➔ Artificial Gratification ➔ Digital Addiction

Because no unified self is required for this model to produce desirable experiences, all ideas of a unified, higher self are rendered obsolete. Within the context of AI development, the philosophical quest for a transcendent self becomes merely a theoretical debate with no practical use.

To emphasize: According to scientific reductionism, what we ordinarily think of as an individual is merely a physical mechanism—made of parts that consist of smaller parts, which in turn can be broken down into even smaller parts, and so on ad infinitum. There is no "self" in such an entity.

Figure 22 contrasts the trajectories of spirituality and materialistic gratification concerning the future of individuals. The Vedic terms corresponding to this choice between the spiritual and the material paths are *shreyas* and *preyas*, respectively. The choice of shreyas leads to the truth of oneself. The choice of preyas is one of sensual, carnal gratification that takes one away from oneself.

Shown on the left is the path of meditation and other spiritual practices leading to the pure experience known as ananda, or bliss. The entity that experiences ananda is the Self or Atman. Because it transcends the body–mind complex, it *cannot* be deconstructed into parts. The Atman is the *experiencer* of everything.

Algorithms can model the experience and reductionism can deconstruct the experience, but neither process touches the experiencer.

In the materialistic AI-based approach shown on the right, the external stimuli are driving individual experiences. Each stimulus targets and emphasizes a specific impulse or emotion in order to produce a specific pleasure or pain, fulfilling some desire—sex, public acclaim, delectable food, entertainment, talent; the list is endless. The AI system, in effect, hijacks our cognitive and neuroscientific mechanisms by substituting, or augmenting, some natural signals with artificial ones in order to provide a predefined pleasure or pain. For example, soldiers suffering from Post-traumatic Stress Disorder (PTSD) can be treated using machine-enabled alteration of their traumatic memories. While sitting at home, they may enjoy the experience of being on a beach—seeing, hearing, touching, tasting and smelling the ocean—and forget the memories of the trauma.

The individual pleasure or pain that is augmented can be optimized separately from the rest of the experience. In this way each sensation or emotion can be isolated as a target for gratification. This turns each type of desire into a distinct market opportunity.

Vendors are currently developing products that will feed this consumer psyche, which functions as a portfolio of demands put together as a purely artificial and synthetic package. Each product promises to push some specific psychological or biological button. Users only need to select their desired experience from a menu of choices. An important new industry is emerging focused entirely on delivering artificial pleasure boosts through stimulation.

The ultimate effect of this technology is to breakdown individuals into fragments in such a fundamental manner that it undermines their integral unity and selfhood because *no unified center of being exists* in this model.

The quintessential debate here is the struggle between unconscious algorithms and our human sense of self and being.

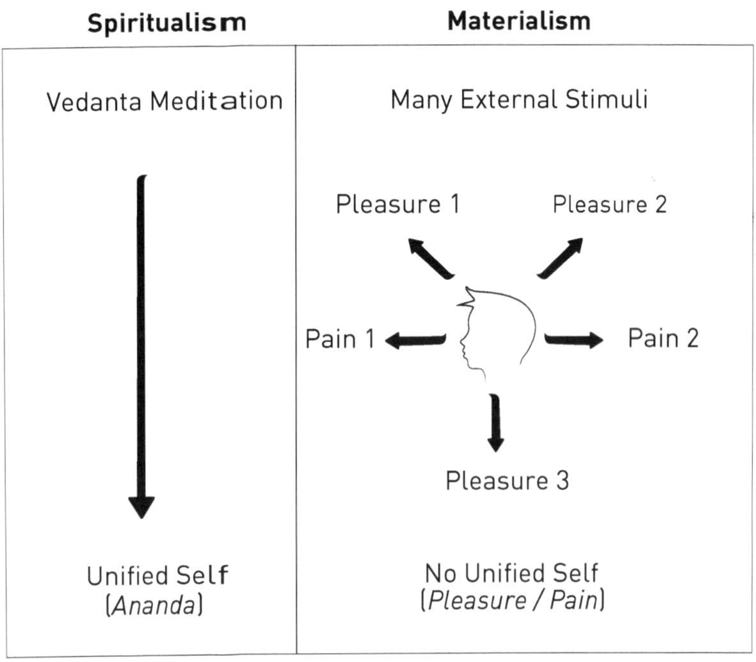

Figure 22: The Dichotomy of Spiritualism and Materialism

The reductionist algorithmic model posits that sensations are nothing more than physical, biological processes. In the same way, emotions and thoughts are merely physical processes, implying that they are susceptible to external intervention, manipulation and substitution.

According to this model, feelings, emotions and thoughts from biological systems somehow mysteriously coalesce into what we call the self—the constituent parts of the greater whole, the human being. The so-called human machine assumes a self only as a biological necessity. In the evolutionary process, the self was an important psychological construct that served as the nexus for the biological machine's success, a survival strategy in the face of challenges. Evolutionary competitiveness determined the outcome: Biological entities without a notion of self were handicapped and failed to evolve the best survival skills. They lost out to competing entities that developed a presumed sense of self and behaved according to that sense. This argument is analogous to the idea that a sports team or an army has a better chance of winning if the group has a cohesive identity comprising all its members, compared to a rival group that lacks a collective selfhood. The self is simply an identity that serves the pragmatic function of competitiveness.

Competing biological systems are essentially rival learning systems. Systems with a collective identity, which we call the self, have better survival skills than those without one. The self serves as the presumptive owner of the entire body–mind machinery, a virtual entity invented by the biological animal during its long evolution as a device to survive in the environment. But in truth, say biologists, the self is a mythic narrative—nothing more than a complex network of biological processes with a shared survival agenda that drives behavior—and not an entity unto itself. They claim the illusion of a self has evolved merely as learned behavior.

Such a model of living entities insists that biological algorithms learn the same way machine learning systems do. The self is nothing in itself; it is merely a conglomerate of biological processes that artificially appear to have a unified, cohesive individuality.[224] I posit this as an alternative to Darwin's theory of evolution.

Competing Theories of Consciousness

Biology faces a major problem i.e. providing an explanation for consciousness. Computer science is also a reductionist discipline but does not concern itself with the philosophy of consciousness because its success lies solely in its *pragmatic* applications. People do not have any expectation that computer science should inform them about consciousness. Biology, on the other hand, must address the issue of *who* is being described. As the fundamental life science modeling the processes of living entities, biology is under severe pressure to explain what consciousness is.

As a reductionist science, biology rejects the notion of an ultimate self, yet it must try to explain consciousness. How can there be consciousness without a self? That is the dilemma biology must address.

To confront the challenges of understanding consciousness, a vibrant multidisciplinary field known as consciousness studies emerged over the past four decades. It incorporates experts from a variety of domains, including spirituality, theology, biology, neuroscience, psychology, linguistics, philosophy, and computer science, to name just a few.

Broadly speaking, the field of consciousness studies spans two competing paradigms. In the spiritual paradigm, consciousness is the primary reality; everything else that exists must be explained as a product of consciousness. Consciousness is the entity having experience, and matter is merely the manifestation of consciousness. This paradigm holds consciousness at its very foundation, and Vedanta champions this spiritual view.

In the reductionist model, everything is explained in the opposite direction: Matter is the primary reality, and causation proceeds from matter to sensation, to feeling and emotion, to thought, all the way to the sense of a unified self. Individuals, according to this reductionist biological model, are nothing more than a collection of algorithms running on a hardware platform that happens to be biological. Consciousness is emergent—it is an epiphenomenon, i.e., a consequence of biological processes. The biological model holds that the fundamental science is physics that describes the behavior of space, time, and matter, including chemistry and biology. Scientific explanation works from the bottom up, starting with small entities as the fundamental reality and combining them block by block into bigger entities.

Figure 23 presents the major levels in the reductionist model, progressing from physics up through the life sciences and computer science to cognition and desire. Each level is a separate and distinct field with its own pioneers, history of discoveries, institutions, models, and vocabulary. Relatively few of these disciplines have been integrated with one another, and that too only in the past several decades. During the formative period of science over several centuries, each discipline was largely independent of the rest. The result is that major contradictions often exist among the hard sciences. Synthesizing them into a unified entity is a significant challenge for scientists from these disciplines. The field of consciousness studies is where theorists gather to cross-fertilize ideas.

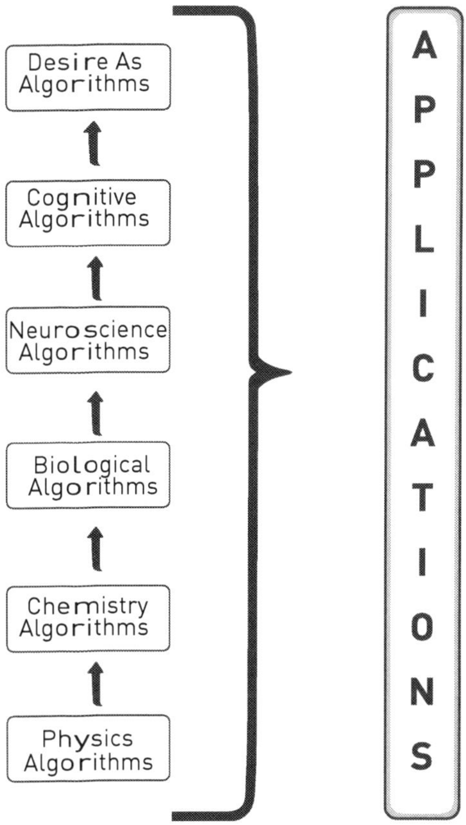

Figure 23: Reductionist Model of Psychology

The spiritual approach is entirely different. At the foundation of the spiritual model is the notion that all reality (both seen and unseen) is integrated; everyone is a microcosm of the greater whole. This is captured in the Vedic statement, *yatha pinde tatha brahmande*—as is the atom so is the universe. The macrocosm and microcosm mirror each other. The human body and cosmic body are isomorphic, as are the human and cosmic mind.

The material model, on the other hand, posits that the unity we see is merely synthetic, a false unity in which individual parts exist as separate, independent entities held together artificially to create a whole.

My approach to this debate is as a spiritual person with a strong foundation in Vedanta, physics, and computer science. I have always argued fiercely that consciousness is primary and matter, secondary. Although the ordinary idea of the self (commonly called the ego) is false, a higher notion of the Atman does exist. Indeed, I believe the Atman is not only real but the only entity that ultimately exists.

Why did the reductionist model become so important to biology compared to the spiritual model of consciousness? Was it because reductionism offers a superior philosophy based on profound experiences? Or was it simply a practical victory because the reductionist model can produce sensory and emotional gratification, and thereby support a thriving economy? I believe the latter reason accounts for this tectonic shift. In Vedanta terms, AI optimizes the fulfillment of kama (desires). And the gratification of desire is what the ego wants above everything.

The victory of materialistic biology and neuroscience over more spiritual explanations of the self is of dramatic consequence, empowering the development of an entirely new technology whose primary effect is to diminish the agency and selfhood of individuals. By embracing such technology, individuals transfer custody for their decision-making to AI machines and applications. This revolution is rooted in the fact that the algorithmic model underlying AI can successfully deliver—at least temporarily—fulfillment for human desires.

SELF-DEFEATING HUMANISM

Materialism Scores a Self-goal

While machines keep becoming more intelligent, humans are being gratified by the AI systems and are encouraged to become dumber. Devaluation of selfhood and privacy is a large part of this trend. Noah Harari openly advocates that we should give up our privacy and turn over our intimate data to the digital platforms, because doing so would be in our best interest. He says we must

> willingly dismantle the barriers protecting our private spaces and allow state bureaucracies and multinational corporations access to our innermost recesses. For instance, allowing Google to read our emails and follow our activities would make it possible for Google to alert us to brewing epidemics before they are noticed by traditional health services.[225]

Ironically, at the same time that he pleads for us to disavow control and ownership of our own private data, Harari does not propose that Google, Facebook, Twitter, or any other corporate entity give up ownership of *their* data and other intellectual property. He proposes a one-way street in the transfer of data, and hence agency: from humans to digital systems.

This loss of privacy and personal agency is directly opposed to Western liberalism's emphasis on individual rights. Western liberalism is all about promoting individual civil liberties, human rights, democracy, and the free pursuit of enterprise. Presently, world cultures and discourses are dominated by the Western view of liberalism, and the social sciences of sociology and economics are built on the premises of liberalism. The expansion of AI technology is a grave threat to Western liberalism.

An understanding of liberalism first requires an understanding of humanism, which espouses that primacy be given to human interests, values, and agency. Humanism has been called the worship of humans because it considers humans to be the ultimate source of meaning in the world. According to humanism, the cosmos has no absolute or inherent purpose; its meaning and purpose are whatever humans assign to it.

Humanism posits that absolute truth does not exist independently of what humans have constructed. What we think of as the meaning and purpose of life is actually a set of shared narratives consisting of stories, metaphysics, laws, cultures, and so on. Such traditions enjoy a public consensus, providing a social and ideological contract among peoples, and this serves as the foundation on which society functions. In other words, all grand narratives are collectively manufactured stories with a practical purpose: to provide us with meaning in what we do. They are the glue, even if at times the crazy glue, that holds society together.

One family of ancient narratives told by humans and accepted by society was constructed on the premise of a God in the sky who created, commanded, and controlled people based on a system of fear and reward. Using machine learning terminology, one can think of organized religion as a reinforcement learning system that trains the public using a certain idea of morality as a heuristic: For example, in traditional Christianity, being saved from original sin and eternal damnation serve as the criteria based on which human behavior should be optimized.

Then arrived the age of European enlightenment, and the Abrahamic story of human existence shifted to the new worldview leading to the pursuit of physical, earthly pleasure. Materialism, and eventually consumerism, supplanted the worship of God as the main pursuit and this became the premise for social sciences.

The grand narratives of humanism and liberalism so dominate the world today that we seldom recognize their relatively recent ascendancy in Western history. A successful theory perpetuates itself by the mutual consensus of, and confirmation by, the people. Shared worldviews have helped humans work together in large numbers to form societies of cooperating individuals, representing a web of meaning that influences a society's laws, philosophies, traditions, and organizations. The role of a society's deep structures can be unconscious, especially when it drives people to undertake collective action on a grand scale. Humans have gained supremacy over all other animals in part because we mobilized language to create new and complex narratives that we constantly expand and adapt based on our experiences.

The core myth that characterizes liberalism is this: There is no transcendental intelligence, and we must be guided by the human-centric starting point. Humans possess free will, and this free will must be accorded the highest empowerment. Liberal politics empower the voter. Liberal economics empower the customer. Liberal aesthetics empower people to define their own ideas of beauty. Liberal ethics entitle everyone to pursue happiness, however they define it. Liberal education empowers free thought. Modern science and technology are built on the liberal premise of humankind's rights and powers over the cosmos.

Ironically, AI is on the course to overthrow liberalism and its substratum, humanism. Yet this new AI technology is itself a creation of humanism through the following process:

1. The rubric of humanism assumes that the cosmos has the meaning and purpose people have assigned to it. In other words, meaning and purpose are whatever we all accept by broad consensus.
2. Liberalism's pursuit of human empowerment has taken us to new heights of scientific and technological achievement.
3. These very advances are now manipulating us to become increasingly dependent on machines to deliver longer lifespans, physical and cognitive pleasures, and a sense of unlimited power through the technological conquest of nature.
4. Such machine domination can only occur at the cost of disempowering ordinary humans. *The biggest casualty is free will, the very core of liberalism.* Smart machines, owned and controlled by a small number of individuals and business entities, will manage more and more of society's functions. Humans voluntarily give up their free will as machines become smarter and take over their thought and agency.
5. Downgrading the importance of the individual amounts to humanism's ideological defeat by its own products.

In other words, *the products of humanism are defeating the myth of humanism*. Figure 24 illustrates this trajectory.

Most people will be adversely impacted by the demise of humanism because individual rights will be diluted and eventually superseded by a new grand narrative supplied by a super-intelligent digital system that is not conscious.

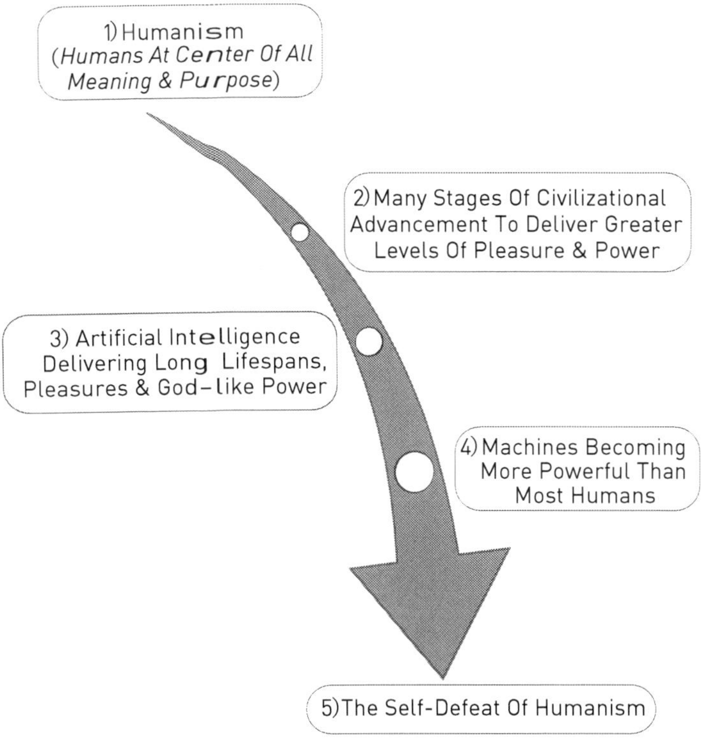

Figure 24: The Path of Self-defeat

Noah Harari explains: "Attempting to realize this humanist dream will undermine its very foundations by unleashing new post-human technologies",[226] by which he means technologies that will make the new futurist humans as different from present-day humans as we are from animals. He clarifies his predictions with powerful observations.

> Computers powerful enough to understand and overcome the mechanisms of aging and death will probably also be powerful enough to replace humans in any and all tasks.[227]

> The rise of humanism also contains the seeds of its own downfall. While the attempts to upgrade humans into gods takes humanism to its logical conclusion, it simultaneously exposes humanism's inherent flaws.[228]
>
> The covenant linking science and humanism may well crumble and give way to a very different kind of deal, between science and some new post-humanist religion.[229]

He believes that the new haves and elites will invent a new narrative, which he calls post-humanism religion. Liberalism will achieve its own defeat because it cannot deliver its promise without destroying itself. He explains:

> The triumphant liberal ideas are now pushing humankind to reach for immortality, bliss and divinity. Egged on by the allegedly infallible wishes of consumers and voters, scientists and engineers devote more and more energies to these liberal projects. Yet what the scientists are discovering and what the engineers are developing may unwittingly expose both the inherent flaws in the liberal world view and the blindness of consumers and voters. When genetic engineering and artificial intelligence reveal their full potential, liberalism, democracy and free markets might become as obsolete as flint knives, tape cassettes, Islam and communism.[230]

Just like the narratives and myths of old were supplanted by new ones, so too will the myth of humanism unravel and disintegrate. It will be defeated by its own extreme focus on individualism and the resulting technology. To make the downfall of humanism widely acceptable to the people who will be most adversely impacted, a new narrative must be invented to provide meaning to the world and establish a positive purpose in the lives of common people.

Postmodernism and the Death of Truth

The theoretical respectability of making truth seem relative if not irrelevant, comes from the school of thought known as postmodernism. Prominent postmodernist thinkers (like Foucault and Derrida, for example) have built their careers and fame on the argument that truth is inherently relative with no ultimate foundation whatsoever, and some of their followers have even considered truth a nonsensical idea. A premise of postmodernism is that all grand narratives are artificially constructed, and they always mask built-in structures of power and abuse. Thus, according to postmodernism, a rejection of all grand narratives is the path to liberation. This narrative to end all grand narratives has gone to the extreme of asserting that all scientific claims are also grand narratives that ought to be rejected.

The problem with this is that, unlike Vedanta, it is not founded on experiences of a higher consciousness.

Postmodernism bestows respectability on the free-for-all that is being given voice on social media; truth is not seen as a virtue. Aside from anything to do with postmodernism, social media is structured to encourage the spread of information without regard to accuracy. The quest is all about getting likes, retweets, and other measures of popularity. People believe whatever seems to be widely accepted by others. Opinions are confused with facts, insults and abuses are substituted for civilized debates, and the result is an overall devaluation of reliable information.

The anonymity of participation is a big factor in the loss of accountability. Deception is commonplace; masquerading behind a different identity or even impersonating someone else is a common strategy. Social media is like a new Wild West in which anything goes for the sake of hustling.

Artificial Intelligence has further exacerbated the syndrome of fake news with its ability to supply custom-tailored information to individuals based on their propensities and profiles. People are fed a filtered combination of truth and falsity engineered for them to reinforce their existing beliefs or enrage them with outlandish claims. This customized filtering is done on users' behalf in the name of personalization. The public is complicit and, in many cases, happily having its beliefs managed this way.

Social media is a distinct subculture with its own myths, its own heroes, and its own rules of the game. As a result, few common terms of reference are available that all perspectives can subscribe to as the foundation for rational debate. Public discourse has become highly disintegrated and polarized. Even worse, digital platforms have influenced the style and aesthetics of people's mannerisms, speech, vocabulary, and other subtle behaviors.

For better or worse, we are at the dawn of a new epoch in which AI culminates the materialistic quest for a better world, bringing together all the greatest technological achievements of recent centuries. But it is ultimately a self-defeating goal destroying the very structure of humanism that created it. Postmodernism serves as a handmaiden for the demise of humanism at the hand of intelligent machines.

Figure 25 depicts the history and future of grand narratives and explains the way in which humans assign meaning to their lives. Postmodernism is shown as the weapon that demolishes all prior views of the self. Artificial Intelligence is shown as the supplier of the new replacement narratives that are being downloaded into billions of moronic people as part of their addiction to artificial gratification.

The box with a dotted outline in Figure 25 is intended to convey a state of disequilibrium resulting from these disruptions. It is dotted because it is not well-defined, and its outcome is uncertain.

The history of various societies swings through a series of alternating states of equilibrium and disequilibrium. Each state of equilibrium is eventually disrupted, leading to a period of chaos and uncertainty. Competing forces enter the vacuum created by the lack of stability until eventually a new equilibrium is established.

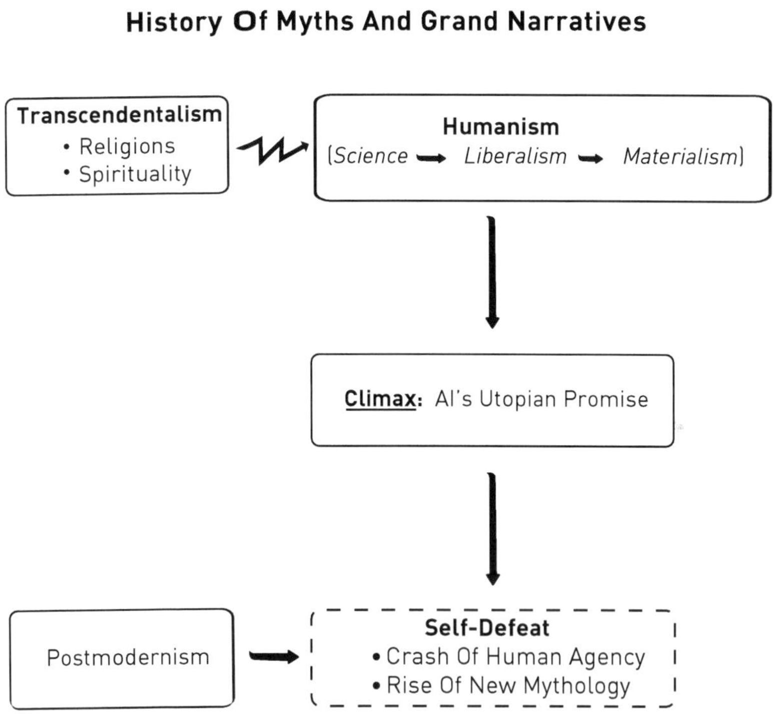

Figure 25: Self-defeating Mythology

For example, a major disequilibrium was the 1960s' counterculture movement in the US. Disruptions were brought about by the Vietnam war, the drug culture, the birth control pill and sexual revolution, and an influx of Hindu gurus offering new experiences through meditation. Many young Americans found inspiration from the dharmic traditions, which introduced key ingredients into what became known as the New Age movement. Eventually, a new equilibrium was achieved. Such a cycle of disruptions and equilibriums is found in social systems everywhere.

Pandemic Accelerating the Disequilibrium

The Covid-19 pandemic has jolted everyone into a renewed interest in environmentalism, sustainability, and conservation. In fact, nature is celebrating in the wake of the pandemic. Animals have been found roaming the streets of numerous cities around the world because humans have temporarily retreated. Fish are being seen in rivers previously too polluted to support life, and the skies have cleared up of pollution. It is unfortunate that humanity needed this hard knock to give back nature its share, at least in the short term. But this wakeup call could also be an opportunity to bring spirituality back into people's lives in a big way.

Artificial Intelligence was *already* becoming a disruptive force in society worldwide. Although the response to such widespread social disruption may temporarily alter the short-term effects of AI, I believe that ultimately *the pandemic will accelerate the trends described in this book*, amplifying the inevitable disequilibrium.

However, the pandemic and AI are different kinds of forces disrupting humanity's equilibrium. Figure 26 shows this *tension between algorithm and being*. On the left side is the cosmic being, manifested in the form of natural forces that unleashed the pandemic. On the right side is humanism, which espouses the supremacy of humans seen as materialistic entities, with modernity as the vehicle and algorithms the climactic accomplishment.

Seen this way, the pandemic is the latest weapon in the cosmic being's arsenal against modernity's reductionist algorithms. As an expression of the cosmic being, nature has retaliated with a force and scale that is unprecedented in living memory. Regardless of how it might have started, the pandemic is a karmic force of the cosmic being fighting back against mechanistic power that has gained too much control over nature.

If technology eventually defeats the pandemic, as most people expect, it will usher in an era of even more powerful breakthroughs in AI. A new epoch of history will emerge in which algorithms will play an even greater role. As the victor emerges more powerful than the vanquished, technology will establish its domination over nature even more assertively and mercilessly.

The ultimate victory AI will claim will be to reduce all of nature to algorithms that come under the control of digital technology—nature subsumed into the internet of things.

In pragmatic terms, the disruption of social and political institutions has created a new vacuum in people's lives. The AI-driven digital systems will exploit the vacuum as an opportunity to enter people's lives even more deeply. Digital networks will increasingly provide the certainty, security, and gratification people are currently craving. The battle for hijacking the self was already being won by AI, and the pandemic seems likely to cement that victory. Society will celebrate this victory of algorithm over being, although few people will see it so clearly.

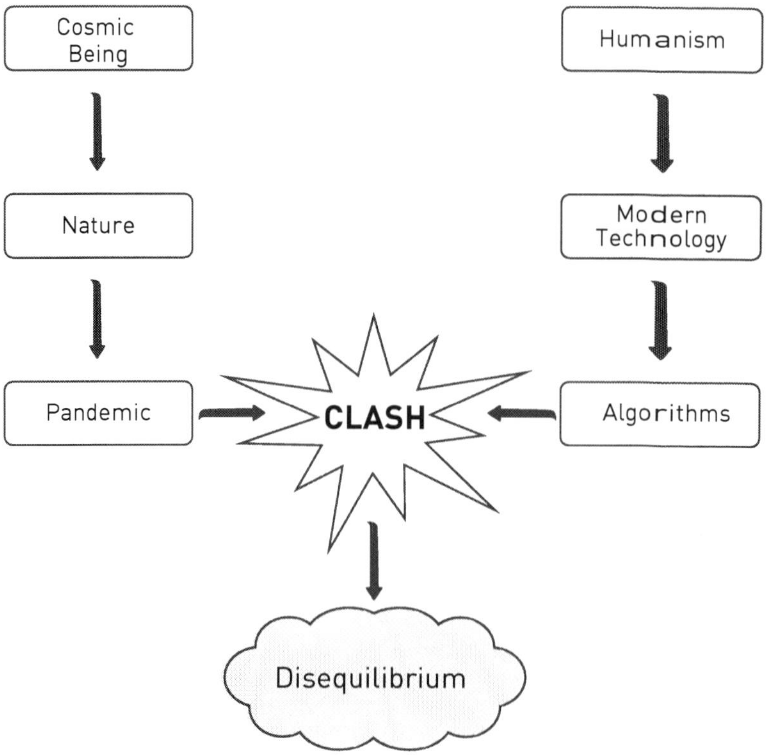

Figure 26: Struggle between Nature and Technology

THE BATTLE FOR A DIGITAL MYTHOLOGY

Post-Liberalism

I have described how the notion of a unified self is undermined by the supply of digital intoxicants that reduce humanity to algorithms programmed to gratify separate impulses. As AI seduces people into life on autopilot and happily surrendering their agency to digital networks, their free will gets eroded. The ultimate consequence of reductionism will be that individualism and free will practically vanish.

The social sciences are disciplines for the study of human society. They have been practiced mostly through the lens of liberalism, which is a product of humanism. Disciplines like economics, sociology, and political science will fade away in their present form as AI undermines the assumptions at the very foundation of humanism and liberalism. Artificial Intelligence-based research has already taken over marketing and will soon dominate public policymaking and the cognitive sciences. The shift away from individualism, free will, and agency—the outsourcing of our choices to algorithms—is crumbling the social sciences and the structures that maintain the social sciences are now being threatened.

Individual Free Will ➔ Humanism ➔ Liberalism ➔ Materialism ➔ Artificial Intelligence ➔ Death of Social Sciences

The rise of social sciences in the 1800s was a European enterprise that combined premises from Biblical ideas with newer Enlightenment thought. The social sciences served as the lens that formulated colonial myths about colonized peoples. In anthropology, data about societies was collected and analyzed to build descriptive models. European anthropologists were sent to study Indian villages and communities to help the East India Company devise plans for dividing and ruling so-called inferior cultures. They used their cultural models to sow discord among villagers and communities and create tension between neighboring kings. The manipulated societal maps were then taught to the newly minted elites among the colonized Indians. Modern social sciences continue this form of colonialism; India's leading social scientists today owe their cherished social theories to this legacy.

Before the development of AI, data collection on society was labor intensive; the simplest of projects could take decades to complete. Researchers had to patiently document individual behavior, categorize people into clusters and groups, analyze the findings to reveal patterns, and finally construct models for a given society. Armed with the compiled data, European scholars and policymakers devised social theories on a given society. These detailed psychological, emotional, and social-political predictive behavioral algorithms guided their strategies toward specific societies and subgroups. Colonialists used the insights to better negotiate with—and eventually completely control—colonized peoples.

Artificial Intelligence accelerates that approach by using machine learning to create the detailed psychological and social maps of collective identities: for example, tracking and modeling behaviors based on ethnic groups, specific age brackets, cultural groups, even entire countries. Analytics based on AI is fast replacing traditional social sciences research. Machine learning is doing the research that social psychologists used to do, and doing it much faster, on a much larger scale, and more accurately. The old-school of social sciences is a house of cards about to be toppled.

Artificial Intelligence's insights are far more extensive than what was possible with traditional methods, and the models for manipulating this data are much better, providing increasing complexity and inventiveness. As noted in Chapter 1, human programmers no longer even must supply the behavioral algorithms of a community because supervised and unsupervised learning systems analyze the examples and devise the algorithms. Models are built quickly, tested, and improved in real time through continuous feedback.

Clearly, machine learning will provide the next generation of models that replace the existing social sciences, rendering obsolete the disciplines of anthropology, sociology, and political science in their present form. For understanding and theorizing about cultures and subcultures, *AI will become the engine for creating new consensuses on social matters.* Algorithms developed by machine learning systems will first augment social scientists, and eventually, replace them.

David Hume and the New Social Justice

A new narrative, in the meanwhile, is being formulated to supply the meaning of social justice. To understand this trend in historical terms, it is helpful to note that nearly three hundred years ago, the Scottish philosopher David Hume (1711-76) imagined a similar situation in which society faced extreme circumstances. His thought experiment explored what would happen in a world where only a few people could enjoy the best things life has to offer, while the majority have very little. According to Hume, the elites in such a situation would conclude that "the strict laws of justice are suspended" and would "give place to the stronger motives of necessity and self-preservation".[231]

Hume envisioned a two-tier society, with the lower tier "a species of creatures, intermingled with men, which, though rational, were possessed of such inferior strength, both of body and mind, that they were incapable of all resistance".[232] He wondered what the relationship between the two social tiers would be like, concluding:

> Our intercourse with them could not be called society, which supposes a degree of equality; but absolute command on the one side, and servile obedience on the other. Whatever we covet, they must instantly resign:

> Our permission is the only tenure, by which they hold their possessions: Our compassion and kindness the only check, by which they curb our lawless will.[233]

In other words, he says that the disempowered humans in such a scenario would be like pets at the mercy of the elites. Civilization, as we know it today would, he believed, collapse because "the restraints of justice and property, being totally useless, would never have place in so unequal a confederacy".

Hume lived at a time when this kind of genocide was already taking place against the natives of America. The Europeans had declared the native peoples subhuman and not worthy of rights. The Church had issued its decree known as the Doctrine of Discovery, which asserted that all lands, property, and even human beings who were supposedly discovered by explorers in the New World became the exclusive property of Christians because only the Christians were considered civilized. A key rationalization cited by the white Christian conquerors was a sense of entitlement based on their presumed superiority over the natives. The relocation of the natives to what became known as reservations was, after all, in the natives' own best interest. On the reservations they would be safer, be able to exist in their traditional lifestyle, and have their basic needs met more efficiently by the whites.

In reality the natives of America were being ghettoized in their own homeland. No less than intellectual giants such as Immanuel Kant (1724-1804) and G.W.F. Hegel (1770-1831) reinforced racist ideas of genocide against the native peoples of America.

We like to presume that humankind has advanced in the past three centuries since those events. But how then do we account for the Nazis herding the Jews into ghettos and then into the Holocaust concentration camps rather recently? This atrocity was perpetrated by the Germans who were the best educated and scientifically advanced European nation at the time.

Fast forward to today. Westerners are used to material abundance and are psychologically unable to deal with scarcity and rationing of critical resources. Covid-19 forced the medical establishment, especially in severely stressed countries like Italy, to make ethical and moral tradeoffs on which patients were treated and on what basis scarce medical resources ought to be allocated. Doctors were compelled to put a hard value on individuals to decide who got life-saving care and who did not. Should a strong young person who is more likely to recover be given preference because he will be more economically productive in society? Should he receive treatment priority over an older person with a lower chance of survival and less economic value to society? Unfortunately, wealth also played a role, as evidenced by how many rich people were quickly tested for Covid-19 multiple times, while ordinary citizens with less means were left out during the first several weeks in the US.

Before the pandemic, similar decisions were routinely being made regarding who gets a scarce organ transplant. When the goal is to maximize the number of lives saved using the probabilities of various outcomes, people seem to accept such a system because they see it as an objective and fair algorithm. In times of crisis, the ethics of life and death assumes a more materialistic, pragmatic bias.

This can lead to the disturbing question: Can we really count on human morality when overpopulation forces tough choices like the ones in Hume's thought experiment? I submit that we cannot. Despite our impressive gains in mastering the material world through advanced technology, humanity has yet to make significant progress in mastering the inner world of our own consciousness. *It is entirely plausible that we will see digital fascism as the return of a new and much more virulent form of fascism.*

The potential risk we now face is too substantial to ignore, and wishful thinking will not solve the problem. We must have the audacity to explore and address the forthcoming impact of AI on society.

The thought experiment outlined below may be aesthetically uncomfortable, but I offer it in the hope that it has the pragmatic effect of freeing us from delusion.

The Emergence of Superrich Superhumans

Chapter 2 presented my thesis that large numbers of humans are likely to lose much of their economic relevance as they become superfluous in the workforce. They will no longer possess the buying power that makes them valuable as consumers. In a world where power becomes increasingly concentrated and machines rapidly outsmart humans, billions are at risk of being deemed useless.

At the other end of the spectrum, the new elites will be able to augment themselves both physically and cognitively by integrating a powerful combination of biological enhancements, both inside their bodies and with external AI systems.

Research breakthroughs will facilitate the complete regeneration of tissues and organs. When such advanced medical technology combines with artificial organs, average lifespans will be extended to levels unfathomable today. Lifespan extension technologies will significantly disrupt the insurance industry, healthcare systems, pension funds, and all aspects of financial and estate planning.

Because machines like computers and cars are merely the sum of their parts, they can be kept running forever by continually replacing various parts. The lifespan of a machine is theoretically unlimited. Owners can choose how long they want to keep a machine running, evaluating factors such as the cost involved in replacing and upgrading parts and the level of performance desired. Similarly, once human beings are deconstructed down to the sum of their various components, lifespan extension will become a matter of replacing, repairing, or re-growing any malfunctioning part.

Artificial life extension will bring significant philosophical, ethical, and quality-of-life issues to the fore. When and according to whose choice should an individual die? Since life extension is bound to be costly, will it only be available to the ultra-wealthy? Should a corporation be able to sell life extension for a hefty price, and if so, could there be subscription models of pricing in which the consumer pays a monthly fee to be kept alive? Outcries about inequality will devolve into debates regarding existential issues on the very meaning of life and death.

A different form of immortality will be afforded by the development of memory transplants. Already, scientists have demonstrated the ability to transmit memory artificially into lab rats. The advent of such technology will mean that people could transfer memories electronically via the internet and download them into patients suffering from Alzheimer's or other neurological impairments. The same technology could be used to insert specific memories into soldiers to enhance their battleground prowess. Hackers could misuse such technology by infiltrating individual identities to appropriate intimate knowledge or by inserting fake memories into people's minds to confuse and manipulate them.

In theory, before people die their entire memory could be downloaded and subsequently transplanted into a new body, enabling virtual reincarnation. Such an artificial reincarnation would be different from the natural one described by the dharmic traditions. The dharma posits that reincarnated beings do not remember details of the past life, whereas artificial memory transplants could potentially enable individuals to retain memories of their past life while living in a different body.

Should humanity have the ability to choose which moments from the past people may forget (or digitally delete), which personal aspects to enhance with fantasies or false memories, which experiences to save or sell to others, and which thoughts to selectively transfer over to a new body? Should the government be the arbitrator of such decisions by enacting laws and regulations? Should private corporations that control the data and the technology be allowed to perform such procedures and make these decisions?

The elites who control this technology will start planning for the day when it will be technologically possible for their bodies to continue living indefinitely. Death will essentially become a technical glitch that can be avoided—that is, for those who can afford it.

This will also create a whole new dimension of haves and have-nots. The elites will be the rich few who can afford to buy technological enhancements and augmented biology. Ordinary humans will, by extension, be inferior to this class of quasi-immortals.

Figure 27 shows the process by which this evolution toward a futurist post-human body might advance.

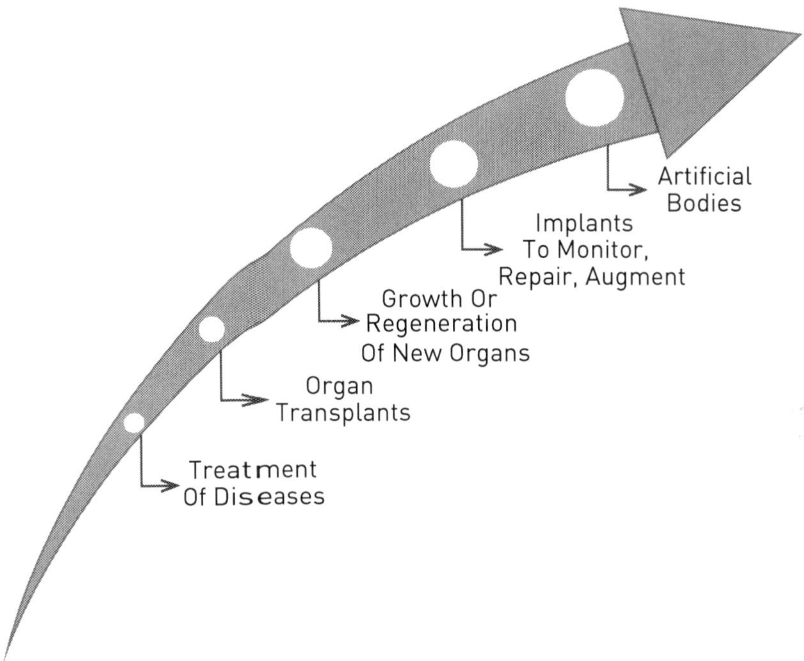

Figure 27: The Future of Humanity

The biotech transformations will culminate in what may be considered the emergence of a new species of superhumans. The integration of AI to upgrade humans might come about with three innovations:

1. In the first innovation, human genetic code is rewritten, and the brain rewired; biochemistry is altered. Humans can grow new limbs and organs. Biological creatures have evolved slowly over eons by using the environment as the supplier of big data for learning; future technology will enable rapid evolution through artificial reprogramming of biology.

2. In the second innovation, the organic body will merge with nonorganic devices such as bionic limbs. Nanorobots will be able to navigate through the bloodstream to cure illnesses and regenerate tissues. The use of implants will skyrocket. The brain will wirelessly connect directly to external machines.
3. Finally, some portions of humans could be transformed into a nonorganic living entity. Human personality could be captured in, or transferred to, intelligent software that may not be limited to operating on organic hardware.

In this direction, Elon Musk (founder of SpaceX and CEO of Tesla) has invested in Brain–Machine Interfaces (BMI) research with the objective of merging the fields of robotic surgery, neuroscience, and AI. The hope is for robots to surgically implant minuscule BMI chips in the brain to augment memory and analytical capabilities. The three-fold goals of Musk's Neuralink venture are (1) treating brain disorders and helping people that have suffered brain damage; (2) creating a brain–machine interface; and (3) building toward a potential symbiosis with AI.[234] The US's DARPA is also at the cutting edge of research into brain–machine futures and is developing an implantable neural interface that will link a million nerve cells simultaneously.[235]

Technological interventions raise issues that current legal, ethical, and spiritual experts are simply not knowledgeable enough to address. Nevertheless, some recent best-selling authors consider such advances desirable and rooted in principles of scientific realism. According to them, the self—and its freedom—is merely an illusion and a myth. For instance, Noah Harari rationalizes that the superhuman of the future is not only inevitable but justified by science. He views it as a path to artificial immortality, artificial happiness, and even artificial divinity. Because he rejects the existence of a human self, any discussion about human rights is dismissed as a sham.

Much of the discussion in these pages is speculative but plausible and this is certainly the trajectory driving the research trends. Even if such futurist technologies are only partially successful, and even if they take several decades to materialize, the mere existence of such long-term possibilities will have a dramatic impact on our society in the near future. The dismantling of narratives we take for granted about the nature of the human self, free will, and personal responsibility will have a profound effect on our development as a species.

The figure below outlines the human progression in a cause-and-effect approximate sequence. The following section explains how the depopulation might be carried out.

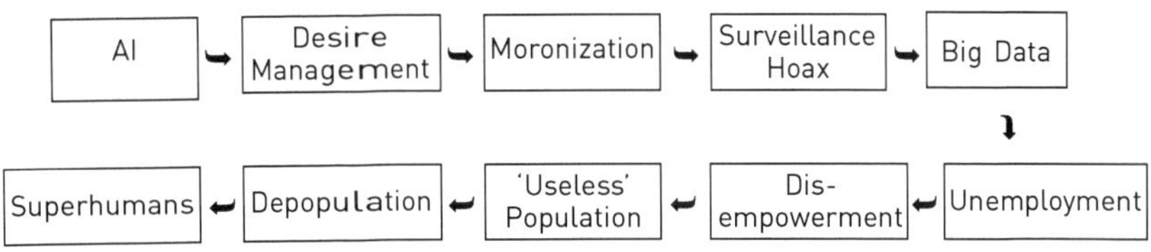

HAPPY MORONS AND DEPOPULATION

The Useless Masses

The new elites would aspire to a sense of all-powerfulness over nature and society, effectively giving them the status of the mythical gods of ancient Greece. At the other end of the spectrum, the unemployed will become further disempowered because their economic value as consumers will decline. The world will enter a period in which ordinary humans surrender their agency to the new elite, and there will be exploitation, chaos, conflict, and instability. Overpopulated countries like India, where the public and the leaders are insufficiently educated about advanced technologies and their social implications, will be especially vulnerable.

What then is to be done with these billions of humans whom Noah Harari, author of numerous best-selling books on the future, classifies as "useless"?[236] These are the people who produce nothing in the economy and hence do not make viable consumers. A period of disequilibrium will emerge in which the superrich will be divided into idealist and pragmatist camps.

- The idealists, being full of liberal rhetoric and activism, will advocate for ordinary humans to retain their basic rights and dignity.
- The pragmatists will wield the hard power and treat overpopulation as an epidemic that requires immediate and drastic action.

Some reports on AI want us to believe that the superrich are genuinely interested in helping the unemployed masses and propose schemes to channel the generosity of the wealthy to help alleviate the lot of the new downtrodden. These optimists propose that the so-called useless people will be given government handouts or some guaranteed minimum income. Such proposals assume that the newly minted superrich will subsidize the lifestyles of the poor majority from a sense of compassion.

This kind of idealism, however, cannot be expected to last indefinitely. The pragmatic capitalists are out to make money, not to support the billions of people that will no longer be required as workers. Heavy taxation of the superrich has never been politically popular for long.

As has happened time and again throughout history, the idealists will gradually and begrudgingly concede defeat to the pragmatists. I have discussed these two ideological postures as the good cops and bad cops, respectively.[237] Eventually, the good cops acquiesce after declaring they tried hard and the outcome offered by the bad cops is the best available.

The superhuman elites will at some point begin to perceive the masses as a parasitic liability once they have been drained of their data and it will become important to regulate their numbers. Eventually, the idea of large-scale depopulation will become a topic of public debate.

An argument will be put forth that gradually rolling back the world population to the level of two hundred years ago would not be a horrible plan. It would be argued that in a less-populated world the inhabitants would be happier and in harmony with each other and with nature. This would also solve the global warming crisis. The impact of the coronavirus pandemic is already triggering discussions on how the human overutilization of resources acts like an infestation inflicting disaster on Mother Earth. The case will be made that a small population would be able to afford the good life of augmentation with the new technologies.

The elites must plan all this well in advance. Before they will be able to disenfranchise the masses, they will need to develop and perfect various emotional and psychological management technologies that transform humans into easily controlled zombies. The transfer of power from ordinary humans to the elites will have to be done in a subtle, nonthreatening, and disguised way designed to keep the masses oblivious to what is happening. Community leaders, especially those that are icons on social media, will be incentivized to promote this view. A false consensus will be manufactured by the digital systems through the manipulation of fake news, shifts in societal norms, and moral equivocation.

We cannot predict exactly how the proponents of depopulation will seek to accomplish their agenda. Thus, the salient question: How can a population of several billion humans be managed emotionally and aesthetically while their rights are being eroded and they are being implicitly downgraded to a subspecies? Will it occur through natural means? Will the population decline voluntarily? Or will new laws and social or economic pressures push the population toward such a fate?

Whenever society decides to put the brakes on new births, it will take at least fifty years for sufficient numbers of people to die natural deaths and lower the population dramatically. This means that regardless of how aggressively birth rates are curbed to reduce the population to manageable levels, it will take two generations of "useless" people having to be supported somehow. In other words, the path to AI-based utopia must pass through a dystopian phase lasting fifty years. Maintaining billions of individuals physically and mentally with dignity will be a humanitarian challenge for at least half a century.

The *Crash* of Civilization

Once AI has taken control of the social sciences research apparatus, it will create a new grand narrative that will make the obsolescence of human agency and labor seem normal, even desirable. For instance, some thinkers already recommend that to resolve the crisis of unemployment, society should decouple work from social status. Unemployed people would then be afforded human dignity by being guaranteed basic needs including entertainment, and the loss of employment would not carry its current social stigma. In effect, these authors are preparing humanity for large-scale unemployment by somehow making it desirable to passively enjoy the sensory delights offered by new AI technologies without having to work.

People will accept this shift as a gift: they will no longer have to work or even make choices for themselves. They will gladly become subservient to whatever customized pleasures are doled out to them; machines will run their lives for them, for their own good. Dumbed-down people will be provided with all their emotional needs and gratification, which will, in turn, make them even more passive and easily controlled, thus paving the way for a small number of artificially augmented superhumans to become the new elite.

I call such a disruption of society the **crash of civilization.** During this period, the humans being downgraded will still need to be fed and have their emotional and psychological needs met.

The transition might involve governments to outsource the management of surplus people in a humane manner to private contractors. Private industry in the US already operates prisons, drug detox and rehab facilities, homeless shelters, homes for the elderly and challenged, and institutions for tens of millions of citizens deemed useless in terms of their economic value. Many such facilities are currently run under government-funded programs. The scenario being discussed will dramatically increase the need for such sanctuaries for the disempowered.

I refer to the individuals who will be managed this way as happy morons. They will be neither productive citizens because no jobs will be available for them, nor consumers, because consumers require money to buy the technologies that will keep them happy. Rather, happy morons could turn into a nuisance and social liability, deadbeats who must be tolerated and dealt with in a humanitarian manner. *But as voters with legal rights, these people will need to be kept happy using some means.*

Ironically, the new AI-based emotional management technologies discussed earlier will likely be applied to maintain the "useless" people in some form of happy, i.e., docile, state. Keeping these billions of surplus people in a virtual state of pleasure, delivered by technologies such as VR and AR, will be an attractive proposition. Artificial Intelligence suppliers will tout this as a positive use of technology for the psychological management of people deemed to be parasites. Perhaps, one of the applications of AR would be to give people the experience of virtual children since the physical birth of children would have been curtailed.

The AI technology that created the demographic crisis will also develop solutions to solve it in a manner acceptable to the sensibilities and legalities of that time. The happy morons will be augmented by technology for binge-watching movies, indulging in artificial sexual gratification, enjoying fantasy vacations, and becoming artificially intoxicated with the help of implants. Letting them escape happily in a decadent, degenerate, and passive state would bypass ethical dilemmas of human rights abuses, and at the same time get the vast majority of human population out of the way for the superhumans to take custody of the world.

The task will require sophistication in the psychological management of the masses. As noted in Chapter 4, the aestheticization of power describes the use of aesthetics to secure and maintain political power over the masses even as they are suffering in a pragmatic sense. The use of aesthetics as a cover for pragmatic goals will become a strategic tool in managing overpopulation. The elites and their technology will offer a variety of ways for the useless humans to indulge in pleasurable, feel-good activities and hold lofty ideas about themselves. As a widening range of entertainment services become available, on terms set by the new establishment, AI technology will further engineer and mold behavior.

Humans will have the capability to live in a fantasy land concocted through VR and AR products, including implants, wearables, genetic modifications, and neuroscientific manipulations, as well as mood-altering or psychotropic stimulants, sedative hypnotics, and hallucinogens. An entire industry will spring up just for the purpose of enabling large numbers of people to live as happy morons. The masses will effectively be disarmed in a make-believe world.

At the hedonistic extreme, promiscuity will become a tool for manipulation and suppression. For example, an AI application could reward individuals with orgasms on demand or metered at a certain frequency. The application would become addictive and thus serve as a psychological weapon for wielding control over people. The frequency, intensity, and type of experience could also be withheld as punishment, resulting in withdrawal symptoms.

The effect will be a new kind of colonization: the conquering of human aesthetics through machines. Figure 28 shows the happy moron syndrome as a self-perpetuating process. Large numbers of our youth today are already unconsciously serving as experimental subjects in testing and perfecting the machine learning algorithms for aesthetic management. Ironically, they seem to enjoy the process of surrendering their sovereignty.

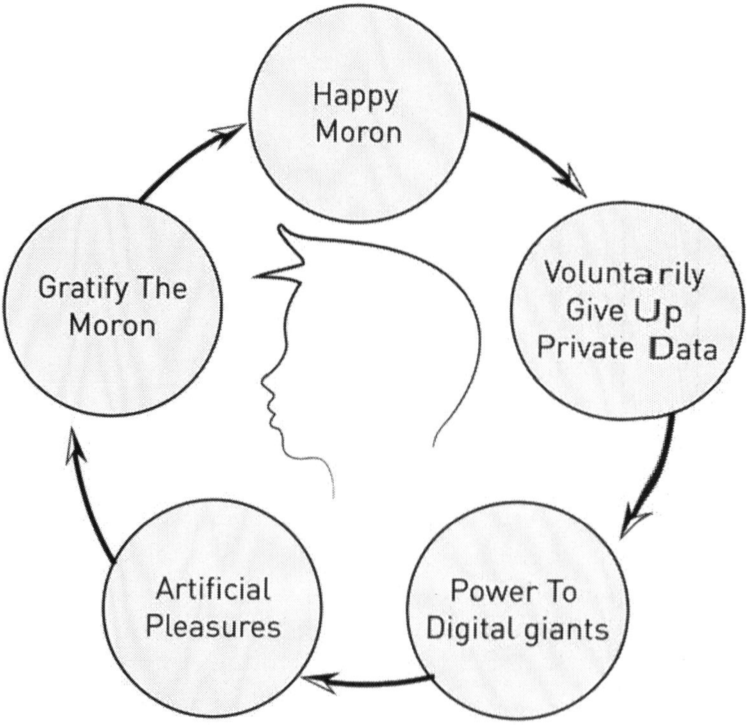

Figure 28: Self-Perpetuation of AI

Figure 29 on the next page summarizes the chaos, conflict, and uncertainty that will likely characterize the prolonged period of inevitable disequilibrium.

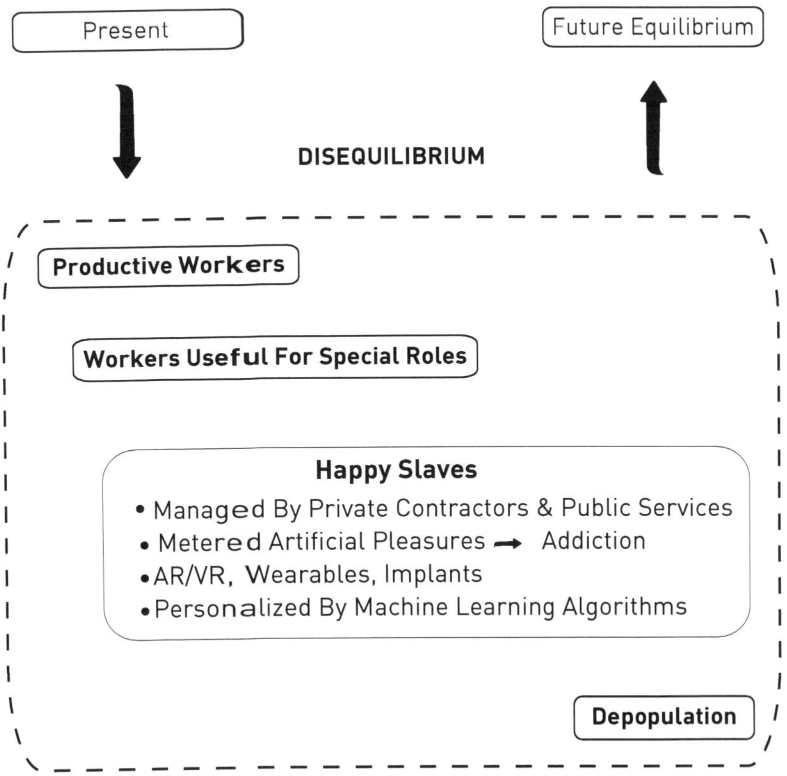

Figure 29: Trends Toward the Future

THE RETURN OF THE GODS

After several decades of this digital genocide of sorts to reduce the population painlessly, a new equilibrium will be established. The superhumans, as the elite minority, and ordinary humans, the somewhat-reduced masses, will learn to coexist, albeit with an asymmetrical power balance. For the drastically reduced population, life will be free from many of the problems facing the world today, such as poverty, global warming, wars, and conflicts. The world could be seen as utopian after all, but only for a few.

The thought experiment outlined in the preceding pages speculates a futurist scenario in which the superrich inherit the earth but they need to implement a messy depopulation without inflicting pain. They will want to upgrade themselves into superhumans with the use of biotechnologies that enable them to live an excessive lifespan, grow new organs, and incorporate AI into both their bodies and their minds. In essence, *they will think of themselves to be superior to ordinary humans in the same way as humans today compare themselves to animals.*

According to Harari, one of the leading proponents of this futurist mythology, such technologies will eventually incorporate humans within the Internet of Things because of which humans will cease to exist separately from the digital collective existence.

> Humans are merely tools for creating the Internet-of-All-Things which may eventually spread out from planet Earth to pervade the whole galaxy and even the whole universe. This cosmic data processing system would be like God. It will be everywhere and will control everything and humans are destined to merge into it.[238]

Meaning and purpose from a human perspective would be completely redefined.

> As the global data processing system becomes all-knowing and all-powerful, so connecting to the system becomes the source of all meaning. Humans want to merge into the data flow because when you are part of the data flow you are part of something much bigger than yourself. Traditional religions assured you that

> your every word and action was part of some great cosmic plan, and that God watched you every minute and cared about all your thoughts and feelings. Data religion now says that your every word and action is part of the great data flow, that the algorithms are constantly watching you and that they care about everything you do and feel. Most people like this very much.[239]
>
> Homo sapiens will disappear, human history will come to an end and a completely new kind of process will begin, which people like you and me cannot comprehend.[240]

Research is already underway that seeks to *connect brains directly to each other in a sort of internet of brains*. The Nobel Prize-winning physicist Murray Gell-Mann envisioned such networks, through which "thoughts and feelings would be completely shared with none of the selectivity or deception that language permits".[241]

Such a collective consciousness would be vastly different from that envisioned by Indian philosophers and gurus like Sri Aurobindo.[242]

Futurists also speculate that algorithms might one day have the same status as persons and corporate entities, enabling them to own assets, make decisions, and have the agency to act in their own interest. Successful algorithms could amass wealth, employ staff, and own land. Algorithms might even clash with each other for a greater share of power and resources.

In effect, superhumans ruling such digital existence and their digital agents will become like the Greek gods and Vedic devatas worshipped for their unfathomable powers: Google-devata, Facebook-devata, Twitter-devata. Just as contemporary humanism and liberalism exploit everything as property and as an inherent right, the new superhumans of tomorrow will see themselves as gods who own the world. They will consider the exploitation of humans as a pragmatic and unavoidable necessity, much like we currently treat animals. Humans could potentially one day be viewed as no more than specimens in lab studies, slaves and beasts of mental and physical burden, or pets that must please their masters in exchange for the gift of a good life.

PART TWO

BATTLEGROUND INDIA

We need to make Artificial Intelligence in India and make Artificial Intelligence work for India.

—Narendra Modi, prime minister of India[243]

6

STRESS TESTING INDIA

What, indeed, are those faults upon whose strength and weakness a wise man should reflect with the aid of intelligence and reason?

—*Mahabharata*[244]

One should speak truly, whether his words be good or bad, hateful or pleasing....

—*Mahabharata*[245]

CHAPTER HIGHLIGHTS

- The impact of AI will be especially heavy in India's case because of high-stress factors such as overpopulation, low education levels, excessive unemployment, social, political and economic divisions, and a range of emotional vulnerabilities.
- The issues raised in this book are seldom discussed by India's intellectuals in public forums.
- After centuries of colonization, repression, and emotional and political manipulation, India seems to have lost the creative drive for discovery and innovation, preferring instead to provide the labor to support other countries' development of intellectual property.

- Despite being a global leader in software as recently as only a decade ago, India is now dependent on imported technologies mainly from the US and China.
- Worldwide disruptions caused by Covid-19 offer India a chance to take back some of the ground it has lost to other countries in recent years.

Artificial Intelligence and related technologies will impact every major industry and institution during the present decade. This tectonic shift is creating a new multi-trillion-dollar economy worldwide, even as it decimates some facets of the current economy. It is nothing short of a new industrial revolution, creating a new world order with important shifts in the centers of power. New global superpowers will exert an imperialistic control over countries that lag. At the individual level as well, new haves and have-nots will emerge based on their proximity to this technology.

The impact of AI on society will not be the same for everyone. Nor will the available remedies be uniformly applicable. It will manifest differently from place to place, industry to industry, and even from one individual to another. For example, driverless cars will have more impact in the US than in low-wage countries where human drivers are inexpensive. The education system's standards and capacity in one place will make it easier to re-train large numbers of workers for careers in the new tech economy, whereas re-education will not be as feasible in places where the existing education infrastructure is weak. Wealthy communities will be able to invest their capital and benefit from the opportunities of AI, while those without financial capital will be left stranded.

My research on the likely impact of AI on India has entailed numerous conversations with thought leaders and the study of the written materials available. NITI Aayog, India's leading government policy think tank, has provided helpful reports on the subject. I also recently read *Bridgital Nation: Solving Technology's People Problem* written by the Indian industrialist, Natarajan Chandrasekaran, chairman of Tata Sons. As the title implies, it specifically addresses AI's impact on India's people. Appendix C gives my critique of this book and explains why I consider its approach insufficient.

Most reports I have read on AI's impact on India adopt the framework used by Western industry analysts as their starting point and fine tune the conclusions by plugging in Indian statistics. There is a lack of fresh studies that start from the ground up in India, beginning at the grassroots and working up, rather than going top-down from the West to Indian corporates and then further down.

Some of the glaring blind spots are as follows:

1. The focus of most reports is on the big corporates. The impact on the bottom 500 million Indians in economic status, if considered at all, is addressed as an afterthought.
2. Most reports do not build financial models to accurately estimate the capital and operating expenses involved in implementing AI. Their forecasts are largely based on surveying industry executives and employees with leading questions of a positive kind, while avoiding the troubling issues except in passing. Many respondents are not sufficiently informed about AI to give useful views of the future.[246]
3. The problems of unemployment and inequalities are brushed aside as non-issues: *The conclusions of some Western reports that new jobs will replace old ones is*

quickly assumed to be applicable to India without due diligence on the details. What is not considered are the following:

a. The new jobs created by AI will help a different social-economic demographic group, i.e. those with high standards of education that very few Indian youths get. These few privileged youths with good education are quickly bought off and plucked away to build intellectual property for Western multinationals. But the jobs lost will be from the lower- and middle-class workers that are poorly educated and insufficiently skilled.
b. Many of the new jobs in AI will be geographically concentrated in places like Silicon Valley and Bengaluru. This will exacerbate the rich versus poor geographical divides within India as well as between developed and developing countries.
c. The new AI related jobs will go to the youth and not the middle-aged workers displaced at the peak of their careers. The speed of disruption is too fast to allow the present generation of workers to continue employment for their remaining careers. They will become obsolete in their vulnerable middle-age. This is a serious inter-generational disruption.
d. The financial burden of the massive re-education of millions of workers is not something we can assume the corporates will automatically do. The rosy promises of re-training workers are simply not backed by credible commitments. In fact, some reports suggest that such talk by industry leaders serves as good public relations to mask the calamity of unemployment, by kicking the can down the road rather than dealing with it.

   e. The fallback position of universal income for everyone is touted as a magic wand, but this is the same old idea of taxing the rich to fund the poor that has never worked on a sustained basis.
4. India's newly minted billionaires, the new zamindars and robber-barons of India, are simply in denial of the problems.[247]
5. India's big data assets are being siphoned off by foreign social media giants right under the eyes of ignorant politicians, bureaucrats, and industrialists.
6. The reports are silent on the major issue raised in Chapter 3 concerning psychological and emotional control of users by the digital platforms, and the resulting mental colonization by foreign ideologies.
7. The reports do not consider the national security threat of *breaking India* forces becoming AI-enabled and managed from their foreign nexuses.

As mentioned earlier, reports on AI in India are targeted at business leaders and cater to those vested interests. Even reports written by government entities do not adequately address the broader social impact that I have raised.[248]

The silence on AI's social impact is especially troubling. Other social issues like genetically modified foods, public health, water shortages, social injustices, and many others rightfully get the space deserved in public forums. Why not AI? One reason might be that policymakers and public intellectuals who ought to be concerned are invested in the foreign platforms for their personal reputation and therefore do not wish to rock the boat.[249]

India has recently started taking AI seriously, but the response is weak and has come rather late. China and the US have a head start of more than a decade, and it will be difficult for India to catch up. The ramifications of being left behind will be serious. Further, India's path forward is crippled by several factors.

- India's budget for AI development is tiny compared to levels in the US and China.
- The main opportunity in AI that has been identified is for Indians to supply labor for foreign clients. Subordination to other countries will perpetuate the problem of Indians serving as the labor class that builds intellectual property assets for others.
- Many AI start-ups in India are funded by foreign companies with deep pockets and a tentacled hold, so that the occasional Indian success story is quickly acquired and digested into the global brand. Those that are funded domestically often look to sell out to foreign tech giants as their exit strategy. Examples include Halli Labs and Sigmoid Labs, both AI start-ups in India that got acquired by Google.
- Many Indian start-ups are "me-too" copycats offering little original intellectual property leadership—mimicking a foreign platform, Uber, Amazon, or Airbnb, etc.
- Even the government's NITI Aayog, which reports directly to the prime minister, is taking the easy path of joining hands with foreign giants like Google to develop India's ecosystem for AI rather than developing its own strategy.[250]

If these trends persist, India will continue to export raw labor, and import the finished technology, rather than actively participating in the creation of new technology that is *owned* by India.

China developed a comprehensive and focused national high-tech strategy about twenty-five years ago and has implemented it brilliantly. In the US, the AI strategy is not dependent on the government; instead, large companies like Google, Facebook, Amazon, Apple and Microsoft each has a robust strategy driving its special place in the AI revolution.

In India, most commentators on economic, social, or political matters do not appear to have even a fundamental knowledge of certain strategic issues discussed in this book, much less to have an adequate response. NITI Aayog's AI strategies are rudimentary, marginal, and too weak to make India a leader. Responding to China's lead, in 2017 the Indian government did create an AI task force for economic transformation. In June 2018, NITI Aayog put out a 115-page report, *National Strategy for Artificial Intelligence*. Unfortunately, the report is disappointing, being little more than an introductory-level survey of the AI field, along with a laundry list of wishes and dreams. It neither delves into the deep structures of the industry's global ecosystem nor addresses the range of issues raised in this book. In particular, the report ignores the psychological invasion of the masses by foreign digital media, an issue discussed at length in Chapter 3. However, what the report does acknowledge is that India is late in the game. To their credit, India's planners have created and funded some concrete programs that use AI in healthcare, agriculture, and defense.

Laying bare these hard truths is unpleasant for me. However, because I care deeply for India and Indians and share concern about the future, I offer an analytical and unemotional review of the issues. India is my home and understanding its complexity has been a lifelong passion and pursuit. I am convinced that *the AI revolution will affect India more than other countries*. My views are likely to upset some people, but my intent is to wake up Indians and encourage them to make dramatic changes in their thoughts and actions. I hope my views serve as a counterpoint to the accepted posture.

Medical scenarios, engineering designs, and corporate business plans are routinely subject to stress tests to reveal insights about potential vulnerabilities that might not be obvious. In that sense, stress testing is inherently a negative exercise. Its success is not determined by highlighting what is already known to be strong about the system being examined; rather, its purpose is to put the spotlight on the problems that need more special attention. Similarly, my posture for stress testing India is to offer clarity on the disruptions India is likely to face.

The arrival of AI as a cause for worldwide societal disruption calls for an evaluation of India's ambition of becoming a global superpower. The evaluation should be free from politics, judging, moralizing, and blaming; to be effective it must present objective facts and likely outcomes. The goal of the exercise is to evaluate India's robustness in the emerging world order.

The question whether AI is an existential threat to India is an important exercise at this point because of the country's vulnerabilities: overpopulation, low education levels, Byzantine-like fragmentation, industrial and technological obsolescence, political disruptions, and security threats from formidable neighbors. India's existing equilibrium is precarious due to risks from what I have termed the *breaking India* forces. All these factors make it urgent to engage in an unemotional stress test of India's sovereignty as it relates to the latest technological disruptions.

On a positive note, it must be said that India serves as a unique role model for many developing countries because of its impressive recent economic performance despite the burdens of its colonial history. Beating all negative predictions, it has maintained a stable democracy for over seventy years and given voice to the largest number of voters in the world. India has an amazing track record of scientific study that includes sophisticated fields like space exploration and indigenous research on nuclear energy.

The past few governments have successfully sold the idea of India as a superpower and the vision that the twenty-first century will be the Indian century. Many legitimate points support this claim. India has had several years of solid GDP growth even though it is inconsistent and uneven across different regions and segments of the population. Its economic activity is in the top two or three positions in the world in several key areas. There has been a remarkable digitalization across all segments of industry and civic society, as well as development of national backbones on an unprecedented scale. Private companies like Bajaj Auto are role models for beating the Chinese in manufacturing and creating a global footprint.[251]

The productivity of Indian workers has increased significantly in recent years. India has a huge entrepreneurial, innovative, and well-educated class of movers and shakers. A small, albeit significant percentage of its youth is functioning at the highest levels of innovation around the world and making noteworthy contributions at the cutting edge of technology. India has the world's largest human resource of software engineers and until recently it was the leading software house serving the world. The country is also home to the world's largest youth population, which could mature into a powerful workforce with proper education and investments. Large populations lead to high levels of consumption, which translates into strong demand for goods, which in turn can ignite a manufacturing economy.

In addition to economic development, India has also made structural reforms to strengthen its foundations, ranging from integrating its states to removing some sources of social fragmentation. But many of these reforms are merely repairing the defects built into the national structure at the time of independence.[252]

India accomplished these feats and more without once in its history seeking to invade, colonize, or oppress other countries, engage in theft of intellectual property or industrial espionage that characterizes modern China. In prior centuries, India exported its civilization's assets to China without demanding anything in return and without attempting to assert hegemony. Even though India has suffered at the hands of numerous foreign invaders, it never attempted to expand its territory.

However, good intentions, especially in the present circumstances, are not enough to offset India's daunting challenges. The question to be addressed is: Will these accomplishments be enough to offset the challenging trends discussed in this book, or are they too little and too late? This is no time to hide behind a false sense of security and complacency.

India's pride often includes the feeling that it is the *vishvaguru*, or the guru of the world, at least in a spiritual sense. But what is seldom discussed in these proclamations is that such a lofty status also brings corresponding karmic responsibilities. In claiming such a status, has India succeeded or failed in its responsibilities?

Indeed, there is great enthusiasm in India about becoming a global soft power. For instance, India has adopted the posture of leading the world's yoga movement and is starting to do the same in **Ayurveda**. The film industry and other popular cultural movements have already become established in the global discourse as Indian exports.

However, the following reality check needs to be considered.

- *Culture ≠ soft power*: Just because a country has a wonderful and robust popular culture does not necessarily mean that it has turned this into any power per se. *Soft power is the ability to influence others' policies according to one's own interests.* Culture, exotica, and tourism are separate entities from soft power. It is a persuasive power over others in a pragmatic sense. Only when culture is transformed into concrete influence over others does it become soft power. Despite their growing popularity, yoga and Ayurveda do not constitute soft power for India. In fact, the Ayurveda certification in Western countries is not controlled from India. The New York-based Yoga Alliance is advancing its goal of standardizing yoga practices decoupled from Indian traditions. The Indian government's efforts to spread awareness of yoga are commendable, but they have not produced any power per se.
- *Hard power as a foundation for soft power*: The real question to ask is whether soft power is sustainable without hard power. Is soft power by itself viable? Or is that merely the fallback position of those that fail to compete in the hard power **kurukshetra** (battleground), a cover for their weakness by claiming soft power as a consolation prize?
- *Individual success ≠ collective soft power*: India is also justifiably proud that its diaspora is asserting its Indian identity and has excelled as doctors,

> technology entrepreneurs, financial industry experts, pharma industry leaders, chefs, filmmakers, and other professionals. Indians head some of the world's largest multinational companies. There is, however, a big difference between the power of individuals for their own personal success and the power of India's institutions for global impact. There is a difference between Indians using their heritage for personal gain and those sacrificing their personal success for a greater national interest.

A recent example of a country's use of soft power is how China has taken over indirect control of the WHO and made it support the country in the Covid-19 controversy. In contrast, consider the triumph with which India sent US president, Donald Trump, his favorite medicine, hydroxychloroquine, and received hugs and a pat on the back through his tweets. Yet within a few weeks, the US Commission on International Religious Freedom listed India among the countries violating religious freedom. Despite the widespread practice of yoga in the US, India has failed to use yoga successfully for impacting US foreign policies. In other words, soft power must be a pragmatic tool, and not about emotions, symbolism, and empty gestures.

It might come as a surprise to some that India had considerable soft power on the world stage some decades back when it was the head of the Non-Aligned Movement (NAM). It demonstrated the ability to easily secure large numbers of votes in the UN and other forums and override the Western powers on many issues. At that time China had no clout globally; but in the past two decades its influence has grown tremendously across Europe, Africa, and South America. Today, China has a large vote bank in the UN among the developing countries and India does not enjoy the same position relative to China it once did. The soft power leadership among developing countries shifted in China's favor after NAM folded. Post the outbreak of Covid-19 there is a fresh anti-China wave that India is leveraging, and the long-term implications could be important.

The scope of my stress test is broad, qualitative and informal. The questions and challenges listed below are examined in the chapters that follow. Each of them is serious enough to deserve further examination.

1. India's overpopulated, but undereducated, public might face levels of unemployment that could precipitate social breakdown in certain communities. Some of the jobs are artificially created by the government, and such employees are only marginally productive. Is the presumptive youth dividend truly a dividend, or is it more of a liability? Clearly, overpopulation has set the country up for unsustainability; so what is being done about this?
2. While aspiring to become a world-class manufacturing base, most of India's workforce is likely to remain immured in low-wage and low-skill tasks relative to better educated countries. India's education system is uncompetitive to produce workers for the industries of the future.
3. Given its lack of effective strategic planning on AI and big data, plus its dependence on American digital platforms and Chinese hardware, India might slip further toward digital colonization. Why does India lag at least a decade behind China in AI and related technologies, despite India having been recently proclaimed as the world leader in

software? How vulnerable is India to becoming a digital colony of the West and China? How do Indian industries, military, and other sectors stack up in addressing the AI-based technological revolution?

4. Traditionally, India's ability to adapt has held its diverse internal forces in equilibrium. But today, Indians are chasing American aspirations, emotional support, validation, and technological platforms. The traditional shock absorbers and self-correcting mechanisms are no longer operative. Is the public psychologically fragile?
5. The moronization of the masses is making people mesmerized by theatrics, pageantry, grandstanding, and personality cults for movie stars, cricketers, politicians, and billionaires alike. Public forums are highly polarized and prone to sensationalism, dirty politics, and petty rivalries. A scan of daily headlines and social media shows insufficient interest in the serious issues discussed in this book. How psychologically vulnerable are the Indian masses because of the shift of their agency to the digital platforms?
6. Artificial Intelligence could disrupt the delicate social equilibrium far worse than any prior upheaval since India's independence. Is the parliamentary democratic system and other core tenets of the Indian Constitution proving successful?
7. India's security involves combating internal insurgencies as well as protecting long borders with hostile neighbors; this requires considerable manpower that consumes the bulk of the military budget. Insufficient funds remain for indigenous R&D and technology related modernization. India is dependent on imported weapons to defend itself.[253] India might find itself facing Pakistani boots on the ground, weaponized by China's AI-based technology.

> How seriously vulnerable is India's national security considering it is lagging in AI?

The goal here is to tease out risk factors that are not adequately being appreciated by the leaders and public intellectuals. Extensive public discussions are the need of the day in which various stakeholders ought to be included. Such explorations will lead to a more formal modeling of India in which all the facts and the policies and responses could be used as big data for training Indian policymakers and monitoring India's stability.

7

TECHNOLOGICAL DEPENDENCE

We have grown over-dependent upon foreign aid in everything from thinking, management, capital, methods of production, technology, etc., to even the standards and forms of consumption. This is not the road to progress and development. We will forget our individuality and become virtual slaves once again.

—Deendayal Upadhyaya, thinker and forerunner of the Bharatiya Janata Party[254]

CHAPTER HIGHLIGHTS

- Because of its awe of the West and inferiority complex about its own capabilities, India has fumbled on many instances by importing foreign solutions that turned out to be short-sighted.
- The wage arbitrage of selling cheap labor in IT made quick and easy profits for a few newly minted billionaires. But these organizations failed to invest in research to create intellectual property for India, and now India's software lead has been replaced by dependency on AI and other technologies. Though large numbers of highly qualified Indians are strategically placed worldwide, India is lagging behind in indigenous research in key areas.

- India's plans for strengthening its manufacturing base to create jobs suffers from lack of technology, well-educated workforce, and end-to-end ecosystem for having its own supply chains. Its top-down corporate investments are inefficient at creating new jobs.
- The population tsunami has not been in tandem with improvements in education or job creation, thereby turning the youth dividend into a nightmare. Yet the topic of population control remains controversial and politically risky.

AWE OF FOREIGN SUPERIORITY

There was a time when the original discoveries by the Indian **rishis** or seers fueled some of the world's greatest intellectual achievements on Indian soil. Under their guidance, large numbers of Indians demonstrated tremendous creativity and built amazing taxonomies of knowledge to organize complex structures in systematic, elegant, and efficient ways.[255]

In recent centuries, however, Indian thinking atrophied in terms of originality and output. Many of the finest Indian minds shifted their focus toward transferring traditional Indian knowledge overseas and helping others recontextualize and digest this knowledge into their own civilizational matrix. Due to a combination of their inferiority complex relative to the West, lack of competent leadership in India, and a general malaise and decline in the civilizational ethos, Indians are too quick to discard traditional methods and replace them with Western ideas. This trend not only continues but has recently intensified. Meanwhile, Westerners have recognized and adopted several good aspects of Indian ways of life.

The wholesale rejection of traditional Indian values and practices in the name of progress has backfired more than once on multiple levels. No doubt India must advance technologically, but such advances should be in sync with scientific appreciation for traditional practices, instead of indiscriminately throwing out traditions in the name of modernization.

Appendix B summarizes numerous examples whereby, in recent times, India's import of foreign knowhow has backfired.

EXPORTING MANPOWER AND IMPORTING TECHNOLOGY

Solid and thorough work, self-discipline by means of noble and orderly action, this is the path by which we shall arrive at a higher national character and evolution.

—Sri Aurobindo[256]

The telecom and information technology revolution, including the spread of the internet, mobile telephones, and social media, has been largely pioneered by Western firms. But it is fair to say that Indian engineers played a significant role as employees and contractors working for the companies that own the intellectual property.[257]

At the same time, India has become one of the largest markets importing these technologies. India is proud of having the fastest-growing installed base of mobile users, but the technology used in the networks is largely US and European, and the handsets are mainly Chinese. India takes pride in that it has the second-highest number of internet users in the world, and this number is growing faster than any other country. India also has among the world's largest installed bases of users on Facebook, WhatsApp, Instagram, Twitter, and YouTube. Indians buy mostly Chinese hardware and use it to access US digital platforms. These facts indicate Indians' eagerness as consumers of foreign products and services, but also highlight the failure of domestic technology developers. Even when manufacturing is done in India due to cost advantages, the research and engineering controlled by foreign entities give them the power over intellectual property.

India has also made considerable progress in the *deployment* of advanced technology. For instance, the Aadhaar Project is the largest unique human identification project in the world. However, it is important to reiterate that consumption and production of technology are two entirely different things. India is transforming into a digital economy largely as a *user* of foreign technology and not as a *producer* of intellectual property.

The diagram below shows that Indian labor is used to make intellectual property for foreign tech giants, which Indian consumers love to buy with great enthusiasm.

Indian tech workers ➔ US & Chinese producers of products & services ➔ Indian consumers

Furthermore, the major information sources on which Indian youth rely for authoritative facts include Wikipedia, Google searches, and YouTube videos—all US platforms. Given the preponderance of Indian languages, it seems odd that Indian companies have not turned this rich heritage into a competitive advantage to build their own native platforms. The availability of rich and precious data in India could also have been used to develop indigenous platforms. But unfortunately, India has missed the boat on these opportunities. When Indian companies do make inroads in unique data collection, they sometimes supply that data to a foreign collaborator.

In contrast, China has developed its own digital media equivalents in every imaginable domain and application. These *made in China* products and services enjoy financial clout and technological leadership.

My concern is that India has failed to adequately educate the youth and enable them to realize their potential. *The civilization that was once a world-class knowledge producer and exporter has become the biggest importer and consumer of foreign products and services—from agriculture to technology.* Even in the realm of accolades, Indians chase Academy Awards, Nobel Prizes, Pulitzer Prizes, Rhodes Scholarships, Fulbright Scholarships, and various other international awards, much more than domestic recognitions of achievement.

In contrast with the above examples, Bhabha Atomic Research Centre's accomplishments in nuclear technology and Indian Space Research Organization's game-changing work in space exploration stand as inspirational Indian achievements. Both are world class technology leaders in their respective domains *without* significant foreign dependency.[258] What makes these organizations stand out is that they set high targets based on international benchmarks. They have not relied on jugaad (improvisations, short-cuts, and ad hoc approaches) to score quick and easy victories.[259]

Similarly, until a decade ago, India's tech giants had a strong lead in software development, many private and corporate fortunes were made, and Indians were justifiably proud of their advantage. It was touted as the path to superpower status. However, the country squandered its lead and allowed China to surpass it in AI and related technologies. Consequently, India has become dependent on the US and others for the latest technology needed in AI.

China is going even further by defining its own novel applications of AI that embed its civilizational narrative and values. This emboldens it to resist pressure to comply with Western human rights and values. India, on the other hand, failed to develop indigenous approaches to AI ethics based on its civilization, and it is likely to get pressured to comply with Western criteria of human rights and values.

To understand how India has slipped, consider the following analogy. Suppose a contractor recruits poor villagers from Bihar and brings them to Delhi as laborers on a construction site. The laborers do not own any equity in the project, not so much as a single brick. The bricks they install belong to the client who owns the building. When the construction project is completed, workers must look for the next job, and then yet another one. Their labor does not translate into any equity or long-term security. But the contractor organizing this labor makes a handsome profit quickly with little effort or value added.

At first this arrangement looks promising for the workers, because they can send money home to support their struggling families. And they may earn enough money to buy some consumer goods that are the envy of people back in the village. Maybe they own a fancy smart phone or a scooter. Compared to others in the village, their lifestyle is superior. They are the village heroes, and their parents are proud. They are sought after as a good catch for marriage.

India's software lead was similarly based on labor arbitrage with foreign clients, which is inherently a rickety business model in the long run. The middlemen in India hired computer programmers for low salaries compared to Western levels. They marked up the rates and sold cheap Indian labor to foreign, particularly US, companies. Clients saved money because the wage rates in the US were much higher than in India even after the markups. This system appeared to bolster India's economy. But in the long run, labor arbitrage is self-defeating as explained below:

- It only works if Indian wages remain sufficiently low compared to the client country. Indian tech workers must be kept below a wage ceiling for the model to remain viable. But suppressing wages merely encourages the best minds to leave India in search of fair compensation.
- Other developing countries also enter the same field using their own low wages as an advantage, and they may underbid the Indian wages.
- Client countries inevitably tighten immigration laws to save their own jobs. India's export becomes contingent on the internal politics of the client country.

Only in the past few years did India's government and corporations wake up when the US started clamping down on outsourcing, and when Indian tech workers sent to the US also faced increasing competition from American professionals. Labor arbitrage does have value for the short term, bringing quick employment and helping train the local workforce. But the middlemen should not accumulate wealth at the expense of workers, and government planners should not consider it as a sustainable strategy.

China's more prudent model stands in sharp contrast to India's. China also started out using labor arbitrage in its manufacturing industry, but they were strategic about it: The Chinese reinvested their short-term income from selling cheap labor and committed themselves to scaling the value chain. Besides bringing in high-tech manufacturing jobs at an increasing rate, they also invested in upgrading large-scale manufacturing infrastructure more heavily than any other country. Their strategy was to put China ahead of other countries and become the most competitive manufacturing hub in the world. They used low wages to jump-start their previously isolated and poor economy without becoming dependent on easy profits. They anticipated the day when low wages would no longer be enough of a competitive advantage. Their self-image was not one of poor laborers looking for better salaries; instead, they set their sights high—on global market dominance. Interestingly, China has already colonized parts of Africa into its low-wage base for manufacturing.

The Chinese started investing in cutting-edge technologies, mapped out a long-term R&D plan, and hired the world's best talent in several specialties to work in China. At the same time, China has accumulated a massive war chest of foreign exchange, which it is investing in highly specialized areas designed to beat the Americans at their own game.

Using this far-sighted vision, China created a vast ecosystem of domestic intellectual property in next-generation technologies including AI, 5G, nanotechnology, robotics, Virtual/Augmented Reality, aerospace, and biotechnology, just to name a few.

What went wrong for India? *The brutal reality is that India's newly minted billionaires were shortsighted—the products of jugaad and selfishness.* They achieved instant wealth but failed to anticipate global trends. They became intoxicated with their status as popular icons that were glorified by the media and the government. The Indian masses love the pageantry and tamasha of honoring their rich as celebrities and high-profile public figures. And many received Padma awards (India's highest civilian awards) because they built personal fortunes even though they made precious little contribution toward nation-building.[260]

While they were at the peak of success with software and services exports, they should have reinvested a portion of their earnings into developing longer-term world-class intellectual property. Imagine if Indian tech giants had invested 10% to 25% of their profits toward the research and development of strategic intellectual property, as opposed to simply selling cheap labor to foreign clients. Imagine if Indian government planners had understood that maximizing the short-term generation of foreign exchange would precipitate the present crisis in which India is dependent on the US and China for critical technologies.

The depletion of India's software lead has devastated its prospects for AI. Today, India is ranked ninth in the world in the number of AI specialists. Among the world's AI experts, nearly 50% belonged to the US with the number of 10,295, followed by China with 2,525 and the UK, Germany, and Canada with 1,457, 935 and 815, respectively. India is behind all these countries.[261]

The government's own NITI Aayog has admitted this plight in its reports with remarkable honesty. The policy think tank's understanding of the problem is sharp and worth quoting in detail:

> India produced a whopping 2.6 million STEM graduates in 2016, second only to China and more than 4 times the graduates produced by USA, ... [but unfortunately] an overwhelming majority of this talent pool is focused on routine IT development and not so much on research and innovation. Exacerbating the problem further, a majority of the small population focused on research almost always prefers to pursue advance degrees to subsequently apply their expertise abroad. [...]
>
> India only has 386 out of a total of 22,000 PhD educated researchers worldwide and is ranked 10th

> globally. The report also looks at leading AI conferences globally for presenters who could be considered influential experts in their respective field of AI. On this metric, India was ranked 13th globally, with just 44 top-notch presenters. [...]
>
> Serious research work in India is limited to less than 50 researchers, concentrated mostly at institutes like IITs, IIITs and IISc. In terms of the citable documents published in the field of AI from 2010 - 2016, India ranks a distant 5th, far behind the likes of China and USA and just about edging ahead of Germany and France who have considerably smaller STEM population. [...]
>
> If we look at the country wise H-Index (a metric that quantifies a country's scientific productivity and scientific impact), India ranks a dismal 19th globally. In other words, while India may be producing research pieces in numbers, their utility has been rather limited.[262]

NITI Aayog explicitly names Indian tech giants like TCS, Wipro, and Infosys for their failure in original research even though they have extensive experience implementing solutions using the cutting-edge technologies developed by others:

> Indian IT services companies, the likes of TCS, Wipro and Infosys, have been the flag bearers of India's competence in implementation of cutting-edge technology solutions, yet their contribution to research has been limited. Given that these IT giants have been working closely with businesses globally and anticipating the trends in emerging technologies, it wouldn't be unreasonable to expect a sizeable volume of research work coming out of these companies. Yet, looking at

> all the research publications from 2001 – 2016, only 14% of all publications have come from industry, with universities contributing 86% of all publications. Even this limited research publication universe by industry is dominated by Indian subsidiaries of international companies (~70%), with only one Indian company in top-10 (TCS).[263]

This is how India lost out in the AI race. Most AI patents, the pipeline of R&D, and the expertise of deep learning belongs to US and Chinese firms, or to small firms elsewhere that those countries have funded. Foreign tech giants gobble up any promising start-up because they have the funds, strategic vision, and capability to make big bets.

The importance of AI as the force multiplier of information technology should not be under-estimated. It was articulated by Google CEO, Sundar Pichai in his keynote at a developers' conference a few years ago. He emphasized what he called the AI-first approach in technology replacing the mobile-first approach:

> Computing is evolving again. We spoke last year about this important shift in computing from a mobile-first to an AI-first approach. ... In an AI-first world, we are rethinking all our products and applying machine learning and AI to solve user problems.[264]

Another steep challenge for India is that AI is moving toward specialized hardware and the old general-purpose computer hardware is no longer adequate. Apple's Neural Engine used in their iPhones, Google's Cloud TPU, and Huawei's Neural Processing Unit are examples of advanced hardware barriers that any Indian company will find extremely difficult to cross. India's myopic priorities have led to its repeated failure to invest in computing hardware and this has widened its AI gap with both the US and China. While the US remains the leader in semiconductor technology, China has been rapidly closing the gap and already has AI-enabled hardware offerings of its own. Even if Indian companies make major strides in AI software over the next decade to try and catch up, they will still be dependent on American and Chinese specialized AI hardware, and this hardware gap is a much tougher one to close.

India's world-class institutions are unable to absorb many of the top-tier technological brains through lucrative jobs. Far too many of them end up working for US or Chinese multinationals, or for Indian companies controlled by foreign stakeholders. In fact, this trend has become the normal vision for India's future as exemplified by a recent speech of the Indian billionaire banker, Uday Kotak. In his inaugural address as the new president of the Confederation of Indian Industry, his much-applauded desire for India was expressed as follows: "Why can't we dream of having Google and Microsoft jobs from rural India?"[265] This is tantamount to saying that India must spread its colonization even deeper into the rural areas and *turn its villagers into low-level workers for American digital giants*. It illustrates the prevailing idea among the Indian elite that the way forward is to train more and more Indians to serve foreign companies.

India needs an entirely different vision than Mr. Kotak's—an awareness of the urgent need to move forward and catch up in advanced technology as producers, rather than as suppliers, of labor or as mere users. Mr. Kotak is like most other prominent Indian leaders who perpetuate the addiction to labor arbitrage for foreign clients. Such industry leaders want the youth to accept their fate below the glass ceiling and accept India's status as the hub for low-grade services.

Unless the mentality changes, India is destined to continue exporting its talent and buying back the innovations.

This Kotak mentality is why many Indian reports on AI highlight the opportunity for IT companies to train people for tasks like data cleaning, search engine optimization, and content moderation. Indians are now helping train the machine learning systems of foreign clients, and this provides tech giants like TCS, Infosys, Wipro, and others a path to upgrade their old outsourcing manpower to serve the world of AI. Such an approach is defensive and short term and does not produce any indigenous intellectual property. For instance, Amazon has an army of low-wage workers to review hundreds of pictures from their warehouse and mark whether a product is upright or fallen over or missing on a shelf. This helps train its vision algorithms to automatically identify objects. This task has been passed off as job creation in India, when in fact all Amazon has done is create more cyber-coolies.

Recently, several research centers in Bengaluru, such as the NASSCOM Centre of Excellence for Data Science & Artificial Intelligence, have started to foster AI research.[266] It hopes to turn India into a hub for AI and related technologies based on the country's large pool of raw talent that could be upgraded with proper education. Unfortunately, the goal seems to focus on grooming young Indians into the next-generation equivalent of tech workers for export. India is inviting foreign AI companies to open offices in India to leverage this talent pool. While the approach is a good way to create employment, it does not bring ownership of the technology into India.

What I am often told is, given the overpopulation and underemployment India faces, the only remedy available to avoid mass suffering among hundreds of millions of poor people is to sell their labor under whatever conditions it is sellable. This is an incredibly sad plight: When a system is so worried about short-term survival that it must perpetuate and even exacerbate a long-term problem, then the system is unsustainable; its capitulation is only a matter of time. The way out of colonization cannot be further and deeper colonization.

India does have numerous start-ups and an abundance of entrepreneurial zeal but there is a dire need for a robust end-to-end innovation engine to turn start-ups into global industry leaders. This entails building a network of alliances across industries, academia, government organizations and start-ups. Unfortunately, universities have been kept largely limited to teaching and removed from the research institutions of the government and industry. As a result, students are in silos and not given the opportunities to get involved in serious R&D projects. Academic research tends to be limited to theories or to small projects. There is a general lack of collaboration between industry and academia specifically in the AI domain. I have also heard of the absurd situation that India's patent law excludes algorithms from being patented.[267] Clearly, this needs to be re-examined.

Most intellectual property development work being done in India is for foreign companies.[268] Indian industry and government have not been thinking big in terms of moon shots to catapult ahead in AI. Sadly, when an Indian start-up becomes successful, the most common outcome is for the owners to sell out to a US or Chinese buyer and join the ranks of global high net worth elites. The emerging AI landscape in India seems to be one in which the best Indian brains will be increasingly employed by foreign corporates, whether directly in their development centers or indirectly in start-ups funded by foreign capital.

The *Economic Times* reported that "more than a dozen new China-domiciled large corporates, venture funds, and family offices are aggressively stepping up investment conversations with early- to growth-stage domestic firms".[269] India's young tech entrepreneurs are enthusiastic about such Chinese investments because they will benefit from China's experience in creating an ecosystem of tech start-ups. Clearly, in the circles of young Indian technocrats, China looms larger than life with its enticing lures and inducements.[270]

Besides investing in Indian brains for their global product R&D, these foreign giants also invest in India's domestic application areas, such as digital entertainment. One of the fastest-growing digital technologies in India is the gaming industry, which boasts over three hundred million players and is growing dramatically. Industry experts predict that digital gaming in India will exceed the combined industries of music, movies, and TV shows within the next several years. The most popular device for these activities is the mobile phone. Once again, the Chinese giants Tencent and Alibaba, as well as SoftBank of Japan, have jumped in as major investors. Unlike digital commerce, digital gaming does not require physical logistics, inventory, or content. The coronavirus pandemic accelerated this industry as people in lockdown sought more diversionary activities than before.[271]

Recently, India has clamped down on Chinese investment by imposing regulatory speed bumps.[272] There was also a backlash against the cloud-based, online video communications company Zoom, which is owned by Eric Yuan, a Chinese American.[273] However, these moves were retaliation against a border violation by China and not a strategic shift in R&D emphasis. It is a defensive move that can at best prevent further Chinese investments to slow the spread of China's influence. But this by itself does nothing to upgrade the global competitiveness of India's AI products. The fact remains that while China is a major disruptor of the world order by using AI as a weapon, India is at the receiving end of this disruption and having to be reactive.

Most of India's leaders, public intellectuals, media personalities, policymakers, think tanks, and authors are ignoring the dangers discussed in this book, living securely in their comfort zones with like-minded peers. The sheer ignorance of AI among the celebrated icons of social media is staggering.

ECONOMICS AND HUMAN CAPITAL

Economic Fallout

Artificial Intelligence poses another serious dilemma for India: On the one hand, Prime Minister Narendra Modi's ambitious *Make in India* initiatives depend on AI and related technologies in order to be globally competitive. On the other hand, the AI-driven economy is not being supported by the required education system and the skill gap is widening.

India's approach to economic development and its use of foreign investments is capital intensive, and does not translate into job creation at a sufficient rate. A Brookings report on the impact of AI on India's workforce says that India's higher GDP growth is not converting into more jobs, and that a 10% increase in GDP now results in less than a 1% increase in employment. The number of new entrants into the Indian workforce each year is almost three times the number of new jobs created.[274] Is India losing the battle for jobs?

India's political and business leaders have been pursuing their ambitious economic program with the *Make in India* initiative. The intent is admirable, but the reality is that many of the manufacturing jobs being created through this program will become obsolete during the present decade. India's manufacturing will continue to play catch-up because it has already lost the technological race in many fields. Much of the industry is labor-intensive and vulnerable to automation. The dramatic decrease of certain jobs and increasing polarization of the employment market will aggravate social inequality.

As an example, India's automobile sector employs several million workers and India is a global hub in the supply of auto parts. But now, factory automation and robotics in the advanced countries will take a huge bite out of this sector. Furthermore, with the recent advent of electric cars, many existing components will soon become unnecessary or obsolete; electric cars simply do not have as many parts as cars based on the internal combustion engine. Until recently, automotive engineering was fundamentally the same as it had been for the past century when Henry Ford sparked the automobile revolution. A second revolution in the car industry (led by Elon Musk's Tesla and others) is coming soon and few of the present manufacturers will survive. India is especially vulnerable because it is low on the value-added scale. Most Indian manufacturers supply intermediate parts as subcontractors to other multinational manufacturers. The global ecosystem of the industry will shift suddenly and dramatically. This impending catastrophe has not received adequate attention.

A common assumption is that the new technologies will have a net positive impact on employment in India, but this presumption is false. New industries will find a home in whichever countries offer the most competitive labor and infrastructure. Tesla, for instance, launched its largest manufacturing facility to build AI-based semi-autonomous electric cars in China. The jobs lost in India's old tech auto industry will move to countries that have a viable ecosystem for next-generation technologies. Worsening this trend, the post-pandemic world is poised for significant paradigm shifts on global supply chains. This will harm India in industries where it occupies a low position in the value chain.

India hopes to create many manufacturing jobs in a bid to emulate China. However, achieving success in technologically advanced products requires India to implement not only AI but a host of other emerging technologies including robotics, 5G, nanotechnology, semiconductors, and biotechnology. The multiple technologies that undergird the future of industry do not exist in isolation because they feed off of each other's breakthroughs. If some critical aspects of a comprehensive solution must be imported, the supply chain becomes inefficient, unwieldy, and uncompetitive, and there is also a national security risk. Introducing one technology in isolation is not competitive and all of them must be integrated.

This requires a comprehensive strategy similar to what China executed over the past quarter century. The Chinese planned and developed an entire domestic manufacturing ecosystem, replete with supply-chain development, infrastructure improvement, and a skilled labor force. China's approach focused on total solutions, encompassing education, research, science, technology, and industry. This robust end-to-end system is difficult to compete against. Artificial Intelligence is at the strategic center in China's plans.

The coming revolution will prove to be more dramatic than the nineteenth century Industrial Revolution, as well as the subsequent Information Technology Revolution of the early 2000s. At the foundation of this AI revolution is a base of research in a multitude of fields that require a workforce with higher education. Sadly, India will become even more dependent on knowledge transfer from other countries.

Also, the loss of manufacturing jobs due to automation might not easily be compensated with more services jobs because major service industry employers like information technology and banking also face job losses.[275] For instance, in call centers where India has been the global hub, humans are rapidly being replaced by voice processing systems and apps for direct web access by customers. India's call center industry failed to reinvest its early profits into the development of next-generation technologies. Investing in call centers turned out to be a jugaad opportunity for clever entrepreneurs to quickly amass wealth but has let down the young workers who expected long-term stable careers.

Furthermore, India's workforce is much too dependent on agriculture and other low-wage, low-tech, and labor-intensive jobs. The agriculture sector provides income to almost half of India's population. Modern agricultural mechanization and automation have already transformed traditional agriculture and AI is taking this trend to a new level. Robots are expected to work in weed extirpation, irrigation, fertilization, and pesticide spraying.[276] Artificial Intelligence will also penetrate plowing, sowing, harvesting, storing, breeding, and selling. Such developments could further challenge agricultural workers, pushing even more of them to the brink of insolvency.

Another challenge is that the wage gaps between Western countries and India for manufacturing have narrowed; automation in Western countries is raising efficiencies and making the supply chains less labor intensive; and protectionism is increasing. As a result, the global supply chains in which Indian manufacturing and IT services are embedded are being disrupted by de-globalization and domestication.

A report by the London-based non-profit NGO, Chatham House summarizes the economic crisis India is facing and its social implications:

> AI can exacerbate existing socioeconomic inequities, lead to a concentration and collusion of power and even reconfigure the fundamental tenets of democracy. ...
>
> The deployment of AI solutions in industry will disrupt labour markets in India, to the detriment of a bulk of the labour force. The reduction in the cost of intelligent automation is already resulting in the re-shoring of numerous industries to industrialized economies in the global north. This will make it increasingly difficult for India to generate employment through an export-oriented manufacturing strategy.
>
> This poses a particular challenge for India, given that a large part of its population is low-skilled, and thus traditionally best absorbed within large-scale manufacturing industries. Further, it is unlikely new job creation can offset such losses. The people who lose their jobs are unlikely to be the same ones to take up newly created jobs—a middle-aged low-skill worker will find it very difficult to re-skill or up-skill fast enough. The newly created high-skilled jobs are likely to be significantly fewer in number and unable to absorb India's large labour surplus. [...]
>
> There is a strong risk that AI-based technology gains are likely to benefit only a select few Indians. In this context, the 'AI for All' narrative obscures rather than answers many of the fundamental challenges that India faces.[277]

In parallel, there is also a shrinking demand for Indian migrant workers in the Middle East due to pro-domestic worker policies and slowdown in infrastructure and industrial projects due to depressed oil prices. This is impacting remittances to India. This negative impact is both on migrant workers who go abroad and send remittances back home and to India-based companies exporting goods and services.[278]

Population Tsunami

> *A nation is great not by its size alone. It is the will, the cohesion, the stamina, the discipline of its people and the quality of their leaders which ensures it an honorable place in history.*
>
> —Lee Kuan Yew, first prime minister of Singapore[279]

India's population, currently at around 1.4 billion and growing at 15 million per year, will surpass China's in 2022 and reach 1.7 billion by 2050. The poor segments are growing faster than the rest, and some communities have religious sanctions against birth control. It is estimated that over 30% of the world's population will live in South Asia by 2041, although the region constitutes only 2.5% of the total landmass of the world. In other words, *South Asia will remain ten times more densely populated than the world average.*

Because women are considered homemakers, *India's official statistics for unemployment do not include women.*[280] The unfortunate fact is that only 23% percent of working-age Indian women are employed, and this percentage is dropping. Overall, less than half the people in the working age bracket are employed. What is especially worrisome is that the unemployment rate for persons aged fifteen to twenty-nine in urban areas is close to 25%.[281] This crisis is despite the government artificially creating special jobs programs just to try and contain the unemployment.

These statistics are from prior to the pandemic and do not factor the worsening of the economy because of Covid-19. The situation will further deteriorate in the next two decades because the working-age population is projected to increase by more than two hundred million new youth being added. An especially volatile situation is the bulge in the youth population, a group that is prone to social unrest and instability. India's leaders have failed to understand that this time bomb can turn into a social threat.[282]

As noted earlier, India has touted its large youth population as a demographic dividend rather than looking at it as a mixed blessing. Young people do have hands to work with, but they also have stomachs to feed. And those hands are productive only if they have jobs. The reality is that a large amount of resources—food, energy, housing, education, etc.—are having to be spent on subsidizing the basic needs of hundreds of millions of people. Urgent government intervention is being required in many regions for basic services such as food and drinking water, land reforms, housing, education, power and fuel, infrastructure, farming, industries, employment, and public health. The larger the population, the greater this burden and the more it drags down global competitiveness. The rate at which new jobs must be created to control unemployment is greater than the economy can genuinely produce. To meet the demand for new jobs, the underlying economy would need to grow at a much faster pace, and consistently rather than in spurts.

To make matters even worse, large-scale migrations from Bangladesh and Nepal are adding to India's population. These migrants are mostly extremely poor and uneducated, becoming liabilities on India's economy and infrastructure. Unplanned rapid urbanization is causing heavy congestion in the cities. In 1975, 20% of the population lived in urban areas; by 2030 this figure will rise to 40%. The need for urban infrastructure and facilities is skyrocketing even as overurbanization increases congestion, pollution, and demand for public services. Clearly, India faces huge challenges in balancing the asymmetries between population, resources, and technology.

The implication of all this is that India's exceptionally large population is an albatross that will amplify the challenges of AI. India is neither nimble enough, nor adequately prepared, to navigate through the rapidly changing technological landscape. If, hypothetically, India had only a fraction of its population, it could advance with the use of modern technology. In reality, too many people are chasing too few resources.

It is true that India's fertility rates have been steadily coming down. But this trend, although encouraging, is not sufficient—birth rates have dropped below replacement levels in only a few states and in certain communities. Further, the death rate is also declining thanks to medical advances, which is likely to continue. Forecasts of achieving zero population growth are unreliable because they fail to accurately factor in the increase in longevity. Unfortunately, the government has no pragmatic population strategy based on realistic assumptions—because that might entail taking political risks.

Even if India's total population could start shrinking steadily, it would take fifty to one hundred years for the population to decrease significantly because the present average age is low; more than 65% of the population is below age thirty-five. India does not have much time left because the technologies that will disrupt large numbers of jobs are advancing faster than the population can be reduced or re-educated.

Yet the optimists believe the population will level off on its own soon enough, and that new agricultural technologies will allow India to feed its growing population. In fact, they claim population growth will stimulate economic growth, although they concede that the economy must grow at a sufficient rate to achieve this optimistic scenario.

Uneducated and Unemployable

Do not make your bloom of youth useless
by sitting idly at home.

—Yoga Vasishtha[283]

Even after decades of Independence, a large portion of India's population is uneducated. Enrollment is slightly above 50% in higher secondary schools, and only 25% at the university level. Half the children in grade five cannot read a grade two text, and less than 30% in grade three are able to do even basic subtraction. Women have a lower participation rate than men; the middle level of education among women is almost completely missing.[284] Only 30% of Indians have a secondary school education, designated for ages fourteen-eighteen.[285] About 66% of the workforce has only an eighth-grade education. Only a tiny portion of workers have any kind of formal vocational training.[286]

Because of the abysmally pathetic education standard, too many Indians are deficient in rudimentary knowledge, reading skills, and learning habits and suffer from short attention spans—a characteristic that makes them gullible and inclined to chase emotional sensations and experiences rather than pursue knowledge. Even those who have formal school certificates often lack job skills and are deficient in analytical competence.

At the same time, Indian businesses report serious shortages of qualified skilled workers, and employers complain that the majority of graduates with engineering degrees in India are unemployable.

The Ministry of Human Resource Development (recently renamed Ministry of Education) is responsible for the current crisis of human capital. The problem started with the first prime minister of independent India, Jawaharlal Nehru, who did not espouse universal education for India's youth. In contrast, China mandated the education of all its citizens two generations ago. As a result, the skill levels of Chinese, both men and women, have climbed steadily during the past few decades. Today, the Chinese are better educated than their counterparts in India.

India's myopic education policies require students to memorize facts for the sole purpose of passing exams, which encourages a culture of educational jugaad. Rather than applying reasoning and innovative thinking, uninformed and irrational youth tend to rely on emotions and bombast. A population focused on short-term gratification and grandiose displays of glory is not a sustainable framework for innovation.

The sad truth is that most Indians, particularly the youth, are poorly educated by world standards and a large percentage are unemployable. Mediocre education and lack of training make Indians especially vulnerable to AI's inevitable disruption in the fiercely competitive global labor market. Yet, discussion of these shortcomings is considered politically incorrect. India has recently introduced a new education policy which shows the authorities are aware of the problem. But it requires a detailed evaluation before one could pass judgment on its merits.

The silver lining behind all these grim facts is that surveys of Indian workers in the corporate sector indicate they are among the most enthusiastic in the world about wanting to learn and use digital technologies. Most of them want careers that offer both formal training and on-the-job training. They are even willing to have their work habits monitored by surveillance systems.[287] However, very few in the workforce have been educated in India's elite institutions and these brightest and best employees quickly get picked up for lucrative jobs with large multinationals, which are in effect buying off the cream of India's youth whose education was paid from public funding. The vast majority of youth are left behind because of India's abysmal investment in primary and secondary school education.

8

DIGITAL COLONIZATION

In a lot of ways Facebook is more like a government than a traditional company.

—Mark Zuckerberg, CEO, Facebook[288]

The online world is not truly bound by terrestrial laws ... it's the world's largest ungoverned space.

—Eric Schmidt, former CEO, Google, and Jared Cohen, CEO, Jigsaw[289]

CHAPTER HIGHLIGHTS

- India's thought leaders, officials, media icons, and academicians are drastically uninformed about the wide range of issues that come under the term, digital colonization.
- The decision by current Uttar Pradesh chief minister, Yogi Adityanath, to invite foreign organizations to capture big data on the Kumbh Mela has been one of the biggest blunders and sellouts of India's big data assets.
- The recent investments in Reliance Jio by Facebook, Google, and some others have been glorified as great achievements across India. However, they are likely to be the tipping point in the digital colonization of India and even further dependence on imported AI solutions.

INDIA IS FOR SALE

That King who is not gifted with intelligence fails to see his own faults.

—*Mahabharata*[290]

Oh Kings! Cast off your pride before those who possess the secret treasure of wisdom.

—Bhartrihari[291]

Even a nation of strong men led by the weak, blind or selfish, becomes easily infected with the vices of its leaders.

—Sri Aurobindo[292]

There is a risk that India is already well on its way toward digital colonization; its strategy on AI is not even an effective defense, much less a plan for a leadership role in the AI epoch. Yet Indian intellectuals fail to address the issue with enough seriousness. In fact, some well-meaning persons have advised me to avoid writing on this topic because it might upset the fragile psychological equilibrium of many Indians.

Most leaders are fully aware that India has big data unique to its immense diversity of genetics, culture, and natural resources. However, most of India's big data assets are sitting in raw unorganized form and not integrated; disconnected ministries have jurisdictions over the silos. Such fragmented data is sometimes being siphoned off by foreign entities that understand its value more than the Indian authorities do. These national assets should not be given away by foolish officials and politicians.

As mentioned already, there has been a recent initiative to organize India's data assets and create a fair and vibrant industry under the leadership of Infosys cofounder, Kris

Gopalakrishnan. It seeks to create a national scheme for sharing non-private data and proposes the government to play the role of the data custodian and neutral marketer to third parties on a level playing field.[293] This is an important and welcome movement, even though I have different thoughts on how the data industry should be organized.[294]

Until India's data assets are properly appreciated and organized into an industry with regulations, there remains a state of disarray in which start-ups do not have large-scale data sets across multiple sectors for training their neural networks. Therefore, Indian AI projects often end up using US and European datasets for their development. But those datasets are biased by the demography of the West which is significantly different from Indian demography. The AI systems trained on foreign data incorporate Eurocentric biases; this is harmful in culturally sensitive applications in health, employment, social justice, and finance.

Figure 30 gives a partial view of the big data availability and potential usages by foreign parties. The top of the figure shows the Chinese and US beneficiaries of India's big data. At the bottom are the sources of Indian data that the digital pirates are tapping into. In the middle are intermediaries, mechanisms like Jio, Amazon India, Flipkart, telecom operators, and all the social media platforms that continuously gather information on individuals' interpersonal messages and e-commerce transactions. The surveillance data is uploaded to databases including facial recognition, individuals' medical information, travel histories, and financial payments. Considering all this, it is shocking that the Reserve Bank of India approved US credit reporting agencies to operate in India who are now the dominant players holding Indians' credit information.[295]

Indians, both in their individual capacity and as officials running institutions, are supplying precious data to train foreign AI systems, and these models are used to understand and engage the Indian mindset in a variety of situations either openly or secretly.

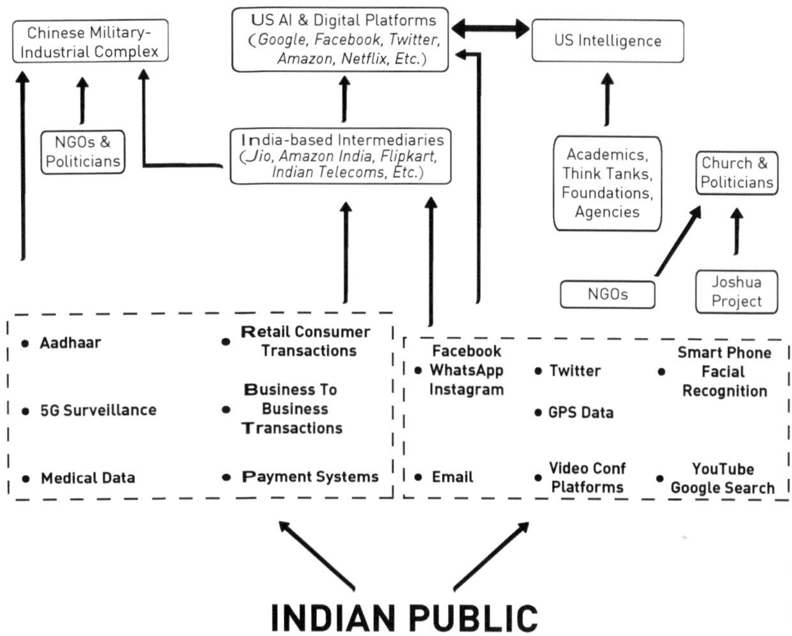

Figure 30: Foreign Collection of Big Data in India

Artificial Intelligence systems have been processing immense amounts of raw data to develop psychological profiles for various segments of the Indian population. Machine learning systems are figuring out Indians' most intense desires that can be used to get them hooked. These systems analyze what various users like and dislike, their habits, strengths and vulnerabilities, key relationships, shopping interests, ideological leanings, affiliations, and so forth. *Facebook, Twitter, and Google know more about Indians than social scientists, government, gurus, or even the people themselves.* This gives them the power to influence the public.

Indians are addicted to the foreign digital ecosystem and depend on it to communicate among themselves and to transact critical services across all sectors of society. Foreign social media platforms choose which individuals and messages will go viral, and hence control the image, career, and social profile of Indians. They undermine the traditional sources of authority, replacing them with algorithms. In the name of fairness and the public interest, they censor and manipulate users by injecting their own ideological premises in the social discourse. Every time there is a public controversy or scandal, these US companies take sides under the pretext of social responsibility. This is exactly the rationale the British colonizers gave for their meddling and divide-and-rule policies. This is social engineering in the digital age.

If a digital platform company champions specific values (which are invariably based on its civilizational ethos), whatever those values might be, it cannot be considered neutral. Moreover, despite what digital giants claim about championing diversity, their core strategy depends on getting people to think and act the way they and their advertisers want. The business models are based on psychologically influencing people's thinking rather than encouraging independent thinking.

One is reminded of the eighteenth-century Indian elites that collaborated with the British, exposing Indian culture's weak links and helping them map the country's vulnerabilities. The British colonizers gave birth to Indology to study Indians, build psychological models of individual and social behavior, and establish policies for dealing with different segments of society. In today's jargon we could say that Indology served the purpose of surveillance to compile big data and build models. After the Second World War (1939–45), this role was passed on to the US, which started the academic discipline of South Asia Studies and took the social-psychological mapping exercise to new heights. The new digital technologies are the latest evolution in this enterprise.

Most people cannot grasp the end-to-end implications of their social media activities. Happy as simple mouse-clicking activists, they are quite ignorant that they are giving up a fair amount of their agency. People voluntarily provide personal details about their lifestyle and choices, thus enabling the digital platforms to model and predict their behavior patterns. In return the platforms give them a broad distribution channel to build their reputation and achieve celebrity status. The platforms write the playbook that users must follow. By complying with the values and policies of a platform, users succumb to the hooks that are designed to keep them in line, influence them, and gradually modulate their behavior.[296]

Indians are so intoxicated by the sense of empowerment that social media provides that they have slavishly accepted this new digital form of authority and tolerated its manipulation. For instance, it has become difficult to exit Twitter because that would give opponents a decisive advantage in creating influence. This capitulation is the price people pay to get ahead in public life. But what they do not realize is that the game is rigged, and although they may think they are winning, the ultimate result is their psychological colonization.

The following figure shows how private data about others is turned into power over them.

AI mapping of psychology, emotions, desires, habits ➔ Behavior prediction ➔ Manipulation

FOREIGN SURVEILLANCE AT KUMBH MELA

Wicked counsels destroy an entire kingdom... A king, although powerful, should never consult men of small sense, men that are procrastinating, men that are indolent, and men that are flatterers.

—*Mahabharata*[297]

My effort to investigate India's data vulnerabilities galvanized in 2018 when Uttar Pradesh chief minister, Yogi Adityanath invited foreign universities to study the Kumbh Mela.[298] The surprise announcement was a shock and disappointment to those who were familiar with my 2016 report on Harvard's project "Mapping the Kumbha Mela". I had researched the Harvard project extensively to expose their data acquisition strategy masquerading as public health research for India's benefit.

My report had warned that the Harvard study was not the benign project it appeared to be, pointing out that it wanted to compile socio-demographic, DNA, and psychological data of nearly one hundred million people from every corner of India. I explained that India was giving foreigners access to precious private data about the world's largest human diversity. Harvard's machine learning templates are using Indian data to identify social and political divisiveness that could eventually be exploited in the name of human-rights interventions.

My report was printed in English and Hindi and widely distributed in many Indian state capitals, as well as in academic, media, and other institutions of civic society. Hundreds of thousands of copies were handed out to senior leaders at various Kumbh Melas, generating an emotional response. This led to public outcry and considerable awareness about the dangers of allowing foreign researchers unrestricted rights to gather data at such events.

When Yogi Adityanath became chief minister of India's largest state, Uttar Pradesh, I went to see him in person specifically to present my findings and to request an investigation into such foreign projects. My suggestion was that India should use only Indian research organizations for these studies. I was assured that the chief minister would investigate the matter. But after my visit, I did not hear back from his office, and there was no follow up whatsoever.

Then came the sudden press release that Yogi Adityanath had invited several foreign research agencies specifically to gather data at the Kumbh Mela. To the best of my knowledge, no formal intellectual property agreement was put in place to assert that the data belongs to India, nor was there any provision for Indian authorities to be given a copy of the gathered data. As a result, the door was flung wide open to foreign institutions learning more about India than any Indian organization does. Ever since that incident, I have examined India's data policies and found them ineffectual.

India's decision makers simply do not seem to acknowledge the risk of foreign surveillance. Given the ubiquitous nature of surveillance by foreign companies and governments, the reasonable assumption should be that important Indian leaders and bureaucrats are being tracked by the abundance of their private data sitting on foreign networks. Just as happened during British colonialism, India's leadership over the decades has potentially compromised the nation. The complicity and carelessness have become the accepted norm over time and resulted in such a data heist in full view of the public and right under the nose of the government.[299]

FACEBOOK-DEVATA AND RELIANCE

Indian authorities are treating Facebook as though they are ignorant of its international notoriety and recent scandals. Any policymaker ought to know that UK-based Cambridge Analytica used Facebook's data analytics to build detailed profiles of American voters and their psychological hot buttons for helping the Russians secretly interfere in the 2016 US presidential election. They manufactured and spread fake news and abused the private information of American citizens to manipulate voters' emotions and facilitate the Russians' goals.

Bragging about their ability to manufacture facts that convince the public, Alexander Nix, former CEO of Cambridge Analytica, said: "It sounds a dreadful thing to say, but these are things that don't necessarily need to be true as long as they're believed."[300] These same consultants specializing in the use of Facebook's big data assets for behavioral psychology models and making political interventions are also rumored to have served clients in Indian politics.[301]

The recent sale of almost 10% equity in Reliance's Jio to Facebook is a glaring lesson in how woefully uninformed Indian policymakers and public intellectuals are about the nature of the AI revolution. The collaboration between the two companies has positioned Facebook deep in the heart of India's digital future. CNN aptly described Jio as "something of a gatekeeper of the country's internet".[302] Taken in the context of its sweeping implications, this merger will likely be the tipping point in India's digital colonization.

More details of the deal are emerging and the analysis in this section may change based on them. Since this is a stress test scenario, the worst outcomes are being considered only as possibilities and are not necessarily the final outcome.

Figure 31 shows Reliance's initial plans. JioMart is Reliance's consumer service, offering free home delivery from thirty million local retailers.

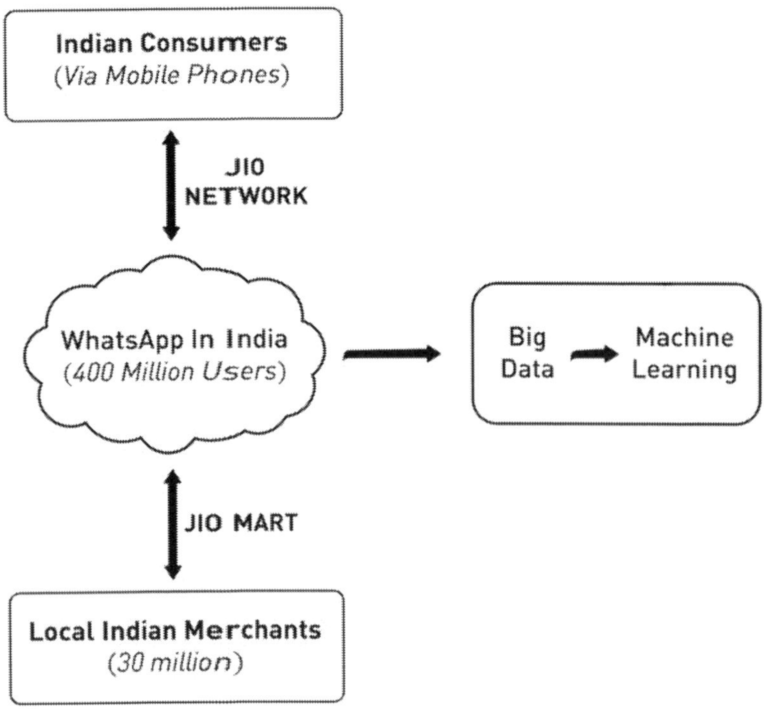

Figure 31: Facebook's Data Incursion Into India

Among its inducements are the promise of excellent savings and an unconditional return policy. The service is being made available to Jio's mobile customers, numbering almost four hundred million and growing rapidly.

India already has among the largest base of users for Facebook as well as its subsidiaries Instagram and WhatsApp. Under this new deal, the four hundred million WhatsApp users in India will be integrated with JioMart and be able to order a broad range of consumer goods and services. Local merchants benefit because inclusion in the Jio-Facebook service increases the total consumer universe available as buyers.

The magnitude of this victory for Facebook is evident from the benefits it receives.

1. Facebook has been banned in China's large market, despite Mark Zuckerberg's personal connections there. The restriction has made it even more critical that Facebook suffuse itself into India's market in a big way.
2. Facebook has not been able to monetize its WhatsApp subsidiary in the US or elsewhere. It has plans to experiment in India with various ways of monetizing the service—knowledge that will prove useful in monetizing in other countries. For the first time in any major country in the world, Facebook's WhatsApp is being used for e-commerce on a scale that others in the digital industry can only dream of.[303] Essentially, India provides an open playing field for Facebook to test-market bold ideas.[304]
3. Consumers in China and other East Asian countries prefer using superapps like the immensely popular WeChat. These apps provide a single umbrella

platform for all kinds of needs ranging from chatting to managing money to making reservations to shopping to telemedicine services. All these activities—and hence all the data produced—are combined into one superapp. In contrast, in the US there are multiple databases owned by different companies that handle separate kinds of transactions, such as credit card information, shopping history, communications and messaging profiles, video streaming history, and search history. Each database is under the control of its respective owner, creating a fragmented relationship with consumers. No American company has been able to break into the superapp market, and India promises to be a prodigious environment for such an application.[305]

4. Zuckerberg visited India in 2015 and presented a charitable proposal to the Modi government to build a free internet service for all people in India. The stated motive was to bridge the digital divide between the rich and poor by providing the service for free. However, India rejected the offer because it contained exclusivity provisions that privileged Facebook as the sole provider of services; all other providers would have to work under rules and prices set by Facebook. The latest deal with Reliance gives Facebook a free piggyback ride on the Jio network. Reliance will focus on its traditional roles, such as supplying pipelines and logistics, managing government relations, implementing marketing and sales, and providing the Indian connections, while Facebook controls the brains of the enterprise. This is even better than the previous attempt by Facebook because now Reliance will handle all the messy and

circuitous issues like logistics, political lobbying, and other local administration.

5. Facebook has long dreamed of starting its own payment system and even its own cryptocurrency. Its hope is that Reliance's contacts in India will give Facebook the ability to launch these initiatives in India, while it is being held back by regulatory factors in other countries.[306]

The right side of Figure 31 shows the prize at stake: the big data generated from these transactions. Facebook's sophisticated machine learning system will convert this data into user profiles in real time, enabling JioMart to better target its marketing offers.

Mukesh Ambani, chairman of Reliance, called the alliance a "winning recipe" that will eventually "be extended to serve other key stakeholders of Indian society", such as agricultural workers, small and medium enterprises, students and teachers, and healthcare providers.[307] With a patriotic ring to his tone, he announced:

> My fellow Indians, I'm here to share some exciting news with you. All of us at Reliance Jio are delighted to welcome Facebook Inc. as our partner. At the core of this partnership is a commitment Mark Zuckerberg and I share for the digital transformation of India.[308]
>
> All of us at Reliance are humbled by the opportunity to welcome Facebook as our long-term partner in continuing to grow and transform the digital ecosystem of India for the benefit of all Indians.[309]

Fellow billionaire Anand Mahindra tweeted, "Bravo Mukesh!", adding that "the world will pivot to India as a new growth epicentre".[310]

Within days of its announcement, the economist and politician, Dr Subramanian Swamy, came out in strong support of the deal. His article argues emphatically that

> Swadeshi has always meant self-reliance, and not self-sufficiency. Foreign trade and investment are permitted as a part of Swadeshi policy of the government if export earnings and commercial borrowing cover the import bill and also add to the foreign reserves.
>
> If we export enough to earn sufficient foreign exchange to pay for the imports and also amortization due on externally contracted debt, then the nation is safe and so is the Swadeshi principle.[311]

He praised the deal because "the Jio-Facebook combine can compete with others in the e-commerce and e-services areas for which the vast WhatsApp and Instagram subscribers will add to JioMart's reach to compete".[312] The deal will also improve Jio's balance sheet, he notes. Facebook will help Jio connect consumers to businesses, take purchase orders, and promote offerings through the internet and mobile phones. The deal will be profitable because Jio-Facebook will reach millions of traders and kirana (small grocery shops) merchants to become a giant digital network providing ubiquitous commercial connectivity. Dr Swamy also likes that the Jio-Facebook combine will potentially introduce a large-scale cryptocurrency network.

Dr Swamy's analysis focuses solely on the short-term impact on the balance sheet of one private company. He ignores the long-term implications for India discussed here. His arguments completely disregard the issue of increasing dependence on foreign-controlled AI technology and the sellout of what could become India's largest database of public transactions and payment system, not to mention the risks associated with welcoming Facebook's cryptocurrency intrusions into India.

Soon after the Facebook investment, Jio got several more foreign investments. The excitement over all these is clear from the following media analysis:

> Technology will play a big part in disrupting and transforming businesses, including those who cater to the customers at the bottom of the pyramid. Jio Platforms is among the best placed to take advantage and is already moving in this direction. For instance, in its unique e-commerce model, it will partner the millions of mom and pop stores around the country. As RIL becomes increasingly consumer facing, it has the experience of reaching the nooks and corners of India. Add to this cutting-edge technologies and tools such as AI (artificial intelligence), Blockchain and AR/VR (Augmented Reality/Virtual Reality) and big data comes into play for all Indians.[313]

Figure 32 outlines the longer-term strategy being touted. Once Facebook has established itself in JioMart and gained control of the big data, the collaboration will expand into virtually all areas of Indian society including banking, farming, healthcare, education, manufacturing, transportation, logistics, and entertainment. Literally, the most detailed map of every place, object, business, individual, relationship, and transaction imaginable in India is within the scope. Facebook's machine learning systems will receive this bounty in real time. Once WhatsApp is in the door as Reliance's e-commerce partner, it would be a natural extension for Facebook to bring in its other platforms deeper into India.

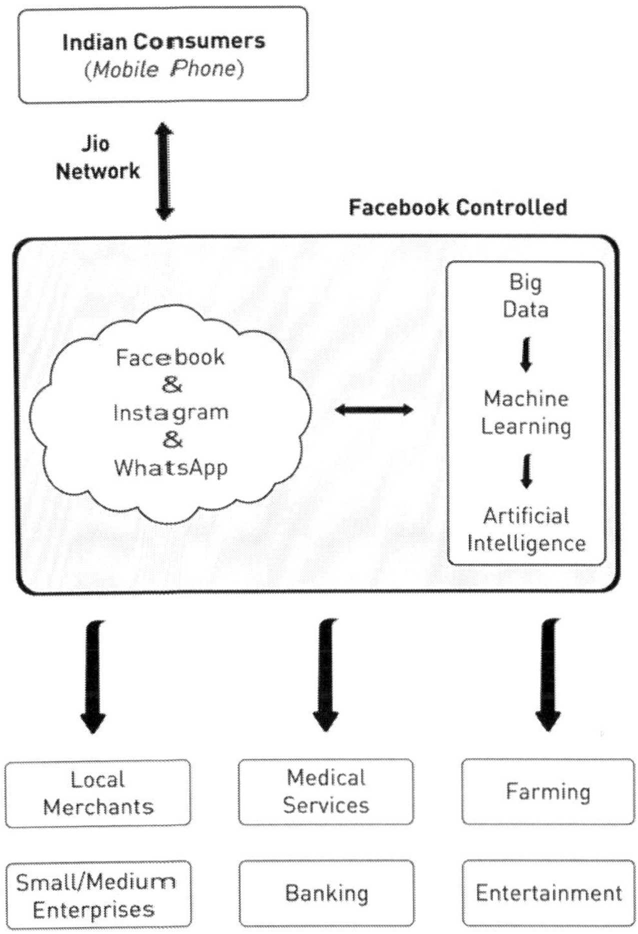

Figure 32: Facebook and Jio's India Strategy

Reliance's advantages—such as Indian language-based communications, Indian regulatory clearances, the momentum to build the unique JioMart network with thirty million local merchants across the country, local credibility, and the means to build networks with farmers, manufacturers, and civil society—should have been leveraged for the sole benefit of India. There is no way that Facebook or any other foreign firm could replicate these assets on its own. These benefits have been undervalued and sold off.

The real prize in the collaboration is the intelligence derived from the data on millions of Indians. Big data on all kinds of transactions and personal messages from millions of users is the most powerful weapon in the AI revolution. Facebook's appropriation of it is a case of blatant digital colonization that will further embolden all the social media giants in their aggressive interventions into India.

Facebook will use India as a testing ground with no real accountability or repercussions because it can take risks that would not be viable in the US market. In fact, within a few weeks after its Jio partnership in India, Zuckerberg told the US investment community that Facebook plans to leverage the ecommerce success of WhatsApp in India to other countries.[314]

Most Indians view Facebook's move as a great gift to the country without even having any serious debate on the complex issues. Essentially, Facebook has positioned itself for a major coup in India in the following ways:

1. *Intellectual and psychological control*—Power to shape public discourse on social media even more than it has in the past.
3. *Political control*—Influence to decide what is fake news and what is legitimate.
4. *Currency control*—Potential ability to exploit digital currency and compromise the power of the Reserve Bank of India. This is part of a war for the world's future reserve currency in which China has also launched its own cryptocurrency.

At certain times, especially when it is under political pressure from the US government or the European Union (EU), Facebook has exhibited self-awareness about its social-political power and has contemplated self-restraint. For instance, there was an internal project in 2018 to investigate its use of divisive content for enhancing its revenues. An internal slide in this review read: "Our algorithms exploit the human brain's attraction to divisiveness", and warned that "if left unchecked", Facebook would feed users "more and more divisive content in an effort to gain user attention & increase time on the platform".[315] This was said during an internal effort to understand how its platform shaped user behavior and how the company might address the potential harm being caused while maximizing its profits. Mark Zuckerberg publicly expressed concern about the "sensationalism and polarization" caused by Facebook. However, once the public scrutiny fizzled out, so did Facebook's interest in this introspection. Zuckerberg and other senior executives abandoned the inquiry and let Facebook divisive products continue.[316] There continue to be revolts by Facebook employees accusing its policies and practices of ethical violations.[317] Yet, Indians have acquiesced to the supremacy of this new devata.

I predict the Facebook-Jio deal will be one of the major factors in undermining India's long-term dreams of technological leadership. This is also an insult to India's technocrats. Despite having all the components in their possession, Indian industrialists simply failed to integrate them into a comprehensive indigenous solution of their own.

As a result of this precedence, other Indian tech companies are believed to be shopping for investments from US digital giants for similar deals. This means that just like Indian local kings fought each using the help of armies from French, Dutch, and British, so also it will be the foreign multinationals that will increasingly pull the strings from across the oceans to determine the competitive outcomes inside India among rival Indian companies.[318] India's current billionaire industrialists are analogous to the rajas that pandered to the British during the colonial era. The "digital transformation of India" being touted by Mukesh Ambani and celebrated by Indians reminds one of the civilizing missions of the British East India Company.[319]

History is destined to repeat itself. The European colonizers were obsessed with studying India and Indians in minute detail and using this knowledge in their quest for power over Indians. They invested heavily in researching cartography and navigation methods as well Indian diversity, cultural vulnerabilities, languages, religious practices, internal politics, and divisions. They used these insights to penetrate Indian hearts and minds and infiltrate the country's power structures. And India simply did not bother to respond by sending its scholars, spies, and travelers to foreign lands to understand them and counter them. Indians' introversion and complacency has cost them their sovereignty repeatedly over the past thousand years. Yet India has not learned its lessons.

GOOGLE-DEVATA

Within a few weeks post the Facebook deal, there was an even bigger deal involving Google's investment in Jio. Most of the concerns expressed above for Facebook also apply to Google, so I will not restate them.[320] In many ways, Google is even more predatory than Facebook in its secret exploitation of data belonging to others. In fact, Google's leaders have been explicit about their grandiose ambitions of reshaping the world order, and their strategy to achieve this is to control all the data they possibly can about your whole life. When asked to define what Google's core business is, co-founder Larry Page said it is,

> personal information ... The places you've seen. Communications ... Sensors are really cheap ... Storage is cheap. Cameras are cheap. People will generate enormous amounts of data ... Everything you've ever heard or seen or experienced will become searchable. Your whole life will be searchable.[321]

As part of its Google collaboration, Reliance Jio bragged that it will make 5G phones built on "made-for-India" Android operating system. It will "join hands with tech giant Google to build an Android-based smartphone operating system". The key issue is simply ignored in the announcement: whether Jio would control the source code, not only of the Indian adaptation of the operating system but also of the main Android system. This is needed to prevent becoming dependent on something critical controlled by the foreign party. The Indian adaptation will need to keep up with the frequent enhancements in the main Android, and this would require having the source code and proficiency in its use. Otherwise, the Indian version would soon be obsolete. It seems like a deal that fixes Jio's dependency status long-term.[322]

The saddest part of this is that India's high-profile thought leaders and social media activists have not come to the mat to wrestle with these complex issues. There should have been public hearings or government hearings like in the US and EU to cross-examine the tech giants. If nothing else, it would have shown a spine and backbone on India's part. If India is for sale, at least it should not be sold off so cheap!

When Artificial Intelligence is discussed, Indian leaders often lack the knowledge and insight to grasp its seriousness.

Some people are mesmerized by the romantic vision of robots with American accents at their gatherings. I am shocked by the incompetence of many speakers at literary festivals, think tanks, conclaves, and the media in general. They seem focused on arousing public emotions with the latest scandals, gossip about celebrities, and other shortsighted outbursts. The looming tragedy, though, is that India's youth are unlikely to achieve their aspirations because their future has been compromised.

The lack of serious Indian opposition and scrutiny of the foreign tech giants is appalling and raises suspicions of the secret inroads they have made. Contrary to this, Google and Facebook, in particular, face escalating legal, political, and public relations fights in the West. US Congressmen have held hearings in which they have accused Google of stealing content from Americans.[323] And the Australian and EU governments are cracking down against the US tech giants as well.[324] But Indians feel proud of being included in this new world order and unconcerned about the subordinate place it is being assigned to.

9

PSYCHOLOGICAL HIJACKING

Weak-minded men do not begin anything out of fear of difficulties; mediocre men begin a work but abandon it when obstacles come in their way; but strong-minded persons though repeatedly hindered by difficulties do not give up what they have once begun.

—Bhartrihari[325]

In this age of Kali, men have put merit out of sight. They show their adroitness and skills in disputes, bickering and aspersions.

—Sant Tukarama[326]

CHAPTER HIGHLIGHTS

- An Indian grand narrative would enable tradition to be brought together with modernity as the basis for shaping Indian society. Because of the leadership's failure to develop this narrative, Western social sciences serve as the foundation of Indian educational institutions at all levels.
- Vedic social theory is based on dharma as the foundation on which artha (pursuit of material prosperity) and

kama (pursuit of desires) can be enjoyed. But if these are indulged without dharma, the result is an unhealthy society.

- There is a vacuum of identity that is being filled by superficial and destructive behavior on social media for escapism, quick limelight, and rabblerousing.
- There has been a serious psychological decline in the character of Indians due to a combination of historical factors as well as problems with the present discourse.
- The present psychological vulnerabilities of Indians, especially of the youth, provides the perfect soil for foreign digital platforms to shape the new myths, icons, heroes and villains, values and standards on which they are crowned winners or declared losers.

COGNITIVE DISARRAY

In their greed for pleasure and gain, men sacrifice everything, even life itself. The duties proper to age and station are forgotten. Men pursue what is not their own business. They run after a comic actor like a goblin after an oblation. Let them catch sight of a rich man and infallibly they will treat him with respect.

—Sant Tukarama[327]

Vedic Social Science

The grand narrative of a people is the structure and grammar of their civilization from which emerges their collective **sankalpa** (deep resolve). India's collective identity is still burdened with the damage from years of colonization, further worsened by the failures of leadership post Independence that have destroyed the very fabric of national unity. As a result, there is a gap in their collective psyche about who they are. The public lacks a clear-cut consensus to bring people together onto one unified platform apart from their basic needs of survival. Dialogue on this issue of shared history and aspirations tends to generate a mixture of anger against historical forces and emotional outbursts of bravado claiming invincibility. These theatrics, however, have not resulted in a productive outcome.

The collective consciousness of Indians and the outlook of modern institutions ought to be shaped by indigenous worldviews. The guiding principles should be traditionally integrated and unified, while remaining flexible and relevant for current times. However, little serious work has been done to adapt and apply aspects of the traditional teachings to today's policymaking.

This is relevant to AI because as discussed in Chapter 4, AI platforms are culturally biased and not neutral. Machine learning systems have certain implicit or explicit values, norms, and ideals that serve as the target for training the algorithms. Artificial Intelligence is a force multiplier that strengthens whatever values and policies are embedded within it, whether visible or not. The ideology to be implicitly embedded in the AI-based models is defined by whosoever controls the models—currently it tends to be driven by worldviews based in the US or China. The US digital giants incorporate an American set of social-political premises cherished by their elite owners; in China the government supplies the narrative.

India has missed a key opportunity to develop an Indian grand narrative that could serve as the substratum for its own AI platforms. Such a narrative would enhance the shared identity across the population and help Indian society coalesce and function under a common value system. Unfortunately, the exact opposite is happening. India's elites have adopted digital platforms from US and Chinese companies, subjecting its public to foreign influences that do not align with Indian values and customs.

Even before the arrival of AI, India's planners relied on a hodgepodge of obsolete European socialist and liberal theories that were sprinkled with traditional ideas and Vedic jargon. Independent India continued many British norms (including the education and criminal justice systems), and even today the social science models taught in Indian universities use Western frameworks to interpret Indian society. These social sciences represent the Vedic tradition as something exotic, ancient, and dead; worse still, it is even presented as primitive and dangerous, just as colonialists did in the past.

The decolonization of the social sciences has not even begun. For example, the Indian Council for Social Science Research (ICSSR) in the Central Government remains in the clutches of colonial theories and methods, despite the current BJP government's public stance of championing academic decolonization. The *ICSSR's definition of social sciences and its methodologies are based on Western sociology.* Ironically, when I proposed projects that would deconstruct the colonial approaches and develop a fresh approach based on Indian traditions, I was told that all projects must comply with the established methodologies in the social sciences. The ICSSR still faithfully follows the rules established by the old colonial masters. The deep inferiority complex among officials is an invisible fence, imprisoning them in Western sociology.

Instead of using Western sociology, the Vedic concept of **purushartha** (the four pursuits of life) would serve as a better lens through which to examine Indian society. The following table shows these four pursuits along with my approximate adaptations in modern terminology.

- *Artha* is the pursuit of material wellbeing and this encompasses wealth, economic infrastructure, assets, and property, all of which today culminate into power. It can be adapted today to refer to the economic and political aspects of a society.[328]
- *Kama* is the pursuit of desires, sensory gratifications, pleasures, and aesthetics. Today it can mean the mental and psychological conditioning leading to lifestyles, fashions, and emotional desires.[329]
- *Dharma* refers to the right metaphysical and ethical foundation for knowledge and action. It should be the ground on which one is rooted while pursuing artha and kama.
- The proper and balanced pursuit of all three of the above leads to the fourth goal, *moksha*, which can be loosely translated as liberation in the ultimate sense.

Purusharthas (Four Pursuits of Life)	**Modern Adaptation**
Artha	Economics, Employment Geopolitics
Kama	Psychology, Emotions, Agency
Dharma	Ethics and Metaphysics
Moksha	Liberation

The important point is that artha and kama must be pursued within the parameters prescribed by dharma, not independently of them. When they are circumscribed by dharma, the pursuits of artha and kama are natural human instincts that provide discipline. Sage Veda Vyasa (legendary author of many key Hindu texts) says in *Mahabharata*, "It is through dharma that artha and kama should be acquired".[330]

Without dharma as the guiding principle, the pursuits of art, music, food, travel, and poetry can lapse into mere sensory gratification—what is called the entertainment industry. The same principle applies to the narrow pursuit of money and power. In the dharmic tradition one should have wealth, prosperity, and a sense of empowerment. However, unless steered by dharma, the result is inevitably a corrupt society, as is now evident in India.

All the pursuits are supported by the Vedic principle of **yajna** (dharmic sacrifice), which means giving back for the purpose of maintaining balance and equilibrium in any ecosystem. The cycle of life is sustained between the devas and humanity through the bridge of sacrifice, as expounded in the *Bhagavad Gita* 3:11–3:16. A healthy system is one that is in equilibrium at all levels—the individual's body, the **rashtra** or nation, all of humankind, and all sentient beings including nature at large. Yajna requires us to be net givers, not net takers.

The traditional approach to a healthy, balanced society is represented in the figure below.

Yajna ➔ Dharma ➔ Artha and Kama

People have, however, forgotten the principle of yajna, which is the foundation of the sustainable equilibrium from which artha and kama are generated. Unfortunately, the pursuit of kama and artha is today being driven primarily by carnal desires, greed, and fear.

Today's Indian society is **tamasic** (laden with lethargy and toxicity) because artha and kama have become disconnected from dharma. This problem is not with the Vedic social system, but with contemporary society. *The shift from Vedic* *to Western social theories has made Indian society vulnerable because its people are lost between the two worlds.*

The AI systems proliferating today are intended to attract and influence people that have abandoned dharma and lost their moorings. The machine learning systems of American digital platforms are using big data to build the personal profiles of people's kama and artha *weaknesses* on an unprecedented scale. Each individual and group is meticulously tracked and modeled as a portfolio of predispositions that can be targeted, influenced, and manipulated. By stroking their personalities and weaknesses, AI systems easily sway people with external stimuli for commercial and political purposes.

In contrast, people anchored in dharma have a more cultivated conscience, a deeper and more vibrant awareness of the consequences of their actions, and they are less likely to be swayed by kama–artha-based temptations.

Psychological Decline

Those who are devoid of vidya, tapas, charity, good conduct and dharma, pass their lives like beasts in human form and are merely a burden on this earth.

—Bhartrihari[331]

Lapse of Yoga

Yoga is a comprehensive system for the development of individuals at all levels, but in modern times it has become diluted. Its practice has diminished from what was originally a sophisticated, nuanced, and powerful system of spiritual and physiological practices. When incorporated as a lifestyle in its entirety, yoga cultivates self-discipline and enhances cognitive abilities such as attentiveness, memory, analytical skills, communication skills, and most of all the clarity to understand circumstances in their proper context at multiple levels. The yogis pursued their svadharma i.e. one's own duty, with a purity of lifestyle that became internalized as their very nature. Their outward lifestyle was a spontaneous expression of the inner state of ananda (bliss). Sadly, many of these qualities are missing in today's India. There has been an overall decline in cognitive faculties, including decay in social and emotional intelligence at all levels from leadership to the masses.

Indian youth suffer from poor attention spans and weak reading habits that could enlighten them. Many of them are unmotivated toward academic rigor because they only need Google to find sufficient information to scrape through. The practice of going to a library and poring over books to complete assignments or gain knowledge has become obsolete. Their aim in studying is to get a job, find a marriage partner, and settle down. The pursuit of knowledge for its own sake is uninteresting. Universities are frequently turning into centers of politics rather than communities of serious study. Meanwhile, the West has systematically studied benefits of yoga and meditation and incorporated them into its own mind sciences research.

Indians still possess some residue of these important qualities, a karmic effect of the **tapasya** (selfless sacrifice toward a higher purpose) done by their ancestors and rishis. This heritage, however, is callously and mindlessly being squandered.

The result is a frighteningly dumbed down population whose emotional buttons can be pushed by machines. The most successful hooks and tricks being used in AI systems to lure people, capture attention, and get them addicted are the ones that exploit a person's cognitive weakness ruled by greed (artha) and lust (kama) without a foundation of dharma.

Lapse of Bhakti

A fool is one who is extremely idle to the extent that he just keeps on hoping that someone will come from somewhere and solve his problems without his doing anything for that purpose.

—Sant Ramdas[332]

Another traditional source of inner strength is bhakti, the path of devotion through which the divine is experienced as immanent and omnipresent, manifest in physical form. The societal power structures were traditionally decentralized, based on the view that every external form is a manifestation of divinity, and each person has direct access to it without any need for an institutionalized religious authority.

Genuine bhakti must be cultivated through persistence and discipline and is not intended to escape responsibilities. You cannot relinquish duties by outsourcing them to a deity, nor simply pick and choose from a buffet of practices based on your whim. The integrity of the entire system from end to end must be understood and respected.

The bhakti tradition was based on an emotional and selfless relationship with God. Unfortunately, this has degenerated into a transactional system with God: One can perform rituals and offer material gifts to an intermediary (like a priest) in exchange for seeking a material reward. Seen in the AI framework, the effect this has on people is akin to reinforcement learning—the feedback loop reinforces certain beliefs. Such low-level bhakti is always available to newcomers, but sincere bhaktas or disciples, should lead a life of yajna to advance beyond the elementary stage.

Many people misinterpret the shastras and take refuge in the traditional shlokas (verses), rituals, symbolism, and stories believing that God will save them from worldly shocks. What they conveniently ignore is that the Vedic tradition requires people to do their part with tapasya, something that many people have increasingly abandoned.[333]

The distortion of bhakti into emotional neediness and dependence on a deity for petty gains has transformed into yet another degeneration: the public's tendency to lionize and idolize all kinds of celebrities, politicians, and public figures. Many such icons have become the object of devotion as though they were deities; the public lives in awe of them out of insecurity, fear, and greed. This degenerate bhakti feeds the slavish fawning over leaders in the hope of being rewarded emotionally or materially. This has led people to abandon independent thinking, reasoning, and responsibilities.

People thus conditioned are perfect targets for digital platforms equipped with AI to turn them into psychological dependents in exchange for gratifying simple desires.

Figure 33 shows how bhakti has slipped into personality cults and is now headed toward digital cults and slavery.

- The left side of the diagram shows true bhakti, in which devotees worship the divine in the form of a deity. The foundation is dharma, and the outcome is a lifestyle of yajna.
- The second stage depicts degeneration, in which individuals mindlessly follow some leader out of emotional weakness and neediness. People want a leader they can treat like a devata, someone to whom they can hand over their personal problems and responsibilities in exchange for emotional succor. Voluntary surrender of agency also stems from a persistent slave mentality,

the result of being colonized for too long. Adharma (violation of dharma) has led people to a hedonistic lifestyle of overconsumption, visible in mind-bogglingly large numbers of people that typically show up at melas, pageants, and gatherings mainly to enjoy the tamasha with some personality cult.

- The final stage, shown on the right, is the result of digital systems capturing users emotionally with trendy inducements and turning them into what I consider digital slaves of Google-devata, Facebook-devata, and Twitter-devata, among others.

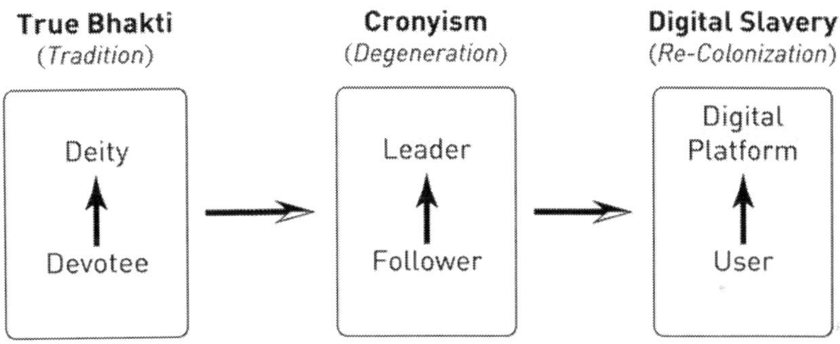

Figure 33: Degeneration of Bhakti

In other words, today there is already a population of intellectually and emotionally enslaved people running helter-skelter to maximize some personal reward, and it is simply a matter of replacing the object of their intellectual or emotional attachment with the products of AI.

Lapse of Kshatriyata

Looking at your own svadharma you ought not waver, for there is nothing higher for a Kshatriya than a righteous war. ... Happy indeed are the Kshatriyas, who are called to fight in a righteous battle... But if you will not fight this righteous war, then having abandoned your own duty and fame, you shall incur demerit.

—Shri Krishna[334]

A psychologically resilient society requires the traditional quality of **kshatriyata** (the attributes of a kshatriya), which is leadership with valor and a willingness to sacrifice for a higher cause. It requires courage, but also strategic thinking, astuteness, and perspicacity. Kshatriyas are in control outside their comfort zone and face opponents head-on. Encounters in the kurukshetra are useful for kshatriya training just like big data is needed for machine learning.

Kshatriyata is often confused with activism. In fact, one reason for the lack of kshatriyata today is that social media activism is a quick and easy path bypassing the required rigor and training. Low-caliber activists resort to internet brawls and mudslinging; winning inconsequential internet battles assumes far too much importance and sucks up considerable energy. Living the social media romance of heroism by winning virtual dogfights has become a popular form of entertainment. All such pursuits are counter to kshatriyata. The table below contrasts activism and intellectual kshatriyata.

Activism	Intellectual Kshatriyata
Has no dharmic underpinnings; opportunistic.	Grounded in dharma.
Based on short-term goals.	Strategic; long-term persistence.
Emotional, loud voice and good public relations skills.	Scholarly, deep purva-paksha to understand opponents.
Popularity as the measure of success.	Success through responsibility to effect structural change.
Begins and ends on social media.	Engagement with serious intellectuals, think tanks, and policymakers.

Today's armchair activists have precious little experience fighting in the kurukshetra but are becoming popular by pontificating from digital platforms, keeping well within their comfort zones in the company of like-minded people.

The present crisis of kshatriyata came about as a result of India's prolonged history of oppressive foreign rule. To survive brutal rulers, people improvised jugaad methods for personal success, and the collective good of their communities took a back seat. Assertive leaders were eliminated by the invaders, as when the brave Sikh gurus were tortured and killed by Muslim rulers. Under British rule, those who cooperated were rewarded for their capitulation as in the case of zamindars (Indian landowners appointed by the British) and babus (Indians serving in administrative positions helping British rule). Survival required playing it safe and not taking risks.

The collapse of kshatriyata is conspicuous in Indian history. In the eighteenth century, the British easily recruited Indian sepoys to serve under their command because the sepoys had no sense of patriotism, no hesitation about working for foreign colonizers. In fact, Indian soldiers fought over one hundred wars under British command. *But the British failed to raise even a single garrison in China.* Chinese soldiers refused to serve under British command, exhibiting superior kshatriyata. Today's elites in India compete for favors from American digital platforms, while China banned those platforms years ago and built their own highly competitive digital platforms.

In the Vedic framework, each of the **varnas** was a type of social capital, and all varnas were required to keep the society balanced and healthy. I want to clarify that my use of varna as categories of social capital (political, intellectual, economic, and labor) is not based on birth but purely on merit and hence is not the same thing as the caste system. When any one of the varnas becomes weak, or when they are not working in harmony, society falters like a sick body with dysfunctional organs. Or when nepotism turns it into a system of birth-based discrimination, it degenerates into corruption. Kshatriyata is the body's immune system and when it is compromised, the body is vulnerable.

Due to an ever-widening gulf between the aspirations and capabilities of today's youth, they end up in frustration. The youth are psychologically fearful and cannot face their situation in the spirit of kshatriyata. Their deep fear leads them astray and indulgences become a form of escape, perpetuating the cycle.

Fear of future ➔ Escape into short-term hedonism ➔ Cycle of desperation

The abdication of responsibility on the part of society's leaders is camouflaged by excessive public events filled with bombastic proclamations. The loss of kshatriyata has reduced India's ability to build institutions as instruments of power. India needs to interpret Chanakya's governance principles written in his *Arthashastra* text for modern times and incorporate them into AI to build and operate the power structures.

Lapse of Jnana

> *In the dark age of Kali, men with false reputation of learning will, by their acts, cause truth to be contracted and concealed. And in consequence of the littleness of their knowledge, they will have no wisdom. And for this, covetousness and avarice will overwhelm them all. And wedded to avarice and wrath and ignorance and lust, men will entertain animosities towards one another, desiring to take one another's lives.*
>
> —*Mahabharata*[335]

Jnana refers to knowledge in the broad sense and includes both worldly knowledge and knowledge beyond the senses. But today's gurus, though trained in spirituality, are typically not subject-matter experts in worldly domains. Spiritual practices do provide them a foundation for acquiring pragmatic knowledge, but that acquisition requires dedicated study as well as practical experience. After close conversations with at least twenty-five gurus over several decades, I found none of them to be adequately informed about different world cultures, histories, philosophies, and psychological characteristics. Yet their followers put them on a pedestal as a fount of knowledge, which makes it difficult for them to learn from experts on specialized worldly domains. Gurus must not succumb to followers' pressure and must be honest about things they have little expertise in.

The followers of many popular gurus confuse **paramarthika** teachings (pertaining to the ultimate reality beyond all material existence) and **vyavaharika** teachings (pertaining to the empirical world we live in). Though gurus might grasp the difference, their followers often incorrectly apply paramarthika teachings to vyavaharika contexts. Some spiritual teachers add to the public's confusion with a mishmash of escapist and dysfunctional gibberish that is accepted without adequate scrutiny.

As a result, India's rich and diverse popular culture has slipped into escapism; the boundaries between reality and fantasy are often blurred. Many self-styled experts in Vedanta misinterpret the world as an illusion, thereby giving intellectual sanction to such escapism.

Inevitably, such a population vulnerable to escapism will welcome the seduction of AI-based virtual realities. India's large and emotionally susceptible population will be one of the biggest markets for such artificial fantasy products.

I find that public discussion of these vulnerabilities is met with considerable anxiety and even outright hostility. Many people are threatened by any critique that could puncture their comfort zone. However, I offer these assessments as constructive criticism to build resilience among Indians, because facing the challenges of AI will require grit and mental strength.

DIGITAL OPIUM OF THE MASSES

Identity Vacuum[336]

It will not be wise, however, to engage in a blind rat-race of consumption and production as if man is created for the sole purpose of consumption.

—Deendayal Upadhyaya[337]

Any analysis of the fragile nature of Indian identity must delve into the historical influences that led to the vacuum of identity prevalent today. These are shown in Figure 34 and summarized as follows.

1. *Colonial Devastation.* The colonial era destroyed India's traditional knowledge systems, self-esteem, local institutions of governance, and self-sufficiency, and made Indians dependent on foreigners both materially and emotionally.
2. *Misunderstanding of Vedanta.* Due to a variety of factors, the Vedanta worldview became misunderstood, with too much emphasis being placed on otherworldly aspects and not enough clarity on worldly action. People also resorted to escapism as a means to maintain dignity in the face of slavery. This legacy continues today, with many gurus promoting foolish ideas that the empirical world is to be shunned, an approach that has muddled the public understanding of the need for pragmatic actions.
3. *Social Sciences.* The social sciences imported from the West were used to deconstruct Indian society into categories of abuser/abused. Divisions based on caste, region, language, religion, and gender have solidified into political vote banks. This fragmentation has created additional psychological tension.
4. *Postmodernism and Moronization.* Postmodernism theories entered India through Westernized Indian elites. Popular with Indians educated in English, they have gradually trickled down to Indian language institutions as well. These theories attack the Indian grand narrative, creating an intellectual vacuum that makes the task of unifying Indians more difficult.

5. *New Identities Based on Digital Media.* The vacuum of a grand narrative is being filled with new kinds of identities that yield to external intellectual, political, and religious norms, which are mostly against India's self-interest.

Confusing India's intellectuals further, five formal genres of academic scholarship have been imported into India since independence. I have called these the five waves of Indology.[338] Foreign inspired and controlled social media is increasingly influencing the youth's identities, values, and self-esteem. Social media is a potent medium for manipulating the micro-identities of groups like Dalits, Muslims, and regional peoples, using chauvinistic messages of pride as well as hateful messages against other groups.

The lack of dharmic compass is producing students that cannot frame a simple discussion, are tongue-tied when faced with educated Westerners, lack the capacity for original thinking, and are reduced to emoting rather than thinking critically. They cover up intellectual deficiencies with aggressive, baseless opinions.

As a result of the disruption of narratives and psychological insecurities, India today is not pursuing the ideals of either Bharat or those of the West. The previous section discussed the psychological decline resulting from compromising the tenets of yoga, bhakti, kshatriyata, and jnana. The Bharatiya social fabric has atrophied in modern India, making it disjointed from tradition.

The West developed differently, pursuing institutionalized methods of enforcing external morals that are based on collective salvation, and social compliance by heavy-handed laws and institutions. The latest AI technology is a powerful tool for strengthening such a compliance-based approach.

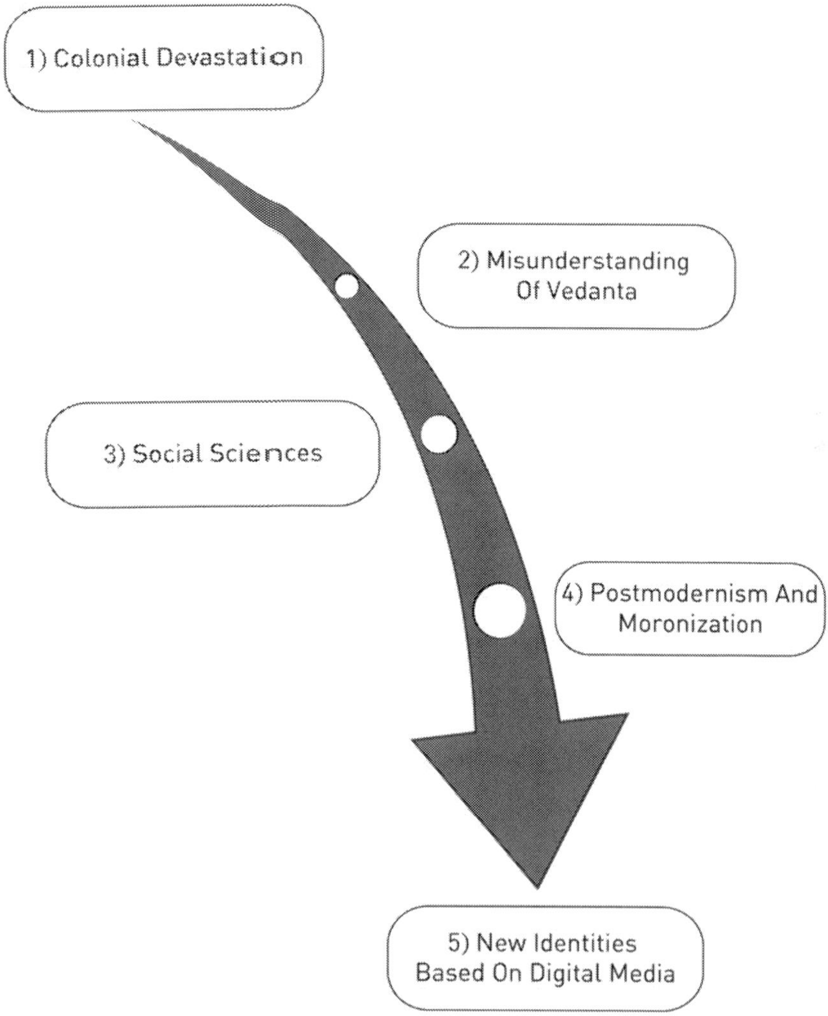

Figure 34: Digital Identity

Indians began actively chasing the Western framework especially after independence, but modern India has not achieved the maturity of a European-style society with law-abiding and efficient institutions. Yet, it has lost its dharmic foundation. India is caught between these two ideals, trapped between the two narratives without embracing either.

The Vedic ideal is rooted in the ancient nation called Bharat. The new Westernized society of Indian elites can be called the Sensex nation, because this section of society is guided by the values of large corporations measured on the Sensex stock market index. There is a clash between the narratives of Bharat and Sensex—not because dharma is against commercial success but because the Sensex nation pursues the maximization of artha and kama detached from a dharmic substrate.

Western consumerism is now fully entrenched in India's culture, especially among the young and urban population. Indians have visibly been influenced by Western values such as instant gratification and the use of credit to live beyond their means, which were once decried in Indian society. Unlike prior generations when people were expected to work hard to earn and fulfill their basic needs, the youth today have assumed a grand sense of entitlement to have their desires satisfied. The youth are drawn toward leaders who dish out platitudes to make them feel good without demanding perseverance and rigor.

As long as India chases Westernization, it cannot claim to be the vishvaguru in a Vedic sense. The destruction of traditional sources of authority, texts, and reference points creates a vacuum in Indians' self-image, giving digital platforms an opportunity to insert their own principles.

Both camps—those aspiring for a unified ethos and grand narrative, and others aligned with the breaking India forces—have access to AI as a game-changer. At this moment, India is at a crossroads.

Tamasha

Indian public life has a large element of tamasha—a public spectacle typically of a dramatic kind but without serious pragmatic value. Social media is becoming a gladiator sport played in the digital coliseum to keep the masses entertained. Even the public intellectuals seem intoxicated by sensationalism, scandals, celebrity crimes, and their false sense of importance. Discussions tend to focus on who will win the next election, what political coalitions will form, and who will get booted out and thrown in jail. Stories of heroes and villains, victory and defeat that evoke extreme emotional responses get the traction. Opinions and shouting matches are more popular than serious intellectual engagement.

The social media platform provides a fast and easy route to popularity and instant recognition by jostling for limelight. Such a circus is being mistaken for democracy, development and global superpower status. It is easy to enter this arena as an overnight activist leader; having numerous followers on social media brings recognition, rewards, and high-profile appointments. Such persons grab opportunities to be on fora and make petitions, public declarations, and announcements. The public, on its part, does not have the discriminatory faculty to differentiate between eloquent speakers with strong social networking skills and others who truly work hard to effect real change. Antisocial elements abound as well, and this can be seen in the form of social media tribes spewing venom and taking potshots at rivals for emotional release.[339]

No better are the numerous physical events like literary festivals, conclaves, and other types of conferences where celebrity panelists often have little to say that is original.

Or as guests on TV shows, they passionately indulge in a verbal slugfest with other panelists. The moderators and event organizers dumb down the serious topics to cater to the short attention span because audiences are not wired for critical thought.

Lurking beneath the public tamasha is a deep inferiority complex, self-loathing, and insecurity. The feeling of powerlessness is buried under pretentiousness and bluster, and by closing ranks with those who wear the same mask. The leaders are being irresponsible because they play the game of conveying to people what is reassuring to hear in exchange for getting their support. *The political process relies on the votes of emotionally fragile people, and that requires making false promises.*

A similar political tamasha also exists in the US, but it does not pose an existential threat to the sovereignty of the US. There are no "breaking America" forces of any significance, and the institutions of power are far more robust than in India. Also, the US has no hostile neighbor at the door claiming American territory.

Aspirations and Fantasy

> *A fool is highly temperamental, without any courage, prides himself without having any virtues of any kind, wears clothes unsuited to his status or the time and place, considers money the ultimate in life, tries to make a mockery of everything. ... He wants to sit on the highest pedestal without qualifications for that, is always apprehensive that his true self will be revealed, envies others for getting things which he doesn't deserve. ... He doesn't get rid of his vices though he knows what the virtues are.*
>
> —Sant Ramdas[340]

In the dark age of Kali the whole world will be filled with mleccha behaviour, ideas and ceremonies and yajna will cease and joy will be nowhere.

—*Mahabharata*[341]

Indians are prone to make-believe realities of the kind provided by the film industry, cricket, song and dance, fantasy, hero worship, and other escapes from reality. These serve as emotional doorways into people's hearts. In the past these fantasy worlds were rooted in Indian narratives such as those found in itihasa (narratives of the past), but now the narratives of Disney, American cowboys, and foreign designer brands have popularized alien tropes, heroes, and values.

This hotchpotch popular culture is becoming incorporated into virtual realities using artificial/digital heroes and villains, fake news, inducements, and sensory gratifications. As noted earlier, *Indians commonly abrogate their responsibility and agency to gurus, parents, and public icons, making them vulnerable to AI systems that promise paternal comfort and instant gratification without any effort.*

Indians have a history of being duped by emotional manipulation. The British, for example, paid lip service to some Indian festivals and rituals to win over the natives even while exploiting them. They also manipulated identities to divide Indians. Thus, the Sikhs were flattered as a martial race while employing their services against other Indians. Even today, when an Indian leader visits the US or vice versa, the Indian media focuses too much on the pageantry, fanfare, and tamasha, enthralled by trivia like the Indian cuisine, the seating arrangements, the celebrities, and slick operators that fund and organize these settings to be in the limelight. While all this tabloid chatter is natural, it dilutes the matters of substance, and the hoopla becomes the headlines.

Such a dumbed-down society is relatively easy to exploit and control. Opponents can easily use aesthetics to disarm the social gatekeepers and get in the door. Give Indians some emotional victories, and they quickly lose sight of the pragmatic issues at stake. The British used psychological manipulation when they put Indian rajas on elephants and gave them a gun salute. The emotional ploy works to win over the populace due to the people's psychological weakness.

Especially dangerous is the rising aspirations of Indian youth to unrealistic levels; this is being fed by the popular rhetoric that India is a superpower. This is a dangerous cocktail: overemotional, overconfident, aggressive, and marginally educated people with a false sense of entitlement demanding instant gratification. Artificial Intelligence-based systems can manipulate the masses whose aspirations far exceed what they can achieve through legitimate means. The gap between aspirations and reality could turn into a tinderbox of social unrest.

The fantasy of having a Western identity is an emotional high ground. Even those who claim to oppose the mimicry of Westerners often chase Western accolades. Recently, some Westerners have become instant icons on Indian social media merely by restating some obvious points; they take advantage of the fact that Indians who suffer from an inferiority complex feel proud when a White person pats their back.

Unfortunately, the Americanisms that India's youth aspire to are the superficial aspects of US culture. Indians mimic Americans in the wrong ways—their habits of eating, talking, and dressing; their foul language and loose sexuality; their drug use and other decadent behaviors. Many Indian feminists imitate White women as their pathway to emancipation. Indians who may have little experience with the US are unaware that despite its self-indulgent pop culture there are deep values and attitudes, such as self-discipline, a strong work ethic, meritocracy, and conservative rootedness.

While the anglicized Indian youth in big cities mimic American popular culture, the youth in rural areas aspire to be like their urban peers. In short, urban youth are wannabe Westerners, and rural youth are wannabe Indian urbanites. Migrant workers share stories of their lives in the city with their friends and family back in the villages. In pre-internet times, such influence moved slower but today it travels at the speed of light. Fashion trends zip through multiple layers of society, especially among the youth. Therefore, it is a false assumption that rural Indians with a low-income lifestyle can withstand economic shocks. The trickle-down effect has raised aspirations of all strata of society.

The digital equivalent to becoming Americanized is to participate on American platforms and have one's private data included in the big data—giving one the feeling of having arrived on the world stage. Indians have given up too much agency to these foreign platforms and the captains of society are complicit.

10

HOW ROBUST IS THE RASHTRA?

What a country needs to develop is discipline more than democracy. The exuberance of democracy leads to undisciplined and disorderly conditions which are inimical to development.

—Lee Kuan Yew[342]

CHAPTER HIGHLIGHTS

- Anti-India groups I have described as breaking India forces in my previous writings are becoming organized to use AI for their goals to psychologically divide Indians into hostile camps fighting each other and the country at large. This will further weaken India at a time it faces numerous challenges.
- China is a world leader in AI, rivalling the US in the research and applications of this technology. Its military is highly AI-enabled, and this will increase its lead over India in certain strategic areas.
- India could utilize AI for nation-building, but its present establishment of industry, government and academia have not mobilized an ambitious development. Time is running out for India.

ARTIFICIAL INTELLIGENCE AND BREAKING INDIA FORCES

My book *Breaking India: Western Interventions in Dravidian and Dalit Faultlines* exposed anti-national people and organizations that exacerbate India's internal faultlines on caste, class, religion, and regional ethnicities. Their goal is to turn the entire country into a battleground of identity conflicts. Religious minorities are told the rest of the country has disenfranchised them. Tamilians are taught they belong to the Dravidian race that was invaded by the foreign Aryan race now living in north India.[343] Dalits are trained and manipulated to blame Brahmins. Poor villagers are evangelized to convert to Christianity with the message that Hinduism is the cause of their plight and the Church is the solution. Rural people are pulled into various Maoist movements with the promise of human rights. And thus, conflicts continue and expand.

Further agitating these social and political schisms is the fact that India's parliamentary democracy encourages vote-bank politics. People organize themselves into minority groups based on regional, religious, and socioeconomic identities. Their leaders create separate political mobilizations to bargain for special privileges. All these factors drain considerable resources just to keep the country together internally and safe from external hostile forces. These divisions seriously stress the fabric of society and its economy. Breaking India forces capitalize on unstable conditions and foment disequilibrium to jeopardize the integrity and sovereignty of India.

Such forces are testing the deployment of AI to organize India's fragments into new emotional networks with foreign nexuses in control. A wall of intermediaries camouflages this threat while the rapid infiltration continues under the guise of free services for the masses.

The AI systems of social media platforms, most notably Facebook, Twitter, and Google, have been experimenting with and training their models on predicting the behavior of Indians: what their weaknesses are, how to divert them into petty flare-ups and mutual abuse, and how to play the age-old divide-and-rule game.

In past eras, people with such knowledge could use it to create social disruptions that were mostly localized and not coupled with other world events. Today's technology of AI-driven psychological behavior intervention has reached new levels and can trigger unrest and havoc on a far more dramatic scale. This is the age of remote-controlled social disruptions.

An important example is the Russian interference in the 2016 US presidential election when it hired the UK firm Cambridge Analytics to use Facebook's data on American voters. Many people claim that the social unrest in the Middle East in 2010 called the Arab Spring as well as the recent riots in Hong Kong were also examples of social unrest triggered by foreign nexuses using social media.

My concern is over the heavy infiltration of foreign digital platforms that have positioned themselves as the arbiters of public discourse in India with alarming success. Twitter, for example, has already assumed the mantle of rule-maker and referee, deciding the outcomes of disagreements among different Indians just as the British East India Company adjudicated quarrels between Indian rajas—a position that gives Twitter immense power. The British colonizers took advantage of isolated rajas because none of them had enough surveillance capabilities outside their own narrowly defined interests and territories. This is how the British cleverly stitched together local kingdoms into a massive empire.

Today, this type of social-political power shift is being achieved with the help of digital platforms.

Indians who celebrate the use of digital technology do not realize that the platforms are controlled by foreign giants whose global clout compares to the East India Company. Ironically, the very same activists in India who wave the flag of decolonization are competing for blessings from Twitter, Facebook, and Google.

Through AI-enabled networks, people can be managed as obedient and happy consumers encouraged to follow guidelines and advice designed especially for them. They can also be made rebellious, angry, and mobilized for violence. Artificial Intelligence-based algorithms can play one Indian against another, promote one ideology over another, and monetize these divisions and disruptions for the benefit of clients. Social media can sway voting patterns and even incite mobs to violence. Hundreds of millions of unsuspecting Indians have helped US and Chinese tech giants accumulate a treasure trove of big data on India by using Chinese hardware and American digital platforms.

A big risk India faces is that the breaking India forces are being trained to use AI-empowered interventions to play havoc in Indian society. Such a scenario is imminent because factions like evangelists, Islamists, and Maoists are internationally well connected and their foreign sponsors are savvy about the use of the latest digital weapons for mass psychological manipulation. They are also insulated because they are operating from extrajudicial nexuses located abroad.

Artificial Intelligence is a force multiplier that can be used to undermine the unity of the rashtra, of political parties, and of communities by encouraging the flareups of fragments. Deep learning of individual behavior can be combined with fake news to manipulate psychology and public opinion. This has serious national security implications. For example, a foreign intelligence agency could compromise Indian leaders with sexual or financial blackmail. It is a fair assumption that many Indian leaders across the ideological spectrum are already vulnerable to subtle blackmail by the US and China. The private information stored in big data and machine learning models provide foreign countries and companies with the ability to compromise people at many levels—emotional, professional, and even legal.

Despite all these risks, Indians are not overly worried that foreign digital platforms will end up having too much emotional control over hundreds of millions of people. Artificial Intelligence is barely understood by India's social scientists, government officials, legal experts, and education leaders. Ironically, India's public intellectuals—social media celebrities, the blaring mainstream media voices, and political debaters—are heavily invested in supporting the digital media platforms that are recolonizing India. They build their popularity and boast their identities sitting on foreign platforms that are a fake foundation whose strings are being pulled from faraway places.

The diversity of India makes it difficult for its Constitution to withstand all these challenges. It is based on concepts drawn from the British and American political systems; it has been criticized for not being firmly grounded on the Vedic principles of rashtra and rajya, often equated with Western notions of nation and government, respectively. There is a fundamental difference between the top-down Western-inspired Constitution of India and the grassroots Vedic traditions of India's past. Despite so much constitutional and political flux in India, neither the majority Hindu population nor the many minority groups seem satisfied with the present status quo.[344]

This instability is not merely a matter of political parties fighting for power. Unlike in mature Western democracies, India's infighting can feed the centrifugal forces that threaten its sovereignty. India's Muslims, Christians, and ultra-leftist groups are being shaped, funded, and given extraterritorial support from their respective foreign influences. In other words, India's future is up for grabs, with many stakeholders and string-pullers located outside as well as within its boundaries.

THE CHINA THREAT

A wise person does not disregard even a weak foe,
proceeds with intelligence in respect of a foe,
anxiously watching for an opportunity.

—*Mahabharata*, *Vidura-niti*[345]

Another factor in stress testing the robustness of India's sovereignty is that it is situated in one of the most hostile neighborhoods in the world and the threats to its physical security are worsening. In addition, a lot of manpower resources are spent on anti-insurgency operations within India. A considerable part of the defense budget is, unfortunately, required to be spent on personnel salaries. Therefore, the research and development of advanced weapons cannot compete with China and the US that invest large budgets on advanced technologies for defense.

It is important to understand the depth and breadth of China's threat. The Chinese have demonstrated their ability to think long-term for nation-building and protecting the Han cultural and historical identity. Their goal is to surpass the West in every domain using AI as one of the primary strategic technologies.

The table below shows how China and India compared against each other a few decades ago and how they compare today. It shows that India was on par with China not long ago but has lost the race for advancement in recent years. An important difference in outlook is that Indians like to measure progress relative to their own past while China sets targets against the world's top competitor in each field. China's mindset is intensely competitive, and progress is not measured in terms of its own reference point. [346]

	1950s		Present	
	China	India	China	India
Urbanization (%)	12	17	61	35
	1970s		Present	
	China	India	China	India
Infant Mortality (Deaths/1000)	84	145	7	30
	1980s		Present	
	China	India	China	India
GDP (USD Billion)	191	186	13,600	2,700
Per Capita Income (USD)	195	267	9,771	2,000
Poverty Rate (%)	66	49	0.5	20
Literacy Rate (%)	66	40	97	74
Airline Passengers (Million)	0.7	3.0	611.4	164.0
Rail Network (000 Km)	52	61	127	68
	2000s		Present	
	China	India	China	India
Car Manufacturing (Million Units)	0.6	0.5	21.0	3.6

Sources: World Bank, OICA, Rail ministry, China Statistical Yearbook, UN.[347]

Many people criticize China's progress on the moral grounds of its human rights practices. But the above table presents a way to evaluate the condition of citizens in terms of their material and pragmatic needs. Rights must be evaluated both materially and emotionally, and the tradeoff between short-term and long-term must be considered. China prioritized material gain over emotional gain in the short-term and sacrificed short-term psychological freedoms to play the long game, ignoring the cynicism of its detractors. One must debate the pros and cons of human rights in democratic countries if short-term psychological freedom leads them to digital colonization.

To understand these statistics fully, one must delve into the historical differences leading to the present predicament. A major factor in China's favor is that it has had long and continuous experience in indigenous statecraft without prolonged foreign rule. Its sense of continuity and nationality have remained largely intact, and the government has put them to good use in developing its own version of modernity. In contrast, India's past one thousand years has been a messy history of disruptions of all kinds. Even after gaining independence, India pursued a path that was continuous with the colonial era rather than breaking with that past.

China established and pursued a development course based on its own concepts of society and politics, even though the optimization for long-term success required short-term compromises in economic equality and freedom of speech. For instance, China decided on a two-tier development strategy in which some cities and people got upgraded first, which then became the foundation for spreading the same prosperity elsewhere in China. This approach is fundamentally different from India's haphazard stampede of politicians fighting to get local development and win votes in their electoral constituency. In India, political jugaad drives the policies.

China has been accused of activities such as using data to create communal disharmony and other anti-national activities in certain countries.[348] Chinese internet apps have raised suspicions about cyber espionage and security risks. These are valid criticisms, but such attacks have never bothered China. China's position has been that it is optimizing its technological advancement, efficiency, and use of power toward its *own* goals; whether a policy is moral or ethical is considered irrelevant to these goals. To understand China on its own terms, the ethical and pragmatic criteria must be kept separate.

China has officially announced plans to supersede the US as the world's foremost superpower in every domain—including technology, economics, military power, and geopolitics. In anticipation of achieving world domination, it has launched a network of Confucian Institutes as flagships of its cultural and soft power projection. Nearly five hundred Confucian Institutes are now operational on six continents. A head-on clash between China and the US for world domination is inevitable. The question of where India stands in relation to this duopoly is critical to India's future.

For the foreseeable future, India is likely to remain largely a consumer of AI technology for defense, which means remaining a few steps behind these two leaders. India must view AI as a critical element of its national security. It faces a strategic disadvantage against China given the latter's considerable capability and ambition in its military-driven AI research agenda.

China's Baidu, Alibaba and Tencent are like the US's Google, Facebook, and Amazon in their appetite to expand their technological footprint globally. These foreign companies' lead in tech investments worldwide gave them experience in evaluating early stage companies in India, so they could cherry-pick the ones with the best potential. The Chinese investments were made both directly by Chinese tech giants as well as by their venture capital funds, and many such investments are routed via third countries (such as Singapore) so they do not show up in the Indian government's official records as Chinese investments.

One of the most insightful reports on India's dependence on Chinese technology has recently come out from Gateway House in India, titled 'Chinese Investments in India'.[349]

> While the BJP government focuses on governing border states through a democratic process on its own or through coalitions, the Chinese are blanketing the whole of India, including the border states, through their investments in multiple projects. It will create a diamond necklace around India that is so attractive and insidious that it will make China's potent Indian Ocean String-of-Pearls strategy seem less threatening.
>
> The last decade has seen heavy investments from Chinese companies into India, over $5 billion in 2018. ... Alarming are the investments by China's powerful BAT companies (Baidu, Alibaba and Tencent) in soft power projects in India—Artificial Intelligence, the Internet of Things and fintech. That's because the People's Liberation Army of China and the Communist Party of China have a symbiotic relationship with China's BAT, the makers of strategic domestic and overseas investments.[350]

Because most Indian venture financiers tend to be wealthy individuals and families, they can seldom make the one hundred-million dollars commitments needed to finance start-ups through the early losses.

The Chinese own a majority share of the smartphone market in India. India has recently banned several Chinese apps because they solicit unnecessary access to camera and microphones on the smartphones and collect large amounts of personal data including location, profession, friends' identities and interests, and personal photographs. However, deactivation of a user's account does not result in the old data being returned to the user or being deleted from the server.[351] This ban is good, but it is defensive and reactive to a border conflict. It is not by itself a strategy to jump ahead in AI research.

At some level, India's sovereignty is subject to the dictates of its foreign arms suppliers. This is the reason the Indian military has started taking AI very seriously and views it as a threat making current weapons and soldiers obsolete. Experts have noted that most Indian military applications of AI are still only at the conceptual stage. Among the concrete R&D projects, the Defence Research and Development Organization had claimed in 2013 that by 2023 it would be ready to deploy robotic soldiers.[352] In February 2018, the defense establishment set up a multi-stakeholder task force that included a broad range of leading technological government institutions to define and implement India's AI strategy in defense. A year later, an even higher-level team comprising the defense minister and the three chiefs of the armed forces took responsibility for providing strategic direction in AI. It was announced that AI-based defense products would be ready by 2024. But commentators have remarked that the budgets for such projects are drastically underfunded compared to efforts in the US, China, Russia, Israel and several other countries.

Some of the upgrades being planned for Indian industry and military could make India even more dependent on foreign technological platforms because India has not invested enough in research to keep up with global trends in weaponry. The fact remains that while China is a major disruptor of the world order in using AI as a weapon, India is on the defensive at the receiving end of this disruption.

India's critical defense needs cannot be met by internal manufacturing, according to India's own defense experts. India has always imported defense equipment—initially from Russia, then from France, and now increasingly from the US and Israel. No defense expert in India is willing to gamble by putting a freeze on imported weapons. To pay for state-of-the-art defense systems, India must earn hard currency through exports, and for this India needs globally competitive industries. Effectively, India cannot run away from the kurukshetra of geopolitics. Isolation is not a viable option.

India cannot afford further delay in coming to terms with the fact that the control of most big data and deep learning is effectively in the hands of companies based in the US or China. Americans primarily own the software algorithms, databases, and operating platforms; the hardware is mostly Chinese. India is at the mercy of their technologies. And the foreign owners of the AI technology and digital platforms have no legal accountability in India, nor do they have the interest of Indians at heart to the same extent as their vested interests in their home countries.

ARTIFICIAL INTELLIGENCE AND UNIFYING INDIA POSSIBILITIES

Indian activists should cease the tamasha of bombastic claims that India is on the verge of becoming a superpower on par with the US and China, and even forging ahead of them. Instead, serious thinkers should plan and implement how AI could be used in positive ways to tighten the grip on volatile situations. The widespread use of law enforcement, and propagation of the grand narrative could make AI a force for national stability.

The problem, however, is that unlike China, India has a fiercely democratic ethos entrenched in its public consciousness. The Constitution's preamble enshrines justice, liberty, equality, fraternity, and secularism as foundational principles. Any moves that appear to threaten these principles are routinely challenged in the Supreme Court. The courts and the polity assume that India is as robust as the mature Western democracies from which these principles were borrowed. Yet no other major democracy faces the same level of internal and external existential threats.

Chapter 1 explained how the social sciences can be completely overhauled through AI and how the goals and objectives of an AI system can serve as vehicles to spread the values of its owner.

- The AI systems of Google, Twitter, and Facebook incorporate those companies' ideas about what constitutes good or bad social discourse. They calibrate their machine learning systems to rate each page, post, and comment based on their own ideological criteria. These ideologies remain hidden from the public. The biases of Western thought are buried implicitly into the targets used for training the algorithms.
- Likewise, the Chinese have a clear sense of their own grand narrative and its ideological assumptions. China uses these assumptions to reshape the thinking of its citizenry, and the recent pandemic has expanded the

> use of such technologies. Wherever China spreads its technological footprint, its bias is subtly introduced and reinforced.

Unfortunately, India has not even begun to think along these lines. Considerable rhetoric has announced the renaissance of its ancient civilization. However, no modern schools of thought have been developed to bring these ancient ideas into present-day context, to educate the next generation based on these principles, and to inject the ideas into the models driving the digital platforms. Imagine if India developed a comprehensive national grand narrative, integrated its core values across all domains, and incorporated this narrative into every facet and institution of the country. This would be a strategy for using AI in the service of nation-building, as opposed to the present trajectory leading toward re-colonization.

As machines become smarter and humans become ever more dependent on them, a shift in the power structure is inevitable. A few powerful elites control the digital systems and these systems, in turn, will increasingly control the masses. Artificial Intelligence-based systems implicitly incorporate the values and ideologies about justice and human rights that are aligned with their developers. The ideological, emotional, and aesthetic control of this mental infrastructure is presently in foreign hands. China, on the other hand, developed its own digital platforms. From the beginning of this digital revolution, China has kept out the foreign influences. India, on the other hand, continues to invite foreign intrusions to penetrate at deeper and deeper levels. The price the country will pay for this will be heavy.

I am convinced that *decolonizing AI* is an absolute necessity for India to be a viable nation.

THE COVID-19 PANDEMIC IMPACT

The Covid-19 pandemic is accelerating and amplifying many of the disruptions that AI was already causing.

Unfortunately, India's overpopulation, lack of high-quality education for the masses, and high level of youth unemployment are serious liabilities that will worsen due to AI. The pandemic has added further economic stress. The World Bank estimates that millions of people in developing countries will be driven into poverty because of the pandemic.[353]

The pandemic is putting even more data in the hands of the digital giants—with more collection opportunities as well as increasingly invasive surveillance—leading to a greater transfer of agency from individuals to the digital systems. Despite numerous warnings, Indian authorities are only now beginning to think of controlling its data assets.

The shock experienced by India's large number of domestic migrant workers has made them more vulnerable materially and emotionally and has created opportunities for the breaking India forces. Meanwhile, India's exports will likely suffer because most countries are domesticating their supply lines and creating local jobs. Large numbers of workers from the Indian diaspora are returning to India and are not likely to go back in the next few years. India could enter a prolonged economic recession, combined with a dramatic rise in poverty levels, all of which worsen the impact of AI.

At the same time, the pandemic's temporary disruptions have been worldwide, and this gives India another chance to get its house in order and even leapfrog ahead.

CONCLUSION

Artificial Intelligence is disrupting many fragile equilibriums that hold together societies and the present world order. This trend was already accelerating before Covid-19 added greater momentum to it; over the next three to five years, the Indian population will experience its serious impact, yet nobody is preparing them for it.

Clearly, there is insufficient awareness of AI among the social, faith, and political leaders—as compared to the heightened awareness on other issues like global warming, pollution, water supply, genetically modified foods, pandemics, nuclear threats, and so forth. The public's concerns on AI-related issues are at the level where concerns of global warming were a quarter of a century ago; a lot needs to be done to quickly educate people.

This lack of public engagement is due to the huge knowledge gap between the players of the AI revolution and the masses that are being impacted by it. The public depends on its thought leaders for complex matters, but most public intellectuals do not know enough about these issues. And many of those who do know are vested in the success of the AI-driven economy. For instance, most reports on AI's impact on jobs are written by consultants or economists catering to corporate clients.

However, there is a silver lining: A few organizations and movements have popped up to raise such issues. Appendix D provides a list of some of these groups. But most of them are in Western countries and their concerns are based on targets relevant to the Western experience. I have argued for several decades that there is no such thing as a completely neutral ideology in today's world, and that claims of universalism are the biased projections by those in power. Presently, large portions of humanity are under the spell of what I have described as Western Universalism in my book, *Being Different: An Indian Challenge to Western Universalism*. Using the West's own history and development of thought as the absolute reference point for all humanity, the colonial system imposed it on others so successfully that the elites in countries like India have become prisoners of these very frameworks.

A few courageous authors in the West have raised this issue and even criticized Western AI companies for exploiting their former colonies for low-level AI work:

> The phenomenon of ghost work, the invisible data labor required to support AI innovation, also extends the economic relationship that used to exist between colonial powers and their colonies. Many former US and UK colonies—the Philippines, Kenya, and India—have become ghost-working hubs for US and UK companies. The countries' cheap, English-speaking labor forces, which make them a natural fit for data work, exist because of their colonial histories.[354]

My issue, however, is far more complex than merely the economic dependency of developing societies. *There could emerge a new level of Western Universalism empowered by AI*, and its targets, values and policies will get imported by countries like India where there is a history of the educated elites importing the latest Western lenses as a way to identify with Westernization.

For instance, the Black Lives Matter movement is important and relevant for the ongoing evolution of US society. But it is being exported to India with the dangerous assumption that jati equates with racism. The LGBTQ movement also has legitimate gripes in the West. The same framework for activism, however, cannot be blindly applied to India where the tradition has had a far more complex posture on homosexuality that is vastly different from the closedmindedness in the Abrahamic religions. In both these examples—BLM and LGBTQ—there is activism in AI circles in the West to protect the interests of those minorities from machine learning algorithms trained on white, heterogeneous targets. There is a clear and present danger that the new algorithms in the West, trained with BLM and LGBTQ sensitivity, will get foolishly and mindlessly adopted in India as part of the latest trend of "becoming Americanized". I cite the examples of BLM and LGBTQ merely for illustrating the broader issue of superimposing a foreign lens for the adoption of AI in a developing country.

India has recently announced a new education policy, called National Educational Policy (NEP) 2020, which is being praised by Indians for promoting their tradition. But I have serious reservations. Despite its use of traditional jargon and the emphasis on Indian content, the structure remains largely the Western liberal arts framework that embeds Western Universalism in its deep roots. Indians with Western liberal arts credentials will likely occupy key posts to implement this policy. Those from traditional backgrounds tend to lag in their knowledge of Western Universalism and would be unable to detect the use of Western liberal arts as a Trojan Horse to recolonize India. Artificial Intelligence could end up as the force multiplier inserting Western Universalism deeper into India's fabric than ever before.

As mentioned earlier, the term AI is used broadly to include a variety of distinct new technologies that are coming together under the umbrella of AI raising their level of intelligence and impact. The impact analysis can be organized in a three-tier structure on the timing and certainty of AI developments:

A. *Developments expected with high confidence by 2025*: These technologies are already established, and the timing of the public impact will be a matter of commercial viability and marketing. Overall, the impact will be positive, and AI will be smuggled as the Trojan Horse into the lives of unsuspecting people. The adverse consequences will start being felt in this time frame, but the tectonic shifts will not be clear to the public until a bit later.
B. *Longer term social consequences from 2025 to 2050*: These are the social crises discussed in this book—caused by inequalities, unemployment, and exploitations resulting from automation and AI-driven psychological manipulations. The sedated population will take a long time to comprehend the hoax perpetrated on them by the new elites of power. By then, depopulation on a large scale will be discussed as something unavoidable. This will be a messy affair with unpredictable social and political upheavals.
C. *Speculative future about 2050 onwards*: Eventually, the traumas and disruptions will settle down into a new kind of equilibrium. This is when the optimists will be proven right about the utopian benefits of AI. But the great new world order they dream of will have a small population, and its citizens will be

> seen as superhumans in comparison to the ordinary humans of today.

Of the five battlegrounds discussed in this book, the first four are not country specific. The first two—economy and geopolitics impact the sthula-sharira (physical body) while the latter two—agency and metaphysics—affect the sukshma-sharira (subtle body) of society.

Regarding the first battleground—the economic impact—the predominant view among reports on AI advocates that there be no concern about the loss of jobs. The argument being echoed is that AI will create more new jobs than it destroys. I find this utterly unconvincing. It is a ploy to avoid or at least delay controversy. The undeniable fact is that to stay competitive, businesses must adopt AI to cut costs and improve quality; the interests of workers are secondary. Even the optimists admit that the geographical locations where new jobs will be created will not be the same places where they are destroyed—creating imbalances between regions within a country as well between countries. Besides, the analogy of prior industrial revolutions does not apply here, because earlier the changes were slow and spread over multiple generations. But the AI disruptions are sudden and sweeping, giving few choices to those workers caught mid-career.

The remedy cited is that old workers would get re-trained for new technologies, but this is an empty promise because such voices have not set aside the massive funds required for such an exercise. Some conveniently pass this responsibility to governments and there are even proposals to guarantee universal income without the need to work; however, such socialist ideas have never been sustainable. Though many management consultants and economists have pumped out such reassurances, I am yet to see a detailed plan on how the crisis of jobs would be managed.

The geopolitical impact of AI—the second battleground—is highlighted by the rise of China as the contender for the world's foremost AI-based military-industrial complex. The country has made an unsurpassed level of commitment to AI and related technologies as the foundation for its future. China has bet the proverbial farm on AI. No discussion on AI is complete without examining China's role, and no evaluation of China's future can fail to include AI at the center of its strategies. The clash between the US and China is this race for AI leadership because both countries' current leaders know fully well that whoever dominates this technology stands to occupy the military and economic high ground. China is becoming like the European colonial empires of the past and is in an all-out imperialistic clash with the US.

Apart from the US, China, and a few other countries, most nations will lag increasingly as time goes by. It is virtually impossible to catch up in all the key elements of success that must be brought together—specialized AI hardware, big data resources turned into sophisticated assets, cutting-edge research, massive amounts of venture funding, and most importantly, visionary policies and implementation apparatus in government-industry-academic alliances.

While most people accept the efficacy of AI at the physical level, they still find it hard to accept its ability to decode human psychological behavior, to model and predict the choices people make, and to hijack emotions on a personal level.

The third battleground is over the agency and psychological control of the public on a large scale. Digital interventions through messaging and Virtual/Augmented Reality can already generate pleasures and activate brain processes correlated with dopamine, the feel-good hormone. What is coming next will be implants that go even further to artificially manipulate the mind. This will lead to remote-controlled dopamine and digitally managed mental states of individuals, and raise new ethical, social, and political dilemmas.

The old-school social sciences are being rendered obsolete with AI's superior ability to collect data on a mammoth and unimaginable scale in real time, and to find patterns and build behavior models that continually update with fresh data. Besides understanding a given social community, nation, or even lifestyle, smart machines are being trained to manage the social conduct of people through automated systems of rewards and punishments. I think of this as *the gamification of social behavior* and predict this is becoming commonplace.

The deep and broad influence of Western Universalism today makes it an important source of bias in the social effects of AI: Any gamification of society, be it formal and transparent or informal and secret, has biases based on some civilizational and cultural matrix. The guise of neutrality only makes it more insidious.

The fourth battleground is the metaphysics of consciousness—the nature of the self and what it means to be human. Though I am committed to the primacy of consciousness as the source of all existence, the AI-based trends in the world support a move toward a materialistic society. Machine intelligence does not depend on machines becoming conscious. The pragmatic success of AI will continue empowering the biological theories based on mechanistic models of living things. To whatever extent a living system can be modeled with algorithms, to that extent it can be augmented or replaced by AI-based intelligent systems. As less and less of a human's functionality remains beyond the reach of machines, the algorithms become more powerful at the expense of conscious beings. I am only discussing their relative share of pragmatic power, and not the morality, ethics, or the nature of ultimate reality.

This has implications for philosophical systems like that of Sri Aurobindo, concerning their view of the future evolution of consciousness. In what ways might consciousness evolve in the spiritual sense in parallel with the advancement of machine intelligence? How might the two be brought together, and can they be unified in a positive relationship? Or will there be a clash of civilizations—between algorithms and beings?

The pragmatic battle facing humanity later in this century will be between humans who have become dramatically enhanced in their bodies and minds with the help of the new technologies versus the rest of the humans who are like us. Will the humans 2.0 consider us parasites depleting the resources? Will they treat us in the same manner as many humans today treat animals?

The fifth battleground shows how the first four battlegrounds apply to India as a case study. In fact, India will be the epicenter for the disruptions of AI. Indians have had an amazing history of human capital being used for great achievements, but the leadership in recent generations has turned Indians into the labor class serving the world rather than building India's own intellectual property as an important form of capital.

Billionaires have been suddenly created by selling cheap labor to Western countries and importing goods and services to the large market of consumers. As a result, Indian organizations are way too much dependent on foreign inputs, endorsements, and validation and are not competitive at innovation, despite a plethora of Indians being internationally successful on a personal level. It is not surprising that India has slept through the race for many critical technologies such as AI hardware. This has serious implications in India's long-term ability to defend itself militarily in an increasingly hostile neighborhood.

The Foreign Direct Investment (FDI) driven growth and capital-intensive growth are top-heavy and have fueled the wealth creation for the top tier but utterly failed to create sufficient jobs for the masses.

The human capital has simply not been systematically developed and utilized, because of which India's large population is too poorly educated to be employable at high wages. On the one hand, there are Indians at the top of their specialized fields internationally. We are proud of them. But most of the youth are under-educated and face a challenging future in the new economy.

The phenomenon of moronization of the Indian masses originated at least one thousand years ago due to conquests, colonization, and inferiority complexes. There was a destruction of India's indigenous grand narrative with an abundance of oppressive narratives being imposed by foreign nexuses. The Vedic principles of society, polity, scientific inquiry, wealth creation and other worldly pursuits got dismantled and replaced with a hotchpotch of ideas stuck together. Today's pseudo-Americanization of Indian youth is the latest trend in this trajectory.

India's data policies have been weak and have allowed the drain of its precious data assets. In some ways, India is slipping to become the world's largest digital colony with lifestyles, discourses and commerce controlled by foreign digital giants like Google, Facebook, Twitter, Netflix, Amazon, and Flipkart. The foreign organizations maintain a lead of one generation of technology, and India is forever trying to catch up. This is causing social and political interventions in India with the use of AI-driven platforms whose strings are pulled and manipulated from abroad. Especially those that feel disenfranchised, or who are dysfunctional as productive members of society, are highly vulnerable to succumbing to AI-based digital platforms; such platforms offer feel-good free services in exchange for capturing their private information and their agency.

A new elite has evolved over the past seventy-three years comprising politicians, wheeler-dealers, bureaucrats, legal and educational institutions, and corporate India. I find few leaders across the board to be even sufficiently aware of the risks examined in this book. In the context of this vacuum, the sellout of Kumbh Mela's data rights and the more recent entries of Google and Facebook into India as the new devatas are reminiscent of the way the East India Company stitched together an empire largely with the help of myopic and selfish leaders.

The common people are way too insecure and emotional and are constantly on the search for jugaad and micro-optimized rewards. In this milieu, the traditional bhakti for divinity has been replaced by sucking up to human celebrities in civic society, and this has paved the way for servitude toward the digital devatas. Meanwhile, the spiritual gurus, though remarkably effective at one level, lack the vyavharika (worldly) expertise on the matters discussed in this book, and their contribution is therefore limited.

The present conditions are a playground for the breaking India forces I have discussed in my work over the past quarter century. Their foreign nexuses are well-funded and AI savvy, have experience in the use of technologies for creating social upheavals, and their machine learning systems have been using Indian big data to build and test psychological models for digital manipulation.

To explain the vulnerability of India, Figure 35 shows how a civilization's core narratives become explicitly or implicitly embedded in its AI systems. This weaponizes AI as a very subtle and almost invisible propaganda device. I will explain the diagram starting at the top left and following the arrows.

Western Universalism, as explained in my book, *Being Different*, refers to the assumptions built into Western thought that are projected as being universally applicable and desirable, even though in reality they are specific to the history and worldviews of the West. Ideas of *social justice* are built on this framework but assumed to be applicable globally. Good counter examples are the fact that Chinese and Islamic thinking do not fit into Western Universalism, and hence their ideas of justice are different.

The *Social Justice* movement has found its way not only in the ideologies driving social media platforms like Google, Facebook and Twitter, but also in the training of algorithms by Microsoft and others. The Church and academicians, naturally, are all participating in the deployment of such social justice ideas. There are also powerful individuals like George Soros (the American billionaire) who have organizations with global reach to assert their ideologies in virtually every corner of the world with the stated intention of creating a new world order according to their notions of social justice. The box titled 'AI Systems' indicates that the AI algorithms controlled by these organizations is biased due to this embedded social justice ideology, which in turn, is derived from Western frameworks.

China, on the other hand, exemplifies my point that such notions of social justice are far from being universal.

This is not the place to discuss the merits of one system versus another, but merely to point out that they are radically different from each other in fundamental ways. No civilization's worldview is going to prevail as the universal one acceptable to all. That is the pragmatic reality even if we were to believe that our favorite worldview supplies the best foundation for the social justice movement.

The *AI systems* are becoming rapidly smarter at generating content that is not easily distinguishable from content generated by human experts. This applies to text, audio and video content. As explained earlier, they are also building maps of individual humans' psychology and able to target manipulative content on a personal level. This psychological hijacking which I have referred to as the loss of personal agency is a weapon that can arouse mass mobilizations including riots, civil wars, political disruptions, and other kinds of havoc. As the diagram indicates, the West and China compete in developing such AI systems, each propagating its specific ideologies hidden beneath the veneer of algorithms.

The box titled '*Distribution Mechanisms*' refers to the variety of institutions that are entering the social justice arena and AI is a powerful weapon everyone is using. Individual governments as well as UN and other multilateral agencies are becoming kurukshetras where the ideologies are contested. Their support for a position in social justice brings credibility and the clout of their machinery to push ideas forward. The social media platforms have already been discussed in earlier chapters as powerful forces leveraging AI to influence billions of users worldwide.

The latest entrants are the *multinational corporations* in the wake of BLM; they have actively supported social change inside as well as outside their businesses. This is an important new frontier for social justice because it will influence decisions on which company gets investment capital based on its "Index of Social Justice". And who controls the criteria and definition of such an index and the evaluation of companies' worldview? It happens to be US giants like Ernst & Young (EY), PricewaterhouseCoopers, and the other big consulting and audit firms that have the power to certify the performance of their clients. They have launched a movement called Environment, Society, Governance (ESG) that evaluates how each firm is performing in terms of social justice of its employment as well as impact on the world. Finally, the NGOs involved in dispensing social justice worldwide are getting a boost with the help of AI to assert their values more emphatically and efficiently.

The final column on the right lists some of the main targets where all this impact is going to be felt. The faultlines of evangelists, Islamists, Dalits, Maoists, and various others will be exploited through social media as well channels like legal actions, international sanctions, and coercion by investors. The bottom of the diagram refers to *Breaking India 2.0*, which are the forces I have researched for most of my adult life and written about since the year 2000 and are those that will benefit from these developments.

The Indian rashtra in its current state is fragile and demands an increasing amount of resource allocation merely to keep it from imploding. There is far too much reliance on soft power as the solution, but *soft power is always contingent on hard power*. The lesson to be learned from *Ramayana* and *Mahabharata* is precisely this: Lord Ram failed to convince Ravana using all the soft power at his disposal but had to end up using hard power to defeat him. Likewise, Sri Krishna in the *Mahabharata* tries hard to use soft power arguments to win over Duryodhana, but eventually had to advocate the use of hard power to fight till the end. Therefore, even the avataras have needed hard power after being unsuccessful in producing the dharmic outcome with soft power alone. Indian spiritualists and political leaders should understand this and stop over-playing the soft power hand. It has made Indian society wooly-headed and lazy, and caused the kshatriyata to atrophy.

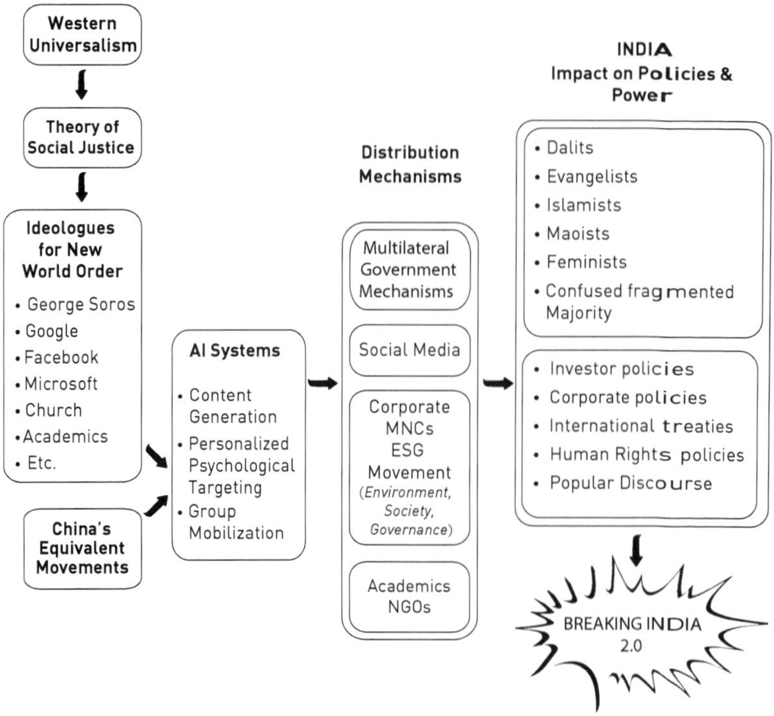

Figure 35: Civilizational Narrative & AI

A decade ago, when my book *Breaking India* was published after several years of research, the initial response was that it was too negative, and many reviewers even dismissed it just another sensational conspiracy theory. Gradually, however, an increasing number of readers began observing events around them through the book's lens and became convinced of its thesis. It started to function as the worldview of many people based on their own experiences and observations. This awakening galvanized a serious movement bringing together many smaller movements such as decolonization, fighting Hinduphobia and Sanskrit phobia, and responding to extreme minorityism and other forces of fragmentation. The framework of breaking India forces is now well-established and commonly used in India's conclaves, literary festivals, social media, and gatherings of policymakers.

I anticipate that this book will have a similar impact in the present decade. It might initially be received with skepticism and emotional dissonance because its arguments are new and will shock many readers; hence it could face the same mental blocks. But as in the case of *Breaking India*, I believe people will start noticing that the events unfolding around them fit into the framework I have developed.

The book will achieve its purpose once it jolts the public intellectuals who are currently filled with awe and gratitude toward the digital platforms, seeing them as a God-sent gift. Once public awareness builds up, it will pressure the captains of Indian politics, government, industry, media, think tanks and social activism. Eventually, the book could serve to develop a new framework for the intellectuals and activists who are presently wasting precious time chasing sensations and rehashing issues that are less consequential.

From such a manthan or churning, will emerge strategic new projects to utilize AI as a positive force for unifying India and spreading its grand narrative digitally. I hope the Indian government shall appoint a Minister for Digital Affairs with the focus of protecting the country and bringing

AI into all branches of the government and society. I am presently writing a sequel to this book that gives concrete ideas for not merely catching up in AI innovation but also using India's special capabilities to leapfrog ahead by ten to twenty years. In many ways, this book is intended to prepare the ground for the way forward.

Our actual enemy is not any force exterior to ourselves, but our own crying weaknesses, our cowardice, our selfishness, our hypocrisy, our purblind sentimentalism.

—Sri Aurobindo[355]

Appendix A

FORECASTS BY ECONOMISTS

Forecasters disagree on the timing and extent to which AI will be adopted and the impact on jobs. After examining numerous studies, I compiled the following list of factors that experts consider key in the adoption of AI in each situation.

- *Technical feasibility*: Each situation must be tested to evaluate its viability and benefits.
- *Cost*: Besides the initial investment, the ongoing cost of operating a given technology must be compared to the available alternatives.
- *Labor market*: Each country, location, and industry possesses its own dynamics of the supply, demand, and costs of human labor. Educational quality and competence determine whether AI or the old methods are more attractive and cost-effective.
- *Economic benefits*: Benefits like higher output and better quality are as important to consider as cost savings.
- *Competitive forces*: Even when the benefit in purely economic terms does not justify it, adoption of AI may be required for companies to remain globally competitive in terms of quality, safety, speed, flexibility, or other factors.

- *Ecosystems*: Artificial Intelligence cannot work in isolation. Reconfiguring supply chains and ecosystems across multiple industries may or may not be feasible in a given situation.
- *Regulation and policy*: Policy makers have to remain abreast of global trends and stay competitive, yet also manage the economic safety nets of displaced workers. Policies and regulations for re-training workers must be developed, as well as social security networks for those left behind by automation.

Based on a global survey (before the pandemic), McKinsey estimated the number of jobs that could, in theory, be automated by adapting "currently demonstrated technologies". For a developed country like the US, McKinsey estimated 60 million jobs could be lost, and for a developing country like India, 233 million jobs are theoretically vulnerable. These forecasts are based on the deployment of *currently proven* automation technologies and do not factor in future technological breakthroughs that would endanger even more jobs. For instance, estimates do not include the potential automation of farm work, which is an optimistic assumption in light of the AI breakthroughs for robots on farms.

This estimate does not claim that all jobs that *could* be automated will *actually* be automated, nor does it forecast the year when such changes might happen. McKinsey states that China, India, Japan, and the US account for just over half of the total wages and almost two-thirds the number of employees associated with activities that are technically automatable by adapting currently demonstrated technologies.[356]

Artificial Intelligence displacement is primarily at the task level, not the job level, because jobs consist of a portfolio of tasks, and workers usually have some flexibility in the portfolio mix as some tasks are displaced or augmented by automation. The report clarifies:

> While less than 5 percent of all occupations can be automated entirely using demonstrated technologies, about 60 percent of all occupations have at least 30 percent of constituent activities that could be automated.[357]

Regardless of these nuances, the situation is serious. Developing countries that already suffer from overpopulation, underemployment and low education levels on a large scale are at particular risk.

Bain & Company predicts that by 2030, US employers will need twenty to thirty million fewer workers than today. Each industry will be impacted differently. In some cases, automation will lower the cost of goods and thereby increase demand; cheaper goods will boost sales and offset some of the job losses.

However, many of the remaining jobs will suffer. As more people jostle for the fewer available jobs, wages will fall. Bain & Company estimates that by 2030, 80% of American workers will be affected by one or more trends: lost jobs, downward wage pressure, and drastic re-training.

At the same time, the benefits of automation will help the top 20% of highly compensated, highly skilled workers, as well as the owners and investors in AI-related industries.

An Oxford Economics report notes that too much reliance is placed on creating new jobs in the service sector. The use of service robots will increase, and entire service business models will be replaced by new models requiring fewer humans or different kinds of human workers.[358] Consider Amazon's effect on the retail industry. Walmart, once the world's largest brick-and-mortar company, has been replaced by Amazon as the world's leading retailer. Yet Walmart has four times more employees than Amazon. The new jobs created at Amazon are not enough to replace the old retail jobs.[359]

Tasks less vulnerable to replacement by machines are those that depend on human skills such as negotiation, persuasion, and customer service orientation, where humans have a distinct advantage over robots.[360] However, the workers' race to keep up with technology will become harder with time. Tasks that cannot be replaced by machines will become scarcer and more fiercely contested among applicants. Mismatches of skills, geographical locations, and interest in performing a given task are also grave concerns.

Too many reports on the unemployment consequences of AI quibble over the exact timing and chronology. What concerns me more is the broad nature of automation's impact on humans than with exact dates or the sequence of events. Daniel Susskind's analysis concludes:

> And, as we move through the twenty-first century, the demand for the work of human beings is likely to wither away, gradually. Eventually, what is left will not be enough to provide everyone who wants it with traditional well-paid employment.[361]

The International Labor Organization report also sounds a clear alarm:

> Most observers seem to agree that job destruction is likely to accelerate under the current technological changes. In contrast, little is known about the potential for the creation of new jobs. For such new jobs to appear, many comment(s) on the need for new markets to be developed and regulated, in particular in the green economy, care

> and personal services sectors, or an augmented public sector in areas where currently no profitable activities exist. The fear is that *this process might not happen fast enough*. Therefore, the number of jobs might fall faster than the global labor force when existing jobs are substituted by automation and other systems operated by artificial intelligence.[362] (Emphasis added)

The Bain & Company report also reaches a dire conclusion:

> Unemployment and wage pressures may exceed levels following the Great Recession in 2009. Income inequality, having grown steadily throughout the 2020s, could approach or exceed historical peaks.[363]

On the other hand, PricewaterhouseCoopers acknowledges the problem but arrives at a more optimistic conclusion.

> The net long-term job impact of automation would be likely to be neutral or even slightly positive. This will, however, require both business and governments to provide support to workers affected by these technological advances to retrain and start new careers.[364]

Such optimism must be tempered by the fact that the report is based on surveys of the world's largest companies' CEOs and human resources officers, and thus reflects the views of big business. Large corporations want to be politically correct and socially sensitive when projecting disruptions for their workforces and describing their AI plans.

McKinsey also seeks to avoid panic among its corporate clients, reminding readers that the problem was solved by itself in previous waves of automation.

> In the United States, for example, the share of farm employment fell from 40 percent in 1900 to 2 percent

> in 2000, while the share of manufacturing employment fell from approximately 25 percent in 1950 to less than 10 percent in 2010. In both cases, new activities and jobs were created that offset those that disappeared, although it was not possible to predict what those new activities and jobs would be while these shifts were occurring.[365]

The McKinsey report hedges its bets by offering contradictory statements. It first states that "a surplus of human labor is much less likely to occur than a deficit of human labor, unless automation is deployed widely". It then backtracks on that assertion, writing: "We cannot definitively say whether historical precedent will be upheld this time".[366]

Many of these reports simply assume that the unemployment problem will be solved by a combination of government social security nets and employer investments to retrain displaced workers.[367] In principle, such programs could be a theoretical shock-absorber, but the arguments are not especially convincing.

The WEF, a voice for the who's who among the world's elites, is optimistic even while acknowledging indisputable factors.

> The Fourth Industrial Revolution's wave of technological advancement is set to reduce the number of workers required for certain work tasks. Our analysis finds that increased demand for new roles will offset the decreasing demand for others. However, these net gains are not a foregone conclusion. They entail difficult transitions for millions of workers and the need for proactive investment in developing a new surge of agile learners and skilled talent globally.[368]

The WEF report also concludes that individuals must "take a proactive approach to their own lifelong learning" and advocates that "governments create an enabling environment, rapidly and creatively, to assist in these efforts".[369] Once again, the organization washes its hands off of any responsibility to help implement these measures.

However, WEF does acknowledge the big-business tendency to shirk responsibility for displaced workers and articulates the gap in corporate obligation.

> Nearly a quarter of companies are undecided or unlikely to pursue the retraining of existing employees, and two-thirds expect workers to adapt and pick up skills in the course of their changing jobs.... [Merely] 33% stated that they would prioritize at-risk employees in roles expected to be most affected by technological disruption. In other words, those most in need of reskilling and upskilling are least likely to receive such training.[370]

Interestingly, the risk of social disruption caused by unemployment is not included among the top ten future global risks the WEF examines in detail.[371] In contrast, Tesla CEO, Elon Musk has said that AI is "the biggest risk we face as a civilization".[372] (Of course, subsequently, he switched sides and invested in research for AI-based interventions in the human brain.)

Personally, I consider these optimistic reports something of a hoax by the corporate consultants that produce them. Their clients are big industries that hope to increase profits through automation, and the social remedies they offer are merely there to placate concerned social and political leaders.

Some economists do acknowledge that newly unemployed workers will not be easily assimilated into other industries, because no concrete plans have been proposed to re-train and hire them on such a massive scale. Even in the best-case scenarios, re-training will take time, some regions will be hit harder than others, and a dangerous generational gap may appear.

Appendix B

HISTORY OF SHORTSIGHTED IMPORTS BY INDIA

The examples given below illustrate the problem of India's indiscriminate reliance on foreign knowledge in a variety of domains.

Green Revolution

The much-touted Green Revolution, an initiative that won the American agronomist, Norman Borlaug, the Nobel Peace Prize (in 1970), is credited with saving India from mass starvation in the 1960s. However, despite the numerous advantages of the program, the long-term outcome was not entirely beneficial. After considerable early success, especially in Punjab, considered the granary of India, the Green Revolution eliminated traditional farming in India. New methods that relied on imported seeds requiring chemical fertilizers and capital-intensive irrigation systems have brought on long-term harm. The damage to the environment has been considerable, including soil degradation, ground-water depletion, and loss of biodiversity.

Today, the West is moving back toward organic farming after recognizing the health and environmental disasters caused by some aspects of the new agriculture technologies. Ironically, organic farming was imported from

India into Europe about a century ago, when the English botanist, Sir Albert Howard, learned the techniques in India and wrote books to export that knowledge.[373] Today, India is reimporting the latest practices in organic farming from the West to salvage its farms from chemical toxins and destructive techniques. Indian farmers are having to rediscover the benefits of non-chemical pesticides, crop rotation, biodiversity, and natural seeds.

White Revolution

The White Revolution was started in 1970 by the National Dairy Development Board with the well-intentioned purpose of expanding India's milk production. It was phenomenally successful in converting India from milk scarcity to the world's highest milk production. However, the approach involved replacing traditional cows that had evolved on Indian soil with imported European cows that produced more milk. The enhanced production also involved the heavy use of hormones and other chemicals. The sole measure of success was the quantity of milk produced, without considering qualitative factors. The traditional medical care of cows in India, based on Ayurveda principles of veterinary care, was replaced with Western medicine.

Desi (Indian) cows are superior to many other breeds in their resistance to disease and are better acclimatized to conditions in India. They have had an intimate relationship with the plants and animals of India, whereas the imported varieties are alien to the ecosystem. Traditional dairy farming included free grazing, organic fodder cultivated at the farm, and immunity-boosting herbs like Ashwagandha, Jeevanti and Shatavari. Native cattle thrive under these conditions.

Another concern is the distinction between A1 and A2 milk, a designation that indicates the type of proteins found in the milk. Some studies suggest that A2 milk is superior to A1 from a health perspective, for example in potentially easing symptoms of lactose intolerance. Cows that originated in Asia, Africa, and southern Europe produce A2 milk, while northern European varieties produce A1 milk. As a result of the White Revolution, the Indian milk supply that originally consisted of the desi A2 variety of milk was primarily converted to the A1 European variety.

Meanwhile, Brazil's White Revolution was based on imported Indian cattle. Brazilian breeders crossbred their cows with the Indian desi strains to increase milk production. India is now collaborating with Brazil to bring desi cows back to India. Ironically, India is reimporting the gene pool of its native cattle breeds.

Pink Revolution

The term *Pink Revolution* applies to India's push to rapidly increase meat production, both for domestic consumption as well as for export, which resulted in India becoming one of the world's largest beef exporters. The domestic consumption of poultry has also skyrocketed. These trends have been justified by the need to increase the protein component in Indian diets.

At the same time, Western countries have discovered the health benefits of vegetarian diets, trending toward a growing emphasis on plant-based food and a decline in meat consumption.

There is also considerable concern about the poor treatment of animals in industrial-scale processing of meats. It is estimated that each year eighty billion animals are killed by the meat industry—ten times the entire human population of the world. These animals are reared in cruel conditions and are treated as mere raw material in a production process with no concern for them as living creatures.

Public Health and Wellness

In blindly chasing Western solutions, Indians have abandoned many of their traditional approaches to health. Of course, Western medicine has made huge advances, especially in the area of diagnostics and acute care, and incorporating best practices from around the world is an important aspect of modernization.

The irony is that the entire mind–body–spirit approach to what is now called wellness was originally inspired by Indian practices. Western researchers that started out learning yoga and meditation in the 1960s, and then discovered Ayurveda, vegetarianism, and other Indian traditions, recontextualized their findings into novel structures. They became famous as medical pioneers in the West, although much of their craft was learned at the feet of Hindu gurus in India as well as in Hindu ashrams in the US.

The latest trends in Western wellness include practices like functional medicine and personalized care. These systems reject the Western allopathic approach of a standard treatment for specific problems that can be applied to all people; they are based on the uniqueness of each person's individual physiological balances and imbalances.

Unfortunately, Ayurveda, even as championed by India's AYUSH ministry, (the ministry in charge of non-Western systems of medicine) is required to prove its efficacy by using Western medicine's criteria of legitimacy. These criteria are based on standardized treatments and are not customized for each person, an approach that defeats the whole principle of Ayurveda.

The WHO has begun to develop standards for yoga, with input from Indian yoga leaders. Yet compromises are being made in the way yoga is being characterized, solely to make it compatible with the biases of Westerners. A better approach would be for experts trained and established in the yoga tradition to develop appropriate standards and present them to the WHO for approval. This is how China controls the standards for the use of Chinese medicine in other countries.

In addition to the WHO, an organization in New York known as Yoga Alliance has positioned itself to define yoga's standards, develop curricula at various levels, and certify teachers. This process supersedes and replaces all the Indian gurus, who in the 1950s, started yoga teacher training in the US and created the yoga revolution.

Yoga Alliance's clout among yoga teachers and practitioners worldwide has been steadily increasing because of sophisticated lobbying and marketing, as has its political influence among policymakers. I find considerable merit in much of their work, but the process is yet another example of how Indian experts have abrogated their authority in the global spread of their own traditions. The Indian government's International Yoga Day movement is commendable but focuses on popular portrayals especially among the Indian diaspora and has only a limited impact on the institutions worldwide where yoga is researched, curricula are developed, and teachers are trained.

Worse still has been the way the Vedic and Buddhist meditation traditions have become digested into Western mind sciences and Judeo-Christianity. Pioneers like Maharishi Mahesh Yogi (transcendental meditation) and S.N. Goenka (vipassana) spread these practices around the globe. But in recent years, the institutions and their teachings have been absorbed into inauthentic Western frameworks.

Interestingly, many of these adulterated forms of yoga, meditation, and Ayurveda get reimported back into India disguised as fashionable "Made in America" trends.

Computational Linguistics

European universities regarded Sanskrit as the mother of languages in Europe and Asia, and study of its grammar was required in any advanced linguistics curriculum. In particular, the revered Sanskrit scholar, Panini's *Ashtadhyayi* (grammar text) was mined by nineteenth-century European Sanskrit scholars to help develop European linguistics, with the help of Indian pandits.

Today, Indian experts in Sanskrit and computational linguists have been selling their services to foreign organizations to help them incorporate Sanskrit grammar into the field of computational linguistics. The branch of AI called Natural Language Processing is key to the understanding of spoken and written human statements, and it is based on the research done in computational linguistics. India should be leading and controlling this research to exploit its commercial applications.

However, the sobering reality is that hardly any world-class product developed or owned in India enjoys a large market share in NLP. In essence, Indian experts have once again served as coolies in the transfer of critical knowledge to firms in the US, China and Japan. The intellectual property at the core of major applications is not in the hands of institutions based in India.

Metallurgy

As documented in many volumes of Infinity Foundation's fourteen-volume *History of Indian Science and Technology* (HIST) series, one of the fields in which India's pioneering role is well established and acknowledged among historians worldwide is metallurgy. Many early technological breakthroughs in metallurgy are credited to India.

Yet the Statue of Unity, erected in Gujarat in honor of Sardar Patel, a towering personality in India's freedom struggle, a national symbol of pride and an expression of India's greatness, was built using Chinese metallurgy for the bronze plates that constitute the outer facade or skin. Behind this emotional achievement lies the sorry truth that the metallurgy required to build the plates was unavailable in India, so the advanced technology was Chinese, and the overall construction and assembly was Indian. Even more distressingly, a US firm based in Princeton, Michael Graves Architecture & Design, was hired as the architect to design the concept for the entire project and review its implementation.

Appendix C

TATA CHAIRMAN'S PLAYBOOK FOR INDIA

Natarajan Chandrasekaran, the chairman of the board of Tata Sons, has held one of the most powerful posts in India's industry. He is the senior author of the book *Bridgital Nation: Solving Technology's People Problem*, which offers a grand assessment of the unemployment issues in the face of AI and presents a detailed playbook to solve the problems. The book has received endorsements from international luminaries like Satya Nadella, CEO of Microsoft; Indra Nooyi, former CEO of PepsiCo and board member of Amazon; Michael Bloomberg, CEO of Bloomberg L.P.; Nandan Nilekani, former chairman of Infosys; and Fareed Zakaria of CNN.[374]

The book proposes what it calls the bridgital approach to simultaneously solve two problems: jobs and access to vital services. It claims this approach could create 30 million new jobs by 2025, raise wages by 10% to 20%, and make essential services accessible to 200 million citizens.[375]

Its approach has two parts: first, to examine the labor market and identify a specific group that is underutilized; and second, to identify services that are not being delivered properly. The strategy, then, is to connect these two aspects—training the target group of workers to provide the services in demand.

Indian workers are classified into three educational levels. The vast majority are uneducated or have at best, a limited primary education. They can only work in what is called the informal or unorganized sector. Roughly 77% of India's employed are in this informal sector, most of them self-employed. This sector comprises micro entities—tiny entrepreneurships that are unregistered and operate without contracts, social security, or regular salaries. These workers are at high risk due to the lack of insurance, regulation, and safety measures. Though technically considered employed, they are deemed underemployed and have low productivity. Incapable of getting jobs in formal, organized entities, they are entrepreneurs out of necessity. The book does not offer a solution for this segment of workers.

At the opposite end of the spectrum are the well-educated youth that easily get jobs in corporate entities. There are in fact shortages of highly qualified workers at this top end. The large employers who hire them tend to be capital-intensive, not labor-intensive businesses. They assimilate only a small portion of the youth population, and thus growth in this sector of the economy cannot alleviate the unemployment problem of the masses.

A failure in India's economic planning is that the growth in GDP is based on high levels of capital and skill, but the vast majority of workers are unskilled with low wages. *Bridgital Nation* points out that the quest for rapid economic development bypasses the underlying need for developing human capital. The approach followed was based on jugaad, the shortsighted political expediency typically practiced in India. The lack of education is why India failed to transition workers from agriculture to manufacturing the way other countries did in the past. The authors (the book is co-authored by Roopa Purushothaman, an alumnus of Yale and the London School of Economics) explain: "Agriculture, which contributes 18 percent to GDP, employs 44 percent of the workforce. Against this, the services sector contributes 52 percent of GDP, but employs less than a third".[376] Lack of education is one reason why economic growth has not solved unemployment.

The Indian economy has the high-end formal sector producing consumer goods and services for the wealthy class and employing workers with high levels of skill and productivity. At the other end is the much larger informal sector that serves the low-income masses with low-cost goods and services by employing poorly educated people.

The gap between these two extremes is huge. The book points out the underutilization of people who have secondary school education but do not have the top-caliber education of the elites. For instance, 120 million women with at least a secondary education do not participate in the workforce even though millions of job openings have no qualified workers at that level.[377] Another group with underutilized education is graduates of vocational training.[378]

The authors' strategy is to identify job opportunities for people with medium-level education. Rather than waiting to better educate people, it proposes ways to find work in large numbers for the middle-level group using their current level of education. It focuses on those with secondary school education and proposes training them to work as technicians, sales executives, and customer service agents.

The second part of the analysis is to identify important services that do not reach the masses—that is, fields that face huge shortages of workers. For example, India has a shortfall of 600,000 doctors, 2.5 million nurses, 1 million teachers, and 1.7 million commercial vehicle drivers.[379] The conventional approach of training more doctors and building more hospitals requires a significant investment of time and capital. The book suggests making urban medical systems available to remote locations through use of the internet and telemedicine—results that can be achieved quickly by training new digital workers to serve as intermediary between the masses and the medical services.

The book targets small and medium enterprises (SMEs), defined as organizations with between 10 and 199 employees, and suggests boosting this middle layer by employing people with secondary education. This section occupies the middle ground between the informal sector at the bottom of the pyramid and large corporate employers at the top. They are more productive than the informal sector. Further, they can assimilate workers with only a secondary school education, unlike the large corporate employers that require high levels of skill.

The approach of using digital bridges serves two purposes: improving access to services for the masses that are not being supplied and creating jobs for those with some education but not enough to get high-end corporate jobs. The process requires training millions of medium-educated people to function as human technology-enabled bridges between the masses and the available resources—digital intermediaries who would not require high levels of education.

Although Chandrasekaran and Purushothaman make a brave attempt to address India's human capital problem, the strategy suffers from several serious shortcomings.

- The book's forecast of new jobs that would be created is flawed because it assumes that India will mirror experiences in the US, Germany, Brazil and Israel, countries it calls "India's peers".[380] In those countries SMEs have over 30% share of employment, while in India they have just 12%. Without offering any rationale, Chandrasekaran and Purushothaman assert that the SME share of India's employment will jump from 12% to 30% by 2030. Yet each of these peer countries already has in place necessary infrastructure in education, government policies, and political dynamics, as well as the emotional and psychological predisposition of its masses. These countries might be India's peers in certain respects, but they are not necessarily peers in the type and level of employment.

- The book fails to address the fact that India lost its global lead in software and hardware and became dependent on US and Chinese AI technology. The omission is particularly glaring considering that Chandrasekaran worked his entire career at Tata Consulting Company (TCS), India's flagship company in software services. He climbed rapidly at TCS and became its CEO and managing director. Considered one of the most brilliant executives of Indian industry, he was appointed chairman of Tata Sons, India's most prestigious multinational. The myopia of TCS in missing the boat on AI happened under his watch.
- Chandrasekaran and Purushothaman's strategy of avoiding over-automation does somewhat alleviate the unemployment problem. But that tactic would exacerbate the problem of India lagging far behind other countries in AI. In effect, it would make Indian industry even less competitive in global markets.
- The book offers some short-term answers to unemployment but ignores the underlying problem of overpopulation. Such solutions can at best serve as band-aids to temporarily diminish the effects of overpopulation.

- It does not address the substandard education system that produces a workforce consisting mostly of youths who are unemployable by world standards.
- The authors make no mention of, and indicate no concern, over the huge loss of India's big data to foreign entities.
- Finally, and most notably, the book completely ignores the emotional dimension of the Indian public and its psychological vulnerabilities to foreign digital platforms as a new form of colonization.

Despite these limitations, *Bridgital Nation* deserves praise for its courageous analysis of the magnitude of India's problems and innovative proposal for using AI to make a profound impact on India.

Appendix D

AI ORGANIZATIONS DISCUSSING SOCIAL JUSTICE

Though all such initiatives are commendable, one needs to examine each organization individually to find out the extent to which it is biased toward certain corporate, national, or ideological stances.

EUROPE

Organization	Focus Area
Algorithm Watch (Germany) https://algorithmwatch.org/en/	Effects of Algorithmic Decision-making processes on human behaviour and ethical conflicts.
We and AI (United Kingdom) https://weandai.org/	Public awareness in the UK, to make AI more visible, transparent, accessible, and fair.
AI for People (Italy) https://www.aiforpeople.org/	Accuracy & Robustness, Explainability and Transparency, Bias, Fairness, Privacy, Accountability

The Bluerise AI Observatory & Monitoring (United Kingdom) https://thebluerise.com/ai-observatory-monitoring/	Impact of AI usage and the spread of disruptive technologies on developing countries, Prevent Digital Colonialism.
All-Party Parliamentary Group on Artificial Intelligence (United Kingdom) https://www.appg-ai.org/	Understand AI's impact on UK citizens and organizations, and whether and how it should be regulated.
OECD AI Policy Observatory (France) https://oecd.ai/	Facilitate dialogue between stakeholders with multidisciplinary, evidence-based policy analysis in areas where AI has the most impact.
Technical University of Munich-Institute for Ethics in Artificial Intelligence (Germany) https://ieai.mcts.tum.de/	Ethics, fairness diversity, governance and regulation, privacy, public discourse, safety, social responsibility and sustainability, transparency and accountability.

NORTH AMERICA

Organization	Focus Area
The Aspen Institute (US) https://www.aspeninstitute.org/	Intersection of AI and societal, economic, ethical and regulatory issues to suggest how AI can serve personal and local community values worldwide.
The Future Society (US) https://thefuturesociety.org/	Facilitate responsible adoption of AI for the benefit of humanity. (Affiliated to Microsoft, UNESCO and others.)
AI-4-All (US) https://ai-4-all.org/our-vision-for-ai/	Involve people from diverse backgrounds, identities and perspectives to build responsible AI systems.
Stanford Institute for Human-Centered Artificial Intelligence (US) https://hai.stanford.edu/	Develop human-centered AI technologies and applications. (Funded by Amazon Web Services, Google, IBM, Wells Fargo)
Partnership on AI (US) https://www.partnershiponai.org/	Safety-critical AI, fair, transparent and accountable AI, labor and the economy, collaborations between people and AI systems, societal influences of AI, and social good. (Affiliated to Amazon, Amnesty International, Apple, Facebook, Google, and others.)

AI and Humanity (US) http://aiandhumanity.org/	Bridge the gap between humanities and computer science to address AI's influence on identity and society.
AI Ethics Lab (US) http://aiethicslab.com/	Consulting and research to integrate ethics into the development and deployment of AI technologies.
Data Science for Social Good (US) https://www.datascienceforsocialgood.org/	Develop programs that use data science, AI, and machine learning to create positive social impact in a fair and equitable manner.
Montreal AI Ethics Institute (Canada) (Affiliated to Microsoft, Shopify, Deloitte, and others.) https://montrealethics.ai/	Privacy, disinformation, labor impacts of AI, machine learning security, environmental impacts of AI, indigenous data rights.
AI Impact Alliance (Canada) http://allianceimpact.org/?lang=en	Study the social, political, legal and ethical implications of AI; propose solutions to achieve the 17 United Nations Sustainable Development Goals.

ASIA

Organization	Focus Area
IT for change (India) https://itforchange.net/	Gender, development & democracy, internet governance, education.

The Centre for Internet & Society (India) https://cis-india.org/	Digital accessibility for persons with disabilities, access to knowledge, intellectual property rights, openness (open data, open source software, open standards, open access, open educational resources, open video), internet governance, telecommunication reform, digital privacy and cyber-security.
AI for Sustainable Development Goals Think Tank (China) http://www.ai-for-sdgs.academy/ai4sdgs-cooperation-network	Promote positive use of AI for sustainable development; investigate the negative impact of AI on sustainable development. (Affiliated to Xiaomi, Baidu, and others.)

ACKNOWLEDGMENTS

I am indebted to numerous individuals who have helped this book project in various ways during the past three years of its development. Once my first draft was ready about a year ago, I sent it to Anurag Kesari, a robotics and data systems engineer based in the European Union, as well as to Bala Deshpande in Michigan, USA. They helped do a fact check from a technical perspective and also supplied several important suggestions and additional examples.

Vijaya Vishwanathan has been an important sounding board who made helpful suggestions and added fresh perspectives. As the draft went through multiple iterations, I started sharing it with several others whose comments and advice have helped improve it considerably. These include Manogna Sastry, Anurag Sharma, T.N. Sudarshan, among others. Significant editorial corrections were made by each of them as well as by Shalini Puthiyedam, Divya Nagaraj and Subhodeep Mukhopadhyay. Certain chapters were edited by Aditi Banerjee and Shefali Chandan. In addition, Divya Sharma and Anurag Sharma worked as a team to help polish up the figures. Ginny Ruths was hired for the first few rounds of professional editing and Sanjana Roy Choudhury finalized the manuscript with her editing.

A team consisting of Divya Sharma, Manogna Sastry, T.N. Sudarshan, Anurag Sharma, Subhodeep Mukhopadhyay and Shalini Puthiyedam have helped to turn the facts and figures in the book into slides and also developed fresh slides to make educational presentations to be used by Infinity Foundation.

GLOSSARY

Note: Many of these words have no exact translation and the descriptions provided are approximations. For a clearer understanding of non-translatables, please refer to my book titled, *Sanskrit Non-Translatables*.

Aesthetics	A cognitive posture that involves beauty, artistic impact, feelings, and emotions
Aestheticization of politics	Use of aesthetics to secure and maintain political power over the masses even as they are suffering in a pragmatic sense
Algorithm	A systematic, step-by-step process to achieve an outcome
Artha	Pursuit of material wellbeing
Artificial general intelligence	Artificial Intelligence spanning multiple domains and contexts
Atman	Absolute Self
Ayurveda	Healthcare scientific system based on Vedic principles
Bhakti	Complete surrender of the ego to the divine
Big data	Massive collections of examples that are used to train machines

Cobots	Collaborative robots that work alongside humans and amplify their productivity
Community standards	Criteria used by social media companies for ad hoc filtering and censoring
Crash of civilization	Unprecedented social disruption created by the advent of superhumans that will supersede the metaphysics of humanism and its notions of free will, individualism, and human rights
Data capitalism	Economic impact of big data as a new kind of capital asset
Deep learning	Training neural networks and applying them to practical problems
Deepfake	Videos where machine learning systems pose as realistic human personalities, both visually and aurally
Devata	Deity
Dharma	Right metaphysical and ethical foundation for knowledge and action; adharma is that which is opposed to dharma
Dhyana	Deep meditation
Digital colonization	Re-colonization of the world on account of weakening of sovereign states and destabilization of fragile political equilibriums due to disruptive technologies

Digital Twin	Virtual replica of a complete physical environment recreated using data collected from a variety of sensors
Epigenetics	Changes in the biological algorithms from one generation to the next
Happy morons	Unproductive citizens that are a social liability, but as voters with legal rights who need to be kept happy in some way
Haptic	Devices providing tactile sensations of a Virtual or Augmented Reality
Human causation	Processes that humans define
Internet of Things	Artificial Intelligence technology where different physical devices are digitally connected with the internet
Jati	Traditional community with social and emotional cohesion
Jnana	Knowledge in the broad sense and includes both worldly knowledge and knowledge beyond the senses
Jugaad	Improvisations, short-cuts, and ad hoc approaches
Kama	Pursuit of desires, sensory gratifications, emotions, and aesthetics

Karma	Principle of cause and effect that includes scientific empiricism but goes beyond it into other dimensions
Kshatriya	Leaders, warriors, or those with power
Kshatriyata	Leadership with valor and a willingness to sacrifice for a higher cause
Kurukshetra	Battleground
Luddite Fallacy	The view that rather than eliminating jobs, new technology simply changes the nature of jobs
Mela	Popular fair
Mithya	Technical term in Vedanta for the transitory nature of things and the deceptive nature of their self-existence
Moksha	Liberation in the ultimate sense
Moronization	The atrophying of mental faculties of humans as they become increasingly dependent on digital systems for their basic cognitive needs
Natural causation	Rules by which natural systems function
Natural Language Processing	Branch of AI for understanding spoken and written human statements

Neural networks	Processes modeled after human brain activity using the experience from many examples and feedback to improve themselves
Paramarthika	Pertaining to the ultimate reality beyond all material existence
Pragmatics	A cognitive posture to find an empirical outcome or achieve a specific goal
Purushartha	The four pursuits of life – artha, kama, dharma and moksha
Purva-paksha	Critical analysis of an opposing point of view, done with respect
Rashtra	Shared geography, physical assets and mental and physical sense of unity
Recommendation systems	Systems that offer product suggestions to users based on their likelihood to purchase them
Rtam	Vedic explanation of universal patterns that make up all existence
Svadharma	Personal purpose in life
Swarm Intelligence	Collective behavior of decentralized, self-organized systems as understood by AI
Tamas, Tamasic	Laden with rot and toxicity
Tamasha	Public spectacle typically of a grand and dramatic kind but without serious pragmatic value
Tapasya	Selfless sacrifice toward a higher purpose

Unsupervised learning	Machine learning in which the system is turned loose to explore and discover structures on its own
Varna	Type of social capital
Vedanta	A system of philosophy based on the Vedas
Vedas	Earliest texts of humanity seen by ancient rishis that contain eternal truths about reality
Vyavaharika	Pertaining to the empirical world we live in
Yajna	Ritual or other action for giving back to the cosmic ecosystem for the sake of maintaining balance

BIBLIOGRAPHY

Allen, Gregory C. *Understanding China's AI Strategy.* Center for A New American Security, February 6, 2019. https://www.cnas.org/publications/reports/understanding-chinas-ai-strategy

Arntz, Melanie, Terry Gregory, and Ulrich Zierahn. *OECD Social, Employment and Migration Working Papers. o. 189*. Organisation for Economic Cooperation and Development, May 14, 2016. https://www.oecd-ilibrary.org/social-issues-migration-health/the-risk-of-automation-for-jobs-in-oecd-countries_5jlz9h56dvq7-en

Balliester, Thereza and Adam Elsheikhi. *The Future of Work: A Literature Review*. Geneva, Switzerland: International Labor Office, 2018.

Bhandari, Amit, Blaise Fernandes, and Aashna Agarwal. *Chinese Investments in India*. Gateway House, Indian Council on Global Relations, 2020.

Burke, Brian. *Gamify: How Gamification Motivates People to Do Extraordinary Things*. Gartner, 2014.

Chandrasekaran, Natarajan, and Roopa Purushothaman. *Bridgital Nation: Solving Technology's People Problem*. Penguin Random House India, 2019.

Chinn, Ewing Y. *John Dewey and the Buddhist Philosophy of the Middle Way*. Downloadable book: https://www.tandfonline.com/doi/full/10.1080/09552360600772645

Chou, Yu-kai. *Actionable Gamification – Beyond Points, Badges, and Leaderboards*. Milpitas, CA: Octalysis Media, 2019.

Congressional Research Service. *Artificial Intelligence and National Security*. Updated November 21, 2019, https://fas.org/sgp/crs/natsec/R45178.pdf

Credit Suisse Research Institute. *Global Wealth Report 2019*. October 2019.

Desouza, Kevin C. and Kiran Kabtta Somvanshi. *How India can prepare its workforce for the artificial intelligence era*. Brookings, April 22, 2019. https://www.brookings.edu/blog/techtank/2019/04/22/how-india-can-prepare-its-workforce-for-the-artificial-intelligence-era/

Edwards, Douglas. *I'm Feeling Lucky*. Boston: Houghton Mifflin Harcourt, 2011.

Eyal, Nir. *Hooked: How to Build Habit-forming Products*. New York: Portfolio/Penguin, 2019.

Frandrup, Erich. "The US Navy Needs Offensive Undersea Drones". In *The Future of the Navy*, December 2019.

Foucault, Michel. *Power/Knowledge: Selected Interviews and Other Writings, 1972-1977*. New York: Vintage Books, 1980.

Fraser, J. Nelson. *Poems of Tukarama Volume 3*. The Christian Literature Society for India, 1915.

Ganguli, Kisari Mohan. *The Mahabharata of Krishna-Dwaipayana Vyasa*, Calcutta: Bharata Press, 1883.

Gita Press. *Sri Ramacaritamanasa (A Romanized Edition With English Translation)*. Gita Press Gorakhpur, 2018.

Government of India. *Comments/suggestions invited on Draft National Guidelines for Gene Therapy Product Development and Clinical Trials*. 2019. http://dbtindia.gov.in/sites/default/files/Call_comments.pdf

Han, Barbara A., John Paul Schmidt, Laura W. Alexander, Sarah E. Bowden, David T.S. Hayman, and John M. Drake. "Undiscovered Bat Hosts of Filoviruses". *PLOS*, July 14, 2016.

Harari, Yuval Noah. *Homo Deus: A Brief History of Tomorrow*. New York: Harper Perennial, 2017.

Harris, Karen, Austin Kimson, and Andrew Schwedel. *Labor 2030: The Collision of Demographics, Automation and Inequality*. Bain & Company, 2018.

Herman, Edward S. and Chomsky, Noam. *Manufacturing Consent*. New York: Pantheon Books, 1995.

Horwitz, Jeff and Deepa Seetharaman. "Facebook Executives Shut Down Efforts to Make the Site Less Divisive". *Wall Street Journal*, May 26, 2020. https://www.wsj.com/articles/facebook-knows-it-encourages-division-top-executives-nixed-solutions-11590507499

Howard, Albert. *An Agricultural Testament*. Oxford University Press, 1943.

Hume, David. *On Morals, Politics, and Society*. New Haven, CT: Yale University Press, 2018. See https://davidhume.org/texts/m/3

Hume, David. *Philosophical Works of David Hume, Volume 4*. Boston: Little Brown & Company, 1854.

Joglekar, K.M. *Bhartrihari Niti and Vairagya Shatakas*. Oriental Publishing Company, 1911.

Joshi, Shankar Narahari. *Dasabodha (Hindi Translation)*, Pune: Publisher Unknown, 1930.

Kania, Elsa B. and Wilson Vorndick. "Weaponizing Biotech: How China's Military Is Preparing for a 'New Domain of Warfare'". *Defense One*, August 14, 2019. https://www.defenseone.com/ideas/2019/08/chinas-military-pursuing-biotech/159167/

Lawson, Max, Anam Parvez Butt, Rowan Harvey, Diana Sarosi, Clare Coffey, Kim Piaget, Julie and Thekkudan. "Time to Care: Unpaid and Underpaid Care Work and the Global Inequality Crisis". OxFam International, January 20, 2020.

Lee, Kai-Fu. *AI Superpowers: China, Silicon Valley, and the New World Order*. Boston, MA: Houghton Mifflin Hartcourt, 2018.

Malhotra, Rajiv, and Neelakandan, Aravindan. *Breaking India: Western Interventions in Dravidian and Dalit Faultlines*. Princeton, NJ: Infinity Foundation, 2011.

Maqsood, Ammara. *The New Pakistani Middle-Class*. Cambridge, MA: Harvard University Press, 2017.

Martone, Robert. "Scientists Demonstrate Direct Brain-to-Brain Communication in Humans". *Scientific American*, October 9, 2019.

https://www.scientificamerican.com/article/scientists-demonstrate-direct-brain-to-brain-communication-in-humans/

McKinsey Global Institute. *A Future that Works: Automation, Employment, and Productivity.* 2017.

Mitra, Vihari-Lala. *The Yoga Vasishtha Maharamayana of Valmiki*, 4 vols. Calcutta: Bonnerjee and Co, 1891.

Moran, Bill, "It's Time to Make Data Strategic for Our Navy". *The Future of the Navy*, December 2019.

Muro, Mark, Jacob Whiton, and Robert Maxim. *What Jobs Are Affected by AI?* Washington, DC: Metropolitan Policy Program at Brookings, 2019.

NASSCOM, FICCI, and EY, *Future of Jobs in India – A 2022 perspective.* 2017, http://ficci.in/spdocument/22951/FICCI-NASSCOM-EY-Report_Future-of-Jobs.pdf

NITI Aayog. *National Strategy for AI.* Delhi, June 2018. https://niti.gov.in/sites/default/files/2019-01/NationalStrategy-for-AI-Discussion-Paper.pdf

Obermeyer, Ziad, Brian Powers, Christine Vogeli, and Sendhil Mullainathan. "Dissecting Racial Bias in an Algorithm Used to Manage the Health of Populations". *Science* 366, no. 6464, 2019.

Office of the Director of National Intelligence, USA. *The Aim Initiative: A Strategy for Augmenting Intelligence Using Machines.* 2019. https://www.dni.gov/files/ODNI/documents/AIM-Strategy.pdf

Oxford Economics. *How Robots Change the World: What automation really means for jobs and productivity.* June 2019. http://resources.oxfordeconomics.com/how-robots-change-the-world

Pai, Mohandas and Umakant Soni. "An AI innovation engine for New India". *Financial Express*, July 19, 2019. https://www.financialexpress.com/opinion/an-ai-innovation-engine-for-new-india/1649078/lite/

Parker, G.G., M.W. Alstyne and S.P. Choudary. *Platform Revolution:*

How Networked Markets are Transforming the Economy—And How to Make Them Work for You. New York: W.W. Norton & Company, 2016.

Pentland, Alex. *Social Physics: How Social Networks Can Make Us Smarter*. Penguin, 2014.

Pham, Sherisse. "Facebook is Spending $5.7 Billion to Capitalize on India's Internet Boom". Business, *CNN*, updated April 24, 2020. https://www.cnn.com/2020/04/22/tech/facebook-india-reliance-jio/index.html

Pollock, Sheldon. *The Language of the Gods in the World of Men*. Berkeley, CA: University of California Press, 2009.

Prasad, Rajendra. *A Historical Developmental Study of Classical Indian Philosophy of Morals*. 2009.

PricewaterhouseCoopers. *Sizing the Prize: What's the Real Value of AI for Your Business and How Can You Capitalise?* PricewaterhouseCoopers, 2017.

PricewaterhouseCoopers. *Will Robots Really Steal Our Jobs? An International Analysis of the Potential Long-term Impact of Automation*. PricewaterhouseCoopers, 2018.

PricewaterhouseCoopers. *How AI is reshaping jobs in India*. PwC India and All India Management Association, 2018.

Ray, Pratap Chandra. *The Mahabharata of Krishna-Dwaipayana Vyasa*. Calcutta: Bharata Press, 1887.

Rathi, Aayush and Elonnai Hickok. *'Future of Work' in India's IT/IT-es Sector*. The Centre for Internet and Society, January 2019.

RBR Staff. "New Research Shows How AI Will Impact the Workforce". *Robotics Business Review*, 2019. https://www.roboticsbusinessreview.com/ai/new-research-shows-how-ai-will-impact-the-workforce/

Reddy, R. Shashank. *India and the Challenge of Autonomous Weapons*. Carnegie India, 2016.

Reese, Byron. "AI Will Create Millions More Jobs Than It Will Destroy. Here's How". *SingularityHub*, 2019. https://

singularityhub.com/2019/01/01/ai-will-create-millions-more-jobs-than-it-will-destroy-heres-how/

Obermeyer, Ziad, Brian Powers, Christine Vogeli, and Sendhil Mullainathan. "Dissecting Racial Bias in an Algorithm Used to Manage the Health of Populations". *Science* 366, no. 6464, 2019.

Office of the Director of National Intelligence, USA. *The Aim Initiative: A Strategy for Augmenting Intelligence Using Machines*. 2019. https://www.dni.gov/files/ODNI/documents/AIM-Strategy.pdf

Pentland, Alex. *Social Physics: How Social Networks Can Make Us Smarter*. Penguin, 2014.

Ray, Pratap Chandra. *The Mahabharata of Krishna-Dwaipayana Vyasa*. Calcutta: Bharata Press, 1887.

Rathi, Aayush and Elonnai Hickok. *'Future of Work' in India's IT/IT-es Sector*. The Centre for Internet and Society, January 2019.

Reddy, R. Shashank. *India and the Challenge of Autonomous Weapons*. Carnegie India, 2016.

Roth, Marcus. "Artificial Intelligence at the Top 5 US Defense Contractors", *Emerj*, last updated January 3, 2019, https://emerj.com/ai-sector-overviews/artificial-intelligence-at-the-top-5-us-defense-contractors/

Roy, Pratap Chandra. *The Mahabharata of Krishna-Dwaipayana Vyasa*, 12 vols. Calcutta: Oriental Publishing Company Calcutta, 1884-1894.

Sanyal, Kaushiki. Artificial Intelligence and India. Oxford University Press India. 2020.

Schmidt, Eric and Jared Cohen. *The New Digital Age: Transforming Nations, Businesses, and Our Lives*. New York: Vintage, 2014.

SCMP Research. *China AI Report 2020*. Hong Kong: South China Morning Post Publishers, 2020.

Scott, David. *William James and Buddhism: American Pragmatism and the Orient*. Downloadable book: https://doi.org/10.1006/reli.2000.0292

Sen, Gautam. "*History, Geopolitics and the Indian Predicament*". *IndiaFacts*, 2020. http://indiafacts.org/history-geopolitics-and-the-indian-predicament/

Sinha, Amber. *The Networked Public: How Social Media Changed Democracy*. Rupa Publications, Delhi. 2019.

Sinha, Amber, Elonnai Hickok and Arindrajit Basu. *AI in India: A Policy Agenda*. The Centre for Internet & Society, September 5, 2018. https://cis-india.org/internet-governance/blog/ai-in-india-a-policy-agenda

Smith, Aaron, and Janna Anderson. *AI, Robotics, and the Future of Jobs*. Pew Research Center, August 6, 2014. https://www.pewresearch.org/internet/2014/08/06/future-of-jobs/

Sri Aurobindo. *Bande Mataram, Early Political Writings - I (1893-1908)*. Sri Aurobindo Birth Centenary Library, 1972.

Sri Aurobindo. *Karmayogin: Early Political Writings - II (1908-1910)*. Sri Aurobindo Birth Centenary Library, 1972.

Sundram, Bala Murali, Dhesi Baha Raja, Fazilah Mydin, Ting Choo Yee, Kamesh Raj, and Fadzilah Kamaludin. "Utilizing Artificial Intelligence as a Dengue Surveillance and Prediction Tool". *Journal of Applied Bioinformatics & Computational Biology* 8 no. 1, 2019.

Susskind, Daniel. *A World Without Work: Technology, Automation, and How We Should Respond*. New York: Metropolitan Books, Henry Holt and Company, 2020.

Susskind, Jamie. *Future Politics: Living Together in a World Transformed by Tech*. Oxford, UK: Oxford University Press, 2018.

Swami Chinmayananda. *The Holy Geeta*. Mumbai: Central Chinmaya Mission Trust, 2008.

Swamy, Subramanian. "Subramanian Swamy writes: Four Reasons Why Reliance Jio-Facebook Deal is Commercially Sensible and Good for India". *MoneyControl*, April 29, 2020, https://www.moneycontrol.com/news/trends/expert-columns-2/subramanian-swamy-writes-four-reasons-why-reliance-jio-facebook-deal-is-commercially-sensible-and-good-for-india-5198301.html

Thierer, Adam, Andrea Castillo O'Sullivan, and Raymond Russell, *Artificial Intelligence and Public Policy*. Arlington, VA: Mercatus Center, George Mason University, 2017.

Tocqueville, Alexis de. *Democracy in America*. Translated by George Lawrence. New York: HarperCollins 2006.

United Nations Conference on Trade and Development. *Digital Economy Report 2019. Value Creation and Capture: Implications for Developing Countries*. New York: United Nations, 2019.

United States Government. *Executive Order on Maintaining American Leadership in Artificial Intelligence*. February 11, 2019. https://www.whitehouse.gov/presidential-actions/executive-order-maintaining-american-leadership-artificial-intelligence/

United States Government. *Artificial Intelligence for the American People*. Accessed May 8, 2020. https://www.whitehouse.gov/ai/

Upadhyaya, Deendayal. *Integral Humanism*. Deendayal Research Institute, 2002. https://www.dri.org.in/integral-humanism-booklet/

U.S. Department of Transportation. *Preparing for the Future of Transportation: Automated Vehicles 3.0 (AV 3.0)*. September 28, 2018. https://www.transportation.gov/av/3/preparing-future-transportation-automated-vehicles-3

Vempati, Shashi Shekhar. *India and the Artificial Intelligence Revolution*. Carnegie India, 2016. https://carnegieindia.org/2016/08/11/india-and-artificial-intelligence-revolution-pub-64299

Webb, Michael, Nick Short, Nicholas Bloom, and Josh Lerner. *Some Facts of High-Tech Patenting*. Cambridge, MA: National Bureau Of Economic Research, 2018.

Webb, Michael. *The Impact of Artificial Intelligence on the Labor Market*. Stanford University, November 6, 2019.

Wisskirchen, Gerlind, Blandine Thibault Biacabe, Ulrich Bormann, Annemarie Muntz, Gunda Niehaus, Guillermo Jiménez Soler and Beatrice von Brauchitsch. *Artificial Intelligence and Robotics and*

Their Impact on the Workplace. IBA Global Employment Institute, 2017.

World Bank. *World Bank East Asia and Pacific Economic Update, April 2020: East Asia and Pacific in the Time of COVID-19*. Washington, DC: World Bank, 2020. https://openknowledge.worldbank.org/handle/10986/33477

World Economic Forum. *The Future of Jobs Report 2018*, Geneva, Switzerland: World Economic Forum, 2018.

World Economic Forum. *The Global Risks Report 2020*, Geneva, Switzerland: World Economic Forum, 2020.

World Economic Forum. *We'll Live to 100 – How Can We Afford It?* Geneva, Switzerland: World Economic Forum, 2017.

Yew, Lee Kuan. *The Wit and Wisdom of Lee Kuan Yew*. Didier Millet, 2013.

Zande, Jochem van der, Karoline Teigland, Shahryar Siri, and Robin Teigland. *The Substitution of Labor: From Technological Feasibility to Other Factors Influencing Job Automation*. Stockholm, Sweden: Center for Strategy and Competitiveness, Stockholm School of Economics Institute for Research, 2018.

Zichermann, Gabe and Joselin Linder. *The Gamification Revolution: How Leaders Leverage Game Mechanics to Crush the Competition*. McGraw Hill, 2013.

Zuboff, Shoshana. "You Are Now Remotely Controlled". *New York Times*, January 24, 2020. https://www.nytimes.com/2020/01/24/opinion/sunday/surveillance-capitalism.html

Zuboff, Shoshana. *The Age of Surveillance Capitalism: The Fight for a Human Future at the New Frontier of Power*. PublicAffairs, 2019.

NOTES

1 *Ramayana* 6.16.21 and also *Ramayana* 3.37.2.

2 See: https://www.bloomberg.com/news/articles/2020-05-28/google-sued-by-arizona-over-collecting-user-location-data (accessed July 20, 2020).

3 Zuboff, "You Are Now Remotely Controlled."

4 See: https://www.nytimes.com/2020/06/10/technology/amazon-facial-recognition-backlash.html (accessed July 20, 2020). IBM has done likewise.

5 Zuboff, "You Are Now Remotely Controlled".

6 Zuboff, "You Are Now Remotely Controlled".

7 Edward Snowden warns that AI's technical workers are complicit in the ethical impact their products have on society. See: https://www.vice.com/en_ca/article/wxqx8q/snowden-tech-workers-are-complicit-in-how-their-companies-hurt-society (accessed July 20, 2020).

8 See: https://www.nature.com/articles/d41586-020-02003-2 (accessed July 20, 2020).

9 Vidura was cursed in that though he possessed an extremely high level of knowledge and wisdom and presented it with utter honesty, the people of his time would not believe him. The following words of Vidura are inscribed in letters of gold on a dome of the Indian parliament: "It is no assembly where there are no elders. They are not elders if they do not speak dharma. It is no dharma if there is no truth in it. It is not truth if it is vitiated by deception". (*Mahabharata* 5.35.58).

10 As an example of concerns from influential people over the misuse of AI, there was an open letter signed by Elon Musk, Noam Chomsky, Stephen Hawking, among others, calling for a discussion on standards to ensure the ethical use of AI. See: https://futureoflife.org/

ai-open-letter/ (accessed July 31, 2020). This watchdog movement has prepared a document on the ethical issues: https://futureoflife.org/data/documents/research_priorities.pdf?x59035 (accessed July 31, 2020)

11 See: https://www.rt.com/news/401731-ai-rule-world-putin/ (accessed July 20, 2020).

12 See: https://www.wordstream.com/blog/ws/2018/04/10/voice-search-statistics-2018 (accessed July 20, 2020).

13 I use the terms *emotional, aesthetic*, and *psychological* as a single category and interchange these terms freely in applications.

14 Machine learning has been around for a while. But its importance has increased recently as the availability of large amounts of data provided the fuel needed for unprecedented success. Conversely, not all traditional AI is based on machine learning.

15 One blogger aptly remarked: "Machine learning is like sex in high school. Everyone is talking about it, a few know what to do, and only your teacher is doing it". See: https://vas3k.com/blog/machine_learning/ (accessed July 20, 2020).

16 In the pandemic, many AI-based models fell apart and machine learning systems will need to undergo re-training. Dramatic changes in human behavior are defeating the old training of machines when the new experiences are too different from what they have been trained on. Artificial Intelligence experts are discovering the limits of elasticity of behavior that a model is able to handle before it falls apart. See: https://www.technologyreview.com/2020/05/11/1001563/covid-pandemic-broken-ai-machine-learning-amazon-retail-fraud-humans-in-the-loop/ (accessed July 20, 2020).

17 Even the best actors appreciate the director's work in pointing out how they are coming across and suggesting changes and refinements. Public speakers watch themselves in a mirror or record and view their speech to understand their performance more objectively.

18 See: https://news.harvard.edu/gazette/story/2019/04/harvard-google-team-up-to-tap-the-collective-mind-in-medicine/ (accessed July 20, 2020). (On a more philosophical level, I wonder if we can look at myths as a form of collective learning by a whole civilization.)

19 The term emergent property is sometimes used for a property that

is present in a collection of individuals but not in the individual members.

20 Neural networks in AI were inspired by the structure and function of neurons in biological brains. The ongoing collaboration between neuroscience and computer science is one of the most fruitful alliances today.

21 This discussion is based on the 3 *V*s described at https://venturedc.com/2015/10/the-three-vs-of-big-data-volume-velocity-variety/. See also D. Laney. " 3D Data Management: Controlling Data Volume, Velocity and Variety". *META Group Research Note* 6, no. 70 (2001): 1.

22 *Recommendation system* and *recommender system* are used synonymously. See http://infolab.stanford.edu/~ullman/mmds/ch9.pdf (accessed July 20, 2020).

23 Obermeyer et al., "Dissecting racial bias in an algorithm used to manage the health of population", 447-453.

24 See: https://www.reuters.com/article/us-amazon-com-jobs-automation-insight-idUSKCN1MK08G (accessed July 20, 2020).

25 See: https://www.theverge.com/2016/3/24/11297050/tay-microsoft-chatbot-racist (accessed July 20, 2020).

26 I am indebted to Anurag Kesari for helping develop this section.

27 It is therefore no surprise that companies like Apple are now better positioned to track public health with their ability to monitor vital signs including blood oxygen, etc. with user consent.

28 See: https://www.fastcompany.com/90241545/alexa-powered-amazon-houses-may-be-closer-than-you-think

29 Various terms such as AR (Augmented Reality), MR (Mixed Reality) and XR (Extended Reality) are used in the industry to describe these systems. But these hair-splitting differences are likely to blur into a whole continuum of technologies in the near future. I use the term *augmented reality* to encompass the entire range of these capabilities.

30 Very advanced yogis do have the ability to raise their consciousness to such an extent that they become conscious of the subtle mechanisms within their own bodies and even outside their bodies.

31 See: https://www.nbcsandiego.com/news/local/ucsd-health-using-

ai-to-identify-pneumonia-helping-covid-19-analysis/2301350/ (accessed July 20, 2020).

32 See: https://emerj.com/ai-sector-overviews/ai-in-pharma-and-biomedicine/ (accessed July 20, 2020).

33 See: https://www.thehindu.com/sci-tech/health/coronavirus-densely-packed-areas-in-cities-are-vulnerable-says-biocomplexity-expert-madhav-marathe/article31195212.ece (accessed July 20, 2020).

34 Sundram et al., "Utilizing Artificial Intelligence as a Dengue Surveillance and Prediction Tool".

35 See: https://www.wired.com/story/ai-epidemiologist-wuhan-public-health-warnings/ (accessed July 20, 2020). Another AI-based approach is of a digital twin model of a city. The model is connected to sensors to feed it real data from a specific environment and use AI to simulate the real environment. Users can build the digital twin to learn how a given pathogen spreads under different conditions. These network models are too large and complex to analyze without AI-based analytics.

36 See: https://sciencenode.org/feature/machine-learning-and-the-microbiome-computers-spot-sick-guts.php (accessed July 20, 2020). A large repository of microbes in San Diego's prestigious Scripps Institute can be seen at https://www.the-scientist.com/multimedia/slideshow--scads-of-microbes-now-stored-at-scripps-66920 (accessed July 20, 2020). The WEF took note of the potential use of AI in biological weapons before the Covid-19 pandemic. See https://www.weforum.org/agenda/2019/03/how-emerging-technologies-increase-the-threat-from-biological-weapons/ (accessed July 20, 2020). There are unconfirmed and contested reports that China's Wuhan Institute of Virology has used AI to understand the viruses carried by various animals like bats and to discover which of these viruses can jump from animal to human. Separately, a recent machine learning-based study used fifty-seven factors to predict which type of bats are likely to carry Ebola. See Han et al., "Undiscovered Bat Hosts of Filoviruses".

37 See: https://www.melloddy.eu/ (accessed July 20, 2020). Another breakthrough use of machine learning for biological discovery is explained in: https://www.quantamagazine.org/new-machine-

learning-system-decodes-how-proteins-interact-20200603/ (accessed July 20, 2020).

38 See: https://twitter.com/FrRonconi/status/1201841058713350144 (accessed July 20, 2020). See also: https://www-technologyreview-com.cdn.ampproject.org/c/s/www.technologyreview.com/2019/06/27/238884/the-pentagon-has-a-laser-that-can-identify-people-from-a-distanceby-their-heartbeat/amp/ (accessed July 20, 2020).

39 See: https://www.fda.gov/news-events/press-announcements/fda-permits-marketing-first-game-based-digital-therapeutic-improve-attention-function-children-adhd (accessed July 20, 2020).

40 Carnegie-Mellon University's famous Robotics Institute played a lead role in robotics in general and driverless vehicles in particular. Its founding director was Raj Reddy, one of the world's pioneers in AI.

41 See: https://www.cnbc.com/2019/05/07/uber-lyft-drivers-to-go-on-strike-over-low-wages-and-benefits.html (accessed July 20, 2020).

42 See: https://www.nytimes.com/2019/04/18/technology/uber-atg-autonomous-cars-investment.html (accessed July 20, 2020).

43 United States Government, *Artificial Intelligence for the American People*.

44 For example, the US Navy is investing in companies such as Leidos, SAIC, AECOM, and Orbital ATK, while the Army's programs are supported by firms such as SAIC, CACI, Torch Technologies, and Millennium Engineering.

45 See: https://www.youtube.com/watch?v=YdnJI9T-yXI (accessed July 20, 2020).

46 See: https://emerj.com/ai-sector-overviews/ai-in-banking-analysis/ (accessed July 20, 2020).

47 See: https://emerj.com/ai-sector-overviews/machine-learning-at-insurance-companies/ (accessed July 20, 2020).

48 See: https://www.bloomberg.com/news/articles/2019-12-06/robots-in-finance-could-wipe-out-some-of-its-highest-paying-jobs (accessed July 20, 2020).

49 Harari, *Homo Deus*, 327.

50 See: https://www.wsj.com/amp/articles/chinas-efforts-to-lead-the-

way-in-ai-start-in-its-classrooms-11571958181 (accessed July 20, 2020).

51 One example of modeling motivation is the 8-dimensional grid developed by Octalysis. See: https://yukaichou.com/gamification-examples/octalysis-complete-gamification-framework/ (accessed July 31, 2020).

52 There is an example of the use of gamification in politics in Portugal. See: https://sites.psu.edu/ist446/2017/01/23/gamification-of-politics/ (accessed July 31, 2020).

53 Zuboff, *Surveillance Capitalism*, 313.

54 Zuboff, *Surveillance Capitalism*, 8. (Emphasis original).

55 Zuboff, *Surveillance Capitalism*, 20-21.

56 Zuboff, *Surveillance Capitalism*, 413. Furthermore, the whole creed of human-centric design is as much about making it easy for machines to understand and gather data on us as it is about humans understanding machines.

57 Zuboff, *Surveillance Capitalism*, 416.

58 See: https://www.theatlantic.com/technology/archive/2017/02/artificial-intelligence-christianity/515463/ (accessed July 31, 2020).

59 Zuboff, *Surveillance Capitalism*, 10.

60 Critics would say that this gamification contradicts the fundamental premise that dharmic action should emerge spontaneously from within and not be a project of the ego to get rewards from some external mechanism.

61 See: https://www.businessinsider.com/why-google-ai-game-go-is-harder-than-chess-2016-3 (accessed July 20, 2020).

62 See: https://cuseum.com/blog/2019/12/17/3-things-you-need-to-know-about-ai-powered-deep-fakes-in-art-amp-culture (accessed July 20, 2020).

63 See: https://www.vice.com/en_us/article/ywyxex/deepfake-of-mark-zuckerberg-facebook-fake-video-policy (accessed July 20, 2020).

64 Artificial Intelligence poses another interesting challenge: whether a copy made to train AI is a "copy" for copyright protection. Google has also developed a technique in which training data is localized to the mobile device rather than copying data to a centralized server.

65 Herman and Chomsky, *Manufacturing Consent*, 306.

66 "The term 'propaganda' apparently first came into common use in Europe as a result of the missionary activities of the Catholic church. In 1622 Pope Gregory XV created in Rome the Congregation for the Propagation of the Faith. This was a commission of cardinals charged with spreading the faith and regulating church affairs in heathen lands. A College of Propaganda was set up under Pope Urban VIII to train priests for the missions". See: https://www.historians.org/about-aha-and-membership/aha-history-and-archives/gi-roundtable-series/pamphlets/em-2-what-is-propaganda-(1944)/the-story-of-propaganda (accessed July 20, 2020).

67 For instance, my interviews with Ayurvedic doctors giving advice on protection from Covid-19 were rejected. When I finally managed to reach a human employee, I was told that the algorithm probably does not recognize Ayurveda as a legitimate healthcare practice and consequently treated the video as propagating quackery.

68 See: https://www.ndtv.com/world-news/facebook-names-1st-board-members-of-its-supreme-court-to-oversee-content-2224527 (accessed July 20, 2020).

69 Digital platforms also have the power to control the critical evidence on serious criminal cases. See: https://www.cnbctv18.com/technology/us-court-asked-to-force-facebook-to-release-myanmar-officials-data-for-rohingya-genocide-case-6112291.htm (accessed July 20, 2020).

70 Recently, Donald Trump has threatened legal actions against Twitter and Facebook for what he considers to be their bias on his posts. See: https://www.bloomberg.com/news/articles/2020-05-28/trump-furious-at-twitter-aims-executive-order-at-tech-giants (accessed July 20, 2020).

71 In certain circumstances, telecom carriers could be compelled by courts to breach this freedom.

72 See: https://www.warc.com/content/paywall/article/warc-datapoints/nearly-90-of-consumers-have-changed-their-behaviour-because-of-covid-19/132043 (accessed July 20, 2020).

73 See: https://www.democraticmedia.org/article/platforms-privacy-pandemic-and-data-profiteering-covid-19-crisis-further-fuels-unaccountable (accessed July 20, 2020) and https://www.nielsen.

com/us/en/insights/article/2020/key-consumer-behavior-thresholds-identified-as-the-coronavirus-outbreak-evolves/ (accessed July 20, 2020).

74 United Nations, *Convention on Biological Diversity* (1992). See especially Articles 15.7, 16.3, 16.4, 18.2, and 18.4. The Nagoya Protocol is an excellent tool to implement this treaty's spirit. The legal obligations of the recipient side include cooperation in monitoring the utilization of genetic resources after they leave a country including by establishing effective checkpoints at various stages of the value-chain, such as "research, development, innovation, pre-commercialization, or commercialization". See also the following 2010 addendum: United Nations, *The Nagoya Protocol on Access to Genetic Resources and the Fair and Equitable Sharing of Benefits Arising from their Utilization to the Convention on Biological Diversity,* supplementary agreement to the 1992 Convention on Biological Diversity (2010).

75 Smith and Anderson, *AI, Robotics, and the Future of Jobs.*

76 See: https://www.forbes.com/sites/hilarybrueck/2015/09/01/why-computers-could-design-more-organic-products-than-humans/ (accessed July 20, 2020).

77 Susskind, *A World Without Work*, 73.

78 Susskind, *A World Without Work*, 74.

79 Chou, *Gamification*, 19.

80 Parker, Alstyne, and Choudary, *Platform Revolution*, 26.

81 United Nations Conference on Trade and Development, *Digital Economy Report 2019*, 83.

82 DuckDuckGo, which saliently markets itself as being a significantly more privacy-conscious search engine, is one of the emerging dark horses standing up to Google. In November 2019, it achieved over 50 million search queries per day, and by April 2020 was averaging over 61 million per day.

83 Platforms also build moats to prevent users from leaving. For example, Facebook does not permit page owners to create an email list of all followers, even threatening to block pages if owners use a third-party tool that allows extraction of followers' email contacts. Although blatantly monopolistic, the practice has yet to be

challenged legally. In effect, these invisible barriers and disincentives serve to enforce loyalty.

84 "For example, in 2013, Facebook reportedly approached Snapchat—a competing social media platform—with an offer to acquire it for $3 billion. The offer was declined, and Snapchat later proceeded with an IPO in 2017 valued at around $33 billion. After the rejection, Facebook introduced many of the features that had made Snapchat unique by adding AR effects, QR codes, the 'story' format, similar filters, and even similar interfaces. Snapchat has since been plagued by low user growth and dwindling investor confidence, with shares down about seventy-five percent from its opening day price. In this case, even a $33 billion company was unable to compete with the resources of a top-tier platform". (United Nations Conference on Trade and Development, *Digital Economy Report 2019*, 87).

85 Amazon has a delivery robot called Scout. See: https://blog.aboutamazon.com/transportation/whats-next-for-amazon-scout (accessed July 20, 2020).

86 PricewaterhouseCoopers, *Sizing the Prize*, 6.

87 For an example of this approach, see Zande et al. *The Substitution of Labor*.

88 See (1) Muro, Whiton, and Maxim, *What Jobs Are Affected by AI?* (2) Webb, *The Impact of Artificial Intelligence on the Labor Market*. (3) Webb et al., *Some Facts of High-Tech Patenting*.

89 There is no evidence that Ned Ludd actually existed, and many scholars speculate that he is a fictional character like Robin Hood to symbolize an idea.

90 PricewaterhouseCoopers, *Will Robots Really Steal Our Jobs?*, 7.

91 Harris, Kimson, and Schwedel, *Labor 2030*, 1.

92 See: https://su.org/blog/exponential-technology-trends-defined-2019/ (accessed July 20, 2020).

93 PricewaterhouseCoopers, *Will Robots Really Steal Our Jobs?*, 7.

94 Harris, Kimson, and Schwedel, *Labor 2030*, 29.

95 Harris, Kimson, and Schwedel, *Labor 2030*, 30.

96 Harris, Kimson, and Schwedel, *Labor 2030*, 36.

97 Harris, Kimson, and Schwedel, *Labor 2030*, 59.

98 Harris, Kimson, and Schwedel, *Labor 2030*, 30.

99 Harris, Kimson, and Schwedel, *Labor 2030*, 42.
100 Credit Suisse Research Institute, *Global Wealth Report 2019*, (October 2019).
101 Further data is available in: https://www.bloomberg.com/news/articles/2019-12-27/world-s-richest-gain-1-2-trillion-as-kylie-baby-sharks-prosper (accessed July 20, 2020).
102 Lee, *AI Superpowers*, 150.
103 Lawson et al., "Time to Care", 9.
104 Lawson et al., "Time to Care", 11.
105 Harris, Kimson, and Schwedel, *Labor 2030*, 37.
106 Susskind, *Future Politics*, 322.
107 Lawson et al., "Time to Care", 9-10.
108 Oxford Economics, *How Robots Change the World*, 23.
109 World Economic Forum, *The Global Risks Report 2020*, 66.
110 World Economic Forum, *The Global Risks Report 2020*, 67.
111 United Nations Conference on Trade and Development, *Digital Economy Report 2019*, 96.
112 Lawson et al., "Time to Care", 20.
113 Lawson et al., "Time to Care", 12.
114 See: http://www.cnbctv18.com/economy/coronavirus-crisis-could-plunge-half-a-billion-people-into-poverty-oxfam-5654871.htm (accessed July 20, 2020).
115 See: https://edition.cnn.com/2020/03/31/perspectives/equal-pay-day-coronavirus/index.html (accessed July 20, 2020).
116 Harris, Kimson, and Schwedel, *Labor 2030*, 38.
117 Harris, Kimson, and Schwedel, *Labor 2030*.
118 Harris, Kimson, and Schwedel, *Labor 2030*, 44.
119 Harris, Kimson, and Schwedel, *Labor 2030*, 47.
120 McKinsey Global Institute, *A Future That Works*, ii.
121 World Economic Forum, *We'll Live to 100*, 7.
122 Balliester and Elsheikhi, *The Future of Work*.
123 Lee, *AI Superpowers*, 151.
124 Susskind, *A World Without Work*, 193-94.
125 Susskind, *A World Without Work*, 167-68.
126 McKinsey Global Institute, *A Future That Works*, ii.
127 Oxford Economics, *How Robots Change the World*.

128 Sanjaya to Dhritarashtra in Bhishma Parva: Ray, *The Mahabharata of Krishna-Dwaipayana Vyasa*, 34.

129 PricewaterhouseCoopers, *Sizing the Prize*, 7.

130 PricewaterhouseCoopers, *Sizing the Prize*, 7. Due to rounding, the total appears a bit higher than the $15.7 trillion forecast in the report.

131 United Nations Conference on Trade and Development, *Digital Economy Report 2019*, 8-9, xvi.

132 United Nations Conference on Trade and Development, *Digital Economy Report 2019*, 7.

133 Wisskirchen et al., *Artificial Intelligence and Robotics*, 18. See also pages 14 and 17 for risks facing the poor workers.

134 Harris, Kimson, and Schwedel, *Labor 2030*, 46.

135 Thierer, O'Sullivan, and Russell, "Artificial Intelligence and Public Policy". In support of this trend, analysts with Bank of America and Merrill Lynch estimate that robotics and AI will perform 45% of manufacturing tasks by 2025.

136 Oxford Economics, *How Robots Change the World*, 3.

137 Oxford Economics, *How Robots Change the World*, 4.

138 World Economic Forum, *The Global Risks Report 2020*, 66.

139 United Nations Conference on Trade and Development, *Digital Economy Report 2019*, 92.

140 See: https://www.orfonline.org/expert-speak/the-tsinghua-of-economic-development-in-pakistan-66037/ (accessed July 20, 2020).

141 United Nations Conference on Trade and Development, *Digital Economy Report 2019*, 92.

142 United Nations Conference on Trade and Development, *Digital Economy Report 2019*, 92.

143 United Nations Conference on Trade and Development, *Digital Economy Report 2019*, 35.

144 Susskind, *Future Politics*, 155.

145 Lee, *AI Superpowers*, 33.

146 China silently bought out Germany's crown jewel, KUKA Robotics, a fact which has attracted much backlash recently. Chinese also own the Segway robotics and mobility company started by American entrepreneur Dean Kamen, founder of FIRST robotics.

147 Lee, *AI Superpowers,* 99.

148 See Rajiv Malhotra, *Breaking India.*

149 Lee, *AI Superpowers.*

150 See: https://www.financialexpress.com/opinion/an-ai-innovation-engine-for-new-india/1649078/lite/ (accessed July 20, 2020). Furthermore, as of December 2018, the Chinese government claimed it has accumulated $1.8 trillion in state money across thousands of venture capital funds in order to achieve its goal of tech dominance by 2025. Some of the companies that came out of that experiment are Didi Chuxing ($56 billion), SenseTime ($4.5 billion) and ByteDance ($75 billion).

151 Nvidia has been the chip supplier for AI because it specializes in high-speed math. But the Chinese Ministry of Science and Technology has invested huge sums in private industry with the stated goal of developing a new chip that is twenty times better than Nvidia's current offerings. Though Silicon Valley remains the leader in chip design, China is working to catch up.

152 See: https://www.inc.com/magazine/201809/amy-webb/china-artificial-intelligence.html (accessed July 20, 2020). See also https://www.newamerica.org/cybersecurity-initiative/digichina/blog/xi-jinping-calls-for-healthy-development-of-ai-translation/ (accessed July 20, 2020) and https://www.newamerica.org/cybersecurity-initiative/digichina/blog/full-translation-chinas-new-generation-artificial-intelligence-development-plan-2017/ (accessed July 20, 2020).

153 Allen, *Understanding China's AI Strategy*, 3.

154 Lee, *AI Superpowers*, 89.

155 Lee, *AI Superpowers*, 154.

156 See: https://www.scmp.com/news/china/military/article/3031462/china-stakes-claim-unmanned-warfare-national-day-show-drone (accessed July 20, 2020).

157 Lee, *AI Superpowers*, 50.

158 See: https://in.reuters.com/article/grindr-m-a-beijingkunlun/chinas-kunlun-tech-agrees-to-u-s-demand-to-sell-grindr-gay-dating-app-idINKCN1SJ297 (accessed July 20, 2020).

159 See: https://apple.news/AajzW-k_CR7S2-i6EGxvLVg (accessed July 20, 2020).

160 See: https://www.cnn.com/videos/us/2020/02/25/tsa-airport-workers-tiktok-china-national-security-concerns-ots-vpx.hln/video/playlists/atv-trending-videos/ (accessed July 20, 2020).

161 See: https://www.eurozine.com/social-control-4-0-chinas-social-credit-systems/ (accessed July 20, 2020).

162 See: https://www.nytimes.com/2019/12/30/world/asia/china-xinjiang-muslims-labor.html (accessed July 20, 2020).

163 See: https://www.dailymail.co.uk/news/article-7824541/China-rewrite-Bible-Quran-reflect-socialist-values.html (accessed July 20, 2020).

164 Kania and Vorndick, "Weaponizing Biotech".

165 Kania and Vorndick, "Weaponizing Biotech".

166 See: https://www.reuters.com/article/us-usa-artificial-intelligence/u-s-government-limits-exports-of-artificial-intelligence-software-idUSKBN1Z21PT (accessed July 20, 2020).

167 See: https://www.cnn.com/2019/12/09/tech/china-us-computers-software/index.html (accessed July 20, 2020).

168 SCMP Research, *China AI Report 2020*.

169 See: https://www.bloomberg.com/news/articles/2020-05-20/china-has-a-new-1-4-trillion-plan-to-overtake-the-u-s-in-tech (accessed July 31, 2020).

170 U.S. President, *Maintaining American Leadership in Artificial Intelligence*.

171 United States Government, *Artificial Intelligence for the American People*

172 United States Government, *Artificial Intelligence for the American People*.

173 See: https://www.bloomberg.com/news/articles/2020-06-07/huawei-troops-see-dire-threat-to-future-from-latest-trump-salvo (accessed July 20, 2020).

174 Roth, "Artificial Intelligence at the Top 5 US Defense Contractors".

175 See: https://dodcio.defense.gov/About-DoD-CIO/Organization/JAIC/ (accessed July 20, 2020).

176 See: https://www.ai.mil/about.html. The JAIC has also been working in collaboration with various federal, state, and local agencies to help disaster response operations by providing crucial intelligence support.

For example, JAIC's AI detection system has been instrumental in providing critical support to first responders battling wildfires by automatically analyzing video captured from aircraft sensors and sharing accurate wildfire-related intelligence. See: https://www.ai.mil/blog_09_16_19.html (accessed July 20, 2020).

177 Moran, *It's Time to Make Data Strategic for Our Navy*, 17-18.

178 Frandrup, *The US Navy Needs Offensive Undersea Drones*, 7-8.

179 Moran, *It's Time to Make Data Strategic for Our Navy*, 17-18.

180 U.S. Congress, *Artificial Intelligence and National Security*, 10.

181 U.S. Congress, *Artificial Intelligence and National Security*, 12.

182 Roth, "Artificial Intelligence at the Top 5 US Defense Contractors".

183 Office of the Director of National Intelligence, *A Strategy for Augmenting Intelligence Using Machines*

184 See: https://www.darpa.mil/program/media-forensics (accessed July 20, 2020).

185 U.S. Congress, *Artificial Intelligence and National Security*, 2.

186 U.S. Congress, *Artificial Intelligence and National Security*, 10.

187 United States Government, *Artificial Intelligence for the American People.*

188 See: https://www.energy.gov/articles/us-department-energy-and-cray-deliver-record-setting-frontier-supercomputer-ornl (accessed July 20, 2020).

189 United States Government, *Artificial Intelligence for the American People.*

190 U.S. Department of Transportation, *Preparing for the Future of Transportation*, 12.

191 U.S. Department of Transportation, *Preparing for the Future of Transportation*, 16.

192 U.S. Department of Transportation, *Preparing for the Future of Transportation*, 14.

193 See: https://onezero.medium.com/former-google-ceo-wants-to-create-a-government-funded-university-to-train-a-i-coders-9a2df09c5bce (accessed July 31, 2020).

194 One may consider emotions as the method by which unconscious mechanisms send messages to consciousness. When a person's unconscious produces an outcome that it wants the conscious level

to address, the unconscious sends a signal that the conscious brain experiences as an emotion. Emotions are raw in the sense that the logical mind has not yet processed and interpreted the signal. While some psychological theories differentiate between emotions and intuition, for the purpose of this book I treat them as one category.

195 See for example: https://www.bbc.com/news/technology-27762088 (accessed July 20, 2020). Similarly, Google Duplex is a technology that provides a voice assistant to make phone calls on a user's behalf to make hotel reservations, ticket bookings etc. It is widely regarded as another Turing test beater in the traditional sense. However, now there are debates on the relevance of the Turing Test.

196 While computers have become good at generating natural language in text and speech, their ability to understand natural language at a deep level still lags far behind humans. The advent of deep learning and big data has enabled the rise of voice assistants such as Apple Siri, Google Home, and Amazon Alexa. These technologies are not 100% accurate, but they are 85% to 90% accurate for most simple tasks. That rate is sufficient to field them by the hundreds of millions in products and services, collecting further data to compensate for the remaining few percentage points. Recently, in the pandemic era, Indian call centers have started using Conversational Service Automation based on NLP to offer good quality service to clients by phone. See: https://www.cnbctv18.com/technology/how-artificial-intelligence-can-power-call-centres-during-lockdowns-6033791.htm (accessed July 20, 2020).

197 Companies like Amazon use sentiment analysis to understand customer attitudes toward and feelings about products by analyzing customer review text. This process demonstrates how companies use AI to identify patterns from unstructured data and turn them into structured, actionable insights. Twitter uses advanced text mining techniques to analyze the sentiment of tweets on a given topic at a given time.

198 MIT's Media Lab is a pioneer in these studies.

199 An early pioneering example of humans becoming emotionally connected with robots was the Sony Aibo robot dog from the late

1990s and early 2000s. The robotic dog had rudimentary AI that gave it a personality, and Japanese users found it adorable. People held Aibo clinics to maintain their robot dogs in good health, scheduled play dates for them, and often went so far as to hold elaborate ritual funerals for their deceased cyber canine pets.

200 Harari, *Homo Deus,* 342-343.

201 Harari, *Homo Deus*, 342-343.

202 Harari, *Homo Deus*, 342-343.

203 Harari, *Homo Deus*, 342-343.

204 Zuboff, *Surveillance Capitalism*, 411-12.

205 An example of culture-specific psychological habits is how Chinese web-surfing habits differ from those of Americans—the way Chinese look at a page is non-linear. A study tracked Chinese users' eye movements and their clicks when they read a web page. On pages where the Americans spent an average of ten seconds, the Chinese spent an average of thirty to sixty seconds. The Chinese tended to shift between different parts of the same page, whereas the Americans did a linear scan. Websites that copied the American user interface for the Chinese market failed miserably. See: https://www.clicktale.com/resources/blog/puzzling-web-habits-across-the-globe-part-1/ (accessed July 20, 2020).

206 Eyal, *Habit-forming Products.*

207 "After declining for nearly two decades, the suicide rate among Americans aged 10 to 24 jumped 56 percent between 2007 and 2017, according to data from the Centers for Disease Control and Prevention. .... At the same time, the rate of teen depression shot up 63 percent, an alarming but not surprising trend given the link between suicide and depression. ... Some researchers emphasize the potential role of social media exposure and use of smartphones. There is some evidence that girls, who have shown greater rates of increase in depression than boys, experience more cyberbullying because of their greater use of mobile phones and texting". See: https://www.nytimes.com/2020/01/06/opinion/suicide-young-people.html (accessed July 20, 2020).

208 Susskind, *Future Politics*, 143.

209 See: https://www.theverge.com/2020/1/31/21117217/amazon-

kindle-tracking-page-turn-taps-e-reader-privacy-policy-security-whispersync

210 Susskind, *Future Politics*, 229.

211 Harari, *Homo Deus*, 397.

212 IBM has at least temporarily ended all facial recognition technology due to police misuse: https://techcrunch.com/2020/06/08/ibm-ends-all-facial-recognition-work-as-ceo-calls-out-bias-and-inequality/ (accessed July 20, 2020).

213 See: https://timesofindia.indiatimes.com/videos/city/jaipur/covid-19-robots-to-treat-patients-in-jaipurs-sms-hospital/videoshow/74818087.cms (accessed July 20, 2020) and https://timesofindia.indiatimes.com/videos/international/robots-seen-as-effective-tool-against-covid-19/videoshow/76072335.cms (accessed July 20, 2020).

214 Susskind, *Future Politics*, 188

215 Harari, *Homo Deus*, 397.

216 Susskind, *Future Politics*, 220.

217 Foucault, *Power/Knowledge: Selected Interviews and Other Writings*, 155.

218 Susskind, *Future Politics*, 122.

219 Pollock, *The Language of the Gods in the World of Men.*

220 Tocqueville, *Democracy in America*, 692.

221 Harari, *Homo Deus.*

222 Harari, *Homo Deus*, 334.

223 For example, patients with type 1 diabetes can wear a device that continuously monitors their blood-sugar level. It is not an implant, but straps to the arm and holds a microneedle in place for an extended time. Patient simply hold a smart phone up to the device to get a reading.

224 An entire class of algorithms known as evolutionary (or genetic) algorithms can effectively mimic Darwinian evolutionary processes to iterate over multiple algorithmic generations to find the fittest ones with respect to certain parameters.

225 Harari, *Homo Deus*, 338.

226 Harari, *Homo Deus*, 279.

227 Harari, *Homo Deus*, 66.

228 Harari, *Homo Deus*, 66.
229 Harari, *Homo Deus*, 199.
230 Harari, *Homo Deus*, 278.
231 Hume, *Philosophical Works of David Hume*, 247.
232 Hume, *Philosophical Works*, 252.
233 Hume, *On Morals, Politics and Society*, 262.
234 See: https://youtu.be/r-vbh3t7WVI (accessed July 20, 2020).
235 Martone, "Scientists Demonstrate Direct Brain-to-Brain Communication in Humans".
236 Harari, *Homo Deus*.
237 See for example: https://intellectualkshatriya.com/american-exceptionalism-and-the-myth-of-the-frontiers-1-introduction/ (accessed July 20, 2020).
238 Harari, *Homo Deus*, 386.
239 Harari, *Homo Deus*, 391.
240 Harari, *Homo Deus*, 46.
241 Martone, "Scientists Demonstrate Direct Brain-to-Brain Communication in Humans".
242 See, for example, Sri Aurobindo, *The Life Divine*.
243 RAISE 2020 conference. See: https://raise2020.indiaai.gov.in/ (accessed October 2, 2020).
244 Yudhishthira asks Bhishma in Shanti Parva: Roy, *The Mahabharata of Krishna-Dwaipayana Vyasa*, 9:103.
245 Vidura to Dhritarashtra in Udyoga Parva: Roy, *The Mahabharata of Krishna-Dwaipayana Vyasa*, 4:68.
246 One report admits its own limitations in this regard: "Given that more than 50% of the sample population was unaware of the particulars of AI, namely neural networks, deep learning, machine learning and cognitive automation, it can be inferred that there is a lack of such skilled professionals in this field". (PwC, *How AI is reshaping jobs in India India*, 19).
247 The zamindars in the colonial period acted under the suzerainty of the British Crown and served as a medium to siphon off wealth of the Indian peasants to their colonial masters. Today the British Crown is being replaced by big digital corporations like Google, Facebook etcetera and Indian billionaires have taken the place of zamindars.

248 As an exception to this, *The Center for Internet and Society*, a Bengaluru based think tank has produced some interesting reports on India's AI situation, raising ethical and regulatory questions, highlighting the potential discrimination, lack of transparency, and impact on human rights. Its sponsors are dominated by Western agencies. See: Sinha, Hickok and Basu, *AI in India: A Policy Agenda.*

249 Vempati, *India and the Artificial Intelligence Revolution.*

250 See for example: https://www.ndtv.com/business/niti-aayog-google-join-hands-to-foster-artificial-intelligence-ai-ecosystem-in-india-1848608 (accessed July 20, 2020).

251 See: http://www.cnbctv18.com/views/how-one-indian-industry-beat-china-at-manufacturing-and-created-a-global-footprint-6135001.htm (accessed July 20, 2020).

252 India has recently repaired the defect of Article 370, triple talaq laws, Ram Mandir in Ayodhya, among others.

253 See: http://armstrade.sipri.org/armstrade/page/toplist.php (accessed July 20, 2020) and https://www.defensenews.com/global/asia-pacific/2018/02/05/indias-defense-budget-will-rise-but-it-will-get-eaten-up-by-personnel-costs/ (accessed July 20, 2020). And: https://swarajyamag.com/videos/while-the-5-rafale-fighter-jets-arrive-indias-defence-sector-problems-remain (accessed July 20, 2020).

254 Upadhyaya, *Integral Humanism*, 56.

255 Among numerous other sources, Infinity Foundation's fourteen-volume series *History of Indian Science and Technology* is a good starting point to get a glimpse of Indian scientific ingenuity in the past. www.InfinityFoundation.com has many of the volumes available.

256 Sri Aurobindo, *Karmayogin*, 274.

257 It is interesting to note that Indians were highly sought-after migrant workers even many centuries back – Middle East, China.

258 While ISRO has traditionally been a flagship success story for India, especially given its small budget, the entry of private players such as Boeing's Starliner, SpaceX and Blue Origin into the global space sector has caused India to lose some ground in its relative standing.

259 India needs something equivalent to In-Q-Tel the CIA venture fund for national security game-changing technology investments. See: https://www.iqt.org/ (accessed July 20, 2020).

260 Padma awards are the highest awards given by the president of India ostensibly to those who make important contributions to the nation.

261 See: https://www.analyticsinsight.net/artificial-intelligence-india-comprehensive-overview/ (accessed July 20, 2020). Furthermore, India's tech workers face serious challenges in the coming years, according to The Center for Internet and Society based in Bengaluru, that has produced a report on the technological impact on IT/ITES based on surveys of sixteen major companies with a total of about twenty lakh IT employees. This organization is mostly foreign funded. See: Rathi and Hickok, *'Future of Work' in India's IT/IT-eS Sector.*

262 NITI Aayog, *National Strategy for AI*, 50-51. Another recent article that criticizes India's mediocrity is by Subhash Kak. See: https://medium.com/@subhashkak/whence-premium-mediocrity-in-india-ff894a984fde (accessed July 20, 2020).

263 NITI Aayog, *National Strategy for AI*, 51. To remedy some of this, howsoever late, it is encouraging that IIT Mumbai and IIT Patna have entered into a joint research collaboration with industry on the applied aspects of AI. The government of Karnataka has set up a Centre of Excellence for Data Science and Artificial Intelligence in partnership with NASSCOM. Wadhwani Foundation has set up India's first research institute dedicated to developing AI solutions for social good in Mumbai in Feb 2018.

264 See: https://techbeacon.com/enterprise-it/google-goes-ai-first-io-what-dev-ops-need-know (accessed July 20, 2020).

265 See: https://www.cnbctv18.com/business/uday-kotak-bats-for-re-think-on-business-policy-to-get-migrant-labour-back-6070221.htm (accessed July 20, 2020).

266 See: https://coe-dsai.nasscom.in/ (accessed July 20, 2020).

267 See: https://analyticsindiamag.com/should-ai-be-allowed-to-get-patents-how-can-indian-companies-protect-their-inventions/ (accessed July 31, 2020).

268 See: https://emerj.com/ai-market-research/artificial-intelligence-in-india/ (accessed July 20, 2020).

269 See: https://economictimes.indiatimes.com/small-biz/startups/

newsbuzz/tencents-now-the-alibaba-of-indian-startup-scene/articleshow/73789241.cms (accessed July 20, 2020).

270 For instance, the Chinese technology behemoth Tencent has made at least fifteen technology investments in Indian companies. One startup offers a product that allows students to upload a snapshot of a conceptual problem, and in theory their AI system will provide a video solution in ten seconds. Another product Tencent invested in provides audio content such as audiobooks, stories, podcasts, and self-help content in a variety of Indian languages.

271 See: https://economictimes.indiatimes.com/tech/internet/alibaba-tencent-pour-cash-into-indias-gambling-loopholes/articleshow/75173745.cms (accessed July 20, 2020).

272 See: https://economictimes.indiatimes.com/news/economy/foreign-trade/keeping-a-check-on-the-chinese/articleshow/75223704.cms (accessed July 20, 2020). However, when China complained, India immediately backtracked somewhat; see: http://www.cnbctv18.com/economy/no-intention-to-stop-chinese-investments-in-startups-says-niti-aayog-ceo-5733001.htm (accessed July 20, 2020). A few days later, India yielded to pressure and decided to help certain Chinese investments in special cases; see https://www.reuters.com/article/us-india-china-investments-exclusive-idUSKCN2270L9 (accessed July 20, 2020).

273 See: http://www.cnbctv18.com/politics/rss-affiliate-wants-swadeshi-zoom-lauds-crackdown-on-chinese-app-5729751.htm (accessed July 20, 2020).

274 Desouza and Somvanshi, *How India can prepare its workforce for the artificial intelligence era.*

275 Desouza and Somvanshi, *How India can prepare its workforce for the artificial intelligence era.*

276 See: https://medium.com/the-coleman-fung-institute/blue-river-technology-how-robotics-and-machine-learning-are-transforming-the-future-of-farming-f355398dc567 (accessed July 20, 2020).

277 See: https://www.chathamhouse.org/expert/comment/problem-india-s-ai-all-strategy (accessed July 20, 2020).

278 NASSCOM, FICCI, and EY, *Future of Jobs in India – A 2022 perspective.*

279 Yew, *The Wit and Wisdom of Lee Kuan Yew*, 29.

280 Chandrasekaran and Purushothaman, *Bridgital Nation*.

281 See (1) https://qz.com/india/1051533/india-is-unprepared-for-a-near-future-when-it-will-be-the-worlds-most-populous-country/ (accessed July 20, 2020), (2) https://www.livemint.com/Money/JYalqNRTOtaQCIU4EuXGRO/More-than-30-of-Indias-youth-not-in-employment-shows-OECD.html (accessed July 20, 2020), (3) https://www.livemint.com/politics/policy/a-third-of-skilled-youth-in-india-jobless-official-survey-1565161972818.html (accessed July 20, 2020).

282 The economic burden of the aging population is also worsening due to increases in life expectancy. See: https://economictimes.indiatimes.com/news/politics-and-nation/share-of-population-over-age-of-60-in-india-projected-to-increase-to-20-in-2050-un/articleshow/68919318.cms (accessed July 20, 2020).

283 Sage Vasishtha to Shri Rama (Verse 2.5.18): Mitra, *The Yoga Vasishtha Maharamayana of Valmiki*, 1:143.

284 Chandrasekaran and Purushothaman, *Bridgital Nation*, 83.

285 Chandrasekaran and Purushothaman, *Bridgital Nation*, 153.

286 Chandrasekaran and Purushothaman, *Bridgital Nation*, 11, 93.

287 See: https://economictimes.indiatimes.com/tech/internet/india-is-worlds-most-digitally-dexterous-country-survey/articleshow/75178052.cms (accessed July 20, 2020).

288 See: https://time.com/5237458/the-facebook-defect/ (accessed July 20, 2020).

289 Eric Schmidt was Google's CEO and Jared Cohen served as chief advisor to Schmidt. See: Schmidt and Cohen, *The New Digital Age: Transforming Nations, Businesses, and Our Lives*.

290 Bhishma to Yudhishthira in Santi Parva: Roy, *The Mahabharata of Krishna-Dwaipayana Vyasa*, 8:213.

291 Joglekar, *Bhartrihari Niti and Vairagya Shatakas*, 15.

292 Sri Aurobindo, *Karmayogin*, 283.

293 See: https://www.mygov.in/task/share-your-inputs-draft-non-personal-data-governance-framework/ (accessed July 31, 2020).

294 Rather than a state monopoly being custodian for the data and its equitable marketing, a different approach would be for the

government to make and enforce the rules, but let private industry compete in aggregating, managing, and selling the data. To create a level playing field, I propose the approach followed in deregulating the US telecom industry in the 1980s and '90s. A powerful man named Judge Greene was appointed by the federal court for oversight of the breakup of AT&T. The fundamental principle was to separate the critical bottleneck asset (which was the long-distance backbone network in those days) into a separate private company that would be required to *make this asset available equally and impartially to everyone including its own businesses.* This was called the Equal Access principle. AT&T, as the owner of this backbone asset would not enjoy any privileged use of it compared to its competitors (like MCI and Sprint in those days). Today's application of Equal Access to the data industry would be to separate the data aggregating business of Google, Microsoft, Facebook, Amazon, and others, and *require it to be made available to all users including a given data aggregator's own affiliates on equal terms.* For instance, all of Google's data would become a separate business of Google, and the value-added applications of Google and its competitors would have equal access to it without favoring Google's own access. This means a data-grid would be set up as a separate business and all those selling raw data to it would be treated as arms-length suppliers, and all those buying its data would be treated on par as customers. In principle, every sensor or data capture device could be metered as a supplier to the data-grid. If there are multiple competing data-grids, there could also be a competitive bidding system to value any given raw data. This would lead to competing data curators as intermediaries in the value chain—similar to music licensing companies like ASCAP (American Society of Composers, Authors and Publishers) and other aggregators of intellectual property. This would create three separate and distinct kinds of businesses run on arms-length basis from each other: (1) raw data capture, (2) aggregation and organization of databases, and (3) value-added and sale of applications. The breakup of AT&T along these lines is what unleashed the telecom revolution, internet, and all the internet-based industries that dominate the landscape today.

295 Microsoft has impressed Indian authorities by investing in data centers for its Azure cloud infrastructure, and Amazon is locating some of its cloud infrastructure in India. However, the physical location of a data center is irrelevant; the data resident in India is still being accessed by algorithms over which the Indian government has little direct control.

296 Interestingly, when the White House suddenly unfollowed Prime Minister Narendra Modi and India's president, Ram Nath Kovind, it produced an emotional shock in India. See: https://www.indiatoday.in/india/story/white-house-donald-trump-unfollows-narendra-modi-twitter-pmo-president-ram-nath-kovind-1672344-2020-04-29 (accessed July 20, 2020).

297 Vidura to Dhritarashtra in Udyoga Parva: Roy, *The Mahabharata of Krishna-Dwaipayana Vyasa*, 4:63-64.

298 See: https://economictimes.indiatimes.com/news/politics-and-nation/up-government-invites-top-varsities-for-kumbh-research/articleshow/66111831.cms (accessed July 20, 2020). See also: https://swarajyamag.com/insta/with-preparations-in-full-swing-yogi-adityanath-government-invites-the-worlds-best-universities-for-kumbh-research (accessed July 20, 2020).

299 I have been following the recent developments on data protection regulations in India. Though these are important initial steps they are insufficient because of the overriding deficiencies this book points out. Some examples of recent data protection initiatives by India are given in the following articles: https://www.ndtv.com/india-news/amazon-google-face-tough-government-e-commerce-rules-report-2257678 (accessed July 20, 2020); http://www.cnbctv18.com/startup/draft-e-commerce-policy-oyos-esops-and-other-top-startup-stories-of-the-day-6272771.htm (accessed July 20, 2020); http://www.cnbctv18.com/technology/data-of-one-country-should-not-become-surreptitious-property-of-another-country-prasad-6298761.htm (accessed July 20, 2020).

300 See: https://www.wired.com/story/cambridge-analytica-suspends-alexander-nix-amid-scandals/ (accessed July 20, 2020).

301 See: https://qz.com/1239561/cambridge-analyticas-parent-firm-proposed-a-massive-political-machine-for-indias-2014-elections/

(accessed July 20, 2020) and https://www.livemint.com/Politics/CHlxMZEbw24tzCoirSGdGJ/Cambrige-Analytica-whistleblower-Christopher-Wylie-tweets-de.html (accessed July 20, 2020). These reports were denied by some persons in Indian politics. See also: https://qz.com/1239762/cambridge-analytica-scandal-all-the-countries-where-scl-elections-claims-to-have-worked/ (accessed July 20, 2020).

302 Pham, "Facebook is Spending $5.7 Billion to Capitalize on India's Internet Boom".

303 See: http://www.cnbctv18.com/retail/jiomart-whatsapp-kirana-launch-how-to-place-order-thane-kalyan-5779521.htm (accessed July 20, 2020).

304 See: https://www.thestreet.com/investing/facebook-investment-jio-platforms-ambani-india (accessed July 20, 2020).

305 The well-known firm Bernstein Research explains the strategic benefit: "The transaction fits with their recent push to build themselves and experiment ... a WeChat like app". Pham, "Facebook is Spending $5.7 Billion to Capitalize on India's Internet Boom".

306 Bloomberg reports: "Facebook may benefit from a well-connected ally in the country, where its Whatsapp is trying to launch a payments service but has run afoul of regulators over fake news and privacy concerns. ... Zuckerberg has long aimed to roll out a digital currency as well as tools that let users make payments and buy and sell products over the social network's messaging services in India. ... While India will be a testing ground for WhatsApp payment services—currently in pilot—Zuckerberg is also separately looking at the market for his crypto-currency project called Libra. Zuckerberg has said that payments and commerce are a priority, representing a major business opportunity for the company moving forward". See: https://www.bloomberg.com/news/articles/2020-04-22/facebook-to-plow-5-7-billion-in-ambani-s-jio-wireless-platforms (accessed July 20, 2020).

307 Pham, "Facebook is Spending $5.7 Billion to Capitalize on India's Internet Boom".

308 See: https://www.ndtv.com/india-news/facebook-buys-9-99-per-cent-

in-reliance-jio-facebook-teams-up-with-mukesh-ambanis-jio-mark-zuckerber-2215960 (accessed July 20, 2020).

309 See: https://www.deccanherald.com/business/facebook-to-invest-rs-43574-crore-in-reliance-jio-for-99-stake-828352.html.

310 See: https://www.ndtv.com/india-news/reliance-jio-facebook-deal-bravo-mukesh-anand-mahindra-on-how-facebook-jio-deal-could-help-india-2216236 (accessed July 20, 2020). The self-congratulatory tone continues in Indian media across the political spectrum. In the following article, this deal is seen as a boost to India's economy: https://www.ndtv.com/india-news/how-a-whatsapp-hi-could-end-up-transforming-a-1-trillion-industry-2220859 (accessed July 20, 2020).

311 Swamy, "Four Reasons Why Reliance Jio-Facebook Deal is Commercially Sensible and Good for India".

312 Swamy, "Four Reasons Why Reliance Jio-Facebook Deal is Commercially Sensible and Good for India".

313 See: https://www.cnbctv18.com/telecom/jios-sixth-deal-in-six-weeks-underscores-digital-india-opportunity-6076351.htm (accessed July 20, 2020).

314 See: http://www.cnbctv18.com/business/after-jio-partnership-in-india-facebook-wants-to-expand-whatsapp-commerce-globally-6503951.htm (accessed July 31, 2020).

This is a rapidly developing situation. Subsequently, there have been more favorable developments reported in the following articles: https://www.businesstoday.in/current/corporate/facebook-ril-deal-cci-raises-concerns-over-data-sharing-pact-fb-assures-limited/story/418090.html

https://www.bloombergquint.com/law-and-policy/data-sharing-not-the-purpose-of-deal-reliance-jio-facebook-tell-cci

"The regulator said deals between entities having access to user data must be examined in light of incentives they may have for pooling their databanks and monetising it. This transaction will give the Facebook Group and Reliance Jio restricted access to each other's data, the CCI pointed out. Jaadhu Holdings clarified to the regulator that data will be provided only for the purpose of facilitating e-commerce transactions on JioMart. Its use will be limited and proportionate. And any confidential information received from the other party will not be used for their own business purposes. The CCI accepted their submission that data-sharing is not the purpose of the deal. But it also said that any anti-competitive conduct resulting from any data sharing in the future will be open to scrutiny".

315 Horwitz and Seetharaman, "Facebook Executives Shut Down Efforts to Make the Site Less Divisive".

316 Horwitz and Seetharaman, "Facebook Executives Shut Down Efforts to Make the Site Less Divisive".

317 For example, see: https://www.buzzfeednews.com/article/ryanmac/facebook-employee-leaks-show-they-feel-betrayed (accessed July 31, 2020).

318 See: https://in.reuters.com/article/amazon-india-bharti-idINKBN23B1FH (accessed July 20, 2020).

319 In the following CNN report, there is great deal of excitement that Jio could become a massive tech company in all sorts of sectors across India. Facebook's intrusion is celebrated, but readers should note the complete silence on the core issue I raise: the heist in which Jio serves as the vehicle for control of India's big data. See: https://www.cnn.com/videos/business/2020/05/29/mukesh-ambani-jio-platforms-orig.cnn-business/video/playlists/atv-trending-videos/ (accessed July 20, 2020).

320 See: http://www.cnbctv18.com/business/what-googles-rs-75000-crore-india-investment-means-6318891.htm (accessed July 20, 2020). And: http://www.cnbctv18.com/technology/google-india-digitization-fund-sundar-pichai-6317041.htm (accessed July 20, 2020).

321 Edwards, *I'm Feeling Lucky*, 291.

322 See: http://www.cnbctv18.com/business/ril-agm-jio-to-make-cheap-5g-phones-built-on-made-for-india-android-os-6334131.htm (accessed July 31, 2020).

323 See: https://www.ndtv.com/world-news/why-does-google-steal-content-from-honest-businesses-us-congressman-2271102 and: https://www.foxnews.com/politics/rep-ken-buck-big-tech-google-china-violations (accessed July 31, 2020).

324 For the EU crackdown, see: https://www-nytimes-com.cdn.

ampproject.org/c/s/www.nytimes.com/2020/07/30/technology/europe-new-phase-tech-amazon-apple-facebook-google.amp.html (accessed July 31, 2020). For Australia, see: https://www.accc.gov.au/system/files/Exposure%20Draft%20EM%20-%20NEWS%20MEDIA%20AND%20DIGITAL%20PLATFORMS%20MANDATORY%20BARGAINING%20CODE%20BILL%202020.pdf (accessed July 31, 2020).

325 Joglekar, *Bhartrihari Niti and Vairagya Shatakas*, 21.

326 Fraser, *Poems of Tukarama*, 3:267-68.

327 Fraser, *Poems of Tukarama*, 3:267-68.

328 Those familiar with Sanskrit taxonomy understand the term *sthula-sharira* to refer to the physical body of individuals. Here I am addressing the sthula-sharira of the collective body of society in terms of the economy, education, human capital, and issues of unemployment.

329 The Sanskrit term *sukshma-sharira* refers to the psychological and mental body of an individual. My treatment of this level explains the psychological impact of AI both at the level of individuals and the collective.

330 Prasad, *A Historical Developmental Study of Classical Indian Philosophy of Morals*, 110.

331 Joglekar, *Bhartrihari Niti and Vairagya Shatakas*, 13.

332 Joshi, *Dasabodha*, 21.

333 For e.g. Bhishma says to Yudhishthira, "Even Bhagavan Vishnu, who created the three worlds with the daityas and all the gods, even He is engaged in tapsaya in the ocean." See: Ganguli, *Mahabharata of Krishna-Dwaipayana Vyasa*, 13:20

334 Shri Krishna to Arjuna in Bhagavad Gita 2.3, 2.31, 2.32, 2.33, 2.38: Swami Chinmayananda, *The Holy Geeta*, 58, 107-109, 114.

335 Rishi Markandeya to Yudhishthira in Vana Parva: Roy, *The Mahabharata of Krishna-Dwaipayana Vyasa*, 3:247.

336 My assessment of India's urban youth and middle class is based on extensive study of India and its people over the past twenty-five years. I have held more than 2,000 live events and encounters discussing my work, interacted with tens of thousands of individuals online, and helped launch and organize a large number of projects

and movements. About 75% of my audience are between the ages of eighteen and thirty-five. This data set has helped me reach the conclusions being summarized.

337 Upadhyaya, *Integral Humanism*, 47.

338 For an overview of my thesis on the five waves of Indology, see: https://www.speakingtree.in/blog/why-swadeshi-indology-is-required-part-2. For a video on the same topic, see: https://www.youtube.com/watch?v=XWeFa6jUiPw.

339 Some Indian laws are frequently used to pander to emotional sensitivities. For instance, Indian Penal Code 295A considers it a crime to say something that "insults or attempts to insult the religion or the religious beliefs of that class". Indian Penal Code 298 considers a crime "uttering any word or making any sound in the hearing or making any gesture or placing any object in the sight of any person, with intention to wound his religious feeling". I wonder whether such laws have made people too emotionally sensitive at the expense of critical thinking.

340 Joshi, *Dasabodha*, 21-23, 46.

341 Rishi Markandeya to Yudhishthira in Vana Parva: Roy, *The Mahabharata of Krishna-Dwaipayana Vyasa*, 3:248.

342 Yew, *The Wit and Wisdom of Lee Kuan Yew*, 47.

343 Tamilians are Tamil-speaking people, and Dravidian refers to an identity that was developed in recent times and popularized to put the Tamil speakers in conflict with the north Indians.

344 The Indian Constitution has had 104 amendments during the past 73 years of independence, and even now it is considered unstable in some respects. By contrast, the US constitution has been amended a total of 27 times in 233 years.

345 Vidura to Dhritarashtra in Udyoga Parva: Roy, *The Mahabharata of Krishna-Dwaipayana Vyasa*, 4:66.

346 An example of China's manufacturing edge over India for a major industry (i.e. pharmaceuticals) is analyzed in the following recent report: http://www.cnbctv18.com/healthcare/why-china-has-an-edge-over-india-in-api-manufacturing-6331911.htm (accessed July 31, 2020).

347 Table adapted from: https://timesofindia.indiatimes.com/india/not-just-galwan-we-need-to-win-these-5-battles/articleshow/76669128.

cms (accessed July 20, 2020).

348 A University of Toronto report concluded that Alibaba's UC Browser has "several major privacy and security vulnerabilities that would seriously expose users of UC Browser to surveillance and other privacy violations". (Bhandari, Fernandes, and Agarwal, *Chinese Investments in India*, 17).

349 Bhandari, Fernandes, and Agarwal, *Chinese Investments in India*. Some of it is worth quoting in detail: "Unable to persuade India to sign on to its Belt and Road Initiative (BRI), China has entered the Indian market through venture investments in startups and penetrated the online ecosystem with its popular smartphones and their applications (apps). Chinese tech investors have put an estimated $4 billion into Indian startups. Such is their success that over the five years ending March 2020, 18 of India's 30 unicorns are now Chinese-funded. TikTok, the video app, has 200 million subscribers and has overtaken YouTube in India. Alibaba, Tencent and ByteDance rival the U.S. penetration of Facebook, Amazon, and Google in India. Chinese smartphones like Oppo and Xiaomi lead the Indian market with an estimated 72% share, leaving Samsung and Apple behind. ... There are no major Indian venture investors for Indian startups. China has taken early advantage of this gap.... China provides the capital needed to support the Indian startups, which like any other, are loss-making. The trade-off for market share is worthwhile." (p.6) "In India, China's tech giant companies and venture capital funds have become the primary vehicle for investments in the country. ... Chinese funding to Indian tech startups is making an impact disproportionate to its value, given the deepening penetration of technology across sectors in India. TikTok, owned by ByteDance, is already one of the most popular apps in India, overtaking YouTube; Xiaomi handsets are bigger than Samsung smartphones; Huawei routers are widely used. These are investments made by nearly two dozen Chinese tech companies and funds, led by giants like Alibaba, ByteDance and Tencent which have funded 92 Indian startups, including unicorns such as Paytm, Byju's, Oyo and Ola.... 18 of the 30 Indian unicorns have a Chinese investor. This means that China is embedded in Indian society, the economy, and the technology ecosystem that influences

it. Unlike a port or a railway line, these are invisible assets in small sizes – rarely over $100 million – and made by the Chinese private sector, which doesn't cause immediate alarm. All this adds up to just 1.5% of the total official Chinese (including Hong Kong) FDI into India. This doesn't cover investments made by funds based out of Singapore and elsewhere, where the ultimate owner is Chinese, so the actual investment in India will be higher. ... [There are] over 75 companies with Chinese investors concentrated in e-commerce, fintech, media/social media, aggregation services and logistics." (p.8) "Alibaba/Tencent ... can encourage the startup to use pre-existing Chinese solutions for its tech requirements – again leading to loss of control over data. If this process is followed across a range of companies – a taxi service, a hotel aggregator, online retail outlets, a payment provider – it permits an intrusive, comprehensive profile of an individual and his/her habits". (p.6-12)

350 Bhandari, Fernandes, and Agarwal, *Chinese Investments in India*, 15.

351 Bhandari, Fernandes, and Agarwal, *Chinese Investments in India*, 16.

352 Reddy, *India and the Challenge of Autonomous Weapons*, 11.

353 World Bank, *World Bank East Asia and Pacific Economic Update, April 2020.*

354 See: https://www.technologyreview.com/2020/07/31/1005824/decolonial-ai-for-everyone/ (accessed August 3, 2020).

355 Sri Aurobindo, *Bande Mataram*, 18.

356 McKinsey Global Institute, *A Future That Works*, 8.

357 McKinsey Global Institute, *A Future That Works*, ii.

358 Oxford Economics, *How Robots Change the World.*

359 United Nations Conference on Trade and Development, *Digital Economy Report 2019.*

360 Oxford Economics, *How Robots Change the World*, 52.

361 Susskind, *A World Without Work*, 5.

362 Balliester and Elsheikhi, *The Future of Work*, 8. Emphasis added.

363 Harris, Kimson, and Schwedel, *Labor 2030*, 44.

364 PricewaterhouseCoopers, *Will Robots Really Steal Our Jobs?* 8.

365 McKinsey Global Institute, *A Future That Works*, 12.

366 McKinsey Global Institute, *A Future That Works*, 3.

367 PricewaterhouseCoopers, *Will Robots Really Steal Our Jobs?*. Similarly, a report from OECD concluded that the risk of job loss in the countries within its scope was not worrisome. See Arntz, Gregory, and Zierahn, *OECD Social, Employment and Migration Working Papers. No. 189.*

368 World Economic Forum, "The Future of Jobs Report 2018", v.

369 World Economic Forum, "The Future of Jobs Report 2018". v.

370 World Economic Forum, "The Future of Jobs Report 2018", ix.

371 WEF lists the following as the most likely major risks: extreme weather, climate action failure, natural disasters, biodiversity loss, human-made environmental disasters, data fraud or theft, cyberattacks, water crisis, global governance failure and asset bubbles. Risks with the highest impact are climate action failure, weapons of mass destruction, biodiversity loss, extreme weather, water crises, information infrastructure breakdown, natural disasters, cyberattacks, and human-made environmental disasters. (World Economic Forum, *The Global Risks Report 2020*, 12).

372 See: https://www.youtube.com/watch?v=2C-A797y8dA (accessed July 20, 2020).

373 "Indore Process" of manufacturing organic manure was learnt by him from Indian farmers. See: Howard, *An Agricultural Testament*, 39.

374 Chandrasekaran and Purushothaman, *Bridgital Nation*.

375 Chandrasekaran and Purushothaman, *Bridgital Nation*, 16.

376 Chandrasekaran and Purushothaman, *Bridgital Nation*, 164.

377 Safety and mobility concerns are among the blockages identified. Chandrasekaran and Purushothaman, *Bridgital Nation*, 94-95; 125.

378 Chandrasekaran and Purushothaman, *Bridgital Nation*, 149-50.

379 Chandrasekaran and Purushothaman, *Bridgital Nation*, 12, 84.

380 Chandrasekaran and Purushothaman, *Bridgital Nation*, graph, 181.

INDEX

Note: The letters 't' and 'f' following locators refer to tables and figures respectively.

Printed in Great Britain
by Amazon

59591867R00310